GENEALOGICAL AND PERSONAL HISTORY

OF THE

UPPER MONONGAHELA VALLEY
WEST VIRGINIA

UNDER THE EDITORIAL SUPERVISION OI

BERNARD L. BUTCHER

Member of West Virginia Historical Society; Organizer and Corresponding Secretary of Marion County Historical Society; former State Superintendent of Free Schools of West Virginia

With an Account of the Resources and Industries of the Upper Monongahela Valley and the Tributary Region

——BY——

JAMES MORTON CALLAHAN

Professor of History, West Virginia University

Together with Various Historical Articles by Staff Writers

VOLUME I

ILLUSTRATED

Southern Historical Press, Inc.
Greenville, South Carolina

This volume was reproduced from
An 1912 edition located in the
Publisher's private library,
Greenville, South Carolina

All rights reserved. No part of this publication may be reproduced,
stored in a retrieval system, transmitted in any form, posted
on to the web in any form or by any means without the
prior written permission of the publisher.

Please direct all correspondence and orders to:

www.southernhistoricalpress.com
or
SOUTHERN HISTORICAL PRESS, Inc.
PO BOX 1267
375 West Broad Street
Greenville, SC   29601
southernhistoricalpress@gmail.com

Originally published: Richmond, VA 1912
Copyright 1912
By: Lewis Historical Publishing Company
Reprinted by: Southern Historical Press, Inc.
Greenville, SC
ISBN #0-89308-952-4
All rights Reserved.
Printed in the United States of America

INTRODUCTORY

THE present work, "Genealogical and Personal History of the Upper Monongahela Valley, West Virginia," presents in the aggregate an amount and variety of genealogical and personal information and portraiture unequalled by any kindred publication. No similar work concerning West Virginia Families has ever before been presented, and it contains much ancestral history never before printed. The object, clearly defined and well digested, is threefold:

First. To present in concise form the history of West Virginia Families.

Second. To preserve a record of its prominent present-day people.

Third. To present through personal sketches the relation of its prominent families of all times to the growth, singular prosperity and wide-spread influence of the Monongahela Valley, West Virginia, and its tributary region.

No other region in the United States presents a field of such peculiar interest for such research. Its history reaches back to the days when it was a part of the State honored throughout the Nation as "The Mother of Presidents." When the Civil War opened, its people held steadfast to the Union, and created themselves into a State which has taken a foremost place in the Great Sisterhood of States. From that day its development has been one of the wonders of the world, and its magnificent resources of mine and forest have given it a leading place in the commercial world. These subjects are treated in an exhaustive manner by a writer of great ability and amplest knowledge—James Morton Callahan, Professor of History, West Virginia University. Besides, various staff writers have contributed articles specially relating to this remarkable region.

There are numerous voluminous histories of the State. The amplification necessary to complete the picture, old and nowaday, is supplied by these Genealogical and Personal Memoirs—a chronicle of the people who have made the region what it is.

Unique in conception and treatment, this work will constitute one of the most original and permanently valuable contributions ever made to the social history of an American community. In it are arrayed in a lucid and dignified manner the important facts regarding the ancestry, personal careers and matrimonial alliances of those who, in each succeeding generation, have been accorded leading positions in social, professional and business life. It is not based upon, neither does it minister to, aristocratic prejudices and assumptions. On the contrary, its fundamental ideas are thoroughly American and democratic. The work everywhere conveys the lesson that distinction has been gained only by honorable public service, or by usefulness in private station, and that the development and prosperity of the region of which it treats have been dependent upon the character of its citizens, and in the stimulus which they have given to commerce, to industry, to the arts and sciences, to education and religion—to all that is comprised in the highest civilization of the present day—through a continual progressive development.

The inspiration underlying the present work is a fervent appreciation of the truth so well expressed by Sir Walter Scott, that "there is no heroic poem in the world but is at the bottom the life of a man." And with this goes a kindred truth, that to know a man, and rightly measure his character, and weigh his achievements, we must know whence he came, from what forbears he sprang. Truly as heroic poems have been

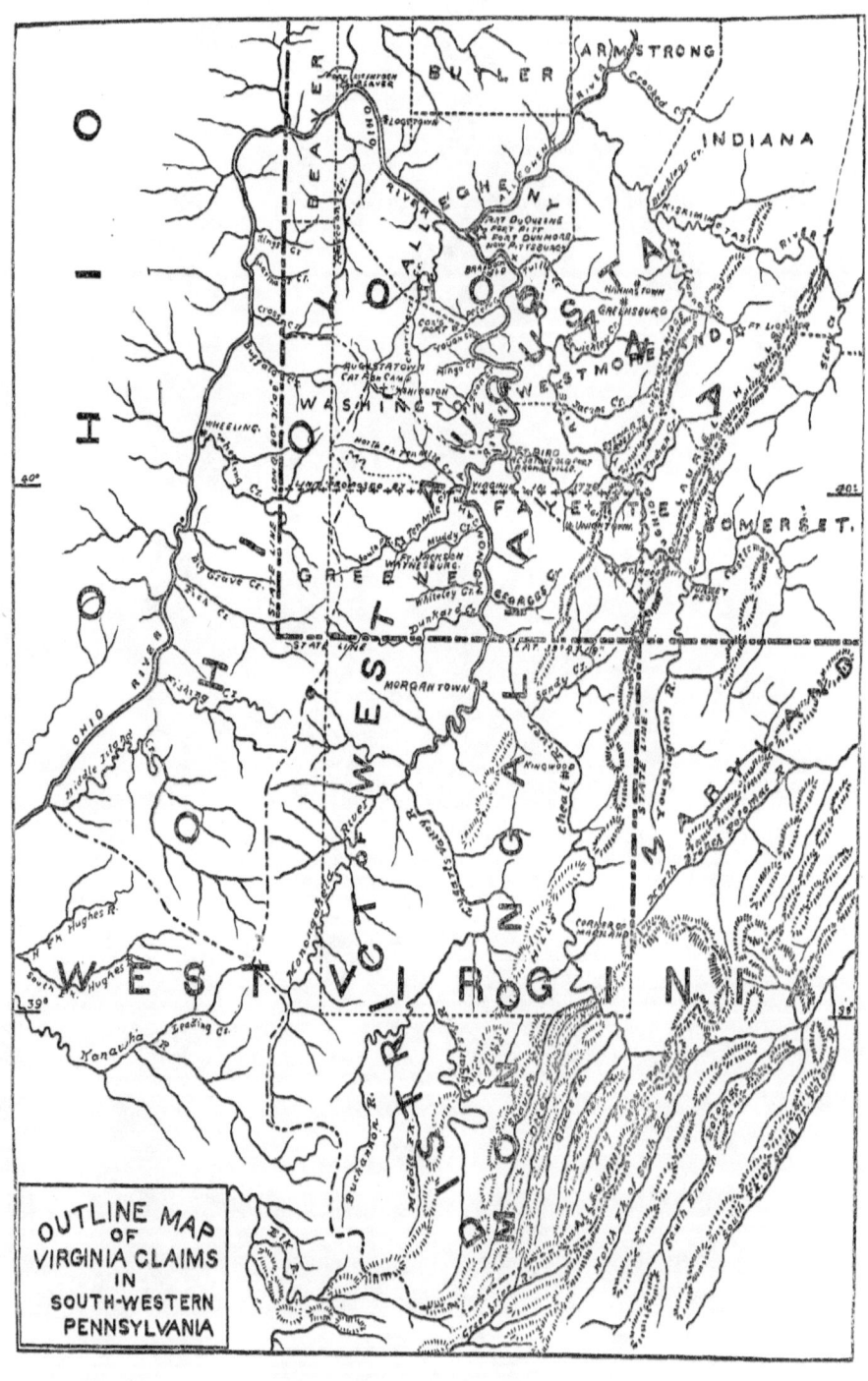

DEVELOPMENT OF SETTLEMENTS AND BEGINNINGS OF INDUSTRIAL LIFE.

INTRODUCTORY SURVEY.

The extent of territory embraced in the drainage system of the Upper Monongahela in West Virginia in 1776 was practically all included in Monongalia county, which was divided in 1784 by the creation of Harrison and later by the formation of Preston (1818), Marion (1842) and Taylor (1844). From the original territory of the Harrison of 1784 has been created Randolph (1787), Lewis (1816), Barbour (1843, from Harrison, Lewis and Randolph), Taylor (1844, from Harrison, Barbour and Marion), Upshur (1851, from Randolph, Barbour and Lewis), and Tucker (1856, from Randolph)—and small portions of its territory contributed to the creation of several other counties which do not belong to the topographical region drained by the Monongahela.

Randolph, Tucker and Preston are largely watered and drained by the Cheat and its tributaries; Upshur, Barbour and Taylor by the Tygart's; Lewis and Harrison by the West Fork; and Marion and Monongalia by the Monongahela below the junction of Tygart's and West Fork. The entire region is picturesque, and still rich in vast and varied resources which largely remained untouched for over a century after the Indian trails of the wild region of sombre shadows and healthy climate first attracted the advance guard of pioneer white settlers. In spite of the general roughness of surface, the soil is valuable, adapted either to various purposes of agriculture or to stock raising, and still capable of large returns under improved methods of cultivation. The iron ores were the basis of earlier active industries; and the abundance of coal, oil, gas, fire-clays, sandstones and glass-sands have recently established prosperous conditions felt by the entire region. The wealth of the woods has largely been depleted in most sections by a system of exploitation which has left in its desolate path nothing more important than the problems of conservation.

On the eve of its settlement by white men, the Upper Monongahela Valley was the hunting ground of tribes of Delaware, Shawnese and Mingo Indians whose permanent settlements or villages were located in Pennsylvania near the confluence of the Monongahela and the Allegheny. Since 1713 they had inhabited the region as tenants of the Iroquois of New York, who claimed the ownership. Several of their trails were distinctly marked. One was the old Catawba war-path between New York and the Holston river leading also through the Carolinas (not an Indian thoroughfare after white settlements were made in Virginia). This path crossed the Cheat at the mouth of Grassy Run, near the Monongalia-Preston boundary line, and farther south passed up the Tygart's valley. Another, the Warrior branch, passed up Dunkard Creek and via Fish Creek to southern Ohio and Kentucky. Another, the Eastern Trail (Great War Path), from Ohio via Fish Creek and Indian Creek and White Day Creek passed through Preston county (near the site of Masontown and Reedsville, and crossing Cheat at Dunkard Bottom) to the South Branch of the Potomac—a route much used by the Ohio Indians in their attacks on the white settlements. A branch starting between Masontown and Reedsville passed southward between Independence and Newburg, via York's Run and south of Evansville to Ice's mill on Big Sandy, where it met the Northwest trail from Maryland via the bridge at Deakin's, on Cheat. Another trail led from Maryland via Big Sandy near Bruceton (Preston county) and via Cheat to the vicinity of Morgantown. There was also a trail from the Ohio up the Kanawha and across the Appalachians into Randolph county.

The trails leading from the Ohio east were well known to the early settlers, who often posted scouts on them near the Ohio to report the approach of Indian war parties.

Indian trail and buffalo trace pointed the easiest way for fur trader and pioneer settler across mountain barrier into the unbroken wilderness drained by the Monongahela. The country gradually became known by reports of hunters and traders who crossed from very early times. Nemacolin's path, following in part an old buffalo trail across the mountains which furnished a pack horse route for traders who had already reached the Ohio before 1750 and was later widened into a wagon road by Washington and Braddock, became an important highway to the lower Monongahela, although the first wagon load of merchandise over it did not reach the Monongahela until 1789.

Farther south, crossing a wilderness mountain region over which no roads were constructed for a century after the early era of settlement of the region drained by the upper Monongahela, were four other trails of no less importance for settlers of the region drained by the upper tributaries of the Monongahela. The McCullough traders' trail led from Moorefield via Patterson's Creek and Greenland Gap across a spur of the Alleghenies to the North Branch, thence to the upper Youghiogheny (west of Ooakland), thence (via Bruceton Mills) to the Cheat near the Pennsylvania line. A branch of it led own Horse Shoe Run to the mouth of Lead Mine Run. The other three were more obscure. The North Branch trail, over which came the larger number of the early settlers on upper Cheat and many on the Buckhannon river, and which probably was the route of the Indians who conducted raids in Hampshire county in 1754 to 1759, continued from Fairfax stone across Backbone mountain and down Lead Mine Run and Horse Shoe Run to Cheat river—connecting here with a down-river branch which crossed Laurel Hill to the Valley River below the site of a Philippi, thence westward to the Ohio, and an up-river branch to the vicinity of Parsons and via the head of Leading Creek to the Seneca trail at Elkins and to the settlements of the Tygart Valley, at the head of which it connected with trails to the Little Kanawha, the Elk and the Greenbrier. The trail to Greenbrier passed through Mingo flats, and west of the present Marlinton pike crossed the mountains—dividing at the top of Middle Mountain into two branches, one of which continued to Old Field Fork and the other to Clover Lick. The Shawnee (or Seneca) trail, although long the chief highway between the South Branch and Tygart's valley, travelled westward yearly by pack horses laden with salt, iron and other merchandise, and later by many droves of cattle driven to the eastern market, ascended the South Branch (passing the McCullough trail at Moorefield), followed the North Fork and Seneca Creek, crossed the Alleghenies twenty miles south of the North Branch trail, and the branches of Cheat above the mouth of Horse Camp Creek, and passed near Elkins and Beverly to the vicinity of Huttonsville in Randolph.

Another path, connecting with the old Shawnee trail from Pennsylvania and Maryland from the head of North Fork, and following the general course of the later Staunton and Parkersburg turnpike, passed up the South Branch to the mouth of North Fork (in Grant county) which it followed to the mouth of Dry Run (in Pendleton county), then followed Laurel Creek to the site of the later crossing of the Staunton and Parkersburg pike, then turned westward, crossed the Alleghenies thirty miles south of the Seneca trail, followed the East Fork of the Greenbrier to the main river, crossed Shaver's Mountain to the Shaver's Fork of Cheat, thence crossing Cheat Mountain to Tygart's Valley, intersecting the Shawnee trail near Huttonsville, and crossing to the head of the Little Kanawha, which it followed to the Ohio.

Two other trails may be noticed. One led from the headwaters of the South Branch via the Sinks of Gandy, to Shaver's Fork of Cheat river, at the mouth of Fishing-Hawk, and across Cheat Mountain via the head of Files Creek to Valley Bend (above Beverly). Another led from the Great Kanawha up the Elk and Valley Fork and down Elk

Water to Tygart's Valley—a meeting place of so many trails and probably a favorite hunting ground of the Indians.

The first direct stimulus to settlement farther west came from the earlier settlements established about 1732 on grants, including the site of Winchester and the site of Staunton. As the lands of the lower and upper Shenandoah valley, and on the James, became more populated, the settlers, following the hunters, began to push their way across the divide to new valleys beyond. The organization of Greenbrier county in 1749 led to the establishment of more western nuclei of settlements such as Frankfort (1769), which later contributed not only to the advance down the Kanawha to the Ohio (in Wood, Jackson, and Mason counties) by 1755, but also to the settlement of the Monongahela region. By 1755 there were also settlements along the frontier region now in Hampshire, Hardy, Grant and Pendleton counties, and the earliest beginnings had been made farther west by settlers penetrating through the wilds to the valleys of Cheat, Tygart and West Fork. Many of the first settlers west of the mountains considered the soils of the region non-supporting, and intended to remain only until the game should be exhausted. The earliest incentive to actual occupation in the Monongahela and Ohio region was furnished in 1748 by the formation of the Ohio Company, which received from George II. a grant of five hundred thousand acres along the Ohio between the Monongahela and the Kanawha, and which planned settlements by which to divert the Indian trade from Pennsylvania. Plans for settlement by Germans from Pennsylvania were prevented by Virginia's laws against dissenters. Four years later, transmontane settlements were encouraged by the house of burgesses through an offer of tax exemption for ten years.

The settlement of the Monongahela Valley region was delayed beyond that of other parts of West Virginia farther south, first by the barrier of the Alleghenies, and later by the uninviting character of narrow defiles and dense wilderness and uncleared valleys beyond—which furnished ample cover for treacherous Indians opposed to the adventurous pioneers seeking to penetrate the wild hunting grounds. Although settlements of short duration were made on Tygart's Valley river in 1754 and on Decker's Creek in 1758, permanent settlements were not made until after the close of the French and Indian war, and until the treaty negotiated with Pontiac at the forks of the Muskingum by General Bouquet rendered peace on the border more certain.

During the early part of the French and Indian war, western settlements were pushed back to Winchester and Cumberland and the Indians held sway west of the Alleghenies. The fate of the Monongahela Valley hung in the balance until the fall of Fort Duquesne opened the way for the new colonization movement—a movement also encouraged and aided by the Braddock and Forbes roads which had been opened to determine the destiny of the West.

In the decade between the French and Indian war and the opening of the Revolution, settlements could be made only in opposition to the policy of the English government.

Although Governor Dinwiddie, in 1754, in order to encourage volunteers to enter military service, had set apart one hundred thousand acres along the Ohio to be granted to soldiers, George III., desiring that the trans-Allegheny region should remain a hunting ground for the Indians, or at least expecting to control the later settlement and government of the territory, on October 7, 1763, issued a proclamation forbidding the colonies to grant warrants, surveys or patents in the territory until it could be opened by treaties with the Indians—thus theoretically extinguishing their titles to lands beyond the proclamation line. Two years later he directed the governors of Virginia and Pennsylvania to remove by force all settlers in that region—an order which was never executed in Virginia. Ten years later, after considering for four years a petition of Thomas Walpole, Benjamin Franklin and others for a grant of land, including the larger part of West Virginia and the eastern part of Kentucky, which they proposed to form into a colony under the name of Vandalia, the king favored the project to organize the sparsely settled Virginia hinterland into a fourteenth colony with a government more dependent upon the crown than those of the older thirteen, but in 1775 the execution of the draft of the royal grant was postponed to await the cessation of hostilities, which finally closed only with the complete loss of English jurisdiction between the Atlantic and the Mississippi.

The people, determined to occupy the land without purchase of Indian titles, during the peace on the frontier from 1764 to 1774, proceeded first to secure tomahawk rights, and soon thereafter to establish settlement rights—pushing the frontier to the Ohio and into Kentucky. A tomahawk right respected by the frontiersmen was often merged into a settlement right. In the decade before the Revolution, while settlers along the Kanawha and the lower Monongahela were advancing to the more distant Ohio, settlements were began at several places along the Cheat in Preston and Tucker counties, along Tygart's Valley river in Randolph, and along the Monongahela and its West Fork and Tygart's valley tributaries in the territory now included in Monongalia, Marion, Taylor, Harrison, Barbour, Lewis and Upshur counties. Although Virginia took no steps until 1779 to sell lands in West Virginia, and no titles can be traced beyond that year, she respected the claims of the earlier settlers, and in fact taxed these settlers on their lands before patents were issued. Pioneers, in order to hold their four hundred acres on a settlement right, erected any kind of a pole cabin or log cabin near a good spring of water. Surveys, both the earlier ones and the later ones, were inaccurate and unsystematic and laid foundations for many future law suits—some of which are still on the court dockets. In early years, speculators patented large tracts—ten thousand to five hundred thousand acres—often overlapping scores of farms; but they could not hold land already occupied, and in many cases the large tracts were sold for taxes or otherwise transferred to the people in smaller tracts.

These permanent settlements, tentatively beginning as early as 1766, became especially augmented both in extent and number from 1772 to 1774. They were seriously affected by the conditions which precipitated the battle of Point Pleasant in 1774, and by the renewed danger of Indian attacks beginning about 1777 and continuing in some sections until the treaty of 1795 following Wayne's victory against the Indians in northwestern Ohio. Was it any wonder that the Indians fought to retain a country which they and their fathers had used for a summer retreat for many generations—a land famous for game and fish, and with abundance of fruits and nuts which could be obtained without toil?

The hardy and rugged pioneer settlers, after conquering the Indians, turned to the conquest of primeval wilds which the Indians had sought to retain unconquered. The problems of sheltering cabin and rude agricultural clearings were soon followed by larger problems of better communication through the almost fathomless depths of almost trackless regions, and of improvements in transportation. At first, following mere trails along the streams or across the bends of the streams or the divides, they opened wider avenues of travel as thickening settlements and multiplying population dictated the formation of new counties. In everything they were bound together by a community interest—fasting, feasting, fighting, praying and cursing, with one common mind. Although always influenced by traditions and customs and laws of Anglo-Saxon civilization, they often became in their isolated communities a law unto themselves. Banded together by neighborly ties and coöperation, and isolated from the touch of orderly law and the refinements of culture, they forged a set of customs which were transmitted like law forming the basis of an unwritten law. Finally, through the fertility of the soil and frugal industry, and the eastern demand for their surplus products, the problems of their primitive life of frugal economy and mere subsistance emerged into the new problems of improved industry and new conditions and standards of life. Their surplus product of energy and labor, through the law of supply and demand, found a sale in the older communities of the East—furnishing them a money commodity of exchange, the means to increase their wants and to improve their homes and farms, and the stimulus to facilitate communication between east and west. With these improvements came the accumulation of wealth and the increase of refinement and culture.

The material advance of the settlements before the era of railroads may be measured by the evolution of mills, by the increase in the number and size of stores, and by the evolution and development of roads and methods of transportation—as well as by the changes in farm implements and machines, and the general development of agriculture.

The earliest mills, the "tub mills," which were built about 1779 or 1780, began to be superseded between 1795 and 1800 by the better water-grist mill (equipped with country stones) which in time retreated before the steam mills. The construction of dams across the Monongahela was first regulated by the Virginia legislature by an act of December 5, 1793, and later by act of February 3, 1806. Many such dams were found along the streams of the settled regions by 1820. When the first official examination and partial survey of the Monongahela river was made in 1820, under the direction of the Virginia Board of Public Works, beginning a mile below the Lewis county court house and continuing to the Pennsylvania line, there were between those points (nearly one hundred and seven miles) ten dams—usually mill dams. There were four below Morgantown (including two old ones), Grey's between Booth's Creek and Little Falls, two (Law's and Conn's) between Great Falls and Middletown (Fairmont), Palsley's at Middletown, one built by an incorporated navigation company five miles below Clarksburg, one at the site of Colonel Benjamin Wilson's saw mill above Clarksburg, one at John G. Jackson's salt works, another below Samuel Clement's, another at John Patton's and another at Edward Jackson's mill about six miles below the present site of Weston.

Stores, established as early as 1785 at Morgantown, at first kept only a few goods which had been carried over the mountains on a pack horse. At a later period they were supplied with larger stock brought by wagon from Eastern markets or (first by wagon and later by boat) from Pittsburgh. With the stores, developed villages and towns, some of which showed considerable economic and social development by 1830 and thereafter.

The development of transportation, confronted with many obstacles, was determined largely by the pressing needs of the growing communities. After the Braddock and Forbes roads, the first road affecting the Monongahela region was cleared from the South Branch to Fort Pitt along the general route of the Braddock road by commissioners appointed by the General Assembly in 1766. The first road connecting directly with the Virginia-Monongahela region was the "state road" from Winchester via Romney to Morgantown, authorized by the legislature previous to 1786, when a branch wagon road was authorized to be opened from a point on this road near Cheat to Clarksburg. Over this route there was probably no wagon traffic for many years. A wagon was driven from Alexandria over the road to Morgantown as early as 1796. In 1786 the legislature also authorized the opening of roads from Morgantown to the mouth of Fishing Creek, and from the state road in Harrison county to the mouth of the Little Kanawha. Among the other earlier authorized roads which at first were little more than mere trails, were one from Morgantown to the mouth of Graves Creek in 1795, one from Clarksburg to Point Pleasant in 1806, one from the Monongahela Glades to the mouth of Buffalo and to the Ohio in 1812, one from Beverly via Clarksburg and Middlebourne to Sistersville in 1817, and a turnpike from Staunton (via Jackson river, Huttonville and Beverly) to Booth's Ferry on Tygart's Valley in 1818.

The first post road was opened to Morgantown, at which the first post office was established in 1794. Morgantown and Clarksburg advertisements and news which before 1797 found their only avenue of newspaper publication in the Pittsburgh Gazette, appeared in the Fayette Gazette from 1797 to 1804, when a paper was established at Morgantown. In 1806, Virginia gave aid to repair a post road in Randolph county. Ferries which began to appear by 1776 were established by 1785 at several points. Toll bridges which began to appear by 1807 were considerably increased in number from 1816 to 1819. The completion of the National Road from Cumberland to the Ohio at Wheeling in 1818 stimulated projects in its vicinity for branch roads to intersect it, and further south for competing roads between Virginia towns and the Ohio.

River transportation to Pittsburgh or to nearer points began at a very early period. In 1793, the Virginia legislature passed the first act for clearing and extending the navigation of the Monongahela and West Fork rivers for the convenient passage of canoes and flat boats. In January, 1800, it declared the Monongahela a public highway. Soon thereafter, both through private individual initiative, and possibly in part through the report of Secretary Gallatin on internal navigation, the question of river improvements to secure better navigation was seriously considered early in the century. The subject received new significance from the development of steam navigation on the Ohio after the trial trip of 1811-12. In January, 1817, the Monongahela Navigation Company was incorporated by the legislature to make the West Fork and Monongahela rivers navigable for flat boats, rafts and lumber, and with authority to cut a canal to divert the waters of the Buckhannon to the waters of the West Fork in order to secure an additional supply of water. A survey from Weston to the Pennsylvania line was made in 1820. The company, under the energetic lead of John G. Jackson, began its work on West Fork even before the survey was made, but soon abandoned the enterprise after the destruction of some of its dams by a river freshet, and finally forfeited its rights and franchises. Steamboats from Pittsburgh began to make regular trips to Morgantown about 1826, but the ascent to Fairmont first made in 1850 was more difficult, although in 1854 and thereafter regular trips were made at periods of high water. Improvement of the river above the Pennsylvania line, strongly urged in the ante-bellum decade, was postponed until the beginning of Congressional appropriations for the work in 1872.

In the decade after 1830, the question of roads, which had already become prominent, assumed a position of dominating importance. The construction of the Northwestern Turnpike and the Staunton and Parkersburg Turnpike stimulated the construction of intersecting roads, and in various ways exerted on the economic and social development, in almost every part of the Monongahela region, an influence which continued until the greater changes wrought by the advent of the railroad. About 1852 many bridges were built across streams at important crossings.

That the route of the first railroad to the Ohio would pass through the Virginia counties drained by the Monongahela was practically determined by the James-Kanawha River enterprise, which largely absorbed the money which might have been used for internal improvements in other parts of the state. Finally, after various delays and the consideration of several different routes, in 1852 the construction of the first line of the Baltimore and Ohio, causing the disappearance of the pack-wolves which had previously roamed through Preston county and the northern part of Randolph, was completed via Fairmont to Wheeling, and in 1857 the Northwestern branch intersecting the older line at Grafton was completed via Clarksburg and Salem to Parkersburg—constituting a rival to the great Northwestern Turnpike. By furnishing improved facilities for transportation, these roads, which touched both the throbbing pulse of the great metropolis of the East and the streams of life in the growing West, soon began to produce wonderful changes affecting the material interests and the social life—and may be regarded as the entering wedge in the larger development of the region through which they passed.

Material development, in the larger sense, which at the opening of the Civil War in the region drained by the Monongahela was largely confined to the immediate vicinity of these railroad routes, became more active and extensive in the second quarter century after the Civil War—both through the improvement and extension of transportation facilities and the increased exploitation and utilization of the vast mineral and forest resources of the region.

The growth of population to 1860 in the ten counties included in the drainage system of the Monongahela is indicated in the following table:

	1790.	1800.	1810.	1820.	1830.	1840.	1850.	1860.
Monongalia	4,768	8,540	12,793	11,060	14,056	17,368	12,357	13,048
Preston	....	....	.....	3,422	5,144	6,866	11,708	13,312
Marion	....	....	.....	.....	.....	.....	10,552	12,722
Harrison	2,080	4,848	9,958	10,932	14,722	17,669	11,728	13,790
Randolph	951	1,826	2,854	3,357	5,000	6,208	5,243	4,990
Lewis	....	....	.....	4,247	6,241	8,151	10,031	7,999
Barbour	....	....	.....	.....	.....	.....	9,005	8,958
Taylor	....	....	.....	.....	.....	.....	5,357	8,463
Upshur	....	....	.....	.....	.....	.....	.....	7,292
Tucker	....	....	.....	.....	.....	.....	.....	1,428
	7,799	15,214	25,605	33,018	45,163	56,262	75,981	92,002

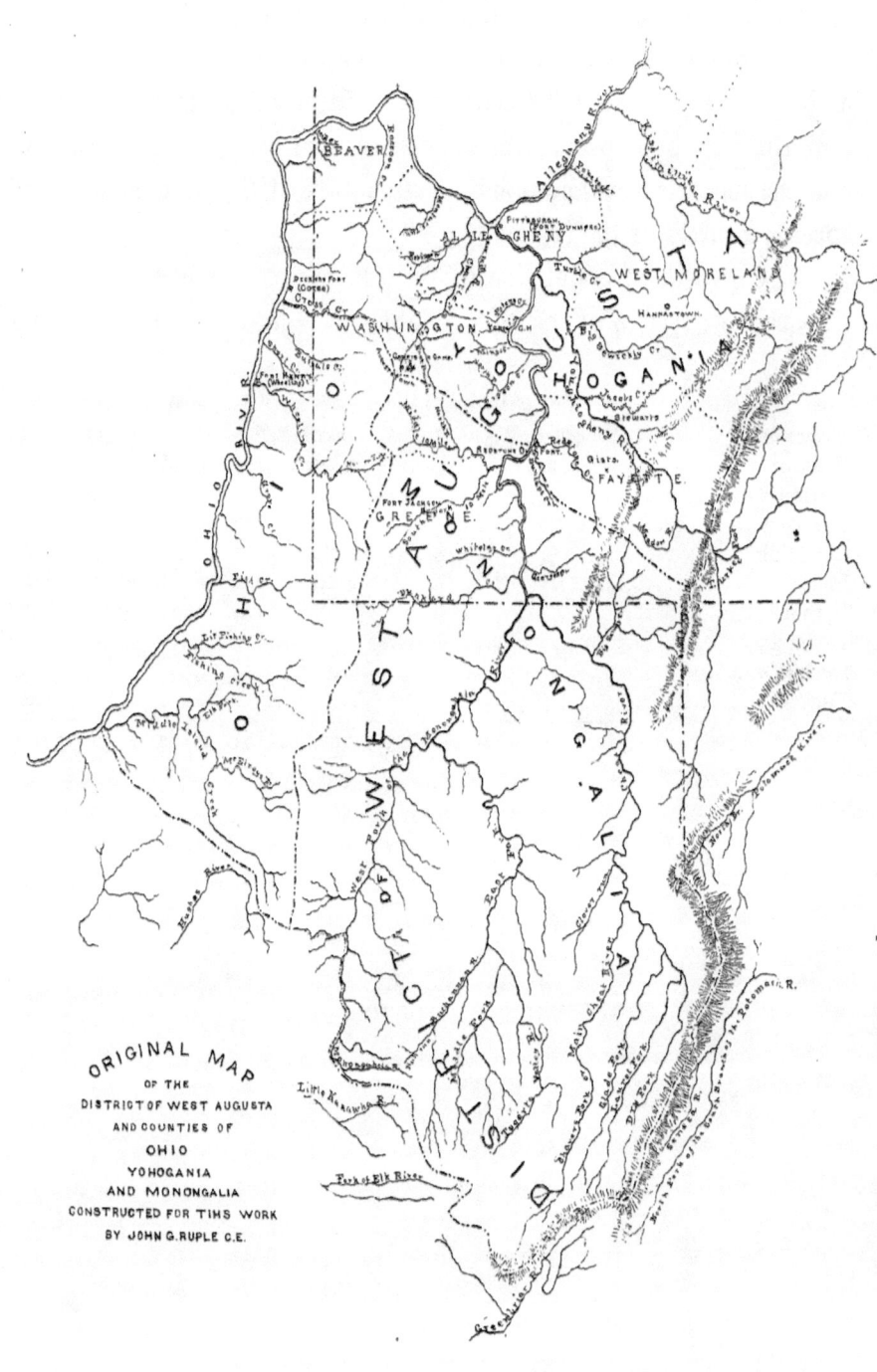

COUNTY DEVELOPMENT

MONONGALIA, PRESTON, TAYLOR, MARION,
HARRISON, LEWIS, BARBOUR,
UPSHUR, RANDOLPH,
TUCKER

ZACKWELL MORGAN.

According to frontier history and tradition, he was one of the earliest settlers of Morgantown, emigrating from Berkley County, Virginia. He first located at George's Creek, Pennsylvania, but in 1768 removed to the site of the town which was established under the name of "Morgans Town" by act of the General Assembly of Virginia in 1785.

In 1784 George Washington, returning from a visit to his western lands, summoned him to Pierponts (three miles from Morgantown) to consult with him in regard to the topography of the country between the Monongahela and the Kanawha.

COUNTY DEVELOPMENT

MONONGALIA COUNTY.

Early origins and later growth of settlements and industrial life can best be traced by counties, each of which has special features difficult to present in a general survey.

In 1758, while General Forbes' army was marching on Fort Duquesne, Thomas Decker and others began a settlement on Decker's Creek (near the present eastern limit of Morgantown), which was broken up early in 1759 by a party of Delawares and Mingoes.

Permanent settlers by 1766 reached the region now included in Monongalia county. At Ice's Ferry on Cheat in 1767 was born the first white child west of the mountains—Adam Ice, who was soon thereafter taken by his parents to the vicinity of Fairmont, and at his death in 1851 was buried at Barracksville. About 1767 or 1768 the first permanent settlement at Morgantown was made by Zachwell Morgan and others on lands for which they received patents several years later (1781) from a commission appointed to adjust claims to unpatented lands. From here David Morgan emigrated to a point further up the Monongahela in what is now Marion county, in which several settlements were made by 1772. In each of the seven years following (1769-75) many settlers, usually from eastern Virginia, arrived and made improvements, built a log cabin and raised corn, which later entitled them to a settlement right to four hundred acres and a preëmption right to one thousand acres adjoining. Stockaded forts and blockhouses were built for protection against the Indians, whose outbreak in 1774 retarded settlement for several years. Roads, which were beginning to emerge, usually followed the tops of the ridges in order to avoid Indian ambushes in the hollows. The leading men of this region in 1774 included Colonel William Morgan, Colonel Charles Martin, Colonel William Haymond, John Pierpont, David Scott, Richard Harrison, Jonathan Cobun, William Stewart, John Statler and Michael Kerns.

While these Monongahela settlements rapidly increased, the boundary between Virginia and Pennsylvania was still unsettled. The line originally claimed by Penn as the southern boundary of his grant would have given him a large part of the Monongahela region which is now included in West Virginia. In September, 1767, the surveyors of the Mason and Dixon line, who had been accompanied by an escort of the Six Nations until they reached Petersburg, Pennsylvania, continued westward from that point alone beyond the western limit of Maryland marking the northern boundary of what is now Preston and Monongalia counties. They were first threatened and finally stopped near Mt. Morris, on Dunkard Creek, at the crossing of the Warrior branch of the Great Catawba war path, by the Delawares and Shawnees, who claimed to be tenants of the country. The survey was not finally completed until seventeen years later. In 1773 Governor Dunmore, of Virginia, sent Dr. John Connolly to Fort Pitt to resist occupation by Pennsylvania, which had just established courts at Hanna's Town (near Greensburg), with determination to exercise jurisdiction over the lower Monongahela Valley. He soon occupied Fort Pitt, changed the name to Fort Dunmore, and established a rival court and rival magistrates precipitating a bitter struggle which was stopped only by the Revolution.

In October, 1776, amid the storm of the Revolution, the first general assembly of the commonwealth of Virginia created Monongalia county by the division of the District of West Augusta into three counties, the other two of which were Youghogheny and Ohio. Its boundaries included all territory drained by the Monongahela in Virginia, and in Pennsylvania south of a southeastward line drawn from the ridge between the headwaters of Chartiers Creek and Ten Mile Creek through Redstone Fort (Brownsville) and along the Dunlap and Braddock roads to the meridian of the head fountain of the Potomac. Under provisions of the act, landholders of the county met at the home of Jonathan Cobun, two miles east of the site of Morgantown, in the following December; and, at an election conducted by the sheriff, voted that the meetings of the county court should be held on the plantation of Theophilus Phillips, two miles from the site of Geneva, Pennsylvania, which was located in the most thickly populated part of the county. The county court, a self-perpetuating body, which then not only governed the county but also both civil and criminal jurisdiction, was composed of justices of the peace appointed by the governor from persons recommended by the court itself. The tenure of office was for life or during good behavior. The members of the court received no compensation for their services, but from their number the governor appointed the county sheriff.

During the Revolution, inhabitants of the Monongahela region, besides manning their feeble stockade forts against Indian attacks, participated in campaigns and battles in the East. The incursions of the Indians along the Monongahela and the difficulty which Colonel John Evans encountered in attempting to guard a frontier of eighty miles, with its scattered settlements at Horse Shoe, Tygart's Valley, West Fork, Dunkard's Bottom and Morgantown, induced Governor Harrison, of Virginia, in 1782, to send a company of militia from Hampshire, which Colonel Evans stationed on Tygart's Valley, Horse Shoe and West Fork. Rejoicing at the news of peace with England, they were not certain of peace with the Indians on the western frontier for over a decade. The final Indian attack in Monongalia occurred in the Dunkard Valley near Blacksville in 1791. Monongalia furnished soldiers for the expedition of General St. Clair, which met defeat in November, 1791, and for Wayne's campaign, which met success in 1795.

At the close of the Revolution, the settlement of the boundary dispute with Pennsylvania reduced the bounds of Monongalia and necessitated the removal of the county seat. From 1774 to 1780 Virginia courts continued to sit on territory claimed by Virginia in western Pennsylvania. An agreement on the boundary was finally reached by negotiations of 1779, which were ratified by Virginia in June, 1780. The temporary survey of the Mason and Dixon line was completed in 1781, and the permanent survey in 1784 (soon followed by the completion of the survey of the western boundary of Pennsylvania northward to Lake Erie in 1785-86). In April, 1782, before the Pennsylvania-Virginia boundary line was run through Monongalia, and prior to the regular administration of civil government had been settled in the disputed territory, confusion was threatened; and between the Youghogheny and the Monongahela, and in the larger part of Washington county, there was (among the settlers opposed to the transfer to Pennsylvania) a strong sentiment expressed in conventions favorable to a proposed new state including the territory west of the Alleghenies from the Kanawha to Lake Erie—a resurrection of the old Walpole grant of 1772 (the abortive *Vandalia*). It was counteracted by an act of Pennsylvania, passed December, 1782, but was revived in 1794 by some of the leaders in the Whiskey Insurrection.

In 1782 the county seat of Monongalia was located at Morgantown by an act of the legislature which made Zackwell Morgan's the place of holding court and designated Morgan's and Boush's Fort (now Buckhannon) as voting places. At Morgantown was built a frame house, which by 1802 was replaced by a brick structure. In 1784, however, Monongalia was divided by the legislature, and Harrison county was created from that part south of a line drawn from Ford Fork on the Maryland boundary to the headwaters of Big Sandy, thence down the Big Sandy and Tygart's to the West Fork, thence up West Fork to Bingamon Creek and up Bingamon to the Ohio county boundary. Monongalia refunded to Harrison her proportion of the cost of erecting the public buildings in Monongalia.

"Morgantown" was established as a town by the legislature in 1785. To stimulate the growth of the town the act of incorporation required every purchaser of a lot to erect upon it within four years a house at least eighteen feet square with chimney of stone or brick. In 1788 an extension of three years was allowed on account of Indian hostilities, and in 1792 a further extension was granted because of difficulty of procuring building material. The first trustees were named in the charter, and not elected, and the governor was authorized to fill vacancies. In 1810 the first necessary step toward self-government was taken by making the trustees elective by the freeholders, and in 1816 they were given power to levy taxes. Not until 1824 was a survey of lots, streets and alleys made and entered in the office of the county clerk. In May, 1828, the town trustees passed town regulations (published by N. B. Madera, clerk) to restrict racing through the streets, to stop the play of long-bullets and the discharge of arms except for slaughtering beeves and hogs for food, to present the throwing of dirt or filth into the streets and to secure correct scales and weights in the butcher stalls of the market house. By the new charter of 1838 a government under trustees of more extended powers was inaugurated resulting in an increasing number of ordinances—some of which, necessitating a serious break with long-established customs, met with fierce opposition. The latter are illustrated by the "hog ordinance," which after a varied career as one of the chief municipal problems was finally settled by the *referendum* in the election of 1852, by which the hogs lost by twenty-five votes.

The industrial development of Morgantown may be presented as a fitting introduction to that of the surrounding region. Beginning with perhaps no more than four log houses, a frame court house and jail, and a store and a grist mill on Decker's Creek beyond the borough boundary, it grew little before 1791. Several new settlers arrived in 1792.

In 1793 the town became the terminus of a post route from Pittsburgh, established under the management of the Pittsburgh Gazette, which was distributed by private post riders both before and after the United States mails reached Pittsburgh in 1788. A post office was established in 1794 and a post route was designated from Hagerstown via Hancock and Cumberland to Morgantown, thence to Uniontown and Brownsville. Ordinaries were licensed in 1796. Henry Dering who came from Lancaster, Pennsylvania, via Hagerstown, opened a hotel before 1800; and John Shisler who came from Winchester, Virginia, in 1796, began to manufacture wagons by 1802. Buggy, carriage and furniture manufacturing works were established in the decade after 1840. Tanbark was used in the local tanneries. The first newspaper printed in the town was established in 1803. The first steamboat arrived from Pittsburgh in 1826.

The town improved more rapidly from 1815 to 1830 largely influenced by growing trade with the region now included in Preston, Marion, Barbour and Taylor counties from which the people came to buy salt, iron and groceries; but in the decade after 1840 it felt a decline of trade resulting especially from the construction of the Northwestern Turnpike in 1838, and the formation of Marion county in 1842—and, after the opening of the B. & O. main line in 1853, it lost the great interior wagon trade and could thereafter depend only on the local county trade until it could secure slack-water navigation or railway connection. Although the streets seemed deserted in comparison with their busy aspect of the thirties, closer touch was felt with the larger world by the establishment of a daily mail by 1854. Trade with the western end of the county was encouraged by the construction of a suspension bridge in 1854 by a company which had been organized four years earlier. Before 1853 Pittsburgh was the main point for exchange of state bank paper, and in the absence of safe mails payments were conveyed to eastern cities by private messengers. After 1853 money was sent by express from Fairmont until 1875 when a

VIEW ON CHEAT RIVER.

nearer express office was established at Fairchance. Telegraph connection was opened in 1866 by a line from Pittsburgh to Fairmont.

Probably the first road in Monongalia followed Deckers Creek from Morgantown to Rock Forge, thence over the general route of the later Kingwood pike and across Cheat at Dunkard Bottom to the site of Westernport, Maryland, and to Winchester. It was probably cleared as a pack horse road between 1772 and 1776, and was later known as the State road or old Winchester road. Over it the early settlers brought salt and iron from Winchester (before the days of local iron works and Conemaugh salt), and after the Revolution it became an emigrant road to the West. Even as early as 1772 Michael Kern kept a boat yard at the mouth of Decker's Creek for the accomodation of westward emigrants who followed this road to Morgantown—from which they continued their journey to Kentucky by the Monongahela and the Ohio. In 1784 the importance of trade with the Ohio, and of political connections between East and West, induced Washington to urge connection from the Potomac by a canal via Cheat to the nearest navigable point on the Monongahela. In 1791 the state road from Winchester was extended to the mouth of Fishing Creek (now New Martinsville) and soon became a wagon road from the mouth of Savage River (Westernport) to Morgantown. In 1800 the Allegheny Turnpike Company was projected to improve the road from the mouth of Savage River to the head of navigation on the Ohio, but failed to organize. In 1812 the Monongalia Glades road was opened to Clarksburg via Smithton.

The first ferry established by law was located across Cheat at Andrew Ice's in 1785, others were established across the Monongahela in 1791 and 1792, and others across Cheat in 1792 and 1805. After January, 1807, ferries were authorized by the county courts instead of by the general assembly.

In the earlier decades after the Revolution, population and development in Monongalia county increased rapidly in spite of the tide of immigration to Kentucky and Ohio. The population of four thousand in 1790 was more than doubled in a decade. This development was doubtless stimulated after 1794 by the establishment of a mail route, with weekly mails, which gave communication with the larger world. In their somewhat isolated homes the people were happy with their work. The discontent resulted in the Whiskey Insurrection of western Pennsylvania in August, 1794, was felt to some extent in neighboring Virginia settlements on the Monongahela; but they sent no representative to the insurgent meeting at Braddock's Field nor to the later meeting at Parkinson's Ferry (Monongahela City), and the people of Morgantown offered a determined resistance against insurgents from Pennsylvania who instigated an attack on the house of the excise collector of the county and later attempted to secure proselytes to their cause. After the military advance into western Pennsylvania, it appears that part of the Virginia division commanded by Governor Henry Lee (father of General Robert E. Lee) went from Pittsburgh to Morgantown, "from thence to Winchester by way of Frankfort."

By 1810 the population had increased to twelve thousand seven hundred and ninety-three, and the iron works on Cheat and on Decker's Creek furnished a basis for prospective increase of material development restricted only by problems of transportation.

To meet the demand for connecting the interests of East and West, and for securing more direct commercial intercourse with the Ohio from which such commodities as salt could be obtained far more conveniently than by the overland route from Winchester or the water route from Pittsburgh, in January, 1812, an act of the legislature authorized the opening of a road from the Monongalia Glades (now in Preston) via the mouth of Buffalo to the present site of New Martinsville which was to connect on the opposite bank of the Ohio with a road from Zanesville. The road, however, did not meet the expectation of its projectors, and in January, 1817, new efforts for better communications resulted in the incorporation of the Monongahela Navigation

Company to secure better facilities in river transportation, but all efforts of the next few years to secure slack-water navigation failed.

The census of 1820 showed a decrease of two thousand in the population—a decrease only partially explained by the creation of Preston county with a population of three thousand in 1818. In 1823, all efforts to secure slack-water navigation having failed, attention was directed toward the question of canal communication between eastern and western waters. Three years later (on April 29) the first steamboat reached Morgantown followed by others which facilitated the escape of indentured apprentices; but merchants who had already been transporting salt from Pittsburgh continued to buy their dry goods and groceries in Philadelphia and Baltimore. By 1830, however, the continued arrival of steamboats from Pittsburgh, causing a shifting of the old dispute between Wheeling and Pittsburgh in regard to which was the head of navigation, stimulated public demand for improvement of the Monongahela. In Congress, Mr. Doddridge obtained a resolution inquiring into the expediency of an appropriation for improving the navigation from Pittsburgh to Morgantown and to Clarksburg.

In 1830 the census showed an increase of three thousand since 1820. Morgantown became an educational centre by the incorporation of Monongalia Academy in 1829 and the establishment of a female academy in 1832. Development in the western end of the county resulted in the establishment of Blacksville as a town; and growth of settlements further up the river, together with the demand for easier access to the county seat, resulted in petitions for the creation of Marion county which was accomplished in 1842.

In the decade from 1830 to 1840 the question of roads was still prominent. Earlier efforts were directed toward securing the survey of a road over the nearest and best route from a point on the Ohio between the mouth of Fishing Creek and Marietta via Morgantown to the national road at or near the Youghogheny bridge, and the establishment of a mail route with semi-weekly stages from Uniontown via Morgantown and Clarksburg to Parkersburg. These enterprises were opposed in 1830 by Kingwood which seemed disposed to enlist Winchester, Romney, Westernport and Pruntytown against the establishment of the proposed new route; and it also met some opposition within the county on the ground that it would prevent other roads of the county from receiving proper attention. The discussion of the question led the editor to suggest that the road leading to all eternity needed most serious attention.

The efforts of Monongalia to secure better means of communication were stimulated by neighboring improvements. In 1831 stages began to carry great western mail from Philadelphia to Pittsburgh in three days. Pennsylvania by her canal, and Maryland by her railroad, were struggling for the western trade. It was evident that the completion of the canal would soon reduce freights and no one yet knew at what point on the Ohio between Pittsburgh and the Kanawha the B. & O. would terminate; but it seemed certain that either the B. & O. railroad or the C. & O. canal would reach Cumberland which would thus become a deposit for western products. Therefore it was urged that Morgantown should push the opening of the road from the mouth of Fishing Creek to Smithfield in the direction of Cumberland (via Monongalia county), and the opening of the navigation of the Monongahela; and that she should secure the establishment of a bank. In 1832 legislative authority was obtained to open and improve the navigation of the Monongahela in Monongalia county and to raise money by a lottery to construct the Maryland and Ohio Turnpike. Four years later a portion of this road known as the Brandonville and Fishing Creek Turnpike was surveyed, and during the following two years efforts at construction were pushed forward. Early in 1833 a line of four-horse stages was started between Morgantown and Uniontown by Colonel Johnson and a year later a tri-weekly mail in two-horse stages was established between Uniontown and Clarksburg via Morgantown. In 1839 the Dunkard Creek Turnpike Company and the Morgantown and Clarksburg (and Ice's Ferry) Turnpike Company were incorporated by the assembly. The latter was completed in 1840 via Smithton to Morgantown and, using the Brandonville and Fishing Creek Turnpike to Ice's Ferry, thence to the Pennsylvania line.

In 1840 the location and construction of turnpikes and bridges were the chief subjects of local interest. The establishment of Ellicott's rolling mill at Ice's Ferry on Cheat (1840) furnished a new impetus to such public improvements, and to new efforts to obtain slack-water navigation, first on the Monongahela and later on Cheat (1847). The Dunkard Creek Turnpike projected in 1839 was revived in 1847 and located to Blacksville from whence it was later extended to Burton on the B. & O. The Morgantown and Bridgeport Turnpike was authorized by act of 1849. The Brandonville, Morgantown and Fishing Creek pike was repaired in 1850. The Kingwood, Morgantown and West Union (Aurora) Turnpike, incorporated in 1848, was completed in 1851 partly on the location of the Morgantown and Clarksburg Turnpike. The Pennsylvania, Beverly and Morgantown Turnpike, incorporated in 1837, was revived in 1853 and constructed via Evansville. From Morgantown to Evansville, it was usually called the Evansville pike. The Masontown and Independence Turnpike, incorporated in 1856, was built from a point on the road one mile west of Ice's Ferry.

Among the various industries of the county besides agriculture, for a half century after 1800, were the manufacture of iron (one of the earliest), the preparation of country millstones, the operation of carding and fulling mills, the manufacture of paper (begun 1839), the manufacture of pottery (which became important by 1830), carriage making (which became prominent after 1851), the operation of foundries, and the manufacture of furniture.

By 1845, Morgantown contained about one hundred and fifty dwellings, several stores and mills, two printing offices, two churches and an academy. Jamestown, Granville and Blacksville were the chief villages in the county; and Jackson's iron works on Cheat were industrially important.

The names and ruins of iron furnaces in the eastern part of the county recall the story of the first early industry—which began in the neighborhood of Quarry Run and on Decker's Creek and Aaron Creek before the close of the eighteenth century. From the early output of the Quarry Run territory came the incentive to establish (nearly a mile below Ice's Ferry) the Cheat Iron Works (and later the first rolling mill west of the Allegheny mountains outside of Pennsylvania) which by 1811 was supplied from additional furnaces to which in 1836 were added the Clay furnace with its eight miles of tramway and in 1845 the Anne Furnace. By 1840, or soon thereafter, the Iron Works (then owned by the Ellicott's) included a nail factory, a rolling mill and a foundry, machine and wagon shops, and a blacksmith shop. Furnishing employment for over twelve hundred persons, when the population of Morgantown was only seven hundred, the Iron Works settlement contained nearly one thousand people whose social and economic needs were supplied by the works, a company store, a daily mail carrier from Morgantown, a school, a justice of the peace and three neighboring churches. The manufactured products, beyond the needs of the neighboring territory centering in the Morgantown market, were sent on flat boats to Pittsburgh. To facilitate transportation the Ellicott's built a steamboat (*The Lady Ellicott*) which was abandoned because it was unable to ascend the Cheat. A gradual decline of the industry, beginning after 1846 and causing the failure of the Ellicott's in 1848 or in 1849, resulted in its termination in 1868.

The construction of the Baltimore and Ohio through Preston and Taylor and Marion counties in 1852 over a route practically determined by the foresight of Thomas Haymond (representative from Marion county in the Virginia legislature) stimulated the industrial and social development of the entire upper Monongahela Valley. Even Morgantown to some extent was benefitted by the construction through Pres-

THE OLD SUSPENSION BRIDGE, MORGANTOWN.

OLD FRANKLIN HOUSE, MORGANTOWN, WHICH OCCUPIED THE SITE OF THE PRESENT MADEIRA HOTEL.

ton; steamboats which reached the town from Pittsburgh brought cargoes of supplies which were transported by wagons from this head of navigation across the country to the great tunnel, and in some instances Irish laborers came by the same route.

The early surveys of the Baltimore and Ohio passed down Muddy Creek in Preston and down Decker's Creek via Morgantown, and the change of route may have been partly due to the opposition shown both in Monongalia county and in Greene county (Pennsylvania) by people who feared the innovation would seriously affect the price of horses and horse feed, and the lives of wives and children and of cows and hogs. "Compel them to stop at Cumberland," they said in their meetings, "and then all the goods will be wagoned through our country, all the hogs will be fed with our corn, and all the horses with our oats. We don't want our wives and our children frightened to death. * * * We don't want our hogs and cows run over and killed * * *."

Monongalia county, regretting the earlier opposition which had been a factor in diverting the route of the road to Fairmont, made new efforts to escape from her comparative isolation. Although the efforts of her citizens secured from the legislature (1852) the incorporation of the Morgantown and Independence Railroad Company which proposed to begin by 1857 the construction of a road to intersect the B. & O., the work failed through lack of necessary subscriptions. Enterprising citizens also urged another road—"The Monongahela and Ravenswood Railroad"—which the legislature incorporated in 1854 to connect Morgantown with the Ohio, but which never got beyond the paper stage of projection. This road was really conceived as a link connecting the Pennsylvania lines with the Ohio at a terminal point which, situated below Parkersburg, was believed to possess advantages over either Wheeling or Parkersburg as a satisfactory head of navigation, and which therefore would give an advantage in securing control of the trade of the Ohio Valley.

At the same time efforts were renewed to secure better facilities for river transportation. A company was chartered by Virginia in 1847 to slack the Monongahela from the state line to Fairmont. In 1851 it became active in its efforts to obtain subscriptions but failed. Its charter was extended by Virginia in 1853 and the Board of Public Works was authorized to subscribe to its stock as soon as the Pennsylvania company completed slack-water navigation to the state line. Morgantown, in March, 1853, became especially active in soliciting aid, and appointed a committee to institute suit against the Pennsylvania company to compel it to complete its work or forfeit its charter—but the suit was never brought. The charter of the Virginia company was revived in 1858, extending until 1868 the time for completing the work of slacking the river to Fairmont—and again in 1860, authorizing the extension of the work to Clarksburg. At that time the Pennsylvania Navigation Company had completed dams (1844), making the lower Monongahela navigable from Pittsburgh to Brownsville and by 1856 to New Geneva; but assurances of aid from the Pennsylvania company came to naught, and civil war postponed the subject until the incorporation of the Marion and Monongahela Navigation Company in 1863, and the amendment of its charter in February, 1867, so as to allow it to collect tolls on lumber and their freight as soon as one lock and dam should be completed. The project was fruitless as its predecessors and nothing was accomplished until Congress began a policy of appropriations in 1872.

PRESTON COUNTY.

The region east of Monongalia had some special advantages of geographical location. Its earlier settlers were Dr. Thomas Eckarly and his two brothers, who, seeking to avoid military duty, left Easton, Pennsylvania, in 1753, and settled on Cheat river—but their settlement was terminated by an Indian attack upon them at Dunkard Bottom.

The first permanent settlement in the territory now included in Preston were made on the waters of Big Sandy in 1769 by James Clark and John Judy—one near the site of Clifton Mills and the other two miles from Bruceton. In 1770, Samuel Worral came from Philadelphia and by settlement right occupied tracts of land on Sandy Creek Glades, and James Walls founded the Walls settlement east of Cheat. Others from Pennsylvania followed and settled under the impression that they were within the boundaries of Pennsylvania. In 1770-73 hunters from the South Branch led the way for Virginia homeseekers who soon began a settlement on Dunkard Bottom two miles from the site of Kingwood, and a few settlers continued to arrive even after the opening of the Revolution. The settlement at Dunkard Bottom was attacked by Indians from the Ohio country in April, 1778, and neighboring settlements in 1780. Later attacks were made at Dunkard Bottom in 1788.

After the Revolution, old settlers obtained patents for the lands on which they had settled, and new settlers arrived in larger numbers, increasing each year. After 1784 Francis and William Deakins selected numerous choice tracts of land in the territory near the Maryland boundary. New settlements were made at Brandonville and in the vicinity of Aurora by 1786. A German settlement called Salem was made in 1787. In 1789 the settlements were growing by immigration from the South Branch, the Valley of Virginia, Maryland and Pennsylvania. Among those who came was Colonel John Fairfax, a former superintendent of Washington's Mt. Vernon estate, who purchased from Philip Doddridge a large tract of land in the Monongalia Glades near the present site of Masontown and Reedsville. In 1790 James Brown, coming direct from Ireland, settled in the vicinity of Kingwood. In 1791 Samuel Morton, of West Chester county, Pennsylvania, owned the first mill on Big Sandy Creek at Bruceton. A ferry was established there by the legislature in 1792. From 1785 the pioneer clearings slowly widened into farms of considerable size. Especially after 1795, when the fear of Indians had ceased by Wayne's victory, the settlements rapidly increased in numbers.

At this time the settlers still obtained iron and salt from the South Branch by means of pack horses which, heavy laden with furs, crossed the mountains by bridle paths on a difficult journey that required several days. At night they encamped and sank to sleep on pack-saddle pillows, often amid the sound of howling wolves or screaming panthers.

By 1800, or soon thereafter, the bridle path and pack-horse road was evolving into a wider immigrant road, and in a few instances wagons were replacing sleds and ox-carts; but the furs, obtained in diminishing quantities, were still carried by pack-horse over the Clarksburg and Winchester road (the Monongalia state road) or the Morgantown and Winchester road (the two names referring to a single road) eastward from its union with the state road near a wooded site which was a noted camping place on the route before the name Kingwood was given to the cluster of houses built there in 1807 and established as a town in 1811. Many of the earlier settlers of Kentucky used this route from Winchester to the fort on the Ohio opposite Marietta from which they took flat boats to Covington and other places at which forts were provided for their protection. Although iron, as well as salt and luxuries such as coffee, was still purchased east of the mountains for the larger number of settlements, the Jackson iron works on Cheat near Ice's Ferry produced considerable iron which in addition to local use was carried on flat boats to the distant New Orleans market. Early in the century, alterations and repairs were made on the Monongalia state road at various points westward to Parkersburg including the section from Gandy's (near the site of Gladesville) to the Tygart's Valley River. In 1812, in order to encourage settlements, and to establish better commercial facilities, the legislature authorized the opening of a wagon road from Monongalia Glades to the mouth of Buffalo and thence to the Ohio at the mouth of Fishing Creek to meet a road under construction between the opposite bank of the Ohio and Zanesville.

Before 1800 competent magistrates in every neighborhood transacted the simple legal business which earlier would have required a trip to Morgantown. Soon thereafter, complaining of the long distance they were compelled to travel to attend court, to vote, and to muster, they began to urge the need of the formation of a new county at the northeast. This need was emphasized by the percipible progress of settlement after 1813, and the division was made by the legislature in 1818 without objection of Monongalia. John Fairfax was president of the first Preston county court—held at Kingwood, the oldest town in the county—and later he became sheriff by seniority of commission as magistrate.

By this time the panther was retreating before the advance of the settlers, although the wolf and the bear were still numerous beyond the margin of the settlements. Cattle raising which had begun as a business to meet the demands of the eastern market, and was encouraged by the completion of the National Road between Cumberland and Wheeling in 1818, brought money into the community and stimulated new efforts toward new improvements—such as the water mills, the introduction of frame and stone buildings, and the beginnings of mercantile business in the small village store.

The frequent passage of immigrant teams on their way to Ohio indicated further improvement in the roads, and increasing travel stimulated new enterprises such as the Northwestern Road Company which was incorporated in 1827 to build a road from Winchester to Parkersburg. In 1828, across Cheat at a point later known as Albrightsville the people of Preston by authority of the legislature built a suspension bridge which remained until its destruction by the Confederates in 1863. A year later (1829) a road from Maryland via Kingwood to the Ohio was authorized—the money to be raised by lottery.

After the Virginia constitutional convention of 1829-30, the legislature authorized the construction of many turnpikes—some of which, because of failures to raise money by subscription or by lottery, never reached beyond the paper stage, although the companies promoting them frequently secured renewals of legislative acts. Among those which were finally completed was (1) the Morgantown and Fishing Creek Turnpike, projected and authorized in 1830, and built by 1836 from the Pennsylvania line near Smithfield (now Somerfield) via Brandonville and Morgantown to the Ohio, and (2) the Northwestern Turnpike constructed by Virginia as a rival of the National (Cumberland) road across the mountains to the Ohio and passing from Winchester via Romney through the southern part of Preston county, across the picturesque Cheat valley, along the waters of Little Sandy and through Evansville (1833), and via Clarksburg to the Ohio. The latter, a toll road completed soon after 1838 after various reverses, became at once a busy thoroughfare of travel and traffic which stimulated the creation of many inns and towns along its route (such as West Union—now Aurora, which sprang up near the Maryland line in 1846) and in many ways influenced the material prosperity and social life of people of the counties through which it passed. In 1835 the legislature authorized the survey of a road from Smithfield, Pennsylvania, via Brandonville and Kingwood to intersect the Northwestern Turnpike near Evansville at a point which became Fellowsville by 1848. Two years later it provided for a survey of Cheat from the Pennsylvania line upward to the Northwestern Turnpike, and also incorporated the Greenville Furnace Company which transported its product by water from Cheat to Pittsburgh and Cincinnati. In 1840 it incorporated the Preston Railroad, Lumber and Mining Company, organized to operate in the lumber and mining business on Cheat.

By 1845 Kingwood had about thirty dwellings and several stores and the chief staple of the county was Indian corn. Considerable sugar and tobacco was also raised. In 1850 one of the first prominent woolen factories in Preston was established at Bruceton (originally called Morton's Mills).

By 1852, the Baltimore and Ohio railroad, that horseless rival to the great Northwestern Turnpike, which had scorned the possibility of competition, was pushing from Piedmont westward across Preston county, parallel to the extensively travelled route whose immense throngs were soon to be diverted to newer routes of more rapid travel. After passing over deep gorges on high trestle work, and over turbulent streams by heavy masonry work, at Tunnelton it passed through the longest railroad tunnel which had yet been constructed in the world and continued westward toward Fairmont creating new towns (Rowlesburg, Newburg, etc.) in a region which was still sparsely settled, and bringing the pioneer prospectors who prepared the way for the later era of great industrial development based on coal and timber.

Just above the site of Tunnelton, on Tunnel Hill, on the pike in the direction of Fellowsville, a hamlet known as Greigsville sprang into existence, grew to a busy town resembling the frontier terminal stations of the later transcontinental Union-Pacific, and melted away with the cessation of the construction of railroad and tunnel. It was the scene of the termination of the "Irish War" of the combined factions of Connaughters and Corkers (about five hundred) against the Fardowners, who, after being driven eastward from the scene of construction camps at Fairmont and partially dispersed at Newburg, were finally relieved from further disturbance at Tunnel Hill by the prompt action of acting sheriff, Colonel J. A. F. Martin, who with a force of one hundred and thirty men dispersed the invading force and arrested several leaders.

Many of the Irish laborers, although in some instances they engaged in disturbing factional fights during the construction of the roads, became permanent residents and contributed a useful element to the citizenship of the state.

The new village of Tunnelton, the neighboring successor to the construction town of Greigsville, was located on the B. & O., ten miles south of Kingwood, at the head of Pringles Run, at a spot on which the primeval forests were first broken in the summer of 1849 by the B. & O. surveyors who announced to the neighboring farmer-pioneers the invasion of steam transportation to the Ohio. It was built on land acquired by Hon. James C. McGrew, who perceiving the advantageous position erected the first house and the first store which furnished the nucleus for the future town largely supported at first by timber and lumber industry to which was added a large tannery in 1858. Later Mr. McGrew, after opening mines and constructing tramways and other structures, began to mine and ship coal to supply the increasing demand in eastern cities, but was forced to abandon his enterprise by a discrimination in freight rates in favor of other mines farther west in which railroad officials were interested, he disposed of all his interests in the vicinity of Tunnelton. The first post office immediately followed the opening of the railroad.

New industrial life began at many points and stimulated new enterprises. The stave industry was begun at Independence in 1853. The first circular saw mill which entered the county began operations at two miles south of Tunnelton in 1854. Another began work at Newburg in 1865 and a third at Austin in 1867 and three years later they were at work in other sections of the county. By 1852 Cranberry Summit and Rowlesburg had also become centers of considerable lumber and timber business and coal mines were extensively operated at Newburg and Austen. Coal mines were opened at Newburg in 1855 and at Austen eleven years later. The Orrel Coal Company which operated the Newburg mines after 1856 also acquired timber lands. The revival of interest in the iron industry is shown by the construction of the Virginia Furnace on Muddy Creek in 1853 by Harrison Hagans, who shipped his product by rail to Cranberry Summit, and the later enterprise of George Hardman near Independence (Irondale) in 1859 and at Gladesville in 1869. The demand for better highways was also increased. The West Union and Morgantown Turnpike was opened in 1854. Brandonville was connected with the railroad in 1857-58 by a turnpike terminating at Cranberry Summit.

The rapid development of the region along the new railroad resulted in an unsuccessful attempt to remove the county seat from Kingwood to the east side of Cheat at the suspension bridge. Kingwood increased its hold on the county seat in 1857 by erecting a fire brick court house to replace the small stone structure. This hold was strengthened a year later by the establishment of Kingwood's first newspaper, although in 1869 when the court house was burned by an incendiary the question of removal to Cranberry Summit (later Portland and now Terra Alta) was agitated.

With the gradual development of the eastern part of the county there was a revival of the old boundary dispute with Maryland which persisted until it was finally settled by the decision of the United States Supreme Court in 1910 and the survey which followed.

In November, 1852, as the B. & O. was pushing westward through southern Preston and via Fairmont to the Ohio at Wheeling, enterprising citizens of Preston and Monongalia counties desiring to develop the great mineral wealth of the region secured from the legislature the incorporation of a company to build a branch railroad from the mouth of the Cheat via Morgantown to intersect the B. & O. at Independence. Although the enterprise failed through lack of general interest and financial means, its inception was prophetic of the great industrial development of the region a half century later.

TAYLOR COUNTY.

West of the southern part of Preston was a region which in 1844 was organized as Taylor county. Although settlements therein had been made as early as 1772, its earlier development had been much retarded. From the beginning of the nineteenth century its timber found some commercial demand for production of charcoal used by the old iron furnaces of Taylor and Preston. After 1820 considerable white oak hewed for ship timber was hauled to the Monongahela and rafted to Pittsburgh. A new stimulus to greater development followed the opening of the Northwestern Turnpike. Williamsport, or Pruntytown, situated near the ferry across Tygart's River was the first village of any importance. Its growth for a while was partly influenced by Rector College, which reported one hundred and ten students in 1840, and by its later selection as the county seat. In 1845, it had grown to a town of thirty dwellings, three stores and two churches.

Wonderful changes in the industrial and social life of the county followed the construction of the B. & O. railroad. Shipments of cattle and other earlier sources of wealth were made with larger profits. Timber resources were utilized, agricultural interests were improved, coal mines and other mineral deposits were opened, manufacturing and commercial interests flourished and thriving business centers were created. Fetterman, bright with prospects of rapid growth, became a way station only through an enthusiastic over-confidence of its citizens which induced them to elevate the price of land beyond that which the railroad promoters proposed to pay. Grafton, founded in the woods at Three Forks—its first house constructed by Mr. McGraw, one of the many "railroad Irish," whose descendants have become prominent and useful in the affairs of the state—grasped the opportunity which Fetterman failed to seize, obtained the location of railroad shops and buildings, became the divisional stop for the change of engines and crews, and later flourished as the terminus of the Parkersburg branch known as the Northwestern Virginia Railroad which, chartered in 1851 and supported by the interests of the B. & O. which made its construction possible, by 1857 was completed to the Ohio, connecting there by steamer with the road from Marietta to Cincinnati and beyond Cincinnati to St. Louis.

Largely the creation of the Baltimore and Ohio, the new town also later received a new stimulus to growth by securing the location of the court house which was removed from Pruntytown. Its railroad facilities attracted capital to the town, gave it excellent manufacturing plants, and made it quite a mercantile center. Before the extension of branches of the B. & O. it was the market for all the timber from Buckhannon and Valley rivers—which was floated down and caught in the boom above the town, but later the timber was sawed nearer its source and the lumber shipped by railroad.

MARION COUNTY.

Near the junction of the Tygart's Valley River and the West Fork centered Marion county, whose development at the coming of the railroad had advanced beyond that of Taylor—although its oldest settlements were probably made no earlier than those of Taylor. By 1772 Captain James Booth and John Thomas settled on Booth's Creek near the site of Boothsville, and David Morgan and others at the mouth of Prickett's Creek, five miles below the site of Fairmont. Their descendants form a considerable part of the population of the county.

At the close of the Revolution many families settled in the vicinity of Yellow Rock Ford on the West Fork, and west of the site of Fairmont. Others followed in rapid succession. For the earliest settlers of this region Morgantown and Clarksburg were marketing centres; but, with the increase of improvements and the erection of mills along the streams, nearer stores were established, and monthly communication with the outside world was later secured by a regular mail route.

In 1819, Middletown (now Fairmont) was legally established and regularly plotted in a laurel thicket on the farm of Boaz Fleming—the roughest and poorest land in the vicinity. Its earliest development was partly determined by the need of a midway stopping-place for travellers between Morgantown and Clarksburg. Its later growth was due to the establishment of various industries in the vicinity. In April, 1831, Barnes and Haymond announced through the Monongalian, of Morgantown that they would begin fulling and carding at Middletown Mills on May 1 and agreed to take grain at Thomas Barnes' on Buffalo and Robert Lynn's mill on Tygart's.

In 1837 Rivesville was laid out upon the land of Elisha Snodgrass. In 1838, across the river from Middletown, was established Palatine at which the Marion machine works manufactured McCormick reapers

ONE OF THE OLDEST HOUSES IN MARION COUNTY: ABOUT ONE HUNDRED YEARS OLD.

a decade before the civil war. In 1839 a town was plotted adjacent to the Boothsville post office which had been established in 1833 at Robert Reed's tavern near the forks of Booth's Creek. The first newspaper of the county was established at Fairmont about 1840. Some of the smaller towns of the county are older than the county, but the larger number were established after the arrival of the railroad.

The attempt to secure the formation of a separate county in 1842, twenty-three years after the plan had first been proposed to the legislature, was successful in spite of considerable opposition in the legislature both from the delegates of Monongalia and those of Harrison. The first county court met at the house of William Kerr, and later sessions were held in the Methodist Church until the first court house was built. The early court days were general trading days for the people of the surrounding country—and by some were often regarded as convenient occasions for disputes and fights. By 1845 Fairmont had seventy dwellings and five stores; and Palatine across the river had twenty-five dwellings and two stores. In the vicinity were located several flouring mills and other mills.

A decided increase in the population of the county began in 1849 through the immigration which followed closely on the heels of the surveying engineers of the Baltimore and Ohio. Some of the immigrants were Irish, fresh from the bogs of Connaught and the lakes of Killarney, who carried with them all their local feuds and prejudices which induced them to transfer their sectional fighting from the old sod to the land of greater freedom and opportunity. In a locally famous riot, in which the Connaughters who were employed at Benton's Ferry attacked the Fardowners at Ice's Mill and pursued them to Fairmont in an exciting chase punctuated by occasional gun-shots and hideous yells, the law abiding citizens of Fairmont proved themselves equal to the occasion by arresting all accessible assailants, eighty-eight of whom they placed in jail where they had an opportunity to study their first lessons in Americanization.

The approaching railroad encouraged other activities which furnished other incentives to industry and progress. These included the construction of three turnpikes, each begun in 1849—one to Weston, another to Beverly, and another to Fishing Creek. In February, 1850, the people were excited with delight by the first arrival of a steamboat —the *Globe*—resulting in the subsequent arrival of others which began to make regular trips in high water during 1852, and also producing local efforts to secure permanent navigation through organization of the Monongahela Navigation Company, and attempts to interest capitalists—efforts which failed largely through lack of sufficient encouragement from the people of the county. A suspension bridge across the river to Patatine was completed in April, 1852, and the completion of the B. & O. from the East to Fairmont was celebrated on June 23 following. In 1853 a state stock bank was organized.

Rafting on the Monongahela to Pittsburgh and lower points which began as early as 1840 continued until about 1890. A few years after the completion of the B. & O. in 1852 much lumber cut by portable mills was shipped from Fairmont, Mannington and Farmington.

Mannington, which receive its earliest stimulus from the construction of the railroad, stands on the site of a clearing first made in 1786 at the fork of Buffalo and Pyles Creek by Robert Rutherford of Winchester, Virginia, who received from Governor Patrick Henry a patent for the lands on which he settled. It is located near the old Indian trail made memorable by the Indian attacks along Buffalo Creek in 1786 and 1787. Its houses were a dwelling built by Wesley Clayton in 1843 and a tavern and store built by Samuel Koon soon thereafter. By 1845, then known as Koontown, it became a center for mercantile transactions. In 1852 it was renamed for James Mannings, a civil engineer of the new railroad, and in 1856 it was incorporated by the assembly. From 1853, it had a tannery and a good trade in timber products and farm products.

HARRISON COUNTY.

South of Marion was a region which, in its earlier history and before the coming of the railroad, could show a higher development than any part of the Monongahela section of Virginia—possibly excepting parts of Monongalia. Even before the Revolution, it was becoming a settled community in the vicinity of Clarksburg and at other points farther west. Its first white visitor was John Simpson, a trapper and trader, who about 1764 left Maryland westward down Horse Shoe Run to Cheat and then travelled via Sandy Creek and Simpson Creek and down Elk to a point opposite its mouth where he built a camp and remained until the country around him began to be settled (about 1772). In 1772, eight years after John Simpson established his camp and two years after Elias Hughes preëmpted land on the West Fork near the mouth of Hacker's Creek, settlers began to locate lands near the site of Clarksburg. The first mill in the community was built about 1776. By 1781, the village—a mere group of log cabins—was named in honor of George Rogers Clark. In 1782 it was protected from the danger of Indian attack by a small body of troops sent from Hampshire county, and, on the creation of Harrison county in 1784, it became the county seat. By 1784 it had several stores. In 1785, it was incorporated as a town—the twin sister of "Morganstown" of Monongalia. Its first court house was built in 1787. In 1788, it was visited by Bishop Francis Asbury who in his official capacity as a bishop had journeyed horseback from North Carolina via Greenbrier county and Tygart's Valley.

By 1790 it had primitive roads connecting it with both East and West. In December, 1784, the Harrison county court ordered a bridle road opened from Clarksburg to Wickwire's Ford (below Fetterman) on Tygart's River. By 1790 commissioners were ordered to mark a road from the state road by Neal's station on the Little Kanawha to the Harrison and Kanawha county line—partly to meet the needs of travellers from Kentucky who left their canoes at "Belveal" and crossed by land from Neal's station, near the mouth of the Little Kanawha, to Clarksburg (often under direction of a pilot to keep them from losing their way). This connection with the Ohio, and another at Isaac Williams' opposite Marietta were made by William Haymond Sr. and others between 1788 and 1790. In 1790 or 1791 cattle were collected at Clarksburg to drive through to the new Marietta settlement. In 1791 or 1792 William Haymond Jr., after a successful hunting trip, carried beaver skins, buffalo skins and bear skins and meat by canoe down the Kanawha and up the Ohio from Neal's station to Marietta where he sold them.

In 1793 Clarksburg was the seat of an academy and by 1797 it contained about forty dwelling houses. By 1798 it had a post office. In the early days it was on a mail route between Gandy's (of Preston county) and Chilicotha via Salem, Webster, Marietta, Athens and Hewitts. By 1804 it had a wagon shop. At a very early day, too, it had a boat yard for the manufacture of large flat boats which before the era of railroads were built at several points along West Fork and floated to Pittsburg loaded with old iron, whiskey, grain, flour, lumber and country produce. Its first newspaper appeared in 1815—eleven years later than the establishment of the first paper at Morgantown. By 1818 its connections with a larger surrounding region was secured by the opening of new roads such as the Booth's Ferry and Ohio Turnpike from Philippi via Clarksburg and Middlebourne to Sistersville. Its larger trade was always with the East, but by 1819 it received supplies of Bulltown salt, and perhaps also supplies of Kanawha salt which by this time found a market at Salem and other points northward. Although its citizens were of old Virginia descendants, its eastern trading and commercial relations were always with Baltimore which was more conveniently accessible than Richmond. By 1820 its most natural markets were either eastward across the mountains to Atlantic cities (two hundred and fifty or three hundred and fifty miles distant) or down the Monongahela to the towns of the Ohio and the Mississippi. The transportation of breadstuffs in either direction was too expensive to yield a profit. Therefore, the surplus grain was fed to horses, cattle or hogs which could transport themselves "on the hoof" to the eastern markets. By some labor the products of the forest—logs, boats, plank and staves—were a fruitful source of wealth if the uncertainties and irregularities of navigation had not prevented them from reaching the market at time to meet the demand. The commercial development of the town was one of the factors which induced the state to make a survey of the West Fork and the Monongahela to the Pennsylvania state line in 1820. The report of the survey stated that the demands of the country imperiously required that some improvement should be made in the navigation of the river both above and below Clarksburg, and with special reference to the greater importance of the ascending batteaux navigation below Clarksburg whose central position made it a suitable place to collect articles for transportation to Brownsville and thence to Baltimore over the turnpike in wagons which returned westward with merchandise. It was urged that this route offered cheapest transportation for Clarksburg.

By this date, other early settlements were growing into towns of some importance. Among these were Salem, located on an early strategic site as a station for troops sent to watch the Indian trail leading from the Ohio up Middle Island Creek and Long Run to the settlements on the West Fork, and named by its first colony of forty families who arrived from Salem, New Jersey, before peace had been established with the Indians. On the site of Bridgeport, which probably received its first settlers (Joseph Davisson and others) between 1771 and 1774, a town was established by legislative act in 1816. Shinnston at which the first settlement was made in 1773 by Levy Shinn and others, sturdy and independent Quakers from New Jersey, was first legally established as a town by legislative act of 1818. West Milford, the site of which had been included in tracts of land granted a decade or more earlier, gradually grew as a village clustering around the Clement's Mill which was erected in 1817, and it received legal recognition as a town by legislative act of 1821.

Municipal improvement at Clarksburg did not keep pace with economic development. Jack Lovegood, in 1819, after a journey over the mountains, wrote from the safe distance of the Youghogheny Glades in Maryland giving some of his impressions of Clarksburg in which he especially urged the need of a better cemetery, a hearse and better facilities for protection from fires. "I wondered," said he, "why the citizens of Clarksburg who are esteemed as a liberal and intelligent people have not a place to bury their dead secured by a fence from the intrusion of hogs and cattle; and was it not that I looked over the files of the Clarksburg newspaper which had many obituary notices I would have supposed that no person had ever died there. I attended a funeral and to my utter astonishment there was no bier on which the coffin could be placed. A wagon was substituted. I frequently observed in the evenings large fires made by the boys in the center of the town to the jeopardy of all the buildings in the neighborhood. Neither engine, bucket, hose, or even a public ladder is to be seen in the town." Perhaps his criticism caused the town ordinance which went into effect three months later prohibiting hogs from running at large. According to J. H. Dis Debar, a French agent for claimants of the Swan lands who visited Clarksburg in 1846, the citizens were "a somewhat exclusive conservative set with all the traditions and social prejudices pertaining to an ancient moss-grown aristocratic town" with pretensions "by common consent founded upon antiquity of pedigree and superior culture and manners."

In 1845, triweekly stages ran from Green Spring to Romney and thence to Clarksburg (one day) and Parkersburg (three days). Stages from Winchester and Moorefield made connections with this line at

Romney. At that time, Clarksburg contained a population of eleven hundred, seven stores, two newspaper offices, two churches and two academies; and the mineral wealth of the county was already regarded as an element of prosperity. Bridgeport contained twenty-five dwellings and two churches. After 1830 Clarksburg began to feel the influence resulting from better means of communication. By a line of coaches or stages established about 1830, a connection was secured with the National Road. At that time merchants reached Baltimore by horseback in six days, and their heavily loaded wagons required fifteen days or more. The town especially felt the influence of the wide Northwestern Turnpike which, chartered in 1827 and began in 1831, crossing the mountains by easier grades and the streams by good bridges, reached Clarksburg in 1836 and was macadamized from Tygart's Valley River to Parkersburg in 1848. In 1840 facilities for travel and news were increased by the establishment of a daily line of stages and a regular mail service which made connection with the Ohio steamers at Parkersburg. Along the route of the turnpike, for the usual local reasons, there was much opposition to the construction of the railroad which later absorbed the slower traffic of the turnpike.

Clarksburg traffic kept in touch with the advancing terminal station of the B. & O. until it reached Fetterman which remained her railway station from 1852 until the tracks of the Northwestern Railroad reached her from Grafton in 1856, opening the way for her later era of larger opportunity and development.

LEWIS COUNTY.

South of Harrison, along the head waters of West Fork, Lewis county, which in the early days had been a part of Harrison, soon felt the touch of changing conditions produced by the railroad crossing the river below. Notwithstanding its greater isolation, its first settlements were made perhaps as early as those of Harrison. In 1772 its settlers on Hacker's Creek invaded and destroyed the neighboring Indian settlement which had been made about 1765 at Bulltown (in Braxton) by a party of Delawares under Chief Bull from Orange county, New York.

The first settlement on the site of Weston was made by Henry Flesher, who in 1784, after an attack by a party of Indians ravaging the settlements on West Fork, discreetly took refuge for a time at the settlement made by Thomas Hughes and others on Hacker's Creek. By 1800 several Virginia families, which later exerted a strong social and political influence, established homes in the Collins Settlement and elsewhere. With the increase in the number of settlers and the development of settlements, the inconveniences of communication with the county seat at Clarksburg found expression in the demand for the formation of a new county. This demand was satisfied in 1816 by an act of the assembly which created Lewis. "Beginning at the head of the left hand fork of Jesse's run; thence a straight line to the mouth of Kincheloe's Creek; thence up said creek to the dividing ridge; thence a west course to the Wood county line; thence to include all the south part of Harrison down to the mouth of Buckhannon River; thence a straight line to the beginning." Under the provisions of the act the first court was held at Westfield, and the location of a permanent county seat was delegated to five commissioners appointed for the purpose— Edward Jackson, Elias Lowther, John McCoy, Lewis Maxwell and Dwight Stringer. These commissioners chose the site of the present Weston which in January, 1818, was incorporated as a town under the name of Preston, on lands of Lewis Maxwell and Daniel Stringer, and governed by four trustees—Henry McWhorter, William Peterson, James M. Camp and Robert Collins. By act of February, 1819, the name was changed to Fleshersville, which by act of the following December was succeeded by Weston which has since borne the honor with no serious opposition. In the following spring the first survey of the West Fork and the Monongahela, with a view to the improvement of navigation, was begun just below the Weston court house.

Gradually, in many instances, the earlier log houses were succeeded by better structures, expressing refinement, social tastes and prosperity. The early settlements of the northern and eastern parts of the county were supplied with lumber from choice yellow poplars and black walnuts prepared by water power saw mills located along the neighboring streams. Many of the earlier buildings are still preserved. Trees which were too large to be easily sawed were split into fence rails or burned in the clearings.

In 1843 portions of Lewis were detached to contribute to the formation of Barbour and Ritchie counties.

The population of the county steadily increased—two thousand each decade—until 1850, after which the total population was considerably decreased by the loss of territory occasioned by the formation of Upshur county in 1851. By 1845 Weston contained about sixty dwellings.

The large development and aspirations of the people of Lewis at the middle of the century found expressions in many ways—the most prominent of which probably were the Weston and Fairmont Turnpike, the Weston and Gauley Bridge Turnpike and the Weston and West Union Turnpike. A branch of the Exchange Bank of Virginia was established by 1853.

On the eve of the civil war, Weston secured the location of the hospital for the insane—the first and only state institution which was located in the transmontane territory later included in West Virginia.

BARBOUR COUNTY.

Southeast of Harrison and south of Taylor to which it had nearer communications, Barbour county felt more quickly than Lewis the more immediate influence of both turnpike and railroad—although Lewis perhaps could claim priority of settlement. The first settlement in the present limits of the county was probably made in 1780 two miles northwest of Philippi—soon followed by other scattered settlements, for which there were many grants of land, especially in 1786-88 and thereafter. As early as 1787, when the Randolph county court ordered the survey of a road from Beverly to Sandy Creek, Daniel Booth probably lived near the site of Philippi, but the original owner of the land on which the town stands was William Anglin who possibly settled there as early as 1783. The place was called Anglin's Ford in 1789 when the Randolph court ordered the survey of the road to connect it with Jonas Friend's (the site of Elkins). The place was later called Booth's Ferry, named for Mr. Booth who established it or owned it about 1800. The old ferry was not abandoned until after the completion of the wooden bridge at Philippi in 1852.

The early scattered settlements were connected by "blazed" trails many of which were distinguished by the kind of tree blazed in order to avoid bewilderment or danger of becoming lost at trail crossings. As early as 1788 the trail from Clarksburg to Winchester, the east and west highway through Barbour and Tucker, crossing the Valley River a mile below Philippi and Cheat at St. George, was mentioned in the records as the "state road"—although it was still only the "Pringle Packroad." The Beverly trail branched off a mile above the mouth of Hacker's Creek, and passed via Sugar Creek and the site of Belington. With the establishment of Booth's ferry, the road from Clarksburg to the Valley River was widened for wagons and steps were taken to open the road toward Beverly via Sugar Creek. By 1803 there was a wagon road constructed on the east side of the river which was later extended to Beverly. The first wagon which appeared in the county was brought over the mountains to Cheat in 1783 via North Branch, Lead Mine Run and Horse Shoe Run before trails had been widened for wagons.

The early economic life was largely confined to the problem of mere subsistance. Ginseng, however, was exported as early as 1789. A tanyard was located above Philippi in 1800, and the first mill at Philippi was erected in 1818.

In 1843 Barbour county was formed from Randolph (and parts of Harrison and Lewis) and the site for the court house promptly selected at Philippi (the old Booth's Ferry of Randolph) which was then only a farm. The new county seat was first called "Phillippa," the Latin feminine form of the first name of Philip Pendleton Barbour. Among the first acts of the court was one fixing the charges for taverns—which was reënacted every subsequent year for over a decade. By 1845 the county was regarded as rather thickly settled at the heads of Simpson and Elk Creeks and on the Buckhannon and Tygart's Valley rivers. Philippi contained only about a dozen buildings, but a basis for later growth was believed to exist in neighboring deposits of excellent coal and iron.

Coincident with improved transportation facilities resulting from the completion of neighboring turnpikes—the earlier Northwestern, and the Staunton and Parkersburg Turnpike completed via Buckhannon in 1847—various signs of improvement appeared. Instances of the introduction of improved farm machinery, occurring by 1840, became more common a decade later. Although the horse power thresher began to appear, perhaps as early as 1846, the first horse power thresher and separator was not introduced until 1852. In 1848 there was an attempt to develop the iron resources of Cove district. At the same time construction of local pikes was begun. In 1850 Luther Haymond, of Clarksburg, completed the survey for the Beverly and Fairmont pike, making changes of route above Belington and elsewhere which caused bitter controversies. In Barbour one of the first steam saw and grist mills was built at Peeltree about 1856 and continued to saw lumber for local use for thirty or forty years.

After the opening of the B. & O. railroad through Taylor county the people from the northeastern part of Barbour found their most convenient shipping point at Thornton. From various points on the Tygart's Valley River considerable timber was floated to Grafton.

The Bank of Philippi, the first bank in Barbour, was established in 1855 and closed at the opening of the war. Its notes were bought by speculators even after the close of the war.

The first newspaper of the county was founded in 1857 and suspended publication in June, 1861.

At the outbreak of the war nearly all the county officers of Barbour sympathized with the secession movement at the South.

UPSHUR COUNTY.

Southward and above Barbour, stretching east and west from the banks of the Buckhannon River, is Upshur county, which at the time of its creation a year before the completion of the railroad through Taylor could have furnished proof of a development almost equal to that of Barbour which had an advantage in geographical location.

The first settlement in the territory now included in Upshur was made by John and Samuel Pringle and two others who, deserting from garrison duty at Fort Pitt, roamed into Maryland from whence in 1764, in the employ of John Simpson the trapper and trader, they went west down Horse Shoe Run to Cheat, and after a quarrel with Simpson continued their journey to the Valley River and up the Buckhannon to Turkey Run (just below the site of Buckhannon) where they established a forest camp. This camp resulted in the visit of several prospective settlers followed by settlements in the Buckhannon valley by several families in 1769. Those settlements, prospering except during the "starving time" caused by a scarcity of corn in 1773, were followed by others at Booth's Creek in 1770 and at Simpson's Creek and Hacker's Creek in 1772. The settlers on Hacker's Creek came from the South Branch settlements. In this region Indian warfare following 1777 was severe, and the settlement at Buckhannon was broken up in 1782 by Indians who also burned the fort.

Several other later settlements made large openings in the original forests long before the emergence of lumbering as a commercial industry in this region. Settlers erected their cabins at Sago in 1801 and at French Creek, and by 1825 families were living in every part of the territory later included in Upshur county.

Hunting of both animals and medicinal plants in the days of the early settlements was a necessary occupation and ceased as such only when the profits arising from it became less than the profits from other labor.

The earlier trails were gradually widened into roads to meet the increasing demands of the settlements—especially after the introduction of wagons. In 1814 the court of Randolph ordered a horseback or pack horse from Beverly to Buckhannon which was later widened and graded and converted into the Parkersburg and Staunton turnpike. In 1800 Jacob Lorentz, Abraham Post and Abraham Carper emigrated from the South Branch, cut an uneven wagon road along the Indian trail, and brought the first road wagon to the region. In the same year goods were transported from Beverly to Buckhannon in a wagon. The second road wagon was brought to the county in 1810 by the New Englanders on their overland journey.

A mill built 1783 above the mouth of Fink's Run near Buckhannon was the only mill in the Buckhannon Valley for a score of years. A second mill in that region was built in 1821. Saw mills for domestic use were established on Spruce Run in 1806, at Buckhannon and Sago in 1810, and at French Creek (Meadville) in 1813.

Cattle were brought by the earliest settlers of 1770 and by almost all later settlers. Better cattle were brought by settlers from New England about 1810. Sheep were introduced from Hardy county and from New England at the same time. Sheep husbandry became an important industry—especially after the close of the hunters period along the frontier. Obstacles arising from the migratory habits of the sheep and the depredations of wolves and dogs were largely overcome with the development of the settlements. In the earlier days there were many and menacing disputes over ownership of hogs—a product which found a ready sale at Richmond, Winchester or Cumberland.

Spinning, knitting and weaving were common home industries. Every family contained its own tailor, usually a woman. Tanning of leather at first was a home process. At first almost every family contained a cobbler. The conditions encouraged native mechanical genius.

Salt, which in the earlier days was brought over the mountains on pack horses and sold at prices which made it too dear for extensive use, was obtained in the county by evaporation after 1839.

Jacob Lorentz, who established the first store in the limits of the county—and for a long time the only store in the entire surrounding region—for many years brought his goods on pack horses from Richmond, Parkersburg or Cumberland. A second store was opened near French Creek in 1820.

Towns emerged slowly. The first incorporated town in the present limits of Upshur was Buckhannon which was established in January, 1816, on lands of Robert Patton Jr. at that time within the jurisdiction of Harrison county. The first trustees were Joseph Davis, Jacob Lorentz, Philip Reger, John Jackson, John Reger, Benjamin Reeder and John McWhorter.

Under the loose system of Virginia land warrants, which often applied to no particular spot, there were many conflicting claims and endless controversies. Many New England settlers, who had been settling in the territory since the first of the century, becoming tired of dilatory courts and adverse decisions, emigrated westward to Illinois about 1830. Many people who remained were compelled to repurchase their lands from rival claimants.

Industrial development and other improvements in the county were especially stimulated by the construction of the Staunton and Parkersburg Turnpike, which received state appropriations for construction of bridges in 1848, and for macadamizing at different points in 1849. This stimulation was increased after 1848 by the construction of the Clarksburg and Buckhannon Turnpike and especially in 1852 by the completion of the railroad to Grafton opening a market for logs rafted down the river.

The first attempt to establish Upshur county, in 1848, met considerable opposition—especially at Weston which disliked the proposal to add to the new county a part of the territory of Lewis. The law creating the new county from parts of Randolph, Barbour and Lewis was finally enacted in 1851. The town of Buckhannon was incorporated in 1852, and the first court house was completed in 1854.

By the census of 1860, Upshur had a population of seven thousand two hundred and ninety-nine—which was about seven hundred less than that of Lewis, and almost fifty per cent. greater than that of the neighboring mother county (Randolph).

RANDOLPH COUNTY.

The region stretching along the head streams of Cheat, forming the extreme southwestern part of the Monongahela drainage system—although it received some of the earliest settlers who passed over the divide from older settled bordering region of Pocahontas on the east, and after reducing its limits several times by the formation of other counties on the west still contained more territory than any other county of the Monongahela section—was retarded in its development throughout the period before the civil war, and scarcely felt the quickening touch of the pioneer railroad which elsewhere had produced great industrial and social changes far beyond the immediate region penetrated.

The first settlement on the waters of the upper Monongahela, made in 1753 by Robert Files and David Tygart with their families, just above the site of Beverly, Randolph county, was broken up later in the year—probably by a party of Indians returning westward over the Seneca trail after a thieving expedition in the region around Moorefield. Remaining untouched for eighteen years after the Files settlement, in 1772 nearly all the land in Tygart's Valley was located—although few patents were obtained for it until ten or fifteen years later. Two forts were built (at Beverly and near Huttonsville) in 1774, and three others (in Tygart's Valley) in 1777. The settlers were attacked by Indians late in 1777 and again in 1779, 1780, 1781 and 1782 after which the Tygart's Valley remained free from Indian invasions with one exception, in May, 1791. The most disastrous invasion of 1781 began by an attack on a party of men who were returning from a visit to Clarksburg to obtain deeds from the land commissioners, and it closed by an attack which almost broke up the settlement on Leading Creek.

Randolph county was formed from Harrison county in 1787 by act of October, 1786. At that time it included half Barbour, half of Upshur, much of Webster and all of Tucker. At its first county court, held in 1787, a county seat contest between the people of Leading Creek and the people in the vicinity of the later town of Beverly was decided in favor of Beverly. In 1788 plans were adopted for a court house which was not completed until ten years later and was not used after 1803. In 1808 contracts were made for a new building which was completed in 1815.

In December, 1790, Beverly was established as a town, by the Virginia assembly, on lands owned by James Westfall. At first, the government was vested in seven trustees who were selected by appointment. In 1811 the number of trustees was reduced to "five fit and able men, freeholders and inhabitants of the town," who were to be elected by the freeholders of the town.

The earliest roads grew from the need of communication between the various settlements, and at first were merely paths of bridle roads. Randolph's first court of 1787 provided for making a way for a wagon road from Leading Creek to Horse Shoe Bottom on Cheat (now in Tucker), but not until 1826 were wagons able to cross the mountains from the direction of the South Branch. By 1800 a score of roads had been surveyed in Randolph county. By 1801 the court ordered a survey from the mouth of Black Fork of Cheat to the head of North Branch—which, although it resulted in no road, was later followed by the West Virginia Central and Pittsburgh railroad from Fairfax to Parsons. In 1814 a pack horse road was ordered from Beverly to Buckhannon. In 1822 aid was voted to open a road from Beverly via Clarksburg to Sistersville. In 1824 the legislature authorized a "state road" from Staunton to the mouth of the Little Kanawha which was built via Beverly over the same general route followed by the Saunton and Parkersburg turnpike twenty years later. In 1826 Randolph coöperated with Monongalia in constructing a bridge across Sandy Creek which was then their boundary and remained so until the creation of Marion county in 1842—after which it became successively the boundary between Randolph and Marion, then between Marion and Barbour (1843) and finally between Barbour and Taylor (1844). In 1832 steps were taken to raise money by lottery to build a road from Beverly to Morgantown.

Development with few exceptions was slow. The first saw mill at Mingo (upper end of the county) was built near Valley Head in 1822 and the wagon which hauled the irons for the mill was the first that crossed the mountains to Mingo. The first grist mill in the upper fifteen miles of the river was built about 1820 or 1822.

Outside the valleys of Tygart's River and Leading Creek the territory of Randolph was occupied but slowly—and a century later much of the forest land remained undisturbed. Even after half a century few houses were built of sawed lumber. A saw mill introduced near Valley Head in 1822 was probably the only one in the county in 1835, and perhaps for several years later. Even in 1840 there were few settlements except along the Cheat and in the narrow lottoms of the larger creeks toward the northern end of the county. In 1853 there were large tracts entirely uninhabited and almost inaccessible.

Changes in markets and transportation are illustrated in the case of David Blackman who, engaged in the mercantile business at Beverly from 1824 until the civil war, hauled his goods first from Baltimore, then from Winchester, then from Cumberland, and later from Fetterman. The chief source of wealth in the county in the ante-bellum period was live stock—a product which exported itself to the eastern market.

The population of Beverly in 1845—three years before it was incorporated as the "Borough of Beverly"—was about two hundred. The population of the (originally larger) county, which reached its highest point in 1840 (two thousand two hundred and eight), suffered a reduction from five thousand two hundred and forty-three in 1850 to four thousand nine hundred and ninety in 1860—due to the loss of territory to form Tucker county in 1856.

TUCKER COUNTY.

The youngest county created in the Monongahela region contained some of the oldest settlements, and across its northern end was penetrated by an early pioneer trail. Emigrants from the South Branch going west by the Horse Shoe Run trail naturally settled in the fine valley at the bend on Cheat. The strategic importance of the route was recognized as early as 1755. Perhaps as early as 1766 a settlement was made on the site of Parsons by John Crouch. With more certainty it is known that a settlement in the Horse Shoe was made by the spring of 1774 by sons of Captain James Parsons who had lived in the vicinity of Moorefield. About the same time John Minear led from South Branch a colony which, after building a stockade and returning to the South Branch, moved (1776) two miles down the river to the site of St. George where he promptly built a saw mill which was probably the first west of the mountains. Soon thereafter, small colonies were established at various points along Cheat. They usually led their cows and brought a few utensils and other "plunder" on pack horses. On the revival of the Indian war, in 1777, the Parsons colony built a fort and soon thereafter a grist mill and a saw mill. In April, 1781, Minear and others went to Clarksburg to obtain their land patents from the land commissioners and while returning, just before crossing the Valley River below Philippi, were attacked by Indians who thereafter turned south and murdered the settlers on Leading Creek. A year later one of three small forces of militia from Hampshire county, sent by the governor of Virginia to protect the border settlements, was stationed on Cheat near St. George. In 1787 and 1789 these Cheat settlements were again invaded by the Indians.

Among the most prominent early men of the county, after Captain James Parsons and John Minear, was the industrious James Goff who settled on Cheat near the Preston county line by 1786 and at one time owned the greater part of the land from the Minear claim to Rowlesburg. Others prominent were the Dumires who settled in the eastern part of the county about the upper tributaries of Horse Shoe Run, and the Losh family—one of whom built a grist mill on Horse Shoe Run at an early date.

At the close of the Indian troubles the few people in scattered settlements along the river turned to the hard work of clearing small spaces on which they cultivated small crops of corn from which to make corn bread. During a part of the autumn they hunted deer and bear. In the earliest years of the St. George settlement buffaloes were found, but they were never as plentiful as they were in the region of Buckhannon, Clarksburg and farther west along the Ohio.

The wealth of the depths of primeval forests was not appreciated by the pioneers of the earlier settlements, who gradually extended the area of cleared bottom lands by the steady and laborious work accomplished by axe and fire. The finest timber was burned or used for fence rails. Gradually with the introduction of a few rude saw mills, a small portion of it found a more appropriate use in a few plank houses which began to replace the more primitive log cabins. At an early date a sash mill was operated in the county by N. M. Parsons and George M. Parsons. Among other later ones was that built on Cheat as early as 1830 by Arnold Bonnifield who operated it continually for thirty-five years. The first commercial demand for lumber outside the county was created by the construction of a bridge over Cheat at the crossing of the Northwestern pike, five or six miles above Rowlesburg. Much of the lumber used in the bridge was sawed by Bonnifield, hauled to the river, and built into rude rafts which were driven by the current to their destination. The first "muley mill," an improvement on the sash mills, was built by Rufus Maxwell in 1865.

Beginning about 1852, and continuing long after the civil war, the timber region along Cheat for twenty or twenty-five miles above the railroad was somewhat developed by an enterprising company, which had mill works located at Rowlesburg and supplied ship timber for the English market.

As late as 1840 there were very few settlers except along the river and in the narrow bottoms of the larger creeks. The region called "Canada" and the land of Canaan—a high basin surrounded by mountains—the Backbone on the west and the Allegheny on the east—was an uninhabited wilderness. From the head of Black Fork to Fairfax stone was an unbroken forest of trees which stood so thick that their branches interlocked for miles completely shutting out the sunlight from the soil below. Bears and panthers travelled through tunnels which they had broken through the thickets in all directions. Although the wilderness of the mountains was largely unbroken, occasionally among the hills appeared the cabin of a settler who was opening a farm. In 1836 settlement was begun about the head waters of Clover Run which later became Clover District. The first cabin was without door, floor or chimney, but it attracted other settlers who obtained lands and by 1840 the neighborhood consisted of five families (including about thirty children) who had begun the earnest work of breaking up the dense forests and its dens of panthers and bears, and had also built a round-poled floorless school house in which their children might be able to obtain some rudiments of an education. Canaan valley and the surrounding plateau country remained practically undisturbed until the forest fire of 1863 which was soon followed by other "burnings" started by hunters.

The people of the northern end of Randolph, long dissatified with the inconveniences of the journey to the county seat at Beverly over bad roads between settlements separated by large tracts of woods, repeatedly agitated the subject of a new county even before the revival of activity which they experienced as a result of the new industrial opportunities opened to them by the construction of the railroad through the neighboring woods on the north at the middle of the century. The decisive step was finally taken in the winter of 1854 by a meeting at the residence of Enoch Minear in the old stone house at St. George—which was then called Westernford. Through the influence of strong petitions and strong lobbying, supplemented by the enthusiastic assistance of Judge John Brannon, of Lewis county, in the legislature, early in 1856 the new county of Tucker was created with the seat of justice at St. George—which remained the county seat until long after the war. Officers were chosen in the following May, and the court was organized in July. Jesse Parsons was the first sheriff, Arthur Bonnifield the first clerk, and Rufus Maxwell the first prosecuting attorney. The size of the county was later increased by the addition of a strip of territory taken from Barbour. The total population in 1860 was only one thousand four hundred and twenty-eight.

When Tucker was created, a few of its citizens foresaw a future of greater industrial prosperity. Abe Bonnifield, dwelling at a point commanding a full view of the principal ridge of Backbone mountain, along the side of which the sugar maples belonging to W. R. Parsons were falling beneath the axes wielded by his slaves, saw the promise of rich grazing plantations. Considering the unoccupied regions of the land of Caanan which had recently come into the market, he expected to see a new tide of emigration. Knowing that coal had been discovered about 1835 on the sugar lands, and about 1855 on the other side of the mountain, he had confidence that the railroad projected (in 1856) up the North Branch from Piedmont on the Baltimore and Ohio would soon be built, and that its terminus would be in the coal lands of Tucker. The realization of his dreams—which came in surplus measure thirty years later—was doubtless postponed in part by the war of secession in which he was a participant in the Confederate service.

STRATEGIC IMPORTANCE OF THE MONONGAHELA REGION IN WAR.

At the opening of the war of secession, the strategic Monongahela region of West Virginia became the theatre of contending armies in a series of introductory episodes which were larger in significance than in size of forces engaged or extent of territory covered. The geographic position of the Baltimore and Ohio railroad, crossing the region of the Monongahela drainage system and connecting Washington with the Ohio, made it of inestimable value as an aid in the military operations of the United States government throughout the war—and at the same time determined to a large extent the theatre of Confederate operations, especially at the inception of the war. The results of the campaign, in which the battle of Philippi occupied a prominent place, determined the control of Northwestern Virginia including the western division of the Baltimore and Ohio railway, contributed largely to the control of the remainder of the Baltimore and Ohio route from the mountains eastward to Baltimore, encouraged the movement for the formation of a new state west of the mountains, and influenced the result of later important military events of the war.

The secessionists very early in the war saw the importance of establishing their lines along the border of Ohio and Pennsylvania which they hoped to make the battle ground. At the same time they underestimated the strength of the opposition which the people of northwestern Virginia would offer to the attempt to join them to the fortunes of the Southern Confederacy. They especially desired to control the Baltimore and Ohio railway which had a geographic position of great strategic importance, and by which they particularly hoped to prevent the concentration of federal troops on Maryland and Virginia.

Therefore, on April 30, 1861, General Lee ordered Major Boykin, of Weston, to call out volunteers and assume command at Grafton, and took steps to control the Ohio terminals of the main road at Wheeling and the branch road at Parkersburg. On May 4th he directed Colonel Porterfield, of Harper's Ferry, to call out additional volunteers to rendezvous at Grafton, to assume general command over Boykin and others in the vicinity, to distribute two hundred muskets which at the request of Boykin had been sent to Colonel Jackson, at Harper's Ferry, and to issue requisitions for additional arms. On May 11 he ordered four hundred rifles and ammunition from Staunton to Major Goff, at Beverly, to be placed at the disposal of Colonel Porterfield for use in the vicinity of Grafton.

In the meantime Boykin had encountered great difficulty in assembling a force in the vicinity, and had made a request for companies from other parts of the state—a request with which General Lee did not think it wise to comply.

On May 16th Colonel Porterfield reported from Grafton, stating that he discovered great diversity of opinion and much bitterness of feeling, and that he was seriously disappointed to find that Major Goff, at Beverly, had received no rifles and had no information that any had been sent. Both at Pruntytown and at Philippi he found a company organized and awaiting arms. At Clarksburg another company was forming but it was without either arms or uniforms. He reported that two companies were marching toward Grafton to aid him; that of Captain Boggess, of Weston, which had only flint-lock muskets, in bad order and without ammunition; and that of Captain Thompson, of Fairmont, which had better guns but little ammunition. Although urging the need of the best rifles, he doubted whether there would be much use of the bayonet in the hills and thought that the rifles which had been in the fire at Harper's Ferry would do if fitted up.

Ordered to advance to Wheeling, Porterfield, before he had time to act and while disappointed with the failure of his appeals to secure adequate arms and ammunition, found it necessary to fold his tents and fall back toward Philippi before a superior force of troops from Wheeling—the vanguard of the army of McClellan—under Colonel Kelly who proceeded to occupy Grafton without firing a shot. He had burned two bridges four miles east of Mannington; but failing in his plans to execute Governor Letcher's order to destroy the railroad at Cheat River, and blow up the tunnel through Laurel Hill, he was unable to prevent the Baltimore and Ohio from falling into the control of the Federal forces which thus obtained a great advantage in the operation of the war.

In the closing days of May, General McClellan's twenty thousand troops had crossed the Ohio at Parkersburg and Wheeling; and on June 1st, about four thousand of these under General Thomas A. Morris, of Indiana, reached Grafton. Early in the evening of the following day, three thousand of these marched by two routes on Philippi (twenty miles southward) where Porterfield had halted with his poorly equipped forces to resist the further advance of the Federals. Just before the dawn of June 3rd, the two columns converged upon the town over muddy roads and fired the opening guns of the first inland battle of the war. The heavy storms which had impeded their march and tested the physical endurance of the young army, had caused the Confederate pickets to retreat from their posts without order to find shelter at Philippi.

The rapid race of the Federals to Philippi, succeeded by the brief battle in which not a single person was killed, was promptly followed by the precipitate retreat of the stampeded Confederates who abandoned their baggage in their narrow escape from capture on the Beverly road and left the Baltimore and Ohio free to transport armies for the preservation of the Union. On June 22nd, McClellan crossed from Ohio with his official staff; and on June 23rd he established his headquarters at Grafton.

General Robert S. Garnett, who superseded Porterfield and reinforced his army to over six thousand by troops from eastern Virginia, completely failed with inadequate force to recover an important strategic position by plans to establish a base at Evansville in Preston county. Later (July 11th), routed at Rich Mountain (five miles west of Beverly) and at Laurel Hill (Belington) where he had constructed fortified positions to prevent the union troops under McClellan from moving south toward Staunton, he returned to Tucker county endeavored to escape by felling tree across the road behind him; but at Corrick's Ford he was overtaken and killed while retreating from a battle which closed the campaign by putting to flight the remnant of his army.

On July 14th, McClellan moved southward and occupied Huttonsville, followed by the line of military telegraph by which throughout his brief campaign he had been able to keep in touch with Grafton and to announce to the excited country the news of his victories—which, although small in comparison with many later victories of the war, were important as a preparation for some of those later victories, and were significant in their larger results which contributed to the integrity of the Union.

Although by the campaign of McClellan southward from Grafton to Huttonsville the Confederates practically lost control of the entire region which so largely controlled the Baltimore and Ohio railway and found no subsequent opportunity to make a serious attempt to regain it, they made several subsequent raids which produced a feeling of uncertainty and insecurity in some sections and severely tested the alertness of the Federal forces and Home Guards. General A. J. Jenkins with five hundred Confederates made a raid through Randolph, Upshur and Lewis (and westward to the Ohio) in August, 1862. General John D. Imboden with three hundred and ten Confederates reached St. George in Tucker county in November, 1862, and planned to destroy the Baltimore and Ohio bridge across Cheat at Rowlesburg and some neighboring trestles, but at the news of approaching Federals he retreated to Pendleton county. In the following spring he directed a double raid—one division of which, led by General William E. Jones, crossed via

Greenland Gap to Preston county, then via Albrightsville to Morgantown and Fairmont, and in Lewis and Upshur formed a junction with the main division under Imboden which entering Randolph had captured Beverly and then had moved through Barbour. From Weston, Imboden moved southwesterly to sweep the Kanawha, and Jones advanced to the petroleum wells in the direction of Parkersburg. In June, 1863, Beverly was again attacked by General William L. Jackson with twelve hundred Confederates, but they were driven back by General W. W. Averell's body of cavalry largely composed of West Virginians —which proved better than the earlier infantry troops in protecting the region through which it moved. Later raids were that of Colonel V. A. Witcher in September, 1864, who started from Tazewell county and penetrated to Weston and Buckhannon, and two later attacks on Beverly—one under Major Hull in the autumn of 1864 and the other under General Rasser in January, 1865.

In their repeated raids, the Confederates were doubtless encouraged by the demoralization resulting from the divided sympathies of the people in the upper counties of the Monongahela region. At the outbreak of the war nearly all county officers of Barbour were Southern in sympathies. For several months after Colonel Porterfield was driven from Philippi there was no execution of the law by the civil authorities, and Philippi was almost deserted. In the following September under the Reorganized Government of Virginia there was an election to fill vacancies. In the winter of 1862-63 the new sheriff, Mr. Trahem, was kidnapped from his home by a detail of Confederates under orders from General Imboden (who was encamped in Augusta county) and sent to Richmond. Although he was released and allowed to return, his capture led to retaliatory acts against the Confederate sympathizers in the county. In the raids under Imboden and Jones, which occurred in the spring of 1863, Barbour was not as much concerned as other counties of the region. In several cases records were carried away, and in Randolph the sheriff (J. F. Phares) was shot. Later, near the close of the war, M. T. Haller in command of the Home Guards in Barbour was killed in an ambush by a Confederate scouting party led by a Mr. Moore.

At the close of the war, in which there had been much waste and destruction of property accompanied by arrested development in regions which had previously begun to feel the pulse of a larger industrial life, the people of the new storm-born state turned first to the work of material reconstruction and then to the larger economic utilization and exploitation of rich but latent resources whose development was possibly hastened by the separation (from the Old Dominion) to which the geographical and political influence of the Monongahela Valley had contributed so largely and effectually.

INDUSTRIAL AWAKENING AND PROGRESS SINCE THE WAR.

GENERAL SURVEY.

The vast resources of the Monongahela Valley, whose development was so long delayed and retarded by lack of transportation facilities, have recently furnished the incentive for many new enterprises which have greatly changed the life of the region. The recent industrial development had its origin largely in the increasing demand for timber, coal, oil and gas, and to the resulting inducements for the construction of railroads and the establishment of certain manufactures, such as glass, iron and steel for which a portion of the Monongahela region furnishes a clean, cheap fuel.

The development of agriculture, as a skilled business in the Monongahela counties, as elsewhere in West Virginia, was greatly retarded by the habits of the people resulting from frontier conditions and long continued lack of transportation facilities. There had been little concentrated or coöperative action for improvement of agriculture before the war. Except in a few counties the people were satisfied with production for bare subsistance and gave little attention to production for exportation. There were few dealers in farm implements even at the close of the war, and the steam thresher did not come into use until about 1880, after which there was a rapid introduction of all kinds of improved implements and machinery. Since 1901 considerable advance has been made through the influence of farmers institutes, better communications and various associations.

Several of the counties in the region annually ship many carloads of cattle for beef to eastern markets, and Harrison and Lewis export some of their finest cattle to England.

CHEAT RIVER VIEW NEAR SQUIRREL ROCK.

CUTTING RIGHT OF WAY—CRANBERRY GLADES.
By Courtesy of West Virginia Geological Survey.

At the close of the war an awakened interest in the latent mineral resources of the region indicated the beginnings of a new era of development. Coal mining companies were formed and coal mining operations were begun in Monongalia county by 1869 and Marion in 1870. Operations were extensive in Marion and Harrison by 1880, and at the same time embryo operations were begun in the coke industry which steadily increased after 1880 and especially after 1890 when machines were introduced for mining. The valuable Pittsburgh vein of coal was easily accessible along the Monongahela, especially cropping out above the water level in Monongalia, Marion, Harrison and Lewis counties.

Petroleum, first obtained in large quantities in 1860 in a neighboring region on the Little Kanawha near Parkersburg where it developed a thriving business which was ruined by the Confederates in 1863 and revived in 1865, was discovered along the western edge of the Monongahela region after the war and has recently been an important industrial factor. There was little extension of productive area from 1876 to 1889, but after 1889 the yearly production which had steadily declined rapidly increased. The traffic in oil, although it ruined some built fortunes for others. By means of a series of pumping stations this product is forced through pipe lines over the mountains to the seaboard cities.

After the opening of new gas wells and the discovery of new gas fields, the practical use of gas became a large factor in the industrial and social development of parts of the Monongahela region, furnishing the inducement for the location of many manufacturing establishments seeking cheap fuel and attracting immigrants desiring a clean and convenient fuel for their homes.

The timber industries became prominent by 1885. For many years after the civil war large rafts of logs were floated down Cheat and the Monongahela to Brownsville and lower points. Portable steam saws generally introduced in some cases about 1860 became more numerous after the construction of railroads. The cross tie industry has been prominent for many years. Lumbering (the lineal descendant of the earlier cutting and rafting of tan bark, hoop-poles and logs), although it developed little before 1865, ranged among the foremost industries of the region in 1900 and even at the close of the decade following.

Among other recent industries are brick works established at Philippi in 1876 (relocated 1887), at Buckhannon in 1890, at Morgantown and Clarksburg in 1891, at Colfax (Taylor county) in 1899 and at Weston in 1900. Tile works were started at Philippi in 1902. In 1903 the Buckhorn Portland Cement Company began the shipment of cement from a mill with a capacity of twelve hundred barrels a day located at Manheim on Cheat, two miles below Rowlesburg.

New forms of wealth are beginning to emerge in the opportunities for valuable water power—which was scarcely utilized before 1870 except for grist mills and saw mills, and which in sections remote from rail or from navigable streams did not recently enhance the value of the surrounding lands.

Bank facilities have been established on unusually good foundations. During the periods of financial stringency in 1893 and 1907 the depression was not seriously felt in the Monongahela Valley. The large number of investments in the region, and the circulation of money necessary for their development, made money usually plentiful.

Both the census of 1900 and that of 1910 indicate a remarkable development of material wealth—including farm property, farm products, manufacturing plants, manufactured products, timber products, coal and coke production, bank resources and bank deposits, and steam railways.

Industrial progress has been greatly influenced by corresponding development of means of transportation. When the state began its separate existence there were few facilities for communication in a large part of upper Monongahela region. Of the few turnpikes the most important were the Staunton and Parkersburg, and the Winchester and Parkersburg ("Northwestern"). Steamboat navigation on the Monongahela above the Pennsylvania line, confined to a few miles in Monongalia, was not yet satisfactory. There was but one railroad, the Baltimore and Ohio, whose immediate influence affected only a narrow strip of territory.

The new government promptly took steps to encourage the construction of railroads. Of the many proposed railways chartered after 1864 several were completed by 1885. In 1872 Congress had begun the appropriation by which slack-water improvements have been extended up the Monongahela to Fairmont. Soon thereafter new railway lines were in progress of construction. In 1886 a line designed to connect the north central part of the state with Pittsburgh was completed from Fairmont to Morgantown, from whence it was later (1895) extended to Connellsville, Pennsylvania, where it connected with a main line of the Baltimore and Ohio from Cumberland to Pittsburgh. From the Charleston, Clendennin and Sutton railroad, which was put in operation up the Elk River from Charleston to Sutton in 1892, a new line was extended to Elkins in 1906. Since 1900 the rapid development of productive industries, and of transportation faculties has been accompanied by great changes in every phase of life, industrial and social, political and educational. It has caused a phenomenal growth of many towns, and great improvement of the conditions of life.

The character of the population has greatly changed since the civil war. The original settlers, whose ancestors were generally English or Scotch-Irish, or perhaps Pennsylvania German, were contented with a life of rural simplicity and hospitality whose economy was in many cases mere subsistence. Their descendants usually lived amiably with their neighbors, maintained their urbanity and self possession in the presence of strangers and, beyond the efforts necessary to secure the necessities of life, were often disposed to leave the improvements of things to time and chance. Always possessing intellect and sagacity capable of high development under favorable conditions, they have gradually responded to the progressive spirit of enterprise and of the strenuous life which received its greatest impulse from immigration from other states and the increased opportunities for communication and intermingling of the people. The development of the vast resources, especially in coal and oil, has caused a large influx of population —at first, largely average American citizens from Pennsylvania, Maryland, Virginia and Ohio, and later an increasing number of foreigners from Europe.

The population has almost trebled since 1860, and has almost doubled since 1880. It has increased nearly seventy per cent. since 1890 and over thirty per cent. since 1900. Although the census of 1870 showed a slight decrease in Marion, every county since 1870 has shown an increase each decade. In the decade from 1890 to 1900 the population increased most rapidly in Tucker (108 per cent.), Marion (56.5 per cent.), and Randolph (51.9 per cent.), and most slowly in Lewis (6.8 per cent.). In 1900 the foreign born were located principally in Marion and Tucker, and the negroes principally in Harrison. In the decade after 1900, immigration greatly increased especially in the manufacturing and mining centers. The largest total increase is shown in Harrison, Marion, Randolph and Monongalia in the order named. The largest percentage of increase is shown in Harrison (74.7 per cent.), Randolph (47.3 per cent.), Tucker (40 per cent.), and Marion (32 per cent.). The smallest total increase was in Lewis. The smallest percentage of increase was in Lewis (7.6 per cent.). The rapidity of the growth of towns may be illustrated by the growth of Morgantown whose population increased from less than two thousand in 1900 to approximately ten thousand in 1910.

The growth of population by counties for each decade since the war of secession is conveniently presented in the following table:

	1860.	1870.	1880.	1890.	1900.	1910.
Monongalia	13,048	13,547	14,985	15,705	19,049	24,334
Preston	13,312	14,555	19,091	20,335	22,727	26,341
Marion	12,722	12,107	17,198	20,721	32,430	42,794
Harrison	13,790	16,714	20,181	21,919	27,690	48,381
Randolph	4,990	5,563	8,102	11,633	17,670	26,028
Lewis	7,999	10,175	13,269	15,895	16,980	18,281
Barbour	8,958	10,312	11,870	12,702	14,198	15,858
Taylor	8,463	9,367	11,455	12,147	14,978	16,554
Upshur	7,292	8,023	10,249	12,714	14,696	16,629
Tucker	1,428	1,907	3,151	6,459	13,433	18,675
Total	92,002	102,270	129,551	150,230	193,851	253,875

EVOLUTION OF RAILROADS AND INDUSTRIAL PROGRESS.

The industrial revolution of recent years has been largely due to the development of railroads which have opened communications with the markets of the world and attracted capital to exploit rich coal fields and valuable timber lands. Every delay in securing transportation facilities postponed the day of prosperity. Every extension of railroad has resulted in great industrial and social changes including large increase in the permanent population.

The awakening spirit of industry and the dawn of a new era at the close of the war was indicated by investments of capitalists in rich mineral resources of the state and the projection of new lines of railroads—such as the proposed West Virginia Central railway (1864) from the Pennsylvania central line either via the Monongahela or via Brandonville, Grafton, Buckhannon, Sutton and Charleston to the mouth of the Big Sandy. While excitement was high along Fishing Creek in Wetzel county, and in Tyler county, oil speculators and well-borers had already been attracted by indications of gas or oil along the tributaries of the West Fork of Lewis county and along the Pennsylvania boundary of Monongahela. Even in the Cheat River valley in Preston they were prospecting and purchasing with expression of confident expectations which materially increased the value of undeveloped tracts of land. Harrison was affected by a strong show of oil on the head waters of Cabin Run (a tributary of Hughes River) in Ritchie, and became excited by an oil strike at a depth of two hundred feet at Clarksburg—which resulted in the beginning of oil leases on town lots, cultivated farms and wild lands. In Taylor too, an oil strike was reported at a depth of three hundred feet. Fortunately the mania for buying "shares" in unknown companies had somewhat subsided. Except in

By Courtesy of West Virginia Geological Survey. GRADE FOR RAILROAD.

a few instances of wild investment in untested petroleum lands, prices continued to rise. In Monongalia considerable excitement caused by the expectation of striking a rich oil field in the spring of 1861, and quieted by the intense excitement of the war, was revived in 1865. Men of thought, aware of other mineral resources foresaw a greater future for Monongalia which at that time included in its exports, cattle, lumber, flour and iron—transported from points outside the county both by railway and steamboat. By 1870, however, there were only two small coal mines in the county and these only represented an investment of $1,200, and employed only three men. Coke-burning which had begun in a small way as early as 1853 did not begin its rapid development until 1902. Industrial development was retarded by lack of a railway to connect with the neighboring trunk lines.

In the decade after the war there were many projected railroads which failed through lack of capital. In 1865, coincident with the revival of projects for a railway along the New River and the Kanawha, the Monongahela and Lewisburg Railway Company was incorporated to build a road beginning at the Pennsylvania state line and passing through Morgantown, and via Fairmont, Clarksburg and Buckhannon to intersect the Chesapeake and Ohio and to give direct connection with the mineral deposit of the Virginias and the cottonfields of the South.

Other roads projected in rapid succession were: The Monongahela Valley (1868) from the Pennsylvania state line to Fairmont, the Uniontown and West Virginia (1869) crossing the Cheat near Ice's Ferry thence via Morgantown, the West Virginia Central (1870) from the Pennsylvania line of Preston county to Charleston, the Pittsburgh, Virginia and Charleston (1870), the Pennsylvania and West Virginia (1870) via Morgantown to connect with the Baltimore and Ohio at Grafton, the Northern and Southern West Virginia (1870) from the Pennsylvania line via Clarksburg and Charleston to Wayne county, the Pittsburgh, West Virginia and Southern Narrow Gauge (1878) from

Washington, Pennsylvania, via Mt. Morris and Morgantown to Grafton, the West Virginia and Pennsylvania (1881) between the Pennsylvania state line and Clarksburg, and the Blacksville and Morgantown Narrow Gauge (1882). The Pittsburgh, Virginia and Charleston Railway, originally chartered as the Monongahela Valley, reincorporated under the new name in 1870 was opened to Monongahela City in 1873, absorbed the Brownsville road (from Mt. Braddock) in 1881, opened the Redstone branch in 1882, but never reached West Virginia. In 1887 it was leased by the Pennsylvania Railroad Company which still operates it.

The earlier activity in connection with projected railways was largely related to the interests of Monongalia and Preston counties—and especially to the interests of Morgantown which had already obtained telegraphic communication with the world by a line erected between Pittsburgh and Fairmont in 1866. In 1871 the legislature authorized the extension of the Iron Valley Railroad (which was constructed from Hardman's on the Baltimore and Ohio via Three Fork Creek to Irondale) via Decker's Creek to Morgantown and to the Pennsylvania boundary, and another line from the Baltimore and Ohio near the mouth of Raccoon Creek via Martin's Iron Works, the mouth of Green's Run, Bruceton and Brandonville to the Pennsylvania boundary on the Big Sandy. In 1873 the legislature appropriated $1,000 for a survey in the general direction of the latter line with a view to connection with the Pittsburgh, Washington and Baltimore Railroad, but plans for financing the construction of the road failed. The county court of Preston, at that time prosecuting an expensive suit against the Baltimore and Ohio for taxes, refused to submit to the people the question of a county appropriation to aid in building the road; and, after the improvement of the financial condition of the county in 1876 by the acceptance of $18,000 by compromise with the B. & O., interest in the proposed road had declined. In 1877 the county court of Preston voted to submit to the people the question of subscribing to the capital stock of a proposed narrow-gauge railway from the B. & O. via Kingwood to Morgantown, but friends of the enterprise decided not to submit the proposition. In 1878 public meetings were held in Monongalia to encourage the construction of a railroad from Morgantown to Grafton. After a period of "hard times" the earlier idea of a railway following Decker's Creek from its mouth and connecting Morgantown and Kingwood with the B. & O. at the point where the short railway from Irondale furnace tapped it was revived in 1881 and a route surveyed.

In her efforts to secure railway connections, Morgantown was partly influenced by lack of adequate facilities for river navigation. Lock "Number 9," although its completion in 1879 was celebrated by fifteen hundred people gathered from surrounding points, proved ineffective until the completion of Lock "Number 8" in 1889 after a delay of ten years during which steamers could not ascend the river above New Geneva.

In 1882 the Kingwood Railway Company was organized to construct a narrow-gauge railway from Kingwood to Tunnelton. Kingwood especially felt the immediate need of a railway connection. She had already endeavored to hold her position as the county seat by neighboring improvements. Among these was a substantial wooden bridge constructed across Cheat at Albrightsville in 1869 and which after being demolished by a furious wind storm in April, 1877, was replaced the same year by a single span wrought iron truss bridge. Additional development of resources in the vicinity necessarily awaited the coming of the railway. Promoters and prospectors were already active in preparation for new industries. In 1882 the Preston Company was incorporated to traffic in minerals and timber lands, to mine and manufacture minerals and to contract for the construction of railways, telegraph lines and bridges.

In July, 1882, Monongalia voted down (by a majority of thirty-two) a proposition to take $150,000 of the capital stock of the Iron

Valley and Morgantown railroad. This adverse vote was especially due to Clay and Battelle districts which claimed that they would derive no benefit from a road on the east side of the river. A later proposition to apportion part of the subscription to a narrow-gauge road from Morgantown to Blacksville was also lost by a large vote. The defeat of the subscription was celebrated by the people of Laurel Point by bonfire, speeches and resolutions. In the meantime, Grant and Cass districts which had been influencial in defeating the railway projects devised by others, proposed (December 27, 1882) a plan for a railroad of their own from the Pennsylvania line via Grantsville and up Davis Run to the Marion county line—a plan which received only one hundred and fourteen votes at a special election called in the two districts.

Construction on the Iron Valley and Morgantown road was begun at Morgantown March 22, 1883, but was discontinued a few days later.

At a meeting held at Fairmont in the fall of 1884, the attempts of the directors of the West Virginia and Pennsylvania railroad to get aid in the construction of that road, also failed.

Although the earlier post-bellum activities to secure railroads were most prominent in the lower counties of Monongalia and Preston, the first actual construction resulting in the opening of new lines of railway was farther south along the valleys of West Fork, Tygart's and Cheat. The construction of a railroad from Clarksburg to Weston (authorized by act of 1866), which also gave the Baltimore and Ohio directors possession of the road from Grafton to Parkersburg, was the beginning of a system of short lines converging at Clarksburg and Grafton—often originally built by independent companies and sometimes constructed as a narrow-gauge which was later widened into a standard gauge—furnishing connections to Buckhannon, Richwood, Sutton, Pickens, Belington and Philippi, opening vast coal fields and timber regions, and penetrating some of the best farming sections. Other lines constructed up the North Branch of the Potomac from Piedmont, and up the Elk from Charleston, pierced Tucker, Randolph, Upshur and Lewis and

BLACKWATER FALLS—TUCKER.
By Courtesy of West Virginia Geological Survey.

centered on the upper Tygart's at Elkins in Randolph and on the upper Cheat above Parsons in Tucker.

The first movement resulting in this remarkable development apparently originated at Weston, the county seat of Lewis, which already becoming a center of local trade before the war was stimulated to a larger growth at its close—first by securing the location of the asylum for the insane, and later by obtaining transportation facilities which tapped its resources and encouraged industrial development.

In January, 1875, the citizens of Lewis, determined to secure an outlet to the world, incorporated the Weston and West Fork Railroad to connect Weston with Clarksburg—and at Weston began the construction of a narrow-gauge line. Three years later, this uncompleted line was leased to the newly incorporated Clarksburg, Weston and Glenville transportation company. Under the direction of energetic Senator J. N. Camden, who was elected president of the new road in 1878, the work begun at Weston was completed to Clarksburg in 1881, and steps were taken to develop the section along the route.

In April, 1882, a movement was begun to connect Weston with Buckhannon by the incorporation of the Buckhannon and West Fork Railroad. This was soon leased to the newly formed Weston and Centreville Railroad Company, and the combination emerged as the Weston and Buckhannon railroad which was promptly constructed as a narrow-gauge—partly by county levy—and opened for traffic in 1883 or 1884. Its superintendent was Dr. A. H. Kunst who in 1888 was elected president of the road (and who was also president of the Clarksburg, Weston and Glenville road). In 1889 this line was changed to a standard gauge as a result of its increased earnings and increasing traffic, and especially to meet the plans of Senator Camden who had purchased large mineral rights on the east bank of the Monongahela for which he proposed to get an outlet to Pittsburgh by constructing the Monongahela River railroad as a broad gauge from Clarksburg to Fairmont.

In April, 1889, the Weston and West Fork and the Clarksburg, Weston and Glenville railroads were merged into the Clarksburg, Weston and Midland railroad, which allowed the stockholders five per cent. of the stock held in either of the other companies, and later in the year absorbed the Weston and Elk River railroad on the same terms. On July 20, 1889, following the last merger, the Buckhannon River Railroad was incorporated to run to Pickens.

The Clarksburg, Weston and Midland, after absorbing the Buckhannon and West Fork and the Weston and Centreville in September, 1889, and the Buckhannon River railroad in February, 1890, was reorganized as the West Virginia and Pittsburgh railroad which was changed to a standard-gauge road with Senator Camden as president, and Dr. Kunst as vice-president and general manager—and soon became a branch of the Baltimore and Ohio. This road extended from Clarksburg via Weston to Pickens in Randolph with another branch from Weston via Flatwoods, and to Camden-on-Gauley in Webster—terminating in each case in a region previously unopened but quickly responsive to the touch of capital.

In making the road a broad-gauge Senator Camden seems to have contemplated a connecting link between the Pittsburgh region and the South by extension of the line to the Chesapeake and Ohio at Covington, Virginia.

Weston received a wonderful forward impetus by the construction of the early narrow-gauge system to Clarksburg, by the later extension and change to broad-gauge, by securing the location of railway offices and repair shops, by the opening of mineral and timber resources, and by the establishment of large manufacturing industries.

From about 1875 to 1890 many poplar logs, obtained at a low price, were floated on the West Fork and its tributaries by R. T. Lowndes and others who manufactured them on circular saw mills at Clarksburg. The larger part of the timber of the virgin forests not removed by the river was cut by portable stave mills and circular-saw lumber

UPPER FALLS—LITTLE BLACKWATER.
By Courtesy of West Virginia Geological Survey.

UPPER MONONGAHELA VALLEY. 85

mills which found an opportunity for most active operations in the Collins settlement and other territory in the southern and southwestern parts of the county. In many instances the product was transported by wagon for twenty or twenty-five miles to reach railway shipping points. From Ireland, after 1906, a private narrow-gauge railway was constructed to carry lumber to Walkersville on the new Coal and Coke railroad. The timber of commercial value has now largely been cut and sold. Practically all the poplar and the greater part of the best oak has disappeared.

At the beginning of the new century industrial development in the western end of Lewis county received a new impetus by the opening of the rich oil fields on Sand Fork of the Kanawha in a region once known as the Camden-Bailey-Camden lands and largely settled by humble Irish who after a period of day labor on the construction of the Baltimore and Ohio in West Virginia decided to invest their small earnings in small farms. The first "gusher" which began to flow on the Copley farm in September, 1900, produced a sudden tide of prosperity which disturbed the social equilibrium for miles around. The increasing flow from two hundred barrels per hour to seven thousand barrels per day, rapidly filling ten large hastily improvised two hundred and fifty barrel tanks and rising rapidly in the bed of the stream which was dammed to save it, and flowing down the stream eight miles beyond the first dams, soon raised the four maiden sisters of a pioneer Irish family from poverty to wealth and created a rapid demand for immediate development on adjacent lands which in the main had been leased by the South Penn Oil Company. The signs of new life were seen in the faces of the crowds of curious visitors, and the active industry of many new operators and speculators.

New industrial activity followed the opening of the Coal and Coke railway in 1906.

In the county there are now about two hundred wells producing oil and five hundred producing gas. The oil and gas industry is principally in the Freeman's Creek, Court House and Hacker's Creek districts. The product from the few wells drilled in Collins Settlement and Skin Creek districts has been very light. In Hacker's Creek district the gas wells have a light volume (one million to ten million feet) but have a heavy rock pressure. In both Freeman's Creek and Court House districts, both the volume and the pressure are heavy. In these districts have been found all the paying oil wells. The coal industry is practically in its infancy. The Jacksonville Coal and Coke Company, organized by citizens of Pennsylvania and operated in a small way at Jacksonville on the Coal and Coke, recently closed business after becoming involved. At present the Kroger Gas Company is operating mines, north of Jane Lew near the Harrison county line, on small holdings. In Freeman's Creek district, about fifteen or twenty miles from the railroad, Pittsburgh capitalists own twenty-two thousand acres of Pittsburgh and Sewickly coal of good quality which they are holding as an investment.

From Weston, eastward over the narrow-gauge, Buckhannon was first reached by passenger train. In 1881 it was entered by the West Virginia and Pittsburgh railway which was later (1899) extended by its new owners (the Baltimore and Ohio) to Pickens. Surrounded by a fine agricultural region and favored by a good country trade, the town had already grown to be an important place even before the advent of the railroad which greatly increased its development. Better transportation facilities gave it new manufacturing plants and made it the home office of several industries (such as the Newlon Coal Works, and the A. J. G. Griffin Lumber Plants) which extended their influence through the counties of Upshur and Randolph and even into Webster and Nicholas.

The first steam saw mill in Upshur had been operated on Cutright's Run (a tributary of the Buckhannon) in 1867. The commercial lumber industry, begun about 1883 as a result of the construction of the railroad to Buckhannon, increased with its later extension up the river.

The Buckhannon Boom and Lumber Company operated large mills at Buckhannon and Ten-mile. Buckhannon received many logs from river floats, and both logs and lumber from Ten-mile by tramroad. Other logs were brought by railroad after the extension of the West Virginia and Pittsburgh line to Newlin in 1891. In 1893 about half of Upshur was still covered with timber, which, however, was rapidly taken out thereafter.

The county seat soon showed the results of the new development. In 1887 it obtained the location of a woolen mill built by Parke Brothers. In 1888 it had its first electric light plant. In 1889 it had a tannery and in 1902 it had a glass plant in operation. By 1894 the town contained a population of about two thousand seven hundred with a strong tendency toward further increase which later became stronger by the completion of new railroad lines—especially by the construction of the short line from Tygart's Valley Junction by the Baltimore and Ohio in 1904 in order to compete with the Coal and Coke.

Below Upshur, on the Tygart's Valley River, the county seat of Barbour also began to feel the spirit of new industrial life. Incorporated in 1871 by the legislature, by 1884 it became the terminal of the Grafton and Greenbrier Railroad—a narrow-gauge road which had projected plans for extension to Charleston, and which was widened to a standard-gauge a few years later and extended up Tygart's to Belington. With its completion began the steady progress of portable saw mills from the line of track towards the heads of streams producing increasing quantities of lumber which found shipping points at Moatsville, Belington, Philippi and Clements. At the beginnings of this new industry, much timber along the river was drifted to Grafton where it was manufactured into lumber at Curtin's band mill.

The development of Grafton, which had begun before the war, was considerably stimulated after the war by timber industries depending upon the surrounding region and especially upon the supply of timber from Tygart's Valley River. By 1870 the manufacture of lumber on a large scale was begun by a large circular saw mill east of Grafton at Westerman. A large water power saw mill was operated at Valley Falls. The latter at first received timber over wooden tramways and later from the river rafts floated from points as high as Philippi. Later a large band mill constructed by Captain G. W. Curtin at Grafton received its supply of logs chiefly from points on Tygart's above the boundaries of Taylor.

In 1872, Grafton seems to have had aspirations to become the capital of the state. A convention of "delegates from six or eight counties and citizens of Grafton," held at Grafton in the early part of the year, and presided over by ex-Governor Johnson, drafted a set of resolutions instructing the delegates of the counties at the Constitutional Convention at Charleston to submit to the people of the state the question of removing the capital from Charleston. Although the town failed to secure the capital it was successful in the contest for the county seat in 1878.

Perhaps the most remarkable industrial changes which have been made in any of the counties of the Monongahela Valley region since the war have appeared in Tucker and Randolph, especially since the first penetration of the railroad into the Upper Cheat and Tygart's Valley country in 1885. In these counties, in 1870, there was a waste of valuable timber which indicated the economic wisdom of the speedy construction of an outlet to the nearest navigable point on Cheat or at Tucker Court House twenty-five miles above Rowlesburg station of the Baltimore and Ohio. In 1870, Diss Debar, the state commissioner of immigration, who issued a handbook to exhibit the various resources of the state, proposed a fifty-five mile double track tramway from the Staunton Turnpike to Tucker Court House (St. George) via the Laurel Fork of Cheat—an enterprise which he said would promote the development of a rich timber region large enough to form a separate county. About the same time (1869) the Randolph, Tucker and Preston Turnpike was projected with a proposed termination at West Union or Chisholm's Mills.

Randolph, although settled a century earlier, remained so inaccessible that few people had settled in its borders. The families of the earliest settlers in many instances still occupied the property of their pioneer ancestors. Although Tygart's Valley region was fairly well settled and properous, other regions were in a wild and unsettled condition resulting from the difficulty of making mountain roads and the distance from railroad connection. The streams as a rule were not navigable for boats and were too swift for any use except to float timber. From 1865 to 1895 many logs were floated on Cheat to Rowlesburg and Point Marion and on Tygart's to Grafton (largely to the Pardee and Curtin Lumber Company). From 1888 to 1896 much spruce timber was floated from Shaver's Fork (almost at the head of Cheat) to Point Marion. The steam saw mill industry began in 1878 with the appearance of a portable mill brought from Virginia to Dry Fork. The more active industry followed the arrival of railroads which made accessible the great coniferous and hardwood forests and after 1894 encouraged the increase of the lumber business by the use of many hugh band mills supplemented by the smaller portable saw mills.

Canaan Vallet in Tucker and the surrounding plateau county remained practically undisturbed until the fire of 1863 destroyed the spruce on a large area, and some parts until the storm of 1877 swept a path through the spruce belt. The lumber industry which had begun by the erection of a saw mill on Cheat as early as 1830 was stimulated by the gradual introduction of steam mills after the close of the civil war, especially after the completion of the railroad through the timber to Davis and westward to Parsons.

For over a decade after the close of the civil war period, although the settlement of the tillable parts of the county developed more rapidly than in the period before the war, Randolph was neglected while the tide of investment and immigration passed by to the far west. By 1880, however, it began to receive new accessions by immigration. In 1879 the main body of the thrifty Swiss colony artfully decoyed into the wilderness of woe by land agents, crossed Shaver's Mountain to Alpina. Food was high, for Webster was then the nearest railroad point and difficult to reach by wagon. Instead of burning spruce-pine logs as the earliest settlers had done, they sawed them into lengths suitable for lumber in hope of placing them on the market—only to find that there was no accessible market.

The construction of a railroad from Piedmont up the North Branch to tap the undeveloped resources of Randolph county was proposed long before it was accomplished. The Potomac and Piedmont Coal and Railroad Company, incorporated by the legislature in 1866 and begun in 1880, secured a new charter in 1881 in its new name, the West Virginia Central and Pittsburgh Railroad Company, which was organized with H. G. Davis as president. Passing over the divide beyond the headwaters of the Potomac, the new road continued south of the Great Backbone Mountains to Davis in the heart of the hardwood forests by November, 1884. Early in 1889 the main line of the road, following the waters of the wild and picturesque Blackwater Run, was completed down the Dry Fork through the mountain gap to Parsons on the main branch of the Cheat—and, later in the year, after turning up Shaver's Fork for a short distance it crossed to Leading Creek and reached picturesque Elkins (previously known as Leadsville) which was established as a town with terminal facilities and has had a steady growth partly due to the proximity of the exhaustless Roaring Creek coal fields. From Elkins (by gradual extensions) one branch followed up the Valley River (sending off a smaller branch at Roaring Creek five miles west of Elkins) and another returned eastward to Shaver's Fork which it ascended until, finding a way through Shaver's Mountains, it crossed to Glady Fork, ascended it to the divide, and descended the West Fork of the Greenbrier to Durbin in Pocahontas. Another line was contemplated from Belington to Clarksburg to connect with the

West Virginia and Pennsylvania Railroad that had been surveyed from Clarksburg to Brownsville, but was abandoned. By 1891 trains were running on extensions to Beverly, and to Belington where connection was made with a Tygart's Valley branch of the Baltimore and Ohio from Grafton. By 1904 connections were made at Durbin.

The new road after passing through Mineral and Grant, penetrated the vast coal fields of Tucker and Randolph. The gigantic lumber plants and rich coal mines, and the propinquity of newly made and growing towns soon furnished evidence of rapid material progress. The opening of mineral and timber resources created towns such as Thomas, Davis, Douglas, Hendricks, Bretz and Parsons in Tucker; such as Montrose and Elkins in Randolph; and such as Belington in Barbour.

At Thomas were located the large Davis-Elkins coal and coke works. Six miles eastward on the branch from Thomas, the coal works and manufacturing industries (a tannery and lumber plants) soon supported a population of fifteen hundred forming the town of Davis with quite a mercantile trade increased by that of the surrounding country.

Elkins, located in a lovely valley, bordering the northwestern bank of Tygart's Valley River, received its first stimulus to growth from the construction of engine and car shops by the railway company, and the erection of homes for many operatives of the road. The resulting activity attracted a good class of merchants who increasingly attracted trade from the surrounding country.

The completion of the railroad through the timber to Davis and beyond furnished an outlet for the timber in the eastern and central sections and admitted portable and stationary saw mills which have since continued to operate. The later construction of the Dry Fork Railroad and its branch to Laneville opened a new field of operations. Everywhere, temporary railroads were forced into the heart of the woods followed by saw mills, tanneries, pulp mills and lumber camps to aid in the campaign of conquest and destruction of the previously unmolested forests leaving behind the desolating tracks and unsightly debris of their triumphant march.

In 1905, along much of the old Fishinghawk packtrail of early days, from Beverly via Files Creek and Fishinghawk to the Sinks of Gandy, the axe of the lumberman was just beginning to break the primeval solitude, and steam whistles were heard both on west and east sounding the death knell of West Virginia's greatest primeval forest. On the forty-three miles of the Coal and Iron railway between Elkins and Durbin there were forty-nine saw mills. The wilderness had been cut in two by the railroad, and again further east by the Dry Fork, and again by log roads, one of which was twenty miles long. At the same time lumber men were advancing from the waters of Greenbrier to attack the mighty forests from that side.

With the rapid disappearance of the timber, there emerges the problems of conservation and replanting. The West Virginia Pulp and Paper Company is already making extensive plantations of spruce on its cut-over lands near the head of Shaver's Fork of Cheat.

Very recently the industrial activity and prospective future of much of the southern part of the Monongahela region have received new promise of importance by the construction of an important outlet for Randolph, Upshur and Lewis counties. The Coal and Coke Railway was incorporated and begun in 1902, and completed in 1906, under management of Senator Henry G. Davis and Senator Stephen B. Elkins in coöperation with the Wabash interests. Its authorized capital was $10,000,000. Conceived as a means in the development of vast coal and timber properties, it fortunately became a connecting link between great trunk lines—especially by the acquisition of the Elk River division of the old Charleston, Clendennin and Sutton railway (begun at Charleston, 1893) with its old established and valuable Charleston terminals adjacent to those of the Kanawha and Michigan, with which track connection was formed. Favored by its geographical location, the road has good connections with both eastern and western markets

MILL AT DAVIS.

By Courtesy of West Virginia Geological Survey.

for coal and coke produced along its line. At the south, it reaches the middle and western states by the Kanawha and Michigan and the Chesapeake and Ohio lines. At the north it has connections with the lakes and the eastern seaboard by the Wabash (Western Maryland) and Baltimore and Ohio systems. The company owns carefully selected coal lands and coal rights along the route of the road in four counties drained by the Monongahela—Randolph, Barbour, Upshur and Lewis—and also in Gilmer and Braxton. The Pittsburgh vein in this region is regarded as a better coal than its type in the Fairmont and Clarksburg districts—being harder and yielding a greater per cent. of large blocks.

While the railway from the Potomac was penetrating westward into Tucker and Randolph, the earlier projects of a railroad along the Monongahela to intersect the earlier B. & O. Lines between East and West, were reviving under more favorable auspices and under more favorable conditions—including the completion of the line from Weston to Clarksburg as no unimportant factor. The construction of the road, by sections which were later combined into a single line, was a great stimulation to industrial and social development in each county through which it passed and also in parts of Preston.

Clarksburg, which had become the terminus of the line constructed from Weston, became the starting point of the Monongahela line to Fairmont; and later it was made the eastern terminal of a short line constructed to the Ohio at New Martinsville. The town, steadily growing under the earlier impetus which it had received from its location on the Parkersburg line of the B. & O., had also been favored by the traffic of the turnpike which served as a prominent thoroughfare from Fairmont up West Fork and to Sutton in Braxton county—and by the limestone soil (and the earlier development of settlements) which at the opening of the war had made Harrison probably the most improved of the inland counties of West Virginia—with a total valuation of live stock exceeded only by Hampshire and Greenbrier, and a corn production exceeded only by Hampshire and Jackson. By the close of the war it was the center of a good coal trade. It received large additional prosperity from the construction of lines later combining to form the West Virginia and Pittsburgh railroad which penetrated southward to the richest coal and timber lands in the heart of the state and northward through great coal fields to the metropolis at the head of the Ohio.

In 1888, seven years after the completion of the Weston line to Clarksburg, the Monongahela River Railway Company was organized to build a road from Clarksburg to Fairmont. It was incorporated by J. N. Camden and others, beginning with a capital of only $5,000 which was later increased. Opened for traffic in 1889 and completed in 1891, it became the property of the Baltimore and Ohio in 1897. It opened rich coal fields which, especially contributing to the success of the large plants of the Consolidated Coal Company which produces an enormous tonnage both of coal and coke, also increased the importance of Clarksburg as a commercial and industrial center. The short line connecting Clarksburg with New Martinsville was incorporated by T. Moore Jackson and others who sold the franchise to the Baltimore and Ohio. Completed by 1902, it opened rich coal fields and timber regions which have contributed to the wealth of Clarksburg and the entire region.

Favored by geographic situation, rich resources, and increasing railroad facilities, the old town of Clarksburg found itself in a state of development exceeding all expectations and exciting larger dreams of future prosperity and greatness. Municipal improvement followed each prominent industrial advance. Illuminating gas was introduced in 1871. Natural gas for heat and light was piped from Doddridge county in 1891. An electric light plant was erected in 1887, and water works were established in 1888. Great changes followed the discovery of oil and gas—in the western end of the county in 1889—which also increased the growth of Salem. Better lighted and better paved streets and the construction of new business houses soon indicated the advent

By Courtesy of West Virginia Geological Survey.

PULP MILL.

MARION COUNTY COURTHOUSE.

of new prosperity. A street car line was constructed in 1900. By 1903 the city was heated by gas from one of the largest wells in the world, and shortly thereafter its facilities as a business center were increased by the construction of the Waldo hotel which ranks as one of the best modern hotels in the state.

The Monongahela River Railroad connecting Clarksburg with Fairmont, completed in 1888 and opened for traffic in 1889, was an important link and a determining factor in the combined Monongahela system. It opened valuable mines in a rich mineral field, including those at Monongah, and gave an industrial stimulus which resulted in the rise of several towns. It supplied coal for both eastern and western markets —and also for local use in Upshur and Lewis. It gave a more direct route for passenger traffic from Clarksburg to Wheeling, and stimulated the construction of the line from Morgantown to Uniontown by which a continuous direct connection was secured with Pittsburgh—in each case superseding the elbow routes via Parkersburg or Grafton.

Fairmont, like Clarksburg, felt the flow of a new life awakened by the construction of connecting lines of railway which opened new industries. Even in the earlier post-bellum period, it began to feel a larger prosperity resulting from the return of the soldiers and others to work on farms which in some cases had long been idle. Its revival of industrial development in a larger sense really began about 1870 by the purchase of large tracts of land by capitalists interested in the mineral resources of the county. Three mines, opened in quick succession by eastern companies soon began to make large shipments of coal, and produced a development in population and wealth which was only retarded by the panic of 1873 and the high freight rates charged by the Baltimore and Ohio. An era of improvement began in 1876, after a fire which destroyed a large part of the principal business section of the town in spite of the efforts of the primitive voluntary "bucket brigade" (of men, women and children) which at that time and place had not been superseded by the modern fire-engine. With some additions to the insurance money which largely covered the losses, the owners of the destroyed buildings were able to replace them with better structures and to secure better street grades. With the new era of development came the demand for the extension of Monongahela slack-water improvement to Fairmont—which Captain Roberts (who made the government survey from Morgantown in 1875) regarded as the head of the navigation of the Ohio.

By 1881, enterprising citizens of the town actively participated in a coöperative effort, through county committees and public meetings, to test the sense of the people on the question of the construction of a railroad up the Monongahela through Monongalia, Marion, Harrison and Lewis counties. With the construction of sections of railway connecting the town with Morgantown in 1886 and with Clarksburg a few years later, enterprising citizens, seizing opportunity by the forelock, organized the "Fairmont Development Company" which contributed greatly to the rapid growth of the town by offering inducements to new industrial plants which were seeking a location. The town was also favored by other advantages such as schools and hotels, and more recently it has been benefitted by the construction of electric lines connecting it with Clarksburg and Mannington.

Fairmont has shared in the prosperity arising from the oil wells in the western part of the county. In October, 1889, an oil well drilled in the Big Ingun sand at Mannington, proved successful, and the development which followed was one of the three developments which attracted the serious attention of the Standard Oil Company to West Virginia. In April, 1890, the first oil was shipped from the Mannington oil field in two tank-cars via Grafton to Parkersburg. Development increased in 1901 and 1902, and the Mannington field soon became one of the largest in the state—and the number of fortunes made continued to increase for several years. From the beginning of the oil industry (1889), Mannington grew rapidly as other oil towns and its prosperity was increased by the development of the neighboring gas territory. Its

STATE NORMAL SCHOOL, FAIRMONT.

population increased from nine hundred in 1888 to five thousand in 1907.

Two years before the Camden line between Fairmont and Clarksburg was built, Morgantown secured connection with the Baltimore and Ohio at Fairmont by a line later extended to connect with the Baltimore and Ohio line via Connellsville and Pittsburgh. Even as early as the latter part of 1883, while the Pennsylvania interests were still endeavoring to secure the construction of a branch line into West Virginia along the Monongahela, the Fairmont, Morgantown and Pittsburgh Railroad Company was organized—apparently backed by the Baltimore and Ohio—to extend the Baltimore and Ohio line from Fairmont to Morgantown and also to connect with its line at Uniontown. Construction was delayed by contests with the West Virginia and Pennsylvania over the right of way—in 1884 at Fairmont, and later at Point Marion and along Cheat where there was room for only one road. The new line, operated by the Baltimore and Ohio, was opened to South Morgantown by January 30, 1886, and to Morgantown a few days later. Three years later, Morgantown secured satisfactory steamboat communication with Pittsburgh by the completion of "Lock Number 8" after a delay of ten years. The first boats which arrived at the wharf in 1889 were greeted by an enthusiastic crowd which the captain entertained by a display of the first electric search light that many of them had ever seen.

The extension of the railroad from Morgantown to Uniontown on which grading began in the spring of 1892 was practically completed early in 1894; and, after some delay occasioned by the bridge across Cheat at Point Marion, was opened to traffic in the following summer —soon resulting in the opening of rich coal fields in Monongalia county. In 1895 the authorized capital of the road which under the incorporation of 1893 had been $1,000,000 was increased to $2,740,000. At first inadequate for the vast freight which it carried, in 1907 the road was improved by equipment with new eighty-five-pound rails and a double track over part of its route.

The completion of railway connections with Fairmont revived the projected railway up Decker's Creek. Grading for this road was begun in the spring of 1887 under the direction of the West Virginia Railway Company which proposed to complete a line via Masontown, Reedsville and Hardman's Furnace to Independence on the Baltimore and Ohio eleven miles east of Grafton, but, on the failure to dispose of its bond, suddenly collapsed in the fall of the same year—producing much anger among its unpaid Italian laborers and resulting in considerable friction in the settlement of its affairs. In the early nineties, the right of way and other properties belonging to the bankrupt company were purchased by George C. Sturgiss at public auction. Before work could be resumed the old grading became almost worthless, the trestles rotten and the property in general was much depreciated in value.

Coincident with the collapse of the Decker's Creek line, the Tunnelton, Kingwood and Fairchance narrow-gauge, surveyed in 1882 and graded in 1883, was completed from Tunnelton to Kingwood (in 1887). Originally constructed largely for transportation of timber, it was changed into a broad-gauge by J. Ami Martin in 1896 in order to facilitate shipments of coal to the East. With this road is largely associated the growth of Tunnelton which until 1873 contained less than a dozen families. The population of one hundred and twenty-five in 1882 increased to three hundred and fifty in 1891 and to four hundred and seventy-nine in 1900 after which the increase seems to have been more rapid. The first mill in the place in 1879 was succeeded by a better one in 1893 and another by 1900. A new era of industrial development for the town began with the advent of the Merchant's Coal Company in 1895. The development in the eastern part of Preston county during the same period possibly was a factor in reviving the long disputed boundary line between Preston county and Maryland which

DOWN THE MONONGAHELA FROM MORGANTOWN.

WORKS OF AMERICAN SHEET AND TIN PLATE COMPANY.

was finally settled by the decision of the United States Supreme Court in 1910, and the surveys which followed.

About 1891 the old expectation of the construction of a road on the west side of the river in Monongalia was temporarily revived. Senator Stephen B. Elkins, who visited Morgantown in 1890-91 to secure options on large tracts of coal lands on the west side of the Monongahela, contemplated for awhile the purchase of the old West Virginia and Pennsylvania rights by the Davis-Elkins interests—but negotiations failed, largely on account of the prices demanded by the promoters.

The previous projects of a railway up Decker's Creek were revived by Hon. George C. Sturgiss in 1898. The Morgantown and Kingwood Railroad was chartered in January, 1899, with a capital stock of $200,-000. The new company opened an office at Morgantown and construction was begun on July 5, 1899, under the superintendence of J. Ami Martin. By November, 1900, the road was completed to the Preston county line, over eleven miles from Morgantown. From this point, after waiting in vain for expected local aid, the road was completed to Masontown in 1902. At this time there were several projects for extensions—one across the Monongahela and down its left bank into Pennsylvania to join with the Wabash system; another up the west bank to Fairmont; another up Dent's Run and over the summit to Little Indian Creek, thence to the Monongahela river; and another up Scott's Run and across Monongalia to some point on the Ohio; and up Robinson's Run to Waynesburg, Pennsylvania. In 1902 the road passed to the control of Senator Stephen B. Elkins and his sons, who also purchased the property of the Cheat River and Pittsburgh Railroad and determined upon eastward extension to connect with the Baltimore and Ohio at Rowlesburg and with the Cheat Valley railroad. The line was completed to Kingwood in 1906 and to Rowlesburg in 1907.

This short line road has proven a very valuable factor in the industrial development of the region through which it passes, opening up valuable coal and timber lands and carrying heavily laden trains of lumber, coal and coke for shipment via the B. & O. at Morgantown and Rowlesburg. The Decker's Creek valley, which before had supported only a small population of farmers, became a bee hive of modern industry with daily shipments of coal, coke, timber, glass sand, and manufactured products equal in value to the entire products of the valley for years previous to the construction of the road. At Sabraton, near Morgantown, is located a large plant of the American Sheet and Tin Plate company. At Sturgisson is located the Sturgisson Crushed Stone and Sand Company. At Manheim is located the Buckhorn Portland Cement Company. The chief coal companies in operation along the line are the Connellsville Basin Coal and Coke Company and the Elkins Coal Company, both of which make large daily shipments.

Coincident with the railroad development solving problems of transportation on which depended the larger usefulness of the vast resources so long stored away in her neighboring hills, Morgantown expanded beyond her ancient boundaries. In the beginning of the larger growth of the town, made possible by new facilities for transportation, an important part was taken by various improvement companies such as the Monongalia Improvement Company which organized in 1884 to bore for natural gas, and obtained from the town council an exclusive right to furnish water and gas within the municipal boundaries for thirty years. The latter was succeeded in 1889 by the Union Improvement Company of which E. M. Grant was manager. In 1890, influenced by the oil production in the western end of the county, construction was begun on the Eureka Line and on a score of oil tanks at Morgantown.

With the erection of new houses resulting from the first signs of a coming era of industrial development, the town council was confronted with many important problems such as sidewalks, street names, street lights, the sale of intoxicants, water works, sewers, and a fire department, which pressed for immediate solution. Many improvements were undertaken under the leadership of Colonel R. E. Fast who was elected mayor in May, 1888. The increase of brick pavements ex-

THE SENECA GLASS WORKS.

hausted the supply of brick. A decision in favor of saloons, by vote of 1889, was reversed by the people two years later. A new court house, begun in 1890, added to the attractiveness of the town.

The earlier development of the town was materially promoted by the organization of a chamber of commerce, and the organization of land companies such as the Morgantown Building and Investment Company which purchased briar fields and (1893) converted them into lots on which Seneca grew.

The completion of direct railroad connections with Connellsville and Pittsburgh, and especially the construction of the Morgantown and Kingwood road, were followed by extensive operations in lumber and coal and by the location of several manufacturing plants which have been important factors in the recent growth of Morgantown—to which may be added the steady growth of the University (largely through its efforts to meet the increasing needs of the state), the extension of street improvements and street railways, and the construction of various bridges over Decker's Creek, and a modern two-span bridge over the Monongahela to replace the old suspension bridge which had served for over half a century. In the decade after 1900, besides many smaller establishments of various kinds, seven new glass manufacturing plants were added to the single Seneca glass factory of the preceding decade, and a large tin plate mill was erected. With new industrial development came many other changes—changes in population, property, prices, public problems and prosperity. At the opening of the second decade of the new century, the bright prospects resulting from the continued growth of established business and population were increased by the extension of electric lines beyond the immediate vicinity of the town and the construction of the "Buckhannon and Northern railroad" on the west side of the river, completed in 1912 between Fairmont and the Pennsylvania line.

JAMES MORTON CALLAHAN.

THE CIVIL WAR

THE STATE OF WEST VIRGINIA

A VIEW ON LOWER CHEAT.

THE RISING WAR CLOUD.

At the general election in 1860, the Republicans had Lincoln and Hamlin as standard bearers; the northern wing of the Democratic party had Stephen A. Douglas, for their presidential nominee; the Consolidated Union ticket was headed by Bell and Everett; the Southern Democracy had for their candidate, John C. Breckinridge. The result, was one hundred and eighty electoral votes for Lincoln and Hamlin; they had a popular vote of 1,866,352, being a majority of 491,195. Breckinridge received 845,763 votes, entitling him to seventy-two electoral votes. Bell-Everett had thirty-nine electoral votes. Stephen A. Douglas polled 1,375,157 votes and had twelve electoral votes.

The census of 1850 showed the following to be the population in the counties now included in the territory of West Virginia:

	Total Pop.	Slaves		Total Pop.	Slaves
Barbour	9,005	113	Monongalia	12,387	176
Braxton	4,212	89	Nicholas	3,963	73
Brooke	5,054	31	Ohio	18,066	164
Doddridge	3,750	32	Pocahontas	3,598	267
Fayette	3,955	156	Preston	11,708	87
Gilmer	3,475	72	Putnam	5,338	632
Greenbrier	10,022	1,317	Randolph	5,243	201
Hancock	4,050	3	Ritchie	3,902	16
Harrison	11,728	488	Taylor	5,367	168
Jackson	6,544	53	Tyler	5,498	38
Kanawha	15,853	3,140	Wetzel	4,284	17
Lewis	10,131	368	Wirt	3,353	32
Marion	10,552	94	Wood	9,450	373
Marshall	10,138	49			
Mason	7,539	647	Total	206,735	8,896

According to the New York *World* of April, 1861, the following estimate was made of the population of Virginia, just before the Federal census had been taken and made public: Virginia had one hundred and fifty-eight counties, with a white population of 1,047,579, and 491,456 slaves. In the forty-eight counties west of the Blue Ridge mountains there were 5,000 slaves. This was in about one-third of Virginia territory, and was only one one-hundreth of the slaves in the entire State. During the decade from 1850 to 1860, slaves had decreased 1,185 in the western counties. The whites had increased during the same decade almost 80,000. The total increase in all Virginia had been only 152,742, fifty-eight per cent. of which was in the forty-eight counties to the west of the mountain range.

But the difference was not altogether this, between the two sections of the Old Dominion. The indifference and hostility to slavery as an institution was not all the motive for wanting to form a new State west of the mountains. The inequality of imposts levied upon the western section by the Richmond government and the higher rate of taxes came in for its share. Then the East exempted all slaves under twelve years of age from taxation. This one act caused one-eighth of the entire tax of the State to come upon the counties west of the mountains. Fully one-half of the building improvements of the commonwealth came out of the people of the western section. This had for years been the burden of contention between the eastern and western portions of Virginia.

THE CAMPAIGN OF 1860.

In West Virginia, which in 1861 was still a part of the "Old Dominion," the State of Virginia, political sentiment and interest was at a high-keyed condition, as well as elsewhere in the country. In fact, it was probably more intense, from the fact of its territory being on the border of the Slave States, and the trouble the eastern and western portions of the commonwealth had been having over taxation, representation, etc., for a number of years prior to that date. The John Brown raid at Harper's Ferry, his trial and execution in 1859, had not been forgotten, and this, with other local causes, made memorable the campaign in Virginia.

The numerous political parties of that memorable campaign each had rousing political mass-meetings at Wheeling and in almost all the larger cities in the State—especially in the western portion. The Bell-Everett ticket was the Pro-Slavery ticket; John C. Breckinridge was the candidate for president of the Southern wing of the Democracy; Stephen A. Douglas was the nominee of the Northern Democrats; and Lincoln and Hamlin were the standard-bearers for the Republican party, the first to be elected on that ticket, John C. Fremont having failed of election in 1856 on the first Republican ticket.

Among the noted speakers who spoke in Wheeling that campaign were Tom Corwin and Breckinridge. Rousing meetings were kept up over the State by the "Douglas Democrats." Hon. Waitman T. Willey, later United States Senator, of Morgantown, supported the Bell-Everett ticket.

What was known in that campaign from ocean to ocean was the organization of Republicans into clubs known as the "Wide Awakes," who were very interesting in their operations at mass-meetings and conventions and did much toward creating sentiment for their party. Their torchlight processions were perhaps as famous throughout the North and East as any other political organization of its character. The first of these companies within the State of Virginia was formed at Wheeling in August, immediately after Mr. Lincoln's nomination. It consisted of seventy members at first, to which many were recruited later. They attended all public gatherings held in Virginia by the Republicans, and also went to Pittsburgh, Pennsylvania, and made a part of a great parade for the "Rail Splitter," which words were inscribed on their banners.

Owing to its geographical location, Virginia was destined to become the seat of a great war, signs of which as early as the autumn of 1859, at least, were to be seen by thinking men both North and South. On her soil were soon to be marshalled contending hosts, and the valleys and mountains were to be crimsoned with some of the best blood the nation afforded in both sections, each contending for what they thought to be right. Two great States were eventually to be where once the Old Dominion stood alone.

Virginia in 1860 was in the wildest state of confusion. Throughout the eastern portion, meetings were held at which enthusiastic thousands heard from eloquent lips the portraiture of Virginia's future destiny, when she should become the chief corner-stone of a newly formed Southern Confederacy. Her people had but recently witnessed the tragic scenes of John Brown's famous raid on Harper's Ferry, and no one could tell, scarce conjecture, what the next move would be upon the part of the Northern faction that did not believe in the slave system of the South. All felt sure, however, that a blow was soon to be struck at that institution, as a natural result of the sentiment in the North. Hence the people of Eastern Virginia nowhere saw safety except as allied with their neighboring sister States to the South, with whom they felt they must share a common destiny. This was the sentiment, largely in East Virginia, but vastly different did the people in the western portion of the commonwealth feel concerning secession, which they regarded as ruinous in effect, and they maintained that safety could only be found beneath the Stars and Stripes of the undivided Union of States. To this loyalty they pledged their sacred honor, their lives and their fortunes. Men of different political faith on all other questions met on one common ground when the question of secession was brought up, and they bitterly opposed such a measure.

The first public meeting for the purpose of expressing opinion along these lines was held in Preston county (now a part of West Virginia), November 12, 1860—less than six months before Fort Sumter was fired upon. The feeling at this meeting was intense. Almost unanimous was the opinion of those assembled that to endorse secession was but treason on the part of an American. One of the resolutions there passed was: "That any attempt upon the part of the State to secede will meet with the unqualified disapprobation of the people of this county."

Twelve days later, a similar mass-meeting was held in Harrison county, and there it was declared: "That the people will first exhaust all constitutional remedies for redress before they will resort to any violent means; that the ballot box is the only medium known to the constitution for a redress of grievances, and to it alone we will appeal; that it is the duty of all citizens to uphold and support the lawfully constituted authorities."

November 27, 1860, two days later, the citizens of Monongalia county assembled at Morgantown, headed by the loyal leaders of all the great political parties, and there resolved: "That the election of the candidates of the Republican party does not constitute or justify a reason for secession, and that the Union of the States is the best guarantee for the present and future welfare of the people."

December 3, that same year, the people of Tyler and Marion counties met at Wheeling and Point Pleasant, and there passed similar resolutions concerning the proposed secession of Virginia. As a State, Virginia was slow to act in the matter. On the west and north was the Federal Union, and on the south lay those who had cast their fortunes with the Confederacy. Not much time was to be lost in determining which course to pursue. Governor Letcher called an extra session of the Assembly, which body convened January 7, 1861, when began the stormiest session in all the State's history. One week later a bill was passed calling for a convention of the people, the delegates of which were to be chosen in the manner prescribed by the election of members of the Assembly. The body was to consist of one hundred and fifty-two members. This action on the part of the Assembly was without precedent in the history of the commonwealth. Before, the people themselves had always called conventions, but now they were to be denied that right. However, the act provided that the action of the convention should be submitted to the people for their approval or rejection. January 21, 1861, the Assembly declared, by joint-resolution, that if all efforts failed to reconcile the difficulties existing between the two sections of the country, "it is the duty of Virginia to unite her destiny with the slaveholding States of the South."

All was confusion and no one knew just what was best to do, and delay could not be had much longer as other sections of the country were rapidly taking a stand for or against the Union. Delegates were elected February 4, 1861, and on the morning of the 13th there was witnessed a scene in and around the old State House at Richmond that has gone into history as being one of the most memorable events. There had convened jurists, wise men, experienced statesmen, not a few of whom had a national reputation and possessed great ability; these included such men as ex-President John Tyler; Henry A. Wise, ex-governor of the State; and many others of high standing in the councils of the nation. It was a time fraught with problems of great importance, and the people west of the mountains sent their best talent and wisest representatives over the Blue Ridge range to take part in the deliberations. The convention organized by electing John Jenney, a delegate of Loudoun county, president, and John L. Eubank, of Richmond, as secretary. A committee on Federal Relations was made up as follows: Robert Conrad, A. H. H. Stewart, Henry A. Wise, Robert E. Scott, W. B. Preston, Lewis L. Harvie, Sherard Clemens W. H. McFarland, William McComas, R. L. Montague, Samuel Price, Valentine W. Southall, Waitman T. Willey, James C. Bruce, W. W. Boyd, James Barbour, S. C. Williams, Will C. Rivers, Samuel McD. Moore, George Blow, Jr., and Peter C. Johnson. Stewart and Clemens asked to be excused, and were dropped from the list.

The final result was seen almost from the beginning. On the second day of the convention, January 14, 1861, credentials of the Confederate commissions of John S. Preston, of South Carolina, Henry L. Benning, of Georgia, and Fulton Anderson, from Mississippi, were received. Four days later, the two last named were heard in speeches of enthusiastic oratory and flourish, but with literary excellence, as they painted a picture pointing out the danger of Virginia remaining longer on the side of the North, and held up a view of a new government of a new nation, of which Virginia should be the corner-stone, should she but pass an ordinance for secession. The next day the committee from South Carolina declared that the people of his State believed the Union unnatural, and that no human force, no sanctity of human touch, could ever compel them to again unite with the people of the North. No such Union would ever be effected unless "the economy of God was changed."

On January 20, 1861, a committee reported from all counties in Virginia, save sixteen, resulting in 52,875 in favor of submitting the action of the convention to the people. January 26, William L. Goggin, of Bedford county, made a speech in which he said that he denied the right of secession, but closed his remarks by adding that "if Virginia went, he went with her." On March 2, that year, John Goodie Jr. (also a delegate from Bedford county), presented a resolution asserting that as the power delegated to the General Government by Virginia had been perverted to her injury, therefore every consideration of duty, interest, honor and patriotism required that Virginia should declare her connection with the government to be dissolved. January 9th the committee on Federal Relations made a lengthy report in which it set forth that any State had a constitutional right to withdraw from the Union whenever the people of that State chose to do so. Ten days later, January 19th, the same committee reported a series of proposed amendments to the Federal Constitution, such as would be satisfactory to the people of the South. By these: Involuntary servitude, except for crime committed, was to be prohibited north of 36° 30′ latitude, but should not be prohibited by Congress or any territorial legislature south of that line; the importation of slaves from places beyond the limits of the United States to be prohibited; the granting of the elective franchise and right to hold office by persons of the African race was forbidden.

On April 6th, Wood Bouldin, delegate from Charlotte, offered a substitute, declaring that the independence of the seceded States should be acknowledged without delay, but this was lost by a vote of 68 to 71. On January 9th, Henry A. Wise substituted a resolution to the effect that Virginia recognizes the independence of the seceded States, which was adopted by a vote of 120 to 20. At length came the crisis. On January 17th the convention went into secret session. Wise addressed the body, and said that events were then transpiring which caused a hush to come over his soul. He spoke well, for then the blaze of fire was around Fort Sumter's walls; the State authorities were then preparing to seize the Federal navy-yard and property at Norfolk, and about two thousand State troops were collected in the Shenandoah Valley and doing the bidding of a mysterious power—were at that very moment attempting the seizure of the government's armory and arsenal at Harper's Ferry,—but the garrison destroyed most of the valuable property, fired the buildings, and fled to the Maryland shore.

At 1.30 p. m. on Wednesday, the vote was finally taken, and the "Ordinance of Secession" was passed by a vote of 88 to 55. Then was East Virginia wild with excitement and glee over the result—but the end had not yet come! All night bon-fires lighted up the heavens in and near Richmond and Petersburg, while cannon were heard loudly booming in the towns and cities in the interior of that part of Virginia. The sounds finally died away in their faint echo, as they rolled back to the eastern base of the Blue Ridge. Enthusiasm reigned supreme from the mountains to the seaboard.

But different were the sights on the western side of the Alleghenies. There the multitudes stood with bated breath, trying to catch some word from Richmond and the final decision of the convention. But the only telegraph wire over the mountain range had been cut at Harper's Ferry, and no intelligence was to be had until the delegates should return. At Morgantown, Weston, Clarksburg, and Wheeling, men stood looking each other in the face, only to see reflected back the same feelings which were locked silent within their own bosoms. But when the delegates did return, the same old jealousies that had been wrankling in the bosoms of the east and west sides of Virginia, again came welling up.

After the election of 1860, the *Lynchburg Virginian*, one of the two leading newspapers of the State, had an editorial containing these words: "So long as the bones of Washington, Jefferson, Henry, Madison, and other illustrious compatriots who cemented this Union, mingle with its soil, Virginia will be true to her memories, she will never desert the Union, with its hallowed associations, until she shall have exhausted every effort of compromise. She knows full well that nations are not born in a day; that republics, when once broken up, are not early reconciled; and that, least of all, it is impossible, when the work of disintegration proceeds from internal dissensions, to cement again the jarring fragments. The sword, a despot, and a throne, are the appropriate symbols of what follows. The North will concede our rights, and the South will be pacified—there will be but two great parties in this country, a Union and a Disunion party, however else it may be named, and with the former Virginia will ally herself."

Notwithstanding this editorial, it was but a few weeks before Virginia followed the foolishness of South Carolina and went out of the Union.

SECESSION, AND ITS RESULTS.

The election of May 23, 1861, resulted in the ratification of the Ordinance of Secession by Virginia, as a whole. The counties now composing West Virginia cast 44,000 votes, of which 40,000 were for rejecting the Richmond Ordinance.

The Convention of Unionists met June 11, 1861, and, on the 19th, passed an ordinance reorganizing the State government of Virginia in the interests of the Union, and on the 20th elected Francis H. Pierpont, governor; Daniel Polsley, lieutenant-governor, and other State officers, and adjourned to meet August 6th, 1861. The members of the legislature of the West Virginia counties who had been elected to meet at Richmond met at Wheeling, July 1st, and proceeded regularly to transact business. On the 29th of the month they elected Waitman T. Willey and John S. Carlisle as United States senators, who were admitted to their seats, thus recognizing the "reorganized" or restored government of the State of Virginia.

The convention reassembled August 6th, and on the 20th passed an ordinance dividing the State, and directed that it should be submitted to the people at an election on the fourth Thursday in October. At such election the result was favorable to ratification, the vote standing 18,408 for, and 781 against. At the same time, delegates were elected to a constitutional convention. Later a constitution was approved by the people, and the President of the United States recognized the same, and in a proclamation it was ordered that the new State should be admitted to the Union, which was done June 20, 1863.

As had been directed by the constitutional convention, an election had been held in May, 1863, for governor, State officers and members of the legislature, hence the new State was now in working order. Thus were the long-cherished hopes of the people realized, and they proceeded in regular order, under well defined legal principles, based solely on the will of the people. Now, after the passing of half a century, it still appears to the rank and file of the citizens of West Virginia that all was guided by a master hand, under Providence.

It will be well to here record the names of the delegates who attended the Second Wheeling convention, the deliberations of which body will ever be referred to by the people of the State as of much historic importance, and children's children will delight in telling of the ancestor of theirs, who had to do with this convention.

The convention was held in old Washington Hall, and the delegates were both elected, and others held seats, by reason of having been elected as members of the Virginia legislature before the opening of the Civil War, and who lived and represented that portion of the State lying to the west of the mountain range. The members were:

Barbour county—N. H. Taft, assemblyman; John H. Shuttleworth, Spencer Dayton.

Brooke county—Joseph Gist, senator; H. W. Crothers, assemblyman; John D. Nichols, Campbell Tarr.

Cabell county—Albert Laidley, assemblyman.

Monongalia county—Leroy Kramer, Joseph Snyder, assemblyman; Ralph L. Berkshire, William Price, James Evans, D. B. Dorsey.

Ohio county—Thomas H. Logan, Andrew Wilson, assemblyman; Daniel Lamb, James W. Paxton, George Harrison and Chester D. Hubbard.

Pleasants and Ritchie counties—James W. Williamson, assemblyman; C. W. Smith, William Douglas.

Preston county—Charles Hooten, William Zinn, assemblyman; William B. Crane, John Howard, Harrison Hagans, J. J. Brown.

Randolph and Tucker counties—Solomon Parsons, Samuel Crane.

Roane county—T. A. Roberts.

Taylor county—Lemuel E. Davidson, assemblyman; John S. Burdett, Samuel B. Todd.

Upshur county—D. D. T. Farnsworth, assemblyman; John D. Smith, John Lane.

Wayne county—William Radcliffe, assemblyman; W. W. Brumfield, William Copeley.

Wetzel county—James G. West, assemblyman; Reuben Martin, James P. Ferrell.

Wirt county—James A. Williamson, assemblyman; Henry Newman, E. T. Graham.

Wood county—J. W. Moss, assemblyman; Arthur I. Boreman, Peter C. Van Winkle.

Alexandria county—Henry S. Martin, James T. Close.

Fairfax county—John Hawxhurst, Eben E. Mason.

Hardy county—John Michael.

Hampshire county—James Carskadon, senator; Owen D. Downing, George W. Broski, James H. Trout, James J. Barracks.

Doddridge and Tyler counties—William I. Boreman, assemblyman; Daniel D. Johnson, James A. Folley.

Gilmer county—Henry H. Withers.

Hancock county—George C. McPorter, assemblyman; John J. Atkinson, William L. Crawford.

Harrison county—Chapman J. Stewart, senator; John J. Davis, John C. Vance, assemblyman; John S. Carlisle, Solomon S. Fleming, Lot Bowen, Benjamin S. Shuttleworth.

Jackson county—Daniel Frost, assemblyman; James F. Scott, Andrew Flesher.

Kanawha county—Lewis Ruffner, assemblyman; Greenbury Slack.

Lewis county—P. M. Hale, J. A. Lightburn.

Marion county—Richard Fast, Fontain Smith, assemblyman; Francis A. Pierpont, John S. Barnes, A. F. Ritchie, James C. Watson.

Marshall county—Remembrance Swan, assemblyman; C. H. Caldwell, Robert Morris.

Mason county—Lewis Wetzel, assemblyman; Charles B. Waggener, Daniel Polsley.

Arthur I. Boreman, of Wood county, was chosen permanent president of the convention, and G. L. Cranmer, secretary. From a transcript of the secretary's original roll, the above list of members has been taken. After two days' deliberation, the following declaration was adopted:

A DECLARATION OF THE PEOPLE OF VIRGINIA REPRESENTED IN CONVENTION AT THE CITY OF WHEELING, THURSDAY, JUNE 13, 1861.

The true purpose of all government is to promote the welfare and provide for the protection and security of the governed, and when any form or organization of government proves inadequate for, or subversive of this purpose, it is the right, it is the duty, of the latter to abolish it. The Bill of Rights of Virginia, framed in 1776, reaffirmed in 1830, and again in 1851, expressly reserves this right to a majority of her people. The act of the General Assembly calling the convention which assembled in Richmond in February last, without the previously expressed consent of such majority, was, therefore, a usurpation; and the convention thus called has not only abused the powers nominally intrusted to it, but, with the connivance and active aid of the executive, has usurped and exercised other powers, to the manifest injury of the people, which, if permitted, will inevitably subject them to a military despotism.

The convention, by its pretended ordinances, has required the people of Virginia to separate from and wage war against the government of the United States, with whom they have hitherto maintained friendly, social and business relations.

It has attempted to subvert the Union founded by Washington and his co-patriots in the purer days of the Republic, which has conferred unexampled prosperity upon every class of citizens and upon every section of the country.

It has attempted to transfer the allegiance of the people to an illegal confederacy of rebellious states, and required their submission to its pretended edicts and decrees.

It has attempted to place the whole military force and military operations of the commonwealth under the control and direction of such confederacy for offensive as well as defensive purposes.

It has, in conjunction with the state's executive, instituted wherever their usurped power extends a reign of terror intended to suppress the free expression of the will of the people, making elections a mockery and a fraud.

The same combination, even before the passage of the pretended Ordinance of Secession, instituted war by the seizure and appropriation of the property of the Federal Government, and by organizing and mobilizing armies, with the avowed purpose of capturing or destroying the capitol of the Union.

They have attempted to bring the allegiance of the people of the United States into direct conflict with their subordinate allegiance to the state, thereby making obedience to their pretended ordinances treason against the former.

We, therefore, the delegates here assembled in convention to devise such measures and take such action as the safety and welfare of the loyal citizens of Virginia may demand, have naturally considered the premises, and, viewing with great concern the deplorable condition to which this once happy commonwealth must be reduced unless some regular adequate measure is speedily adopted, and appealing to the Supreme Ruler of the Universe for the rectitude of pure intentions, do hereby, in the name and on behalf of the good people of Virginia, solemnly declare that the preservation of their dearest rights and liberties, and their security in person and property, imperatively demand the reorganization of the government of the commonwealth, and that all acts of said convention and executive, tending to separate this commonwealth from the United States, or to levy and carry on war against them, are without authority and void; and that the offices of all those who adhere to the said convention and executive or judicial are vacated.

On the 14th, the convention at Wheeling took up the work of reorganizing, or rather restoring, the government of Virginia, and it was during that day that a committee reported the subjoined Ordinance, which was adopted five days later, without a dissenting voice:

ORDINANCE FOR RESTORATION OF THE STATE GOVERNMENT.

The people of Virginia, by their delegates assembled in convention at Wheeling, do ordain as follows:

1. A governor, lieutenant-governor and attorney-general for the state of Virginia shall be appointed by this convention to discharge the duties and exercise the powers which pertain to their respective offices by the existing laws of the state, and to continue in office for six months, or until their elected and qualified successors be elected, and the general assembly is required to provide by law for an election of governor and lieutenant-governor by the people as soon as in their judgment such election can be properly held.

2. A council to consist of five members shall be appointed by this convention to consult with and advise the governor respecting such matters pertaining to his official duties as he shall submit for their consideration, and to aid in the execution of his official orders. This term of office shall expire at the same time as that of governor.

3. The delegates elected to the General Assembly on the 23d day of May last, and the senators entitled under existing laws to seats in the next General Assembly, together with such delegates and senators as may be elected under the ordinance of this convention, or existing laws, to fill vacancies, who shall qualify themselves by taking the oath or affirmation hereinafter set forth, shall constitute the legislature of the state, to discharge the duties and exercise the powers pertaining to the General Assembly. They shall hold their offices from the passage of this ordinance until the end of the term for which they were respectively elected. They shall assemble in the city of Wheeling on the 1st day of July next and proceed to organize themselves as prescribed by existing laws, in their respective branches. A majority in each branch of the members qualified as aforesaid, shall constitute a quorum to do business. A majority of the members of each branch, thus qualified, voting affirmatively, shall be competent to pass any act specified in the twenty-seventh section of the fourth article of the state constitution.

4. The governor, lieutenant-governor, attorney-general, members of the legislature, and all officers now in the service of the state, or of any county, city or town thereof, or hereafter to be elected or appointed for such service, including the judges and clerks of the several courts, sheriffs and commissioners of the revenue, justices of the peace, officers of the city and municipal corporations and officers of the militia, and officers and privates of volunteer companies of the state not mustered into the service of the United States, shall take the following oath or affirmation before proceeding to the discharge of their several duties:

"I do solemnly swear (or affirm) that I will support the constitution of the United States and the laws made in pursuance thereof, as the supreme law of the land, anything in the constitution and laws of Virginia, or the ordinances of the convention assembled at Richmond on the thirteenth day of February, eighteen hundred and sixty-one, to the contrary notwithstanding; and that I will uphold and defend the government of Virginia as vindicated and restored by the convention which assembled at Wheeling on the eleventh day of June, eighteen hundred and sixty-one."

5. If any elective officer, who is required by the preceding section to take such oath or affirmation, fail or refuse to do so, it shall be the duty of the governor, upon satisfactory evidence of that fact, to issue his writ declaring the office to be vacant, and providing for a special election to fill such vacancy at some convenient and early day to be designated in said writ; of which due publication shall be made for the information of the persons entitled to vote at such election; and such writ may be directed, at the discretion of the governor to the sheriffs of the proper county, or counties, or to a special commissioner to be named by the governor for the purpose. If the officer who fails to or refuses to take such oath or affirmation be appointed by the governor, he shall fill the vacancy without writ, but if such officer to be appointed otherwise than by the governor, or by election, the writ shall be issued by the governor directed to the appointing power, requiring it to fill the vacancy. ARTHUR I. BOREMAN, President.

G. L. CRANMER, Secretary.

The next day's proceedings—those of June 20, 1861—of the Wheeling convention, was connected with the election of officers for the restored Virginia government. The office of governor coming first in the list, Francis H. Pierpont, of Marion county, was unanimously elected; Daniel Polsley, of Mason, was elected lieutenant-governor; and James S. Wheat, of Ohio county, was elected attorney-general. The following were appointed members of the governor's council, as provided in the ordinance: Peter C. Van Winkle, of Wood; Daniel Lamb, of Ohio; William Lazier, of Monongalia; William A. Harrison, of Harrison; and J. T. Paxton, of Ohio county. James S. Wheat discharged the duties of adjutant general for a month, when H. J. Samuels, of Cabell county, was appointed and held that office until the formation of the new State.

Another ordinance provided for the election, as soon as expedient, of an auditor of public accounts, a treasurer, and a secretary of the commonwealth.

Concerning the formation of a new State from out the counties west of the mountains, the convention had not taken definite action, but they had left the way clear for such a change, as will be seen by page 63 of the First West Virginia Reports, which reads as follows:

> Having recognized the government as reorganized (or restored), and elected a chief executive officer, and provided for the election of all other officers, civil and military, the labors of the convention were evidently drawing to a close. Nothing had been done that appeared to directly inaugurate the popular movement for the formation of a new state. In reality, however, the true theory had been adopted, and the only legitimate mode of arriving at the most desirable result had been conceived and acted upon by the convention. If the government thus restored, was acknowledged by the Federal authorities as the only government of Virginia, then the legislative branch of it could give its assent to the formation of a new state, as provided for by the constitution of the United States. Leaving the great question to be adjusted at a subsequent day, the convention adjourned on the 20th of June, to meet on the first Tuesday in August.

As provided in the ordinance passed June 19, 1861, the new General Assembly convened July 1st of that year, the members being made up of the men elected at the general election held May 23d that year. It convened at Wheeling, and held its session in the Custom House, where the officers of the restored State had been holding their offices. On first roll call thirty-one members responded. A speaker and clerk were chosen, after which the governor's message was read. In that document he reviewed at length the action of the Richmond convention, the history of which movements led to the reorganization of the State government and his own election. He also informed the House that he had been in correspondence with President Lincoln, and informed him of the circumstances surrounding the loyal government of Virginia, and through the Secretary of War had received from the President assurances that all constitutional aid would be promptly rendered. The attention of the Assembly was called to the fact that President Lincoln had declared vacant the seats of all representatives from Virginia in the Congress of the United States, by reason of their participation in the effort to overthrow the Federal government, and he recommended that the Assembly at once proceed to fill such vacancies by the election of members who should apply for seats in the National Congress as representatives of Virginia under the restored government.

An election was held in the General Assembly on July 9, 1861, in joint-ballot session, and elected L. A. Hagans, of Preston county, secretary of the commonwealth; Samuel Crane, of Randolph, auditor of public accounts; Campbell Tarr, of Brooke, treasurer. Next came the election of United States senators, which resulted in the election of John S. Carlisle, of Harrison, and W. T. Willey, of Monongalia county. These were to succeed Senators R. M. T. Hunter and James M. Mason, who had resigned their seats in that body. The newly elected senators, together with Representatives William G. Brown, Jacob B. Blair and Kellian V. Willey, from the three congressional districts west of the mountains in Virginia, who had been elected at the same time the members of the General Assembly were chosen, at once made haste to go forward to Washington, where they were admitted to seats in the respective branches of Congress from Virginia.

STATE GOVERNMENT OF WEST VIRGINIA ORGANIZED.

May 9th, 1863, forty-one days before the final admission into the Union, a State Convention was assembled at Parkersburg for the purpose of nominating officers for the incoming State of West Virginia. On the same day, General Jones, at the head of the Confederate forces, was only about forty miles from Parkersburg, and one member made a motion that the convention adjourn to Marietta, Ohio, to hold its convention, but this motion had no supporters—West Virginia soil was good enough for West Virginians!

The convention proceeded to make its nominations, resulting as follows: For Governor, Arthur I. Boreman, of Wood county; Auditor, Samuel Crane, of Randolph county; State Treasurer, Campbell Tarr, of Brooke county; Secretary of State, J. Edgar Boyers, of Tyler county; Judges of the Supreme Court of Appeals: Ralph L. Berkshire, of Monongalia county; William A. Harrison, of Harrison county; and James H. Brown, of Kanawha county. On the fourth Thursday of that month, all were elected without opposition; also the judges of the circuit courts for the districts of the State, as well as all county officials. Elections being held in all counties except those occupied by the Confederate forces at arms, June 20, 1863, the machinery of the new State was set in motion.

Of the "Restored Government of Virginia," it may be stated in this connection, that Governor Pierpont, who had held his seat by virtue of appointment, was on the fourth Thursday of May, 1863, elected governor of Virginia for a term of three years beginning with January 1st, 1864, and as such continued in office as the head of the restored government in Virginia until even long after the expiration of his three year term. After the organization of the West Virginia government, he immediately removed his headquarters to Alexandria, on the Potomac, where he continued until the close of the Civil War, May 25th, 1865, when he removed the effects of his office to Richmond. From that date on the Restored Government of Virginia was known as the authorized government in the Old State of Virginia, the Confederate States government having ceased to exist, when the last act of of the War had been taken. Let it be ever remembered that Governor Pierpont was a fairminded and broad-minded man, who used every possible effort to aid those who had lost their fortunes in the war. He appointed men to various public positions, regardless of their party connections and past political record, considering only their fitness for such public places. Men came in from all over the State and poured into his ears their woes and their losses and their grievances, and wherever possible he aided them. The General Assembly had placed at his disposal quite a sum of money with which he speedily relieved the distress of the inmates of the Deaf, Dumb and Blind Institute, as well as the Lunatic Asylum. He served until April 16, 1868, when he was succeeded by Henry H.

Wells. It was the province of Governor Pierpont to materially aid in the healing of many a bitter animosity that had grown up as a result of the Civil War.

Jefferson and Berkeley counties were not included in the original counties of West Virginia at the time the Constitution was ratified. The Assembly under the restored government passed an act January 31, 1863, to have Berkeley county admitted, and another similar act for Jefferson county, which acts provided that an election should be had the following May in these two counties, at which the legal voters thereof might express their desire as to coming within the new State or not. If they so voted by a majority, then the governor was to certify the same to the governor of West Virginia. Such an election was held, and all went well. This was the situation up to the autumn of 1865, when the returned Confederate soldiers desired to be counted in Old Virginia, and not in the new State. Preparations were made in the two counties in question, to hold an election at which this question should be settled. Governor Boreman, hearing of this, issued a proclamation warning all persons against engaging in such an election. General W. H. Emory, in command of the District of West Virginia was also asked to assist in the execution of the laws in those counties. This ended the proposed submittal of the question.

But the end had not yet been reached. In December, 1865, the General Assembly of Virginia, at Richmond, repealed the act of 1863, by which the counties in question were transferred to West Virginia. The authorities of the new State then appealed to the Thirty-ninth Congress and that body, on March 2, 1866, passed an act declaring the counties of Berkeley and Jefferson to be a part of West Virginia, the same as though they had originally been a part of the proposed territory. Then the State of Virginia brought suit against the State of West Virginia before the United States Supreme court, for the recovery of the two counties. The case was heard by that tribunal in December, 1866; no decision was rendered at that time, and the case was again called up in December, 1870, when a decision was rendered in favor of the State of West Virginia. (See XI. Wallace, U. S. Reports, pp. 38-39). The same decision carried with it the boundaries of the new States. Many changes had been asked for, including the embracing of the counties of Accomack and Northampton, and, on the Eastern Shore, Garrett and Allegany, the two western counties of Maryland, but all such projects failed. The original territory of West Virginia embraced forty-eight counties taken from old Virginia, and then Berkeley and Jefferson were added as above shown, making an even fifty counties in the State. But in 1866, two more were organized—Mineral and Grant; and in 1867 Lincoln county was created and in 1871 Summers county, making fifty-four in all.

PRESENT STATE BOUNDARIES.

The legalized and present boundaries of West Virginia are as follows: Beginning at the mouth of Oak creek, where the western boundary line of Pennsylvania crosses the Ohio river; thence with the meanderings of that stream and including its islands, to Virginia Point, at the mouth of Big Sandy river; thence with that stream to the mouth of Knox creek, a corner of the States of Kentucky and Virginia; thence with a line of and including the corner of McDowell and Mercer counties to the top of East River mountains; thence with said ridge and with Peter's mountain to the Allegheny mountains; thence with the top of the same to Haystack Knob, a corner of Virginia and West Virginia; thence with the south line of and including Pendleton county to the top of Shenandoah mountain; thence with the same and Branch mountain to a corner of Hardy and Rockingham counties; thence with the line of and including the counties of Hardy, Hampshire, Morgan, Berkeley and Jefferson to a point on the Maryland and Virginia line where the Potomac river intersects the Blue Ridge; thence with the meanderings of the Potomac to the confluence of Savage river and the North Branch of the Potomac; thence with the meanderings of the latter to the head springs thereof at the "Fairfax Stone"; thence due north with the western boundary line of Maryland, to the point on the Pennsylvania line, a corner of the States of Maryland and West Virginia; thence west with the southern boundary line of Pennsylvania to the southwest corner of the State, and thence with the western boundary of the State to place of beginning.

This territory includes an area of 24,645 square miles, or a tract of land as large as the States of Rhode Island, Connecticut, Delaware, Massachusetts and Vermont.

ADMISSION OF WEST VIRGINIA TO THE UNION

The General Assembly met in extra session at the call of Governor Pierpont in Wheeling, May 6, 1862, and six days later an act was passed giving its consent to the formation and erection of a new State within the jurisdiction of Virginia.

The scene of final action, however, was to be enacted in the National capital, where it was hoped by the friends of the movement to have the new commonwealth admitted before the adjournment of the Thirty-seventh Congress, but it failed at the hands of its supposed friends. Hon. Waitman T. Willey, United States Senator, and his colleague, Hon. John S. Carlisle, with Congressman Kellian V. Whaley, William G. Brown and Jacob B. Blair, of Virginia, under the reorganized government, were each relied upon as firm friends of the measure—but among the number were some unfriendly to the movement as will presently be observed. The committee appointed to bring the matter before Congress were: John Hall, of Mason county; James Paxton, of Ohio county; Elbert H. Caldwell, of Marshall county; Peter G. Van Winkle, of Wood county; and Ephraim B. Hall, of Marion county. They were armed with the necessary documents, and appeared in Washington City, on May 22d, 1862, accompanied by several citizens who paid their own expenses and wrought much good by their presence. Among the number was Lieutenant Governor Daniel Polsley, of Mason county.

The party was introduced to senators and representatives from Ohio by Hon. Ralph Leete and John Campbell.

May 25th the matter was presented to the United States Senate by Senator Willey and the same was immediately referred to the Committee on Territories, of which committee Benjamin F. Wade, of Ohio, was chairman, and John S. Carlisle, of Virginia, the other United States Senator, from Virginia, was also a member. To the last named gentleman was assigned the task of preparing the bill for admission of the State. In 1861 Mr. Carlisle had been foremost in the measure of having a new State created, but it appears that his views had materially changed, and through him the measure was greatly delayed in Congress, and nothing more was heard of the bill until the 23rd of June, when it came from the committee, and it was then to be seen that he was opposed to its passage. It was styled Senate Bill No. 365 and will be found on page 2942 of the *Congressional Globe* for 1862. The promoters of the measure were thunder-struck. All that had been done in good faith had been undone, it seemed to them. Provisions had now been ingeniously worked into the bill so that fifteen other counties were to be made a part of the new State, instead of the counties named in the previous plan. These counties were: Berkeley, Jefferson, Clarke, Frederick, Page, Shenandoah, Rockingham, Augusta, Highland, Bath, Rockbridge, Botetourt, Craig, Allegany and Warren. A second provision was that when an "Enabling Act" should be passed, these counties, as well as the others to the west of the mountains, should elect members to a convention to be held, and should then have power to frame a constitution to be submitted to the people of the several counties for ratification, and if by them ratified, and the Assembly of Virginia pass an act assenting to the formation of the State of West Virginia, then the governor of Virginia should certify the same to the President of the United States, who should by proclamation announce the fact, and West Virginia should become one of the United States without further action upon the part of Congress; but in all this there appeared the fatal clause which provided that "all children born of slave parents within the new State after July 4th, 1863, should be free." When the bill was drawn, it was certainly known to Mr. Carlisle that the fifteen valley counties he proposed to add to the list already agreed upon, that the people of such counties were hostile towards such an act, and would never allow it to become a law, as it really looked toward the gradual emancipation of the slaves. It may be said that it "was a trick of the trade." It was designed to defeat the whole measure for a new State.

That "peculiar institution"—slavery—was greatly in evidence in this whole matter of new Statehood. On June 26, 1862, Hon. B. F. Wade, of Ohio, in the Senate, called the bill up, whereupon Hon. Charles Sumner, then in the Senate, arose in his seat and protested against the gradual emancipation clause, and proposed that the exact wording of the Ordinance of 1787, providing for the organization of the Northwestern Territory, which reads as follows, should be inserted instead: "Within the State there shall be neither slavery or involuntary servitude other than punishment of crimes whereof the party is convicted." This, it was believed by many would not be sanctioned by the voters within the territory proposed to become the new State. Its friends were dismayed. Mr. Carlisle now had come to openly denounce the measure. Senator Willey stood firm, but the members of the House, Brown, Blair and Whaley, were forced to believe that the Lower House would not vote for it. But Senator Willey put forth another heroic effort, and on July 1st called up the bill. A heated debate ensued, in which Senators Wade, Hale, Collmar and Willey took part. Willey closed his speech with what later was styled the "Willey Amendment," which was in reality a substitute for the Carlisle Bill. It omitted the fifteen counties sought to be added to the former list, and also contained Senator Wade's amendment, "that all slaves under twenty-one years July 4th, 1863, shall be free on arriving at that age."

Senator Carlisle then delivered a speech favoring the postponement of the matter until the first Monday in December following. This was replied to in eloquent well-timed speeches by Senators Wade and Ten Eyck. The vote was taken, and resulted in twenty-three for and seventeen against the bill, giving a majority of six.

AN ACT FOR THE ADMISSION OF WEST VIRGINIA.

The following is the complete text of the Bill as it came up for final action in the United States Senate:

WHEREAS, the people inhabiting that portion of Virginia known as West Virginia, did by convention assembled in the city of Wheeling, on November 26, 1861, frame for themselves a constitution with a view of becoming a separate independent state; and, whereas, at a general election held in the counties comprising the territory aforesaid, on the 3d day of May last, the said constitution was approved and adopted by the qualified voters of the proposed state; and, whereas, the legislature of Virginia, by an act passed on the 13th day of May, 1862, did give consent for the formation of a new state within the jurisdiction of the said state of Virginia, to be known as West Virginia, and to embrace the following named counties, to wit: Hancock, Brook, Ohio, Marshall, Wetzel, Marion, Monongalia, Preston, Taylor, Tyler, Pleasants, Ritchie, Doddridge, Harrison, Wood, Jackson, Wirt, Calhoun, Roane, Gilmer, Barbour, Mason, Putnam, Kanawha, Clay, Nicholas, Cabell, Wayne, Boone, Logan, Wyoming, Mercer, McDowell, Webster, Pocahontas, Fayette, Raleigh, Greenbrier, Monroe, Pendleton, Hardy, Hampshire and Morgan. And, whereas, both the legislature and the constitution aforesaid have requested the new state shall be added to the Union, and the constitution aforesaid, being republican in form of government, Congress doth hereby consent that the said forty-eight counties may be formed into a separate and independent state. Therefore, Be it enacted by the Senate and House of Representatives of the United States of America, in Congress assembled: That the state of West Virginia be and is hereby declared to be one of the United States of America and added into the Union on an equal footing with the original states in all respects whatsoever, and until the next general census shall be entitled to three members in the House of Representatives of the United States; Provided, always, that this act shall not take effect until after the proclamation of the president of the United States hereinafter provided for.

It being represented to Congress that since the convention of the 26th of November, 1861, that framed and prepared the constitution of the said state of West Virginia, the people thereof have expressed a wish to change the seventh section of the eleventh article of the said constitution by striking out the same, and inserting the following in its place, namely: "The children of slaves born within the limits of this state, after the fourth day of July, 1863, shall be free; and that all slaves within the said state who shall at the time aforesaid be under the age of ten years shall be free when they arrive at the age of twenty-one years; and all slaves over ten and under twenty-one years shall be free when they arrive at the age of twenty-five years. And that no slave shall be permitted to come into the state for permanent residence therein." Therefore,

Section 2. Be it further enacted, That whenever the people of West Virginia shall, through their said convention, and by a vote to be taken at an election held within the limits of said state, at such times as the convention may provide, make and ratify this change aforesaid, and properly certify the same under the hand of the president of the convention, it shall be lawful for the president of the United States to issue his proclamation stating the fact and thereupon this act shall take effect and be in force from and after sixty days from the date of said proclamation.

The vote in the Senate stood on the final passage—twenty-three to seventeen, in favor of admitting the new State.

The earnest workers and advocates for this Bill in the United States Senate were: Hons. Willey, of Virginia; Wade, of Ohio; Hale, of New Hampshire; Fessendon, of Maine; Ten Eyck, of New Jersey; Pomeroy and Lane, of Kansas; Wilkinson, of Minnesota. The opposition was head by leaders: Carlisle, of Virginia; Bayard, of Delaware; Trumbull and Wilson, of Missouri, and Sumner of Massachusetts.

On July 16, six days after the passage of the bill, the senate reported it to the house. An adjournment was near at hand, and the same day it was postponed until the second Tuesday in December by a vote of 63 to 33, but the friends of the measure were not disheartened—it had already passed the senate, and they had faith in the complexion of the house. December 9, 1862, the General Assembly of Virginia, in session at Wheeling, passed a joint resolution "That feeling the greatest anxiety and interest in the successful issue of the movement for a new State in West Virginia, we earnestly request the House of Representatives of the United States to take up and pass, without alteration or amendment, the bill which passed the United States Senate on the 10th of July last." This resolution was telegraphed to Washington that night and in the morning following it was called up by Congressman William G. Brown, in the house, it having been placed in charge of

Hon. John A. Bingham, of Ohio. The bill was debated all that day and far into the night hours, when a vote was had resulting in ninety-six votes for and fifty-five against.

It is related that when the bill was finally passed and sent to the President for his signature, he requested the opinion of the members of his Cabinet in writing as to their opinion in the new State matter. Harlan, of Iowa, was absent, and Seward, Chase and Stanton wrote out their approval, while Blair, Wells and Bates disapproved of the measure, whereupon Mr. Lincoln remarked that it only illustrated what he had long since believed—"that a President was as well off without a Cabinet as he was with one."

Congressman Jacob B. Blair, who had been untiring in his efforts to have the bill become a law, went to Mr. Lincoln on the evening of December 31, 1862, and told him his great desire, and was told by the good President that he should call the following morning—New Years—and that he would have a "New Year's gift" ready for him. Full of interest in the long delayed matter, Mr. Blair went to the White House at a very early hour, before the doors of the mansion had been unlocked to the public. The President saw him coming, and met him at a window, and, exhibiting the bill with his signature affixed, remarked: "Here is the New Years gift I promised you."

All was over now, save the submission of the required changes above named in the Constitution, to the people, concerning slavery within the new State gradually being done away with. This having later been accomplished and the fact certified to the President, who only then had to make proclamation of the fact, and within sixty days West Virginia would become a State. The convention was called together at Wheeling by President Hall, February 12, 1863, but, Mr. Hall not being present, the convention elected A. D. Soper, of Tyler county, to act in his place. The constitution was changed as ordered by the congressional act, and the day of election at which the people would have opportunity to ratify or reject its provisions, was set for March 26,

1863; it was held, and resulted in a vote of great numbers, and on the final count it was shown that there was a majority of seventeen thousand for the New State. The soldiers voted in the field wherever it was possible. At Vicksburg, in the trenches, an improvised ballot box was provided, and soldiers with arms in hand, watching the enemy, cast their vote for the measure.

On account of his conduct against the bill that he had once favored, United States Senator Carlisle was asked to resign his seat in the Senate, but this he refused to do, and it was now his turn to thwart every plan looking toward an immediate admission of West Virginia, by delay and cunning tactics. On February 14th he presented a resolution setting aside the original bill until such times as the counties of Boone, Logan, Wyoming, Mercer, McDowell, Pocahontas, Raleigh, Greenbrier, Monroe, Pendleton, Fayette, Nicholas and Clay, then in possession of the Confederate States and over which the restored government of the State of Virginia had not been extended, should vote and ratify the constitution. His resolution, however, was lost by a vote of twenty-eight to twelve.

The result of the amended constitution vote was certified to the President of the United States, who on April 20th issued his proclamation declaring that after sixty days the State should be admitted into the Union, which made the final date June 20, 1863.

WEST VIRGINIA STATE SEAL.

On the third day of the session of the legislature of the New State Government, convened at Wheeling in the old Institute building, June 20, 1863, a committee on State Seals was appointed, those on the part of the senate being Farnsworth, Maxwell and Slack. On the 26th of September it made the following report, which was adopted:

The disk of the Great Seal to be two and one-half inches in diameter. The obverse to bear the legend, "State of West Virginia," the Constitutional designation of our republic, which, with the motto *"Montani semper liberi"*—Mountaineers always free—is to be inserted in the circumference. In the centre a rock with ivy, emblematic of stability and continuance, and on the face of the rock the inscription, "June 20, 1683," the date of our foundation, as if "graved with a pen of iron in the rock forever." On the right of the rock a farmer clothed in the traditional hunting-shirt, peculiar to this region, his right arm resting on the plow handle, and his left supporting a woodman's axe, indicating that while our territory is partly cultivated, it is still in process of being cleared of the original forest. At his right, a sheaf of wheat and a cornstalk. On the left of the rock, a miner, indicated by a pick-axe on his shoulder, with barrels and lumps of mineral at his feet. On his left an anvil, partly seen, on which rests a sledge hammer, typical of the mechanic arts, the whole indicating the principal pursuits and resources of the State. In front of the rock and the figures, as if just laid down by the latter and ready to be resumed at a moment's notice, two hunter's rifles, crossed, and surmounted at the place of contact by the Phrygian cap, or cap of liberty, indicating that our freedom and independence were won and will be defended and maintained by arms.

The above to be also the legend, motto and device of the less seal, the disk of which has a dimension of an inch and a half.

The reverse of the Great Seal to be encircled by a wreath composed of laurel and oak leaves, emblematic of valor and strength, with fruits and cereals, productions of the State. For device a landscape. In the distance, on the left of the disk, a wooded mountain, and on the right, a cultivated slope with the log farm-house peculiar to this region. On the side of the mountain a representation of the viaduct on the line of the Baltimore & Ohio railroad, in Preston county, one of the great engineering triumphs of the age, with a train of cars about to pass over it. Near the centre a factory, in front of which a river with boats; on the bank and to the right of it, nearer the foreground, a derrick and a shed, appertaining to the production of salt and petroleum. In the foreground a meadow with cattle and sheep feeding and reposing, the whole indicating the leading characteristics, productions and pursuits of the State at this time. Above the mountain, etc., the sun emerging from the clouds, indicating that former obstacles to our prosperity are now disappearing. In the rays of the sun the motto *"Libertas et Fidelitate"*—Liberty and Loyalty—indicating that our freedom and independence are the result of faithfulness to the principles of the Declaration of Independence and the National Constitution."

THE NEW STATE GOVERNMENT.

The 1908 issue of Virgil A. Lewis' report to the State as Librarian and Archivist, refers to the beginning of this new State government as follows:

June 20th, 1863, was a remarkable one in the history of West Virginia. In Wheeling, a vast multitude thronged the streets; thousands of flags fluttered in the breeze. The display of bunting was the most attractive ever seen in this "Western Metropolis." It threatened rain—June showers; now all the beauties of a clear sunlight were shown, then a cloud chased all away. There were June showers—little ones— not enough to drive the people from the streets. A procession marched through the principal streets and then halted in front of the Linsly Institute. It was filled with people; the streets were filled with men, women and children; the yards, windows and roofs were filled with eager faces. A large platform had been erected in front of the Institute, and thither the officers—officials of the two governments—were conducted as they arrived. Hon. Chester D. Hubbard called the multitude to order. Thirty-five tastily attired little girls, representing the thirty-five States of the American Union, sang the "Star Spangled Banner;" Rev. J. T. McClure addressed the Throne of Grace. Then came two governors—Francis H. Pierpont, the head of the "Restored Government," and Arthur I. Boreman, chief executive of a State just then beginning to be. The first delivered a valedictory, the second an inaugural address. The sovereignty of the Restored Government of Virginia was terminated on the soil of West Virginia. Governor Pierpont retired with the Restored Government to Alexandria. Three cheers were given for West Virginia; the little girls then sang "E Pluribus Unum;" the band played the "Star Spangled Banner," and thus terminated the ceremonies of the inauguration of West Virginia as a Free and Independent State."

"RESTORED GOVERNMENT" MOVED TO ALEXANDRIA.

At high noon on June 20, 1863, West Virginia began her legal existence, and at once set in motion the wheels of government, which have ever since been revolving for the good of the masses.

It had been exactly two years since Governor Pierpont had taken his oath of office and entered upon his duties. Now the seat of government—the capital of the Restored Government—must needs be removed beyond the limits of West Virginia. On the fifth of February, 1863, it was provided that whenever the governor should deem it expedient for the public good that the offices of auditor and treasurer should be kept at the city of Alexandria, or in any other place in the Commonwealth outside of the city of Wheeling, he should make proclamation thereof; and he was authorized to convene the General Assembly at such place as he should select for the seat of government. He chose Alexandria, making proclamation accordingly. Alexandria was that old city on the banks of the Potomac river, nine miles below Washington City. It had been Washington's military headquarters in 1754, when he was a colonel; it was also the scene of the landing of Braddock's ill-fated army in Colonial days. At the date of Governor Pierpont's removal there it was being governed by a mayor and common council of sixteen members, and had been incorporated since 1784. It was now to be graced with what there was left of the "Restored Government" of Virginia.

Remarkable, indeed, was this change of governmental base. Daniel Polsley, its lieutenant-governor; Henry J. Samuels, its adjutant-general; Samuel Crane, its auditor of public accounts; Campbell Tarr, its treasurer, and James S. Wheat, its attorney-general—all resigned when the time for removal came, and Governor Pierpont left with but two members of his official family—Lucian A. Hagans, his secretary of the commonwealth, and Lewis W. Webb, who had been appointed auditor—proceeded to Alexandria. There he occupied a brick building with his Restored Government. There he filled the vacancies by his appointment. Leopold C. P. Cowper was made lieutenant-governor, and a Mr. Smith, treasurer of the commonwealth. May 23d preceding Governor Pierpont had been re-elected for the full term of four years beginning January 4, 1864. At the same time members of the General Assembly were chosen in that part of Virginia outside of West Virginia which gave adherence to the Restored Government, or rather that part which was under control of the Federal armies. These members thus chosen constituted the Second General Assembly under the Restored Government. The regular session of the assembly just mentioned went into session December 7, 1863, and closed its labors February 6, 1864. It was made up as follows: Senators—From Accomac and Northampton, James H. Kellam and Samuel W. Powell, who contested his seat; Alexandria and Fairfax, Thomas P. Brown; Loudoun, W. F. Mercier; Norfolk City, C. W. Whitehurst; Hampton District, T. S. Tennis; Norfolk and Princess Anne counties, F. W. Lemosey.

The delegates were: William H. Gibbons, Thomas H. Kellam, John R. Birch, James W. Brownley, Enoch Haislip, Richard E. Nash, Allen C. Harmon, Reuben Johnston, Andrew L. Hill, J. Madison Downey, J. J. Henshaw, Robert B. Wood and Job J. Hawxhurst.

Both houses received the message of Governor Pierpont, in which was briefly reviewed the history of the "Restored Government" while its capital was at Wheeling. He especially urged in this message the calling of a convention to frame a new state constitution. This was accepted and acted upon, and a bill passed for calling such convention.

January 24, 1864, resolutions on the death of Edward Everett were adopted, and Governor Pierpont was directed to transmit copies thereof to the governor of Massachusetts.

On February 5, 1864, a joint session of the two houses was held for the election of state officers. Samuel W. Powell nominated Lucian A. Hagans, the present incumbent, for secretary of state of the commonwealth. The total vote was sixteen—six in the senate and ten in the house. Hagans received all of the votes, and was declared elected. C. W. Whitehurst nominated Lewis W. Webb for auditor of public accounts, and he was elected without opposition. T. S. Tennis nominated W. F. Mercier for treasurer, and another candidate was John J. Henshaw, who was elected.

CONSTITUTIONAL CONVENTION AT ALEXANDRIA.

The convention for framing a new constitution met at Alexandria February 13, and lasted until April, 1864. LeRoy G. Edwards was president and W. G. Cowing was secretary. The document was framed and its twenty-seventh section had an article (No. 4) which read as follows: "The General Assembly shall provide by law for the adjusting with the state of Virginia the proportion of the public debt of Virginia proper to be borne by the states of Virginia and West Virginia respectively; and may authorize, in conjunction with the state of West Virginia, the sale of all lands and property of every description, including all stocks and other interests owned and held by the state of Virginia in banks, works of internal improvements and other companies, at the time of the formation of the state of West Virginia. It shall not provide for the payment of any debt or obligation created in the name of the state of Virginia by the usurped and pretended state authorities at Richmond."

The small number of delegates attending this constitutional convention was owing to the fact that most of the territory in old Virginia was still within the Confederate lines, and the Civil War was progressing in her domain.

This constitution was adopted April 7, 1864, but was never submitted to the people or ratified by them. In later years Governor Pierpont wrote concerning this matter: "Objection has been made to the proceedings of the constitutional convention of Virginia under the Restored Government, on two grounds—

"1st.—That the number constituting the convention was too small.

"2d.—That the convention did not submit its action to the people for ratification or rejection. The answer to the first is that all were represented which were in the Federal lines. More than one-tenth of the state was represented. The answer to the second is that it was wholly useless to submit the constitution thus amended to the people for ratification or rejection. Suppose there was only one-eighth of the state represented; the adoption of the constitution by that eighth would be no expression of opinion of the other seven-eighths. No person is so silly as to maintain that the adoption or rejection of the constitution by one-eighth thus made by the convention would have been an expression of the public sentiment in the state."

SECOND GENERAL ASSEMBLY AT ALEXANDRIA.

The second General Assembly convened at Alexandria, December 5, 1864, and adjourned March 7, 1865. The same organization perfected in the previous session was continued in force. Governor Pierpont delivered his message to the members, and in it he remarked: "The condition of the commonwealth, as far as I can learn, is deplorable, indeed. The fires of the Civil War have lighted nearly every neighborhood in three-fourths of it." He then went on to detail the difficulties of recognizing the counties then under Federal control, because of the hostility of General Benjamin F. Butler, commandant of the Military District of Virginia and North Carolina.

December 8, 1864, the assembly elected, in joint session, a United States senator to succeed Senator Lemuel J. Bowden, deceased; and another to succeed Hon. John S. Carlisle, whose term was to expire March 4, 1865. Sixteen votes were cast. Joseph Segar, of Elizabeth City, was elected to succeed Bowden, and John C. Underwood to succeed Carlisle, but neither was ever admitted to his seat in the United States senate.

Another year had passed away, and the assembly proceeded to elect an auditor of public accounts and a treasurer of the commonwealth. For the first-named office John W. Kelley received two votes and Lewis W. Webb thirteen votes, and was declared elected. For treasurer James P. Barlow received five votes and Warren W. Wing received eleven votes and was declared duly elected. This was the last of the Restored Government of Virginia at Alexandria.

THE RESTORED GOVERNMENT AT RICHMOND.

While still in session at Alexandria the General Assembly had passed the following resolution on February 25, 1865:

> Resolved, by the senate and house of delegates of Virginia, That the governor of this commonwealth be and is hereby authorized to change the seat of government of this state to Norfolk, or any other convenient place in this state, whenever in his opinion the interests of the state would be promoted by such removal. Provided, however, that nothing in this resolution shall be (so) construed as to authorize the location or detention of the seat of government, at any other place than the city of Richmond when the city of Richmond can be safely occupied as the seat of government of the state.

Under the above provisions Governor Pierpont, on May 25, 1865, removed the capital of the Restored Government to Richmond, the recent capital of Virginia and of the late Confederate government. He was at once waited upon by representative men from all parts of the state, who told him of their trials and losses occasioned by the devastation of war. He learned of many that but few in any of the counties, and none in some of the counties, could hold office because of the disqualification imposed upon them by the Alexandria constitution for the participancy in the Confederate cause as against the Federal cause. With the removal of the seat of state government to Richmond, the personnel of the Restored Government was again almost entirely changed. Lucian A. Hagans, secretary of state, had resigned, and was succeeded by Charles H. Lewis. The auditor of public accounts, Lewis W. Webb, had been followed by William F. Taylor, and Francis J. Smith was made treasurer of the commonwealth instead of Warren J. Wing. The new adjutant-general was David H. Strother, of Martinsburg, West Virginia, the "Porte Crayon," of *Harper's Weekly,* who had risen to the rank of brigadier-general in the Federal army. He was immediately sent by Governor Pierpont to every county that had representatives in the General Assembly at Alexandria, summoning them to Richmond, in 1865, their legal terms ending July 1st ensuing. When they were gathered before the governor in his reception room at Richmond he informed them that without the repeal of the disfranchisement laws he could not reconstruct the state as there were no persons to vote; that they had no power to remove this disability, and, with their consent, he would call them in extra session, and to this they all agreed. The extra session was called, and the third session of the second assembly convened at Richmond. It was opened Monday, June 19, 1865, and ended Friday, June 23—five days of deliberation. Its historic character entitles it to show the transcript of its roll of membership and officers, which is as follows:

Senators: Accomack and Northampton, Samuel W. Powell; Loudoun, F. W. Mercier; Norfolk City, C. H. Whitehurst; Norfolk and Princess Anne counties, F. W. Lemosy; Hampton Senatorial District, T. S. Dennis. Leopold C. P. Cowper, lieutenant-governor, president; R. F. Walker, Richmond City, clerk; F. V. Sutton, sergeant-at-arms;

Miles C. Eggleston, Henrico county, doorkeeper; Alfred Thornton, custodian of senate chamber.

Delegates: Accomack county, William H. Gibbons and Thomas H. Kellam; Alexandria, Allen C. Harmon and Reuben Johnston; Northampton, John R. Birch; Prince William county, Enoch Haislip; Norfolk, Andrew L. Hill; Loudoun, J. Madison Downey and John J. Henshaw; Elizabeth City, Robert Wood; Fairfax, Job J. Hawxhurst. J. Madison Downey, speaker; P. H. Gibbon, Richmond City, vice George Tucker, resigned, clerk; Thomas L. Kendall, Northmapton county, sergeant-at-arms; Robert Somerville, page; Alfred Thornton, custodian hall of delegates.

In five days this body, hastily called together, removed the disability to vote, and by resolution the next General Assembly was given authority to remove the disqualification to hold office. With the fund in the treasury of the Alexandria government, appropriated by the assembly, Governor Pierpont rehabilitated the Western Lunatic Asylum and the Institution for the Deaf and Dumb and Blind at Staunton; also the Eastern Asylum at Williamsburg, all of which institutions were destitute of supplies.

Dr. Brock, the Virginia historian, wrote in 1882 of Governor Pierpont:

> He also found, upon his arrival at Richmond, the United States marshal busy looking after the property of the late Confederates for confiscation. A few days afterward President Johnson issued a proclamation confiscating the estates of certain classes unless pardoned. It was stipulated that all petitions should be recommended by the governor. He soon perceived that the president was temporizing, and was led to apprehend that the "Pardon Mill" was a farce. He accordingly determined to investigate all petitions offered him. He next protested to the attorney-general against the further iniquity of libeling property which was never designed to be confiscated, and which only entailed grievous expense on its owners. His protest was effective. He next interposed for the suppression of the classes of pardon-broker harpies, who obstructed the due course of the executive clemency as provided. He refused to recommend any petition which would pass into the hands of a broker, and this threw this species of thieves out of business.

He next interposed for the relief of citizens who were under civil indictment for offenses which were within the province of military authority, and recommended leniency and conciliation to the courts.

Governor Pierpont, as said elsewhere, continued in office beyond the time for his term to expire, and even until April 16, 1868, when he was succeeded by General Henry H. Wells, appointed provisional governor by General John M. Scofield, commandant of the Military Department of Virginia. He left a balance in the treasury (at least, it was that amount October 1, 1865) of $98,083, after carrying on the state and aiding the public institutions of the same. For his ability and genuine goodness as a man and citizen, who saw both sides of all perplexing problems, he had no equal as a state official in the two Virginias, and will ever be cherished by his people and admired by the reader of United States history. Peace to his ashes.

GOVERNOR PIERPONT'S STATUE.

The first suggestion that a statue of Governor Pierpont should be one of West Virginia's contributions to the National Hall of Fame, was contained in a resolution adopted by the Society of the Army of West Virginia at its meeting in Fairmont, in 1900. At the ensuing session of the legislature that body passed Senate Bill No. 96.

The sum of $5,000 was then appropriated for carrying out the provisions of the bill. But later, when a clay bust had been made, the deceased governor's relatives and friends added to the amount $3,000, that the work might be done in pure marble. The work was executed in Rome, Italy, by Franklin Simmons. His work was completed in the autumn of 1903. Congress had become much interested in the matter by that date and for various reasons—the matter of inscription, etc.—the final work was delayed until March 8, 1910.

THE CIVIL WAR IN WEST VIRGINIA.

When the Civil War broke out that portion of Virginia now within the limits of West Virginia, in common with the bordering states, was a scene of wild excitement and great confusion. Men and parties were taking sides either for the Union or for the Confederacy of the Southern States of America. In each case, men were loyal and true to their own convictions of the rights they sought to maintain, under the state or the United States Constitution, as they interpreted it. But this brought county against county, neighbor against neighbor, family against family, and, in some cases, brothers who had been rocked in the same cradle in infancy, beneath the old homestead roof, were seen taking up arms one against another in battle fierce and deadly. Thousands of men enlisted under the Stars and Stripes, while hundreds found their way over the rugged sides of the Blue Ridge mountains, where they enlisted under the flag of the Confederate States of America under "Stonewall" Jackson, or some other daring Southern leader. The one fought for the rights of a United States, while the other took up arms in defense of "State's Rights," especially for their own native state, for which they bravely drew forth their sword and freely shed their life's blood.

Sentiment was greatly divided, both east and west of the great mountain ranges, but, for the most part, at the east the people stood for secession on the grounds of "State's Rights," while on the western side of the state a large majority was for upholding the Union, and hence were early in the field to take part with the Northern states in putting down the rebellion of the South, which had first showed itself by the firing on Fort Sumter, in South Carolina, April 12, 1861.

On Virginia soil there were three distinct governments during the Civil War period—the state government of the Old Dominion, at Richmond, under control of the Confederacy; the "Restored Government" of the state, with its seat of government at Wheeling, and the West Virginia state government (after the territory had been admitted into the Union in 1863).

Soon after Fort Sumter was fired upon, the demand for flags and bunting in Virginia, in common with every part of the loyal states, was so great that it was soon exhausted. Every one wanted at least one United States flag, and prices soon went up. Flags floated at every cross-roads, on every public building and on many of the residences and business houses in what is now West Virginia. Every stationer carried large supplies of envelopes and letter paper with the Stars and Stripes printed thereon. Red, white and blue neckties for men and boys at once became very popular.

The sentiment of this people may be known from the reading of the following letter addressed to the *Wheeling Intelligencer*, from Grafton, the same being written by an old man, a resident and native:

> I love Western Virginia as I love my own mother. Here are enshrined the memories of the past; here are the exciting scenes of the present, and around them cluster the hopes of the future. In this land was I born; in this land I have spent my life until today—here have I worshiped and wept; have loved and wedded; have expected to spend a peaceful life and lay me down to die. But war has broken this peace, and now stalks through the land with a drawn sword. Men tremble and women shrink and scream and finally faint; fraternal blood has drenched the land which our fathers died to defend. I am persuaded that Virginia is to be the battle-field. She will constitute the great encampment for Jeff Davis's army. Virginia produces grain, cattle and provisions to feed Davis's soldiers upon, and the cotton states do not; besides, no cotton could be raised when vast armies are devastating these states. Western Virginia has no interest in Jeff Davis and his oligarchy, politely called the "Southern Confederacy." The West is not in favor of secession. We will never join that band of traitors who seek to establish a new form of government on our sacred soil. We will stand by the old flag.

In May, 1861, the sentiment in Western Virginia was pronouncedly for the Union. Mass meetings were held everywhere, and resolutions were passed favoring the Union and denouncing the Richmond Ordinance of Secession. At Wheeling and other cities the taxpayers refused to honor the demand of the state tax collector—they would not pay money into the Richmond treasury for state uses. So strong was the feeling that the collector of state revenues had to resign for safety.

A Fast Day was ordered by the mayor of Wheeling on a Thursday in May, 1861, and places of business were closed and services held in all of the churches of the border city. These services were solemn, and each speaker breathed out the true spirit of Union.

On May 6, 1861, General George B. McClellan took command of the Department of West Virginia, while General Garnett held a similar position in the Confederate army. The latter was at Beverly, Randolph county, and McClellan endeavored to force him to the east side of the mountains. He divided his troops into two wings; the one on the left began at Grafton to march, via Philippi, under the command of General Morris, while his right went by the way of Clarksburg and Buckhannon.

The first regiment of Federal troops organized in what is West Virginia was mustered in for three months, and these soldiers were in rendezvous on Wheeling Island, at the city of Wheeling, under command of Colonel B. F. Kelly, having been mustered May 15, 1861, as the First Virginia Federal Volunteer Infantry Regiment. This command was joined by the first union troops to cross the Ohio river—an Ohio regiment commanded by Colonel Lander. About the same date a Confederate force was organized under Colonel Porterfield, near Grafton. The Federal troops went via the Baltimore & Ohio railroad, while the Confederates went back to Philippi, being followed up by the Federals, and on June 3, 1861, occurred the first engagement on West Virginia soil. The Confederates were compelled to retreat, but neither side lost many men. Colonel Kelly was wounded in the breast, but recovered, and later was promoted to the rank of brigadier-general. This was the first military engagement west of the Allegheny mountains in the Civil War.

WAR INCIDENTS.

On May 20th, 1861, seventy soldiers of the state troops came into Clarksburg. They were there for the purpose of recruiting for the Confederate army. They had come in from Romine's Mills, and marched up the main streets with rifles in hand. In a short time they were joined by another similar band of soldiers who came in from the surrounding country. They were commanded by N. M. Turner, Norvil Lewis, Hugh H. Lee and W. P. Cooper. The loyal citizens of Clarksburg were incensed at this act, and at 6 o'clock the bell of the courthouse rang out as a warning, and the two home military companies were soon in line. These were commanded by Captain A. C. Moore and Captain J. C. Vance. A military column was at once formed, with flags unfurled and bands of music playing. This display frightened the "green" Confederate troops, who after a time asked if they might be allowed to leave in peace, when they were told that they could remain until morning providing they would stack their arms, which, after 8 o'clock, they concluded to do.

RAID IN UPSHUR COUNTY.

In September, 1863, between one hundred and fifty and two hundred rebels surrounded a company of militia at Centerville, capturing all save four, who made good their escape. Captain Daniel Gould was among the prisoners taken. They were taken on in the direction of Pocahontas, where it was believed there was a larger rebel force awaiting them. There were sixty men taken and fifty-five good horses. Some of the rebels were known to the citizens. A band of guerillas made a dash into Troy, Gilmer county, about the same date; they robbed and captured three citizens of the place.

The following editorial comment appeared in a Wheeling daily:

When will West Virginia have protection? She has given, according to her population, more volunteers to fight for the cause, than any other state in the Union, and yet is to be destroyed for want of protection. Is it not high time the government should know that West Virginia is virtually without any protection? Surely the government cannot be fully appraised of our situation, or else it would not suffer these things to be. We have all confidence in the general government that it will crush the rebellion—but certainly the powers that be at Washington do not know of our true condition in West Virginia.

In April, 1863, the Confederates, having driven a small force of Federals from Beverly and Philippi back to Grafton, crossed the railroad at several points between Grafton and Rowlsburg, and went on to Kingwood, thence to Morgantown, which place they reached on Monday, the last week in April. The following day they went down the east bank of the river to within eight miles of Fairmont, where they were met by another body of troops, which later crossed the railroad. The whole force then went back to Morgantown, where they greatly alarmed the citizens, destroying property and plundering the place. They took every available horse they could find en route. They then marched on to Fairmont, where they were to concentrate Wednesday morning, crossing Buffalo creek, approaching the town of Barricksville on the Mannington pike. Their forces numbered about five thousand strong. In the meantime many weak-kneed citizens of Fairmont, fearing being taken prisoners and forced into the Southern army, had left for Wheeling and points in Ohio and Pennsylvania. Two companies of militia came from Mannington and brought all the guns they could find. Not to exceed three hundred men could be counted upon in an assault—these were four companies of the One Hundred and Sixth New York Regiment; two companies of the One Hundred and Seventy-sixth Virginia Militia, consisting of 175 men; thirty-eight men from company A, Sixth Virginia, and a few from Company N, of the Sixth Virginia Regiment, together with about forty or fifty citizens.

The Confederates were in command of General William E. Jones, who later declared his force consisted of seven regiments of cavalry, one of mounted infantry, three hundred mounted sharpshooters—in all about six thousand men, many of whom were of the famous Ashby's cavalry.

Wednesday morning dawned in a wet, foggy atmosphere. The Federal scouts came darting into the town, reporting that the enemy was out about three miles. One company of militia and most of the citizens around the place went out to meet them. Pickets commenced firing at each other about 8 o'clock. The Confederates, finding the Federals well protected, prepared to attack them as they came down Coal Run. This had the desired effect, and the Federals fell back. The men from the hillsides retreated, some to the main force near the railroad bridge, a mile above town, and some to the Palatine end of the bridge. The latter made a gallant stand and resisted the enemy crossing for nearly an hour. They took shelter in a foundry and fired from the windows upon the Confederates, who were mostly sharpshooters at that point. They dismounted and took their shelter in vacant buildings, stables and behind trees. A soldier from Bingamon was fatally wounded, and soon all but a dozen had straggled away. The remainder ceased firing, and each one took to looking after his own safety. Soon as the firing ceased a white flag was seen rising from a house. It had been set up by the Confederates, who sent a man with it to treat for a surrender, but to their utter astonishment they found no one there to receive it. The enemy then hastily replaced the planks on the bridge, over which a full thousand men soon crossed and pushed their way to get in rear of the Federals at the railroad bridge.

While the fight at the suspension bridge had been going on the Confederates had disposed their main force for attack at the upper bridge. The Federal force, two hundred and seventy-five men, were at the bridge, and had taken position a half mile or so to the north, but within gunshot of the roadway leading to Pruntytown. As the Confederate cavalry dashed along the road to reach the bridge they were exposed to a raking fire, which unhorsed about a dozen. Having got across at the south bridge and occupied the heights at the eastern end of the railroad bridge and gained the river above, the Confederates had the Federals completely surrounded. General Jones, observing the situation, called out: "Why in hell don't you surrender?" The Federals sent back the yell to their own men to "Rally." Then began one of the most desperate unequal contests known in all the four years' warfare. The Federals were in open meadows, protected somewhat, however, by small ravines, but exposed to the Confederate sharpshooters behind rocks and trees on the bank of the river. Inch by inch they were forced back to within two hundred yards of the bridge, all the time coolly loading and firing at concealed Confederates. Finally they saw their case was hopeless, and just as the Confederate cavalry were ready for a charge which would have destroyed the Federals, a white flag was raised from one of the houses near by, and the firing ceased. Scarcely had the formality of capitulation been completed when two pieces of ordnance from Colonel Mulligan's command at Grafton opened upon them from the opposite side of the river. Then they double-quicked their prisoners to the courthouse, where they were kept until that evening, when they were paroled. The Confederates on the left bank of the river were soon shelled out of range, but those on the same side as the battery made a desperate effort to tear up the railroad, on which stood Mulligan's car with the battery upon it. They took up a few rails and piled several cords of wood on the track, but after a short engagement they were driven off by eighty men of Company B, One Hundred and Sixth New York Regiment, and a few rounds from the Federal cannon. While the train bearing this battery was behind the hill, protected from being cut off and captured, the Confederates completed the destruction of the railroad bridge, then said to be the finest in the United States, its cost being half a million dollars, and its length nine hundred feet. It was an iron structure supported by four piers of massive masonry. The iron work was supported by tubular columns of cast iron. In these columns kegs of powder, brought for the express purpose, were placed, and thus the noble bridge was hurled into the river below, causing the greatest single loss sustained by the Baltimore & Ohio road during the Civil War. This battle was fought Wednesday, April 29, 1863. The great odds in the contending forces, the time fighting was going on and the few Federals killed, was almost unheard-of in war—only one man killed and four wounded on the Federal side, while the enemy lost about sixty men killed and as many more wounded, as stated by General Jones himself soon after the engagement.

The Confederates pursued the retreating Federals and had a running fight for a dozen miles till they were in sight of Grafton. Having plundered and destroyed the bridge, the main object of the raid, the enemy left Fairmont and proceeded to Philippi and so on to Beverly, Randolph county.

In writing of this raid in a Wheeling daily the next week a citizen of the place, an old-time citizen of Fairmont, and loyal to the cause of the Union, had this to say of the disloyal part of the community there:

> Let us for the future take prompt and effectual measures for the removal of every disloyal person, male or female, old or young, south of our military lines. What else can be done with the women who fired from houses on our brave soldiers when compelled to retreat from a hard-fought battle-field?—those who waved their handkerchiefs and cheered the sight of the thieves and robbers as they came in sight, and jeered and laughed at our gallant boys defending their town, though they had been captured as prisoners of war. What should be done with rebel men and boys who spent the day in riding about the town showing the enemy certain private houses they wanted destroyed? These people are not poor as church mice, for they have plenty with which to prepare sweet cakes and pies several days in advance of the raiders coming. If something is not soon done with these *home* rebels, companies will be organized who will undertake to dispose of them in a way that may be deemed more hempy than red tape!

April 18, 1863, Major Thomas Armsey and Lieutenant Daniel Davis, of the rebel army, were arrested near Clarksburg, and upon their persons were found papers authorizing them to recruit a company of soldiers for the Confederate army. They had formerly lived in

Harrison county, near Clarksburg, and had served as spies. They were taken to Baltimore and on to Fort McHenry, tried, convicted and sentenced to fifteen years' hard labor at Fort Warren.

FIRST THANKSGIVING DAY IN VIRGINIA.

Strange as it may seem, yet it is true, that never had the commonwealth of Virginia kept Thanksgiving Day, as had most of the states in the Union, until the reorganized state government at Wheeling was set up by Governor Pierpont in 1861. That year he issued a proclamation to the citizens of his state to keep the day, as had been suggested by the President of the United States for many years. At Wheeling the day was kept sacred, and the churches were nearly all thrown open and religious services held, and many eloquent speeches delivered. The *Intelligencer* had an editorial paragraph reading thus:

Various and threatening the dangers through which we have passed. In contrast is our position to that of our Southern brethren; we cannot but admit that we have much to be thankful for, and hence we assemble ourselves together to acknowledge our dependence on and gratitude to God. We are glad to see that our whole people have united, not only making the acknowledgment to the Giver of all good for His manifold mercies, but in praying also that peace and happiness might be speedily restored to our country by the defeat and dispersion of the rebels and traitors in arms against us.

PRESIDENTIAL ELECTION.

The National Union Convention was held at Baltimore on June 8, 1864, for the purpose of nominating a president and vice-president. General Kramer, one of the delegates, cast the vote for West Virginia straight for Lincoln and Johnson, this commonwealth not forgetting Mr. Lincoln's regard for it when, only the year before, its people asked him to sign the bill admitting West Virginia into the Union. The new state had ten delegates in that convention. The vote was as follows:

Upper Monongahela Valley.

County*	Lincoln	McClellan	County	Lincoln	McClellan
Barbour	593	298	McDowell	..	..
Boone	..	..	Mercer	..	..
Braxton	..	..	Monongalia	1,321	705
Brooke	464	401	Monroe	..	..
Berkeley	726	..	Morgan	205	..
Cabell	191	..	Nicholas	148	..
Calhoun	..	..	Ohio	2,188	2,008
Clay	73	..	Pendleton	211	..
Doddridge	..	..	Pleasants	267	215
Fayette	..	..	Pocahontas	..	..
Gilmer	224	..	Preston	1,612	569
Greenbrier	..	..	Putnam	388	109
Hancock	224	..	Raleigh	..	..
Hampshire	163	7	Randolph	177	50
Hardy	254	..	Ritchie	678	216
Harrison	1,323	863	Roane	275	31
Jackson	769	190	Taylor	56	36
Jefferson	174	91	Upshur	819	60
Kanawha	1,421	26	Wayne	76	..
Lewis	649	448	Wetzel	329	755
Logan	..	..	Webster	..	..
Marion	1,082	511	Wirt	262	209
Marshall	1,470	770	Wood	1,496	591
Mason	1,346	362	Wyoming	..	..
			Total	23,228	10,487

*On account of the progress of the War, several counties made no returns, if indeed elections were held—hence the blanks above noted.

END OF THE CIVIL WAR.

Both Unionists and Southern sympathizers alike in West Virginia were rejoiced to see the long conflict at an end. The *Intelligencer*, of Wheeling, the leading state paper, complete files of which are now in the State Library collection, carefully preserved in glass cases in the historical department, contains the following pointed sentences on the ending of the war. The date was May 2, 1865. It reads: "The war is ended. The rebellion is overthrown. The country is saved. Sherman's army is marching home. Read its order this morning. Peace is at hand. Jeff Davis and a few other friends are fleeing for their lives—trying to escape their fate like Booth and Harrold. Who can realize the mighty change? The days to come are to be days worth seeing."

As would naturally be expected, at the close of a civil conflict like the war between the states, it took some time to restore peace and quiet. The radicals on both sides still held bitter feelings one against the other. In nearly all the counties in the northern part of West Virginia meetings were called and long sets of radical resolutions were adopted concerning the return of Confederate soldiers. Before the legal reconstruction acts had gone into effect the affairs, as in other border states, were in anything but a peaceful condition. But little by little the matter was finally understood, and peace was again restored. These animosities were made all the more bitter on account of the assassination of President Lincoln—this the loyal people could not forget.

One instance—and there were hundreds of like character—may suffice to explain the situation. It appears that one Rundle, formerly editor of the *Valley Star,* and who served in the Confederate cause, was about to return to his old home in the Kanawha Valley. He published a notice to the public reading thus: "If you (the Union men) will treat us right and not insult us, we will keep quiet; but if you don't these hills will be filled with sharpshooters."

COUNTING THE COST.

Immediately after the adoption of the Ordinance of Secession, April 17, 1861, the enlistment of troops for the National, or Union, army began at Wheeling, and speedily spread to all parts of the territory of the loyal sections of the state, then in sympathy with the "Restored Government of Virginia." Not less than 28,000 soldiers served in the Federal army from the territory known as West Virginia now. All told, it is believed that there was $2,000,000 paid out for bounties and other expenses connected with the various counties within present West Virginia. On the day that West Virginia was admitted into the

Union as a state—June 20, 1863—12,000 men within the bounds of the state had entered the volunteer service of the Federal army, as shown by the adjutant-general's reports for 1863. The total enlistments in the Union army were about 28,000.

West Virginia did her full share in caring for her soldiery in way of liberal bounties and caring for the families of those in the army. General Pierpont, under direction of Governor Boreman, made inquiry concerning the amounts raised in all the counties, but the report of the adjutant-general shows that not all of the counties responded to the call for making up this list; from what counties did make the statements to the adjutant-general, it is known that more than a million and a half dollars were sent for the above purpose—in fact, it is all but certain that the amount reached two million in all the counties. The counties within West Virginia that made report at the close of the war are given below, and the greater part was for soldiers' bounties:

County	Amount	County	Amount
Barbour county	$46,684	Wirt county	$27,975
Brooke county	85,155	Mason county	40,110
Doddridge county	71,355	Harrison county	258,438
Gilmer county	3,698	Ohio county	334,959
Jackson county	14,000	Preston county	135,700
Kanawha county	9,400	Upshur county	55,843
Lewis county	28,575	Wetzel county	65,478
Monongalia county	154,425	Hancock county	60,830
Marion county	103,075	Putnam county	12,630
Pleasants county	37,900	Wood county	187,791
Ritchie county	30,270	Cabell county	3,600
Tyler county	16,330		
		Total	$1,966,000

During the years of the Civil War, there were two hundred and twelve colored soldiers enlisted from West Virginia in the Federal army, but there being no regular organization for colored troops from the state, these enlisted men were assigned to the Forty-fifth Regiment United States Colored Troops, in which they were mustered to the credit of West Virginia.

More than three thousand men laid down their lives in the service of their country from 1861 to 1865 from the territory now known as West Virginia. Of this number, 820 were killed in battle; 108 accidentally killed; 2,296 died of wounds or diseases—making a total of 3,224 deaths among the Federal troops.

There were forty-five companies of "State Guards" organized for the protection of the various counties. They were paid by the state. Many of them were in service nearly two years, and some a much longer period.

The question of how many men served in the Confederate army from the territory now comprising West Virginia, will, in all probability, never be known; only approximate figures can be had. There was, indeed, a strange scene during the enlistment days of the civil strife, when it was no uncommon thing to see one set of men recruiting in a neighborhood for the Federal army, and at the same time and place another set equally bent upon getting men for the service of the Confederate States of America. This was especially true all along the northern border line and in the Panhandle district of Virginia.

However, most of the Federal soldiers were enlisted from the northern portion, while most of the regiments represented in the Confederate cause were from the New River region, in the Greenbrier Valley and the lower Shenandoah Valley, where the population was largely secessionists. For example, Mason county, on the Ohio line, sent more than one thousand men into the Union army, while only sixty-one men enlisted in the Confederate army from that county. About the same was true of Hampshire county as to numbers, only the cause for which they fought was reversed—more than a thousand brave men went into the Southern army, while but seventy-three were in the Federal army from that county. The Northern Panhandle sent its thousands to the Federal cause, while the Eastern Panhandle sent its thousands into the Southern army.

There were twelve companies of West Virginians in the famous Stonewall Brigade in the Confederate army — four from Jefferson county, two from Berkeley county, two from Greenbrier county, one each from Hampshire, Hardy, Monroe and Ohio counties. The entire Twenty-second Regiment was composed of West Virginia companies; nine companies of the Twenty-first Regiment Light Infantry were from West Virginia, as were six companies in the Thirty-sixth Regiment Virginia Infantry; while the remaining companies enumerated above were widely distributed for service in various regiments. It has been stated by historians that more men from Mercer county entered the Confederate service than there were voters in that county. Pendleton county sent to the Confederate army over seven hundred soldiers. More than five thousand Confederates returned to their homes in the Kanawha Military District. It is believed from all that can be learned that there were approximately seven thousand men from West Virginia in the Southern army.

The population of what is now West Virginia when the war broke out was placed at 360,000, and allowing that 28,000 men enlisted in the Federal cause, as has been seen above, and 7,000 in the Confederate army, making a total of 35,000 soldiers in both armies, this was equal to nine and two-thirds per cent. of the entire population, men, women and children.

Again, it has been shown that 3,200 men lost their lives as soldiers in the Federal service from West Virginia, or eleven and three-sevenths per cent. of the whole number of enlistments. And now, assuming that the loss was as heavy (it was doubtless more) in the Southern army from West Virginia, the total number of men who sacrificed their lives on the altar of their country—the Blue and the Grey—there must have been 4,024 men lost in the combined forces of the Federal and Confederate armies from West Virginia. The average age of these men was under twenty-one years—the very prime and flower of the manhood of the state.

The well-chosen words of Professor Virgil A. Lewis, of the State Library, in writing on the soldiery of this state, may here be quoted:

So reads the long death rolls and records of battle-scarred veterans of the Kanawha Valley, some wore the Blue and some the Gray, but the dead and the living died and suffered alike for what they believed to be right. They were soldiers in the full meaning of the term, and were descended from a pioneer ancestry of whom it was said: "They are farmers today, statesmen tomorrow, but soldiers always," and the performances of the men in the late war lend honor to their ancestral heritage, and maintain the reputation of the soldiers of this state. With the return of peace these men came home, laid by the military trappings, donned the citizen's garb and united in an effort to secure the intellectual and industrial development of the state.

SOLDIERS IN THE SPANISH-AMERICAN WAR.

April 23, 1898, the congress of the United States declared war against Spain, and immediately President William McKinley called upon Governor George W. Atkinson, of West Virginia, for a regiment of infantry to be formed as far as possible from out the National Guard of the state. On May 2d, that year, he ordered the brigade under Brigade-General B. D. Spillman to mobilize at Kanawha City, on the south side of the Great Kanawha river, about one mile above where the steel bridge spans that river, at the city of Charleston. This was readily responded to, and within a few days the eighteen companies composing the two regiments of the brigade were at the designated rendezvous, and had spread their tents at Camp Lee.

The state responded promptly to every call of the president and governor, and the patriotism of her citizens. Not only did she fill her quota at once, but also tendered the adjutant-general two thousand additional men should they be needed to conquer Spain—the nation that had, as it was believed, sunk our warship, the "Maine," in Havana harbor, which gave this country an opportunity to intervene in behalf of the oppressed people of the Island of Cuba, who had been held in an iron grip by the Spaniards for two hundred years and more. It was stated at the time that, had ten thousand men been called for from West Virginia, they would have been forthcoming.

The total number of troops furnished by this state for that war was as follows: First Regiment West Virginia Volunteer Infantry, 1,385; Second Regiment, 1,322; Companies E and G, Fourth United States Infantry, 152; Companies L and M, Eighth United States Infantry, 145. A total of 3,004.

EDUCATIONAL PROGRESS

EDUCATIONAL PROGRESS.

That the State should concern itself with education as a function of its own is an entirely modern idea. Education was fostered in old times by the State, but with the idea of producing scholars, not valuable citizens. The idea of making of the youth by a system of public instruction worthy citizens, valuable to the State as well as to themselves, was one of the contributions of the Dutch to civilization. Out of the silt of German rivers the sturdy Netherlanders had for hundreds of years built for themselves a home, dyked by an incredible industry and patience against the onslaught of the ocean. So also they had, after a long struggle with Spain, built up out of the blood of heroes and the ashes of martyrs, a State whose free institutions they had the wisdom to see needed to be dyked by a system of free schools.

This idea of schools supported by the State was brought over to the American colonies by the Dutch colonists, and was in the air here when the great men who were building the foundations of the republic sought for those institutions which would insure the permanency of the commonwealth. English and French statesmen also took up about this time the question of the incorporating of educational functions into the duties of the government, and we find the minds of the leaders of public opinion both here and abroad strong in the advocacy of the State's taking upon itself the office of foster parent as well of that of law-giver and judge. European sojourn and their own political common sense taught such statesmen as Benjamin Franklin, Thomas Jefferson and James Madison the wisdom of such a measure, and we find all through their writings the lessons they had drawn from their experience in France of a nation whose citizens were not yet educated up to the burdens of freedom. They advocated, therefore, a system of schools where the State might inculcate those principles of democracy, that respect, nay, hunger for truth and righteousness, upon which the very life of a republic depends.

In the compactly built and distinctly marked classes of the old world infection did not pass from one to another as in the freely moving liquid of a republican commonwealth where the health of a part was the health of the whole. There have been times when the yeomanry of England retained its sturdy virtues and maintained the English fame when the upper class and court had become incredibly corrupt. These statesmen saw that without such bulkheads, society here needed for its own protection, even for its preservation, a bulwark of intelligent citizens. Jefferson had noticed—and only those who have thoughtfully studied the history of nations can fully understand the force of his words,—that the history of every nation and of every age "teaches the awful lesson that no nation is permitted to live in ignorance with impunity." In another place, writing to a friend, Jefferson spoke of his urging the legislature of Virginia to push the project of a State University and says: "The efforts now generally making through the States to advance their science, is for power; while we are sinking into the barbarism of our Indian aborigines, and expect, like them, to oppose by ignorance the overwhelming mass of light and science by which we shall be surrounded. It is a comfort that I am not to live to see this."

In another place he calculated the square miles of several States—Virginia 70,000 square miles, Massachusetts 72,000, Connecticut 4,900, Delaware 2,100, Rhode Island 1,250, and remarks: "By this it appears that there are but three States smaller than Massachusetts; that she is the twenty-first only in the scale of size, and but one-tenth of that of Virginia; yet it is unquestionable that she has more influence in our confederacy than any other State in it. Whence this ascendency? From her attention to education, unquestionably. There can be no stronger proof that knowledge is power, and that ignorance is weakness. *Quousque tandem* will our legislature be dead to this truth."

The economic aspect of the question was dwelt upon by a friend of Jefferson, the Rev. John Rice, of Virginia, the editor of a literary and religious periodical in Richmond. He pointed out that instead of saving money by not having institutions of learning of her own, and thus compelling the youth to go to other States for instruction, she gained less than she lost. He then related that he had instituted investigations and had discovered that during the ten years previous to this (1820), the amount of money carried out of Virginia for education alone, exceeded $250,000. He then computed, at an average of a quarter of a million each year for the preceding twenty-eight years, that the amount would be $7,000,000. But, by adding to that what would have come in from adjoining States had Virginia been furnished forth with the school advantages her resources and her position demanded, another seven millions should be added to this sum, and the total loss might be placed at fourteen millions of dollars. This was a vast sum of money at that time, but the cogency of the facts remains the same, and as an economic argument has had weight with legislators who were deaf to the intellectual appeal.

It must not be supposed from the difficulty Jefferson had in gaining the appropriations from the legislature for a State University that the Virginians were an uneducated people. The political history of the country is proof to the contrary. William and Mary College, chartered in 1693, and, after Harvard College, the oldest in the country, had been *alma mater* to many of the most prominent men of the State. But a large number of these men had not received their education from any public institution. There were many academies and schools scattered through the counties, and these furnished the rudiments of learning, chiefly in the classical languages, to their pupils. But most of the planters and the professional men received their education at home from private tutors or from older members of their own families, and the plainer people obtained the mere elements of learning from country schools, known in Virginia parlance as "old field" schools. Some of the more wealthy planters sent their sons to England to be educated, but these were few. Professor Adams' remark is correct: "The Virginians, if they could afford it or cared to do it, educated their children after the immemorial custom of Old England, by a combination of home training under competent tutors, or local clergymen, with college training and public life. County government played the same role in the political education of the people as it had always played in England."

For many years the history of West Virginia is a part of the history of Virginia, and the one is included in the other. To attempt therefore to give an account of the development of education in West Virginia, it will be necessary to make a brief recapitulation of the early story of the Virginia colony and show what steps were taken by the Mother State in furtherance of educational plans.

The projectors and first members of the Virginia Company of London were not only business men, but among the foremost scholars and literary men of England, at that time, and George Percy, John Pory, Alexander Whitaker, George Sandys and John Rolfe, who came out to the colony, were all men of broad education. It is not therefore to be wondered at that the company, immediately after establishing representative government, hastened to found at Jamestown, in 1619, the first educational institution on the continent north of Mexico. This was to be called the College of Henrico, and was to be built on the James river, near what is now Richmond. Sir Edwin Sandys, the treasurer of the company, recommended the setting aside of fifteen thousands acres of land for its support, and the installment upon them of one hundred tenants for their cultivation. The king, James I., was a warm friend of the project and authorized the raising of contributions for its furtherance. This met with enthusiastic response from all quarters, donations and bequests in cash, books, equipment and furniture, coming from many interested friends. Gabriel Barker, a member of the company, gave five hundred pounds for the education of Indian youth in the institution. The proposed conversion of the savage within its walls had, indeed, been one of the most emphasized features of the plan, and had probably added materially to the enthusiasm with which it had been received. The year after the conception of the plan, George Thorpe arrived, took up his residence at Henrico, and began work on the institution. He was thus the first English schoolmaster in America. In 1621 Sir Francis Wyatt, governor of the colony, arrived with further instructions, among them being that he should see to it that every borough and town "have some children fit for the College." It is therefore probable that schools were established for this purpose.

But besides this officially sanctioned college, another effort was made at this early date to found a school in Virginia. A contribution raised by the Rev. Patrick Copeland, chaplain of an East Indiaman, among the passengers and crew of the ship "Royal James" on a homeward voyage, amounted to over seventy pounds. This was made the nucleus of a fund for the establishment of a preparatory school at Charles City, in Virginia, which was to be called from its origin the East India School. This scheme also found substantial support from individual donors and from the Virginia Company, the latter deeding to it a thousand acres of land, with five tenants for its cultivation. The company also brought over a large number of mechanics to assist in the erection of the necessary buildings. The Rev. Patrick Copeland, the originator of the plan, was appointed rector of the school. Everything was in full swing, and, had not a terrible calamity overtaken the colony, the College of Henrico, with its preparatory schools in running order and its equipment already partially contributed, would have begun work fifteen years before Harvard, seventy-two years before the opening of William and Mary, and eighty years before Yale came into existence. This calamity was the terrible Indian massacre of 1622, when three hundred and forty-seven of the settlers were treacherously murdered, and the infant colony almost wiped off the map. This staggering blow arrested for years the growth of the colony and stayed the work of education in Virginia.

In 1624, two years after the great massacre, the Virginia Company was dissolved, and the colony thereafter became subject to officials appointed by the Crown. A hundred years were to pass before any settlements were to be made beyond the mountains. During this period the records made by historians of any educational establishments are exceedingly scanty. From legislative annals, however, some light is to be gained. In these it is recorded that in 1643 Benjamin Symns devised a freehold of two hundred acres on the Pocosin river, in Elizabeth City county, with the milk and increase of eight cows, "for the maintenance of a learned, honest man to keep upon said ground a free school for the education and instruction of the children of the parishes of Elizabeth and Kiquotan from Mary's Mount downward to the Pocosin river." This bequest was confirmed by the House of Burgesses, the legislative body of the colony. A similar bequest was soon after made by Thomas Eaton. The example of these men was frequently followed, and here and there all over the State of Virginia, even at the present day, are to be found these old free schools, a legacy to the neighborhood of some long dead lover of the light. Instances are also known of the grafting upon these ancient stocks of modern industrial schools where many of the old trades that have fallen into neglect have been revived.

In 1675 Henry Peasley devised by will "six hundred acres of land in Gloucester county, together with ten acres and a brood mare, for the maintenance of a free school to be kept by a schoolmaster for the education of the children of Abingdon and Ware parishes forever." After this school had been in existence eighty years it was represented to the House of Burgesses that the location of the land was such as to defeat the intention of the donor to afford schooling to as many children as possible. The House accordingly created a corporate body called the "Peasley Free School," of which the ministers, wardens and vestrymen of the two parishes were made stockholders, with full power to devise, lease or grant, for twenty-four years, the Peasley estate, and establish a free school in each parish. This then was the first free school incorporated in Virginia.

The check that was caused by the great Indian massacre retarded the educational development of the colony to such an extent that thirty-three years elapsed before the time the House of Burgesses first took steps for the establishment of the College of William and Mary in 1693. This college is therefore the oldest institution of learning south of the Potomac. Set as it was in Williamsburg, the old capital of the State, the College of William and Mary was within a stone's throw of the spot where Patrick Henry uttered his epoch making speech. The college was a very hotbed of patriotism, and sent forth son after son to swell that little band of men who, choosing the motto *sic semper tyrannis*, broke off the yoke of kings, and built up a State upon principles then new to the world.

Burke, the Virginian historian, writing of the condition immediately preceding the Revolution, says: "Although the arts by no means kept pace with commerce, yet, their infant specimens gave a promise of maturity and glory. The science of education had gradually become more liberal, and men of erudition, attracted by the rising fame of the colony and the generous patronage of the legislature, abandoned their counties, and came as teachers to Virginia."

With the close of the Revolution, the Established Church came to an end, and the titles to its property and glebe lands became vested in those counties in which these were situated. This gave rise to the Charity Schools, established by funds arising from these properties, and applied to the building of schools and employing of teachers for the education of poor children. The name "Charity Schools" arose from this circumstance.

This rapid survey of the history of education in Virginia, the Mother State, would not be complete without some account of the establishment of the University of Virginia, that darling project of Jefferson's. Mention has already been made of the passionate urgency of his advocacy before the legislature and in letters to men of influence, of measures to be taken by that body to put on a sure footing not only secondary education but, in a State supported university, provide an institution for moulding public opinion along the new democratic lines. His plea for secondary education was finally successful when, in 1796, the General Assembly passed what was known as the "Aldermanic Law." Of this later mention will be made.

The long agitation of educators in favor of a State University was crowned with success when, in 1818, the cornerstone was laid with pomp and ceremony in the presence of a distinguished company, including three men who had held the office of President of the United States. Jefferson had not allowed the simplicity and frugality of his political philosophy to lead him astray, and, when the University became an assurance, his vision was a splendid one of an institution worthily housed that should "appeal to the sentiments and attract to itself the most famous teachers with crowds of scholars. He knew that the Muses could not be enticed to take up their abodes in mean and squalid habitations. He sought therefore to reproduce on the American frontier a vision of the architecture and art of Greece and Rome. He seems to have been his own architect, and almost his own builder. It would be strange indeed if the results had altogether escaped criticism; but it is no mean tribute to the merit of the original design that, after the lapse of three-quarters of a century, it was reproduced and perpetuated in the restoration made necessary after the great fire of 1895." The doors of the University were finally opened on March 7, 1825, in the presence of all the professors and forty students, which number was increased during the session to one hundred and twenty-three. The University of Virginia was at its inception known as the Central College, Jefferson having with characteristic modesty refused to allow his name to be used in connection with it. The term

Central was due to the argument used with success by Jefferson for its location at Charlottesville, he showing by graphic representation that that town was not only geographically the center of the State, but its centre of population as well.

The control of the University was vested in a board of visitors appointed by the governor and confirmed by the senate; and this board appointed the faculty and its chairman, to whom the details of instruction, discipline and administration were committed. Jefferson opposed the office of president, and the question has not been revived until recent years. The University opens October 1, and closes June 29 each year. Lectures have always continued on Saturday as on other days of the week, and were suspended only on Christmas Day, until recently, so that it is believed that the length of the session was unique in the history of education. According to a recent report of the students somewhat less than fifty per cent. were from Virginia, and more than sixty per cent. were church members. In a summary of the work done in this institution one may use the words of Theodore Roosevelt, then President of the United States, in an address he delivered at the University:

> The University is not old in years, as years are counted in an older world, but there are very few institutions of learning in Europe, which, however old, have such an honor roll of service in the State, in the council chamber of the State, and of service on the tented field, which have such an honor roll of statesmen and soldiers as the roll can be furnished by reading a list of the graduates of the University of Virginia. The University has been peculiarly prolific of men who have gone into public life; but it is not only in public life that the record made by the University is imperishable * * * its importance also lies in the fact that the University, both by its conscious and unconscious influence, has sought to implant the primary virtues of American citizenship—the virtues or honor, of honesty, of common sense, and of that high and devoted courage which will not flinch from the forces of evil, whether they be physical or moral.

The conditions of the early history of West Virginia were not favorable to education of the higher grades. Yet the feeling of the people as regards education is shown in the large number of academies and schools which were later found all over the State. The pioneer character of the settlers continued longer perhaps in this State than in others of the east. This was due in a large measure to the fact that the expansion of the country took the line of least resistance, and West Virginia was left to the side in the great tide of emigration that in the early decades of the nineteenth century sought homes and fortunes on the great plains of the west. The discovery of its wonderful mineral resources, and the later coming discovery of the value of its petroleum and gas, brought with it wealth and an enormous influx of population.

During this early pioneer period which, as already pointed out, lasted till the memory of men now living—men too, of no great age,—the stalwart settlers kept alive the flame of learning in many a little log school house, and when these were inaccessible the children were taught at home and learnt their lessons after the day's duties were done, by the light of the fire on the hearth. These mountaineers were of a sturdy and ambitious stock, and, though they had sought a home in the wilderness, they brought with them the virtues and the aspirations of the best type of American immigrant.

The history of West Virginia begins with the first settlement in 1727. In that year the Welshman, Morgan ap Morgan, built the first cabin of a white settler within the bounds of the State. From that time until 1794, when General Wayne broke the power of the Indian tribes at the battle of Fallen Timbers, on the Maumee river—a period of sixty years—there was little else in West Virginia but constant warfare with the savages. The people were confined in frontier forts, block houses and stockades, and it is small wonder there was little opportunity for education. Yet even then there might have been seen little log school houses in the depths of the wilderness. The first record of a school house during that period is an entry in the journal of George Washington, in 1747, when he was surveying the lands of Lord Fairfax on the upper Potomac. He wrote in that of surveying a certain tract beginning at a station in the "school house old field." It is conjectured that this was in Hardy county, at what is now known as "Indian Old Fields."

The first Virginia school law that affected West Virginia was enacted by the General Assembly in 1796. At that time ten of the West Virginia counties had existence; these were Hampshire, Berkeley, Monongalia, Ohio, Greenbrier, Harrison, Hardy, Randolph, Pendleton, and Kanawha, and were found in the order named. This act, called the "Aldermanic School Law," was the late coming legislative answer to the provision for a complete scheme of free common schools recommended by Jefferson as far back as 1779, when he was called upon by the General Assembly of the State to draw up a code of laws. It provided for the election in each county of three men to be called aldermen of the county. These aldermen were to divide the county into sections that would equalize the number of school children. They were to establish schools in these sections, and in every way be responsible for the instruction of children, all of whom were to have three years instruction, gratis. This law went into operation in 1797, and soon everywhere throughout the ten counties of Western Virginia sprang up what came to be known as the "Old Field Schools." The day of the Indian wars was past; the frontiersmen, now that the day of midnight raids and sudden war whoops was over, assembled, selected sites and erected the rough log school houses, usually on some old abandoned clearing, hence the name.

In 1809 an act of the Assembly of Virginia made an appropriation for school purposes of "all escheats, confiscations, forfeitures, and all personal property accruing to the commonwealth," and this was called the Literary Fund, and was to be used for the promotion of learning. In the same year the governor, lieutenant-governor, treasurer, attorney-general and the president of the court of appeals, were created into a corporate body under the name of the "Directors of the Literary Fund," for its management. The auditor of public accounts was made the custodian of this fund. The power was given to the directors to appoint an attorney to collect in each county money due the fund, and to report the failure to pay money owing to it from any source. In 1812 the State loaned a sum of money to the Federal government for the prosecution of the war with Great Britain, and in 1816 it was enacted that when this sum was repaid it should be added to the Literary Fund. The income of this was now to be used for the promotion of literature, and it was provided that it should be appropriated to the benefit of a school or schools to be kept in each and every county of the Commonwealth, subject to the regulations which the General Assembly might prescribe. It was declared that "whereas this object is equally humane, just, and necessary, involving alike the interests of humanity and the preservation of the institution, laws and liberty of the good people of the Commonwealth, the General Assembly solemnly protests against the use or application of the fund to any other use than the education of the poor."

Such was the use now to be made of the interest or proceeds of the Literary Fund. In 1817 an act was passed which made important changes in the "Aldermanic School Law of 1796," which had been in operation twenty-one years. It provided that for the purpose of applying the Literary Fund to the object of its institution—the education of the poor—the courts of the several counties should each appoint not less than five or more than fifteen discreet persons to compose a board of school commissioners for the county. A majority constituted a quorum; a treasurer was selected from the body, who gave bond in the penalty of two thousand dollars, and then received and disbursed, on the order of the board, the quota of the Literary Fund due his county, this being based on population, and forty-five thousand dollars being the amount annually disbursed, at that time. It was the duty of the board to determine the number of poor children in the county; how many of them it would educate; what sum it could pay for their education; to send these to school, having first secured the consent of the parents or guardians, and supply them with materials for writing and ciphering. This board made an annual report to the directors of the Literary Fund, showing the number of indigent children in its county; the number of schools in operation; the number of indigent children being educated in these schools; and what further appropriation from the Literary Fund would in their opinion be sufficient to furnish the means of education to all indigent children. At this time, eighteen of the present West Virginia counties had an existence; and the Aldermanic Law of 1796, changed by the enactments of 1817—by which the three years free tuition was repealed—continued to be in force for thirty years. In 1833 twenty-five of the counties now embraced in West Virginia had an existence. Three of these made no school report, but on October 1st of that year it was shown that in the other twenty-two there were 655 schools in operation, with pupils in attendance to the number of 5,874; tuition of all these was paid by the Literary Fund.

An act for the establishment of a district public school system was passed by the Virginia Assembly in 1846. Its principal provisions were: that a county school commissioner should divide the county precincts, each containing as many school districts as the number of children in the precinct warranted; that in each precinct there should be annually elected a school commissioner, these to form a board of school commissioners for the county. In each of the districts three trustees were to be appointed in whose hands should be placed the duty of establishing, maintaining and supervising the schools of the district. The total expense of these county schools was to be defrayed as follows: 1. By the quota of the county from the Literary Fund. 2. By interest on the Glebe Land Fund, if there was any. 3. By fines and forfeitures. 4. By donations, bequests and devises. 5. By assessment upon the same subjects of taxation from which the revenue of the State was raised.

This free school system offered by the State of Virginia to West Virginia counties was by most of them rejected. Thus it was that in 1860 but three counties west of the mountains had free schools. There were then fifty West Virginia counties, and in forty-seven of them, with slight modifications, the old system had continued for nearly a century, and the "old field" school house, built of logs, used alike for school purposes and Divine worship, was present in every neighborhood, and in neither cause were they void of results. Rough without and within, these "old field schools" played an important part in rearing the hardy body of Americans that has formed the basis of the West Virginia commonwealth. The teachers were often very highly educated men. In these rude cabins the children learned discipline, as well as to spell, and read, and write, and cipher. But the noble independent manhood they gained was due as much to contact with the fine self-sacrificing personality of the teacher as to the hardy exercise of their out-of-door lives. Many who had been educated at these schools remained in their native State and helped to replace the old ways of life by the arts of modern society. Others went away to make names of whom the State may justly be proud. Four early governors of Ohio were furnished by the "old field schools" of Berkeley county. Reuben Chapman, governor of Alabama, had attended when a boy the "old field schools" of Randolph county. Lorenzo Waugh, who went to California and gathered together the first Methodist congregation ever assembled in the Sacramento Valley, received his first schooling at the "old field schools" of Pocahontas county. James T. Farley, a United States senator from California, was once a boy in the "old field schools" of Monroe county. Thomas A. Morris attended an "old field school" in Cabell county, and later became a distinguished bishop of the Methodist Episcopal church. Thomas and Samuel Mullody were two brothers who attended the "old field schools" of Hampshire county. Thomas was for a time tutor to the Crown Prince of Naples, and died as president of Georgetown University. Samuel, the other brother, became the president of Worcester College, Massachusetts. Stonewall Jackson attended in his boyhood an "old field school" in Lewis county, won distinction in the Mexican war, and died at Chancellorsville, a hero of the Confederacy. From one of "the old field schools" of Ohio county came Jesse L. Reno, who won his spurs in Mexico, and died fighting for the Union as, a major-general, he led the Ninth Army Corps at South Mountain, Maryland. These are a few of the names to show the type of men, the first trend of whose character was determined by the training of the rough little cabins of "the old field school." Judge, hereby, the vast influence of that little lever.

COLLEGES AND ACADEMIES.

Among the most potent agencies in the early educational development of the State were the many academies which were chartered institutions. These were scattered throughout the whole region, their control being in the hands of the foremost men of the community, and were an incalcuable power for good. The oldest of these was the Sherpherdstown Academy, in Jefferson county. Though its establishment antedated the Revolution, the exact date is not known. Another old incorporated school is Randolph Academy, in Clarksburg, Harrison county, which was the first institution of learning incorporated west of the Allegheny mountains. It had among the members of its first board of trustees, Edmund Randolph, Benjamin Harrison, George Mason, and Patrick Henry, and as part of its revenues it received one-eighth of the surveyors' fees of the counties of Harrison, Monongalia, Ohio and Randolph, which sums had formerly been paid to the support of the College of William and Mary. The act of incorporation declared that the school was established for the benefit of the people of these counties, which embraced all of what is now West Virginia north of the Little Kanawha river. George Gowers, a graduate of Oxford, England, was its first principal, and for twenty years he taught Latin, Greek, Hebrew and the sciences within its walls. Its work extended over more than fifty years, and among its teachers in 1830-40 was Francis H. Pierpont, afterward governor of West Virginia under the reorganized government.

The Monongalia Academy, incorporated in 1814, was for many years the most flourishing institution of learning on the banks of the Monongahela river, and in 1867 its property, including that of Woodburn Seminary, founded in 1858, the whole valued at $51,000, was donated to the State by the people of Morgantown in consideration of the location of the University of West Virginia in that place. Another important school is the Morgantown Female Seminary, incorporated in 1839. The Preston Academy, Kingwood, Preston county, began its work in 1841, under the leadership of Dr. Alexander Martin, who was afterwards the first president of West Virginia University, and it was long a power for good. The Brandonville Academy, at Brandonville, incorporated in 1843, is another useful institution in Preston county.

In Taylor county, an important institution of an educationally corrective character is the West Virginia Reform School at Pruntytown. The school came into existence by virtue of an act of legislature passed in 1889. In the year 1909 this body further appropriated $30,000 for a farm, and the average of 267 boys accommodated annually by the school has shown the benefits of agricultural labor as a discipline for reform. In addition to farm work, other industries are taught, though the emphasis is laid upon practical agriculture. The scope of the school is indicated by the recommendation of the principal that the name be changed to that of "West Virginia Industrial Home for Boys." Another institution in Pruntytown is Rector College, a college of the Baptist denomination that had its origin in the "Western Virginia Educational Society" of that place. It was incorporated in 1838. In 1849 the Assembly provided that scholarships should be established in this institution, which in 1850 had three professors in its faculty, fifty students and a library of two thousand five hundred volumes.

In the town of Buckhannon, Upshur county, is the West Virginia Conference Seminary, established by the Methodist Episcopal church in 1890. The school has grown with great rapidity. The debt with which the institution began its work has been replaced by an endowment of $100,000, and its standard is such that its graduates are admitted into the higher classes of the best colleges and universities. It owes its foundation to the Conference of the Methodist Episcopal Church in Clarksburg, in 1885, a board of trustees being then elected who were empowered to collect funds for the establishment of the college. Forty-three acres of land were accordingly purchased in Buckhannon, and the building was completed in 1890. In that year Rev. B. W. Hutchinson, A. M., was chosen president, and the work of the institution began with an enrollment of seventy students, a number which increased before the close of the year to one hundred and one. Its standard is high and it has done valuable work in the community.

Another school of Buckhannon is the Male and Female Seminary, incorporated in 1847.

In Clarksburg, Harrison county, is situated Broadus College, now under the auspices of the Baptist church, but originating in 1871 at Winchester, Virginia, where it was known as the Winchester Female Institute, with the Rev. S. T. Chaplin as its first principal. In its third year the name was changed to Broadus Female College, in honor of a famous Baptist minister of Virginia. In 1876 this school was removed to Clarksburg, and since that time the school has steadily increased both in its financial status and in its patronage and influence in the community.

Another important institution located in Harrison county is Salem College, situated in the town of Salem. This establishment is the property of the Seventh Day Baptists, and was opened in 1889, with the Rev. S. Maxton as its first president, under a charter granted by the State of West Virginia. Although organized under denominational auspices, it is in no wise sectarian. As people of all religious faiths joined in its establishment, so students of all creeds find a welcome within its walls. It is doing an excellent work for the young people of central West Virginia, and sends out every year a goodly number of teachers who are invaluable to the community through their efficient work. A well known school at Clarksburg is St. Joseph's Academy and Day School, under the Roman Catholic church, organized in 1872. The Northwestern Academy at Clarksburg is another school of Harrison county; it was incorporated in 1842. Randolph Academy, already mentioned as one of the two oldest schools in West Virginia, is another of the schools of Clarksburg.

A school of a reform character at Salem is another institution of Harrison county. This is the West Virginia Industrial School for Girls, established by an act of legislature in 1897, and opened for use in 1899. Since that time three hundred and three girls have been received. The aim of the school is to give such industrial education to girls whose environment has been unfavorable, as may help them to become members of society. When this moral and industrial training is considered sufficient, they are paroled and placed as domestic servants in homes over which the school exercises oversight. This is one of the institutions under the management of the State Board of Control.

In Lewis county, the school incorporated in 1847 as the Lewis County Seminary was so successful that after ten years it was erected by act of legislature as Weston College.

In Marion county is located the State Normal School, at Fairmont. This is an institution under the State Board of Control, and began its existence in 1865 as an enterprise of the citizens of Fairmont. In 1867 the legislature united with the town in the construction of a building which for a long time was used jointly by the State Normal School and the Fairmont public schools. Its first president was Dr. Blair, and his splendid management of the institution gave it an excellent standing, especially in the northern part of the state. In 1893 the school acquired its present grounds and building. There are two buildings for the use of the school. The auditorium in the school building is one of the largest and most satisfactory assembly halls in the State. From the

BIRD'S EYE VIEW OF UNIVERSITY CAMPUS AND MORGANTOWN.

tower of this building a view may be had of the beautiful Monongahela river and of all the region round about. It was here that the first training school for teachers within the State was opened. The first principal was Professor J. N. Boyd, and his aim was to train those in attendance not only in the subject matter of the common branches, but in the best methods of teaching them.

The State Normal School at Fairmont is one of the five branches of the State Normal School at Marshall College, in Cabell county. The four other branches are at West Liberty, Ohio county, at Shepherdstown, Jefferson county, at Glenville, Gilmer county, and at Athens, Mercer county. The State Normal School, with its five branches thus enumerated, has wrought a mighty work in West Virginia. The State has spent a million dollars on them, but probably no other million of the commonwealth's expenditures brings in such significant returns. Hundreds of graduates have gone out, trained men and women, to become principals, county superintendents, instructors in institutes, lecturers, writers, editors, and leaders in educational progress. These have been a vast power for the intellectual, moral and spiritual uplift of the State, bringing back incalculably valuable returns in the higher life of the whole people. Two other important schools of Marion county are the Fairmont Academy, incorporated in 1852, and the Fairmont Male and Female Seminary, incorporated in 1856.

UNIVERSITY OF WEST VIRGINIA.

Standing at the head of the educational system of the State, and bringing as it were into one focus all the work of the lower departments, the University of West Virginia is well worthy of an honored place among the country's higher institutions of learning. The State University offers free instruction to all residents of the State, and instruction at a merely nominal price to students from other States. In July, 1862, Congress passed an act donating public lands to the several States and Territories that would provide colleges for the benefit of agriculture and the mechanic arts. The quantity was to be equal to thirty thousand acres for senator and representative in Congress to which the several States were entitled under the census of 1860. In conformity with this and succeeding legislation, the sum of $90,000 was secured for the establishment of the University. On January 9, 1866, the board of trustees of Monongalia Academy tendered to the State the buildings, property and funds of the said academy, including the property known as the Woodburn Female Seminary, the value of the whole amounting to $51,000. This was to be held and used by the State of West Virginia, on the condition that the contemplated Agricultural College be located permanently at or near Morgantown. After considering the claims of a number of other places, the legislature, January 31, 1867, decided in favor of Morgantown. By an act of February 7, 1867, Governor Arthur T. Boreman was directed to appoint a board of regents composed of one member from each of the eleven senatorial districts, to establish and control the proposed Agricultural College. He named Z. H. Logan, D. B. Dorsey, G. M. Hagans, Samuel Billingslea, W. E. Stevenson, J. Loomis Gould, W. W. Harper, Mark Poor, Samuel Young, Joseph T. Hoke, and James Carskadon. These gentlemen assembled in the Hall of Woodburn Female Seminary at Morgantown, on April 3, 1867, organized the Agricultural College of West Virginia, and that day elected the Rev. Alexander Martin, D. D., as its first president. At the recommendation of Governor Boreman the legislature changed the name, December 4, 1868, to that of the West Virginia University.

Through its direct predecessors, the institution reaches back over a period of nearly one hundred years. As Monongalia Academy it had existed since 1814, as the Agricultural College it had an existence of two years. The institution has had a phenomenal growth. It stands to-day in what was little more than a century ago the rough pathway through the forest along which marched the pioneers of this region, down the valley of the Monongahela to Fort Pitt, there to choose the

VIEW OF CAMPUS OF WEST VIRGINIA UNIVERSITY. FROM LEFT TO RIGHT: MARTIN'S HALL, WOODBURN HALL, SCIENCE HALL, EXPERIMENT STATION.

PRESIDENT'S HOUSE, WEST VIRGINIA UNIVERSITY.

first representative from the region west of the Alleghenies, for a seat in the Continental Congress. In 1867 its property was valued at fifteen thousand dollars; now it is worth eleven hundred thousand dollars. Then its faculty was composed of the president and the four professors; now it numbers nearly seventy members whose *almae matres* are the leading colleges and universities of the world. Then it had fewer than thirty students; now it has near by a thousand, among them being representatives from every county of the State, nearly a hundred from Pennsylvania, together with many from other States and from various foreign countries.

But it is not only as a plant, or business organization controlling important property, that an institution is to be valued. It is upon the principle "by their fruits ye shall know them," that a school should always be estimated, and, taking this rule as a standard, the University of West Virginia has done a splendid work. Among the seven hundred and fifty graduates who have gone out from its halls are five college presidents, forty-seven college professors, three State superintendents of free schools, ten normal school principals, twenty-five normal school teachers, ten bank cashiers, ten judges, forty-five ministers, twenty-eight doctors, six United States army officers, one United States senator, four members of congress, one governor, one attorney-general, one State geologist, ten State senators, thirty-five members of the house of delegates, sixty-four engineers civil, mechanical, mining; forty-three superintendents or principals of high schools and schools of similar grade, sixteen editors, hundreds of business men and farmers, and more than one hundred and twenty-five lawyers. This list includes also the first sheriff of Manila, a clerk of the Supreme Court of the State, a clerk of the State senate, a clerk of the house of delegates, a chief mine inspector, and a weather bureau director of South America. These almuni live in thirty-seven States, besides Austria, Mexico, Japan, Siam, India, the Argentine Republic, Bulgaria, and the Philippine Islands.

The organization of the University consists of the following colleges and schools: the colleges of arts and sciences, of engineering and mechanic arts, of agriculture, of law, and of medicine; the school of music, of fine arts, of military science and tactics; the commercial school, and the preparatory school.

It has ten buildings besides those of the Experimental Farm, and has a number of thoroughly modern laboratories, libraries, and shops. The grounds are of more than twenty acres, and so fortunately located as to afford a magnificent panorama of the Monongahela, with all its wealth of scenic beauty and historic association.

In 1910, Thomas Edward Hodges, D. Sc., LL. D., was elected president of the University, and under his able leadership an era of even greater growth and usefulness is to be expected. A scholar of the ripest culture, he has shown in his brilliant educational record the statesmanship and the power to move and inspire to noble ends which are needed for the guidance of a great and beneficent institution. It was James A. Garfield who, when asked what in his opinion constituted a university, said it was a very simple thing—it consisted of a bench with Mark Hopkins at one end and a boy at the other.

Two preparatory schools constitute part of the work of the University. One is situated at Montgomery, Fayette county, and was established by act of legislature in 1895. The other, at Keyser, Mineral county, was founded by the same body in 1901.

The State University may be taken not only as the culmination of the series of academies long at work in the State, but also as the keystone of its system of free schools. Considered as such, the foregoing brief account will serve for a link between the survey of the academies and a short sketch of the work being done by the free public schools. Before going on to notice the work being done in each of the counties of the Monongahela Valley, a short summary would be well of the educational work planned and accomplished during the new era.

EXPERIMENT STATION, WEST VIRGINIA UNIVERSITY.

FREE SCHOOL SYSTEM.

The statehood of West Virginia began June 20, 1863. On that day the first legislature of West Virginia assembled, and four days later a senate and a house committee on education was appointed. The joint work of these two committees was the first school law of the State, and was passed December 10 of that year, and entitled "An Act providing for the Establishment of a System of Free Schools." It was largely the work of Mr. Ross, of the house committee, himself an efficient and experienced teacher who had served sixteen years as professor of ancient languages in Bethany College, and later as principal of West Liberty Academy. This law provided for the election of a State superintendent of free schools, and this was carried into execution June 1, 1884, when William Ryland White was elected for the term of two years.

The administration of the school system is simple and easily understood. Territorially the divisions are: the State; the county; the magisterial district; the sub-district; the independent district. The grades of the schools are: primary schools; graded schools; high schools; the State normal schools; the State University; schools for the deaf and blind. The officers of the system are: the State superintendent of free schools; the county superintendent; the board of education in magisterial and independent districts. The board of education consists of a president, two commissioners, a secretary and three trustees. The law provides for a State board of examiners which issues State certificates, and for State uniform examinations, qualifying through county certificates.

Under the provisions of this law, school attendance is compulsory for children between the ages of eight and fourteen years. Failure to do this is a misdemeanor and punishable by fine. A truant officer is also required in each magisterial and independent district whose duty it is to enforce the provisions of this law.

The education of the youth is the chief business of the State, and for this her people expend more money annually than all other purposes combined. The money with which to do this is derived from three sources; viz.: 1. Interest on the school fund. 2. Distribution of the general school fund. 3. Local levies in the magisterial and independent districts.

The school fund, sometimes called the irreducible school fund, is that portion of the Literary Fund previously mentioned which at the time of the separation of West Virginia from the old State constituted the portion of West Virginia. At the time of the reorganization of the State, the West Virginia share of the fund amounted in value to $120,000. By a constitutional amendment in 1902 the fund was limited to $1,000,000, and all money accruing to its credit over and above this sum is added to the general school fund.

The sources of the general school fund are: (1) a levy of ten cents on each hundred dollars of valuation; (2) the net proceeds of all fines; (3) the proceeds of all capitation tax; and (4) the proceeds of the invested school fund. Local levies are raised in the magisterial and independent districts when the board of education of these districts meet on the first Monday in July and lay levies for the "teachers' fund" and the "building fund," the purposes of which are indicated by the names.

Provision has been made since the installation of the new school system for the instruction and inspiration to be gained by teachers from their meeting together under the leadership of experienced instructors. The "Institutes" thus formed have been organized as a part of the system of education, and the county has been found to be the most convenient unit to be used as a basis for classification. The law requires that each teacher shall attend an institute for at least five days in the year in which he teaches. The programmes of these institutes have shown a tendency in the last few years to concentrate upon a few topics for discussion in preference to dissipating energy upon many. Much valuable work is being done by these organizations.

Another phase of educational effort has been the fostering of school libraries. Although the revised school law provides that boards of education may spend as much as $1,000 annually for each school in its district, the public school libraries of West Virginia have been purchased almost entirely with money secured by entertainments and contributions. Believing in the principle that it pays to advertise, the State Superintendent has designated the first Friday in December as Library Day. The enthusiasm and liberality with which teachers, pupils and patrons have taken up and carried forward the library movement has attracted attention beyond the borders of the State. Indeed, West Virginia has been given credit with the highest percentage of increase in number of volumes added to the public school libraries in the last ten years of all the States of the Union.

An organization of prominent educators and men interested in education has in the last two or three decades done valuable work in gathering together these men and discussing various subjects of educational importance. The formulation of and the dealing with these problems of school work by men of breadth and experience has done much to quicken and vitalize this work in the State. This is the West Virginia Education Association. The meetings for the past three years have been as follows: 1908-09, at Clarksburg, president, Joseph Rosier; 1909-10, at Charleston, president, H. B. Work; 1910-11, at Bluefield, president, M. P. Shawkey.

SOME COUNTY STATISTICS.

The school enrollment for Upshur county, in the latest report, was given at 4372, with 52 enrolled in the high school of the county. Mr. J. H. Ashworth, the county superintendent, reported that the previous year had been the best one educationally in the history of Upshur county. A deep interest in all lines of work had been evinced by pupils as well as teachers. Eighty-eight pupils had completed the course, that being twice as many as had done so in any previous year in the county. The district institute had also met with marked success. The instructors were Superintendent L. M. Jones, of Brookville, Pennsylvania, and Mrs. Harriet Lyon, Huntington, Pennsylvania. Three successful summer normal schools were also taught within the county, and in every line of activity advance was shown. In the direction of school architecture, Upshur county may also have reason to be proud. More than one new school building has been shown in recent reports to exemplify the very latest improvements in the building of school houses.

Mr. Dellet Newton, superintendent of schools for Taylor county, gave in his last report the total number of children enrolled in the county as 3290 in the 118 schools. The number of pupils doing high school work in the three high schools was 221. The number graduating in this county was small, being but thirteen, but good work was done nevertheless, the educational work of the county steadily going forward. The district institute was a success in every particular, having been conducted by the able leaders, Professor J. F. Marsh, and Superintendent T. J. Humphrey.

The enrollment of children attending the common schools of Preston county was given in the last report as 214, with 148 besides doing advanced work in the five high schools of the county. The work of the institutes is such as to be a matter of congratulation, working as they have done for efficiency of the highest type. The instructors of the Preston County Institute held at Terra Alta, were in the last sessions, Dr. Susan F. Chase, Buffalo, New York; Superintendent Joseph Rosier, Fairmont; and Mr. A. W. Martin, Bridgeport. The county superintendent of schools in Preston county is Mr. A. W. Carrico.

The number of children taught in Monongalia county in the common schools were according to the last report 6994, and in the high school were enrolled 130 more. The condition of the schools in general was reported to be one of progress. Mr. Jesse Henry, the county superintendent, reported a graduating class of two hundred, that being the largest in the county since the year 1876. Some good up-to-date school houses were also built in the county. One of the most encouraging features of the work was the marked increase of interest shown by parents in the education of their children. The institutes were conducted by Professor J. F. Marsh, of Charleston, and Mrs. Anna R. Bourne, of Bethany, and their success was a matter of satisfaction to those interested in the educational work of the county.

The enrollment of pupils in the schools, 109 in number, of Barbour county, was given as 3515 in the last report of the superintendent of schools, Mr. A. F. Shroyer. In the two high schools 56 pupils were enrolled. The schools were in a highly satisfactory condition of improvement. Two modern school buildings had been recently erected, and new furniture and equipment purchased for some of the schools. Several new libraries had been started, and about 2000 books bought by the different schools. There were forty-six children graduating. Marked intellectual growth was to be noticed in the teaching force as a result of the institutes and work in the reading course. These institutes held at Philippi were conducted by Dr. Susan F. Chase, Buffalo, New York; Professor F. B. Trotter, Morgantown; and Miss Grace Anne Jewett, Bluefield.

Mr. L. Wayman Ogden, the superintendent of schools for Harrison county, gives in his latest report 9287 children as the enrollment in the 299 schools of his county. There were 360 pupils in the six high schools. The institute held at Clarksburg was in charge of the well known Professor J. F. Marsh, the Assistant State Superintendent of Schools, Charleston; Dr. C. H. Minnich, Oxford, Ohio; and Mr. J. H. Francis, of Charleston. An account of the public schools of Harrison county would be incomplete without a notice of the fifteen excellent schools in the Clarksburg Independent School District, with a teaching force of sixty-six carefully trained instructors. The school population of the district, as shown by the latest enumeration is 2943. The buildings are large and comfortable, and abundantly equipped with maps, charts, libraries and laboratories.

The enrollment of school children in Lewis county is 4374, in the report of Mr. Lloyd G. Losh, superintendent of schools of the county. There are 141 schools in the county, and one high school of the first grade, with 73 pupils. The last institute held at Weston in the charge of Dr. Waitman Barbe, Morgantown; Mr. William H. Culbertson, New Concord, Ohio, did important work in organizing and clarifying the ideas and methods of the teachers in attendance.

Marion county has 159 schools of the lower grades, and an enrollment of 8856 school children. There are three high schools with 384 pupils—an unusually large percentage of students doing the more advanced work. The county institute held at Fairmont was conducted by Dr. C. H. Keyes, Hartford, Connecticut; Miss Keyes, Hartford, Connecticut; Mrs. Gertrude Dobson, Fairmont; Dr. J. N. Deahl, of the State Board of Education, Morgantown.

Mr. W. J. Long, the Superintendent of Schools of Randolph county, gives for his enrollment in the latest report, 5584 pupils in the 205 schools of the lower grades, with 72 in the two high schools of the county. Progress is reported along several lines, the daily attendance being especially satisfactory, and a marked interest has been shown by patrons and other adults in school matters. The institutes conducted at Elkins have elicited the interest and coöperation of many. The last one was under the charge of Prof. A. W. Nolan, of Morgantown; Prof. J. F. Marsh, of the State Department of Schools, Charleston, and of Mrs. Gertrude Dobson, Fairmont.

The enrollment of pupils in the 115 schools of Tucker county is given by Mr. Harry S. Shaffer, the County Superintendent, as 3797 in the common schools, with 45 additional in the two high schools of the county. The last institute, held at Davis, was in the charge of Principal L. B. Hill, of Middlebourne, and Prof. D. D. Johnson, of Morgantown, and has done excellent and stimulating service to the whole community.

The foregoing county statistics are taken in each case from the last (1910) Biennial Report of M. P. Shawkey, State Superintendent of Free Schools.

INDIAN OCCUPANCY AND EARLY TRADITIONS

INDIAN OCCUPANCY AND EARLY TRADITIONS.

When the territory now embraced in the limits of West Virginia first became known to white men it had not an Indian within its borders who considered the region his permanent home. At any rate, if there were any such, their presence and location were never discovered. What is now the State was then an expanse of forest, with scarcely a break in its continuity, and with no inhabitants, except the wild animals that roamed the woods, the fish of the rivers, and the birds that came and went. The early settlers who took up land and established homes in the wilderness that stretched from the headwaters of the Potomac river to the Ohio, met the Indian to their sorrow at almost every turn, but the enemy that harrassed them was not a resident of the region. He came from without and the places of his abode and the manner of his coming and going will be discussed in a future part of this history. The present chapter deals with the Indian's origin and undertakes to present a few facts to explain the causes leading him to make war upon all people who interfered with his hunting grounds and fishing camps. The reason why land from the Blue Ridge to the Ohio river had no inhabitants will be given.

The heading of this chapter indicates that the storehouse of tradition will be opened to supply what history does not furnish. Yet that store will be drawn upon sparingly. Tradition is reports which have come down to us from the past by word of mouth, passed from one individual to another, from one tribe to another, from one generation to another until the actual facts have become so obscured, and so mixed with fiction that it is impossible to be certain where truth ends and error begins. It is not the purpose to deal very extensively with material of this kind in speaking of the Indian's origin. It is unnecessary to do so, for, concerning the origin of this strange and interesting people, tradition is totally worthless. It cannot possibly reach back to a time remote enough to deal with any facts concerning the matter. The

Indian wrote no books, placed no dates on monuments, constructed and preserved no genealogies, and he was in America so long before the white men came that no memory of the early years of his sojourn in this country was preserved in tribal lore. No tradition, therefore, which pretends to deal with the origin of the Indians is of any value.

The only place where tradition can with any reason be consulted—and then only in the absence of history— is in unraveling and revealing some of the complicated series of migrations and wanderings which placed some of the tribes where white men found them. Evidence furnished by tradition should always be accepted with caution, and not at all unless known facts render it possible.

Though West Virginia had no resident Indians when first known, it is clearly established that there was a time when the region was occupied with towns and settlements. The evidence of this will be presented in future paragraphs of this chapter. The origin of the Indians, the place where they had their beginning, and the time and manner of their appearance in America, are no more known than the origin of the animals of the forests and the fish of the rivers is known. They were here always, that is, as far in the past as we can penetrate. There is no reason to suppose that the inhabitants of America were not on the earth as early as those of Europe and Asia. There is no doubt that America had inhabitants at a period more remote than the time reached by the first authentic or traditional history of the old world. In fact, there is as much reason to believe that the old world was peopled from America as there is that the Indians came from the old world to these shores. Theories are many which seek to account for the red man's presence in this country, and most of the theories are worthless. The most plausible is that a relationship in race exists between the Indian on this side and the Mongolian and kindred people of Asia, but if such kinship exists, its precise nature has not yet been discovered. That is, no one knows whether the Indians came from Siberia across Bering Strait into this country, or whether the Chinese and their Tartar relatives reached

Asia by crossing Bering Strait from America, or if neither happened. The inhabitants on both sides of Bering Strait cross and recross whenever they please, and they probably have done so since time immemorial. It is therefore certain that America has received a few immigrants by that route, and Asia has received a few from this country; but it is not known what effect that migration to and fro has had on the Indians as a whole, or on the Mongolian people who live on the other side. It does not seem probable that the question of the origin of the American Indians will ever be settled.

It would be easier to tell how the Indians may have come by any one of several routes than to account for the remarkable condition in which they were found when America was first visited by Europeans. They occupied all parts of both North and South America, an area of about twelve million square miles, extending nine thousand miles north and south and four thousand east and west in its widest part. This extensive area consisted of mountains and plains, forests and deserts. Yet, over all of it, from Labrador to Terra del Fuego, the same race existed, and in nearly the same degree of barbarism, though there were different stages of savagery even among the Indians. Such a remarkable sameness never existed in historic times in any other part of the world over an area so extensive. In the old world, there were nations and peoples, differing in color, customs and character; but in America all were of the same color, all had the same general characteristics. This fact is proof that the Indians had lived in America during an enormous period of time. Otherwise they could not have spread to every nook and corner of such an extensive region.

If the Indians as a people are as old as the people of the eastern hemisphere, and they probably are, there must be a reason why the Americans made no advance in culture above a low order of barbarism, while civilizations developed in Europe, Asia, and Africa thousands of years ago. Physically and mentally, the Indians rate high among barbarians, and it was not due to any defect or weakness of mind or body that they developed and maintained no areas of culture in all the broad expanse of the two American continents. It was the fault of the land in which they lived. Fertile and abounding in natural resources as America is, it was unsuited to the development of centers of civilization. When a country is occupied by a savage population, all on about the same level, and one portion makes a beginning in culture, and as a consequence accumulates a little more property than their savage neighbors, the chance to obtain by plunder the coveted possessions, tempts the more barbarous people to rob the industrious. A few experiences of that kind discourage the workers, and they lapse into barbarism again. In the old world the early civilizations developed in situations measurably secure from inroads by plunderers. Greece was a peninsula not easily invaded; Egypt was a fertile valley surrounded by deserts not readily crossed by bands of plunderers; England was a island; Italy was a peninsula; and the enumeration of instances might be carried on indefinitely. In every instance where a nascent civilization sprang up, some geographical condition of the surroundings protected it against raids by bands of robbers. When nations become powerful they can defend themselves anywhere; but in the feeble beginning there must be protection or there can be no ultimate success.

America lacked protected areas large enough to maintain nascent centers of civilization. There are peninsulas in abundance, and no lack of fertile valleys; but they all lack something. Nova Scotia and Newfoundland were too cold; primitive people could not grow crops there, and no civilization is possible without agriculture. Lower California was too dry; Florida was too poor in soil; and the many valleys of both continents had no protective mountain rims to keep barbarians out. If all parts of America are searched, feature at a time, not one extensive area will be found affording the conditions essential to the beginning of civilization. Two regions were found which in part fulfilled the required condition, the elevated valley of Mexico, and the high basin of Peru; and in them crude and strange civilizations were found, the Aztecs in Mexico, and the Incas of Peru.

RAIDS AND MIGRATIONS.

Having spoken of the origin of the Indians, as far as there is any warrant for speaking on a subject of which so little is known; and having alluded to the reasons why civilization had made little progress in America, it is in order now to come more directly to the Indians who once had their home in West Virginia but who were gone when the region first became known to white men. The Indians of the eastern and central parts of the United States were wanderers. Their wanderings were not such as individuals or small companies indulged in as a diversion or pastime, but were carried out upon a scale large enough to be classed as raids or migrations. In some instances long excursions were made for hunting purposes, but the most extensive of their movements were in war, and were executed partly in hope of plunder but more for the mere love of excitement. The savage inhabitants of the eastern United States were probably the most warlike people in the world. They were seldom long at peace among themselves. Tribe fought tribe with fierceness and cruelty never surpassed. Sometimes several tribes combined in a confederacy and carried on war into distant regions where they fell on peaceful villages and hunting camps, and utterly destroyed them. The cause of their quarrels were often as trivial as some of the causes which have led civilized nations to take up arms. The encroachment of one tribe upon another's hunting ground frequently started trouble which continued until both sides lost sight of the original question, but fought on until one or the other was exterminated, or had moved off to some distant region.

When the whole tribe, or a considerable part of it, departed in a body with no expectation of returning, it was a migration. Indian history abounds in such movements, but generally it is impossible at this day to trace them fully because the Indian leaves no written record. Dependence must be had upon tradition, assisted by such guides as names of places left behind, which names mark the original homes, and the route followed by the tribes in their wanderings.

When a tribe took its departure, the region where it had lived was usually left vacant. Though pressure of war may have forced the tribe to depart, the victors did not always take possession, though they often set up a claim to the territory, and based it on the right of conquest. The conquering tribe was generally too weak in numbers to occupy the depopulated area; but, though unable to hold it by occupation, the tribe was ever ready to attack any people who undertook to move in.

VISIBLE REMAINS IN WEST VIRGINIA.

The Indians who once occupied the territory now embraced in West Virginia left visible remains to bear witness to their presence. These remains consisted of burnt woods, old fields, trails, graves, and arrowheads and other stone implements. There is nothing to show that the whole of the State was the home of a single tribe of Indians, or that any one tribe occupied it during a long period of time. The opposite must have been the case. The territory is divided into valleys; mountain ranges transverse it, and there was no reason why different tribes might not have lived in it at the same time. Neither is there any reason to suppose that a single tribe occupied it during all pre-historic time. On the contrary, it would have been strange if a single tribe had been able to maintain its hold there during a very long period. All known history of the Indian in this part of the United States shows that tribe succeeded tribe at rather frequent intervals.

Graves and Arrowheads—Flint arrowheads are found in all parts of the State. They are most numerous along streams and near springs in situations suitable for villages and camps. Long residence in such spots would naturally strew the ground with these arrow points that might be dropped and lost in the leaves and rubbish of an Indian camp. In some localities the plow turns up multitudes of flint scales and chips, the refuse of the arrow-maker's shop. Such relics are less plentiful now than in early years of settlement when the plow turned up soil which the share had never before disturbed.

The chips of flint are evidence that the manufacturing of the arrow points occurred on the spot, and that the complete weapon was not brought to the region as an article of commence. Flint was a peculiarly fitted material for the making of points in the Indian's way. It broke easily, and the maker's skill was such that he did not spoil many in the process of making, which is evident from the small number of broken points left with the refuse.

Flint is not abundant in West Virginia. It is found in two or three localities, and is in thin ledges. The Indians used all the mechanical means with which they were familiar in quarrying flint. They pried apart the enclosing ledges with wooden levers, and there is evidence that they employed wooden wedges to split apart pieces too heavy to carry. One of the largest flint quarries within reach of West Virginia Indians was at Crab Bottom, on the head of the South Branch of the Potomac, in Virginia, but only a few miles over the Pendleton county line. The old Indian pits may still be seen there scattered over many acres of pasture land. The savages carried rough blocks of flint from the quarries to their camps and there worked them into the finished product. The museum connected with the West Virginia Department of Archives and History at Charleston has an exceptionally fine collection of Indian arrow points gathered in the State. The labor expended by the savages in making the points shown in that collection probably exceeded the labor required to build the State capital.

Indians left other stone relics on the sites of their old encampments. Pipes were fairly numerous, though it is questionable whether the West Virginia Indians smoked tobacco in the pipes. They probably substituted dry bark, buds, leaves, and roots of plants more convenient.

Discoidal stones have been found in rather small numbers. They are as large as a saucer, double concave, with a hole through the center, and their making must have cost the Indians much labor. One such stone picked up near an Indian mound at the mouth of Elkwater creek, in Randolph county, was of highly polished quartzite. It is not known that quartzite is found nearer to Elkwater than Cumberland, Maryland, about one hundred miles distant.

Indian stone graves and earth mounds are found all over the State, the mounds not being as numerous, however, as the graves. The largest mound, and one of the largest anywhere, is at Moundsville, in Marshall county. This is one of the best known mounds in the country, and a stone with hieroglyphics found in it many years ago led to wide discussion among scholars in many countries. It was for a time hoped that its interpretation might be discovered and that it would threw light on the origin of the Indians. The stone was finally pronounced a hoax. It was probably engraved by some joker while the mound was being excavated, and was dropped into the opening when the workmen were temporarily absent. It may be stated that the belief once common that the mound-builders were a people distinct from the Indians, is no longer held by scholars. This matter will be referred to again in a future paragraph. Small Indian mounds were found in several localities. Several still exist in Randolph county in the Tygart's valley above Beverly. Some have never been opened, and others have yielded a few bones and pipes.

Stone graves were most numerous. Some appear to have had only one occupant, while others held many. In some instances, perhaps in most, the body was laid on the ground, and a loose heap of stones was thrown upon it. In others the opening of the stone heaps revealed the bones of many skeletons, old and young, all in promiscuous confusion, as if dejointed skeletons had been thrown in a heap and covered with stones.

Trails—When explorers, traders, and settlers entered Western Virginia they found numerous old Indian trails, and some of them were put to use, and others were forgotten. It would be impossible at this day to make a list of all the roads of Indian origin in the State, nor would it be profitable to attempt it. Early travelers spoke frequently of paths of that kind, before white people had entered the country to make it their home. The Alleghany range of mountains that crosses the region nearly north and south was covered with forests so dense and the ground was so thickly matted with briars and vines that it was next to impossible for human beings to cross without making or following trails. The Indian was a good woodsman, but he was forced to follow paths in order to pass to and fro across those mountains. Both east and west of the chief ranges, the woods were more open, and the mountains were not so continuous and lofty. Accordingly, it was found that the Indians, in times probably beyond the reach of history, established a few routes across the mountains, and the paths there were well worn; but east and west, and particularly west, where the country was less forbidding, the paths divided and went in many directions, some following valleys where the bottom land was level while others passed along the tops of ridges, for the want of valleys leading in the desired direction.

One trail crossed from Greenbrier county to the headwaters of the James river on the east. Another made the passage by way of the upper Greenbrier river to the head of the North Fork of the South Branch of the Potomac. That trail followed the present Staunton and Parkersburg turnpike where it crosses the summit of the main Alleghany mountains in Pocahontas county. Thirty miles further north, the Seneca trail passed from the present site of Elkins, Randolph county, to the North Fork of the South Branch at the Seneca Rocks in Pendleton county. A fourth trail crossed the mountains some thirty miles north of the Seneca path. Its course lay from near Moorefield, Hardy county, through Greenland Gap, over the Alleghanies near Mount Storm, thence crossing the North Branch of the Potomac near the village of Gorman, it reached Cheat river at Dunkard Bottom, Preston county. In crossing the mountains this path followed the general course of the Northwestern turnpike. The path became known as McCullough's, because it was used in early times by an Indian trader of that name.

General Washington followed that path part of the way in his journey to the west in 1784. All of these trails will receive further mention in the course of this history, for they played an important part. One of them, the Seneca trail, can be seen to this day at certain places where it passes through laurel thickets east of Shaver's Fork of Cheat river. During the Civil War it afforded an avenue of escape for a detachment of Confederate troops cut off from General Garnett's army at the battle of Rich mountain, five miles west of Beverly. Two years later, in 1863, the Confederates under General Imboden sent to the south by that route several hundred horses and cattle captured in West Virginia in the great raid which extended almost to the Ohio river.

It is not the purpose to dwell further in this chapter upon the part played in the subsequent history of the region by those old trails which the untutored Indians left behind them when they departed from West Virginia almost a hundred years before the first settlements of white people established themselves west of the mountains. The Indians were excellent road engineers. They found the best routes. In the preceding discussion of those paths, they have been spoken of as if they simply crossed the mountains. That was their chief importance in West Virginia, but some of them reached remote regions. The Seneca trail, for example, extended from western New York to Northern Georgia, and in its course crossed West Virginia. Its very name was ominous in early times. It was the great highway over which the Iroquois or Six Nations whose seat of power was in western New York, sent their warriors south to wage a war of extermination upon enemies six hundred miles away. The name by which those terrible tribes of the north were known to many people upon the frontiers was Senegars, which in literature became Senecas, and their highway across the West Virginia mountains was known as the Seneca trail. The path, a creek which it followed down the eastern slope of the main Alleghany range in Pendleton county, and a remarkable cliff at the mouth of the creek, were all named Seneca. Some of the old men who live in the region have remembered the pronunciation of the name as handed down by their ancestors, and they still speak of the "Senegar Rocks," and "Senegar Creek."

Old Fields—The Indian population was very small in comparison with what the region now sustains. Some sort of census or estimate was made at different times by traders, missionaries, government agents, and others. Their figures could not have been exact, compiled as they were under circumstances as adverse as can well be imagined, but all such estimates place the number of Indians very low. The population of that portion of Virginia between the Alleghany mountains and the sea at the time European settlement began near the coast, has been estimated by James Mooney in his book "The Powhattan Confederacy Past and Present," at 17,000. That allows approximately two and a half square miles, or 1600 acres, for every man, woman and child. It is less than one per cent. of the State's present population, and appears ridiculously small; yet few regions of the United States, within historic times, had Indian population as dense as Virginia's. It was a center of population compared with many other areas of like extent. The average for the whole United States is believed to have been about one individual to 8000 acres, or about one six hundredth part as dense as West Virginia's present population.

Few as the Indians were in the forested regions on both sides of the Alleghany mountains and among the valleys and hills enclosed among the ranges, they could not have subsisted on the products of the chase, supplemented by such berries and wild fruits as they could procure in the unbroken woods. They were compelled by necessity to clear patches of ground here and there and raise corn. The following fruits, nuts, and berries grew wild in West Virginia woods: Strawberries, blackberries, raspberries, gooseberries, huckleberries, buckberries, elderberries, mulberries, services, plums, grapes, black haws, red haws, wild cherries, pawpaws, crabapples, hickory nuts, butter nuts, walnuts, chestnuts, hazel nuts, and some kinds of edible acorns. This list is long, and it suggests abundance of food, such as it was; but even that kind was doubtless scarce in the unbroken forests, for it is well known that food-bearing trees and plants do not yield much in deep and unbroken woods, but only about the margins where the sunshine can reach the ground. George P. Marsh in "The Earth as Modified by Human Action," says on this subject: "In a region abundantly covered with trees, human life could not long be sustained for want of animal and vegetable food. The depths of the forest seldom furnish either bulb or fruit suited to the nourishment of man; and the fowls and beasts on which he feeds are seldom seen except upon the margins of the woods, for here only grow the shrubs and grasses, and here only are found the seeds and insects, which form the sustenance of the more carnivorous birds and quadrupeds. The wild fruit and nut trees, the Canadian plum, the cherry, the many species of walnut, the butternut, the hazel, yield very little, frequently nothing, so long as they grow in the woods; and it is only when the trees around them are cut down, or when they grow in pastures, that they become productive. The berries too—the strawberry, the blackberry, the raspberry, the whortleberry—scarcely bear fruit at all except in cleared ground."

The Indians were, for the reasons stated, compelled to clear land and plant corn to ward off the ever threatening famine.

A good deal more is known of the Indian fields in the eastern part of Virginia than west of the mountains. In the east, the settlers came in direct contact with the natives, and slowly pushed them out of the country, and had opportunity to see how many and how extensive the Indian fields were. The natives raised corn by the thousands of bushels. West of the mountains the opportunity for observation was not so good, because the barbarians of that region had taken their departure from seventy-five to one hundred years before the first colonists crossed the mountains. The cornfields, surrounded by woods, would relapse into forests in a century, except where the clearings had been very large. Old fields would be fewer, and would receive less mention from travelers. Taking that view of the matter, it is safe to conclude that the natives cleared fields in Western Virginia the same as in Eastern Virginia, but the majority of such clearings had been overrun and had disappeared by the time the settlers began to arrive. In spite of the long period that passed between the migration of the West Virginia tribes and the coming of the settlers, there were many remnants of old fields visible at the time white men came.

The clearing of ground for garden and fields cost the Indians much labor, which was performed by women. Small undergrowth was pulled out by the roots, or burned or broken off, and the larger trees were killed by bruising the bark at the base of the trunks and removing it. Stone mauls were used for that purpose. Occasionally rings of fire burned the bark off. The trees which were subjected to such injury speedily withered, but the fall of the trunk might be delayed ten years. Meanwhile the Indians cultivated the ground, clearing away each year the fallen limbs and trunks. The chief crops were corn, beans, pumpkins and melons.

One of the earliest accounts of Western Virginia was written in 1671 by Robert Fallows in a journal which was sent to the London Royal Society by Rev. John W. Clayton in 1688.

In 1671 the New river, a tributary of the Kanawha, was reached, at a point near the present Virginia-West Virginia line, but the exact spot is unknown. The exploration was carried on by what has usually been called the Thomas Batts expedition, though practically all that is known of it is contained in the journal kept by Robert Fallows who accompanied Thomas Batts and Thomas Wood. On September 13, 1671, the explorers camped in a valley near New river where were many "brave meadows and old fields." Rev. Clayton added an explanatory note saying: "'Old fields' is a common expression for land that has been cultivated by the Indians and left fallow, which is generally overrun with what they call 'broom grass'." Two days later Fallows wrote in his diary: "We understand the Mohecan Indians did here formerly live. It cannot be long since for we found cornstalks in the ground."

The next day the diary further refers to cleared land: "We went ourselves down to the riverside, but not without great difficulty, it being a piece of very rich ground whereon the Mohecans had formerly lived, and grown up with weeds, and small prickly locusts and thistles to a very great height that it was almost impossible to pass. It cost us hard labor to get through."

That was the farthest point west reached by the explorers. They proposed to go on, but their Indian guides balked and refused to proceed through fear of the "Salt Indians." But for that unfortunate circumstance, eye witnesses might have left a record of conditions at that time beyond the mountains in Virginia, the region which is now West Virginia. It was at that very time passing through a crisis. Its inhabitants were being swept away, and the region between the Alleghany mountains and the Ohio river was henceforth to remain an unpeopled wilderness until its settlement by white people a century later. It would be instructive to know what that region's condition was at that time, but the fear of the "Salt Indians" caused the expedition to turn back, and we must be satisfied with a few glimpses into the forbidden, transmontane provinces of Virginia. Indians who were sufficiently civilized to manufacture salt, and make of it a commercial commodity, might be presumed to be skilled in agriculture also, and the few extant scraps of information concerning them show that they were.

Robert Beverley who wrote about 1705, commented upon the passages in the Fallows journal relating to the farthest point west reached by the expedition, and said: "Near these cabins (on the New river) were great marshes where the Indians which Captain Batts had with him made a halt and would positively proceed no farther. They said that not far off from that place lived a nation of Indians that made salt and sold it to their neighbors, that it was a great and powerful people which never suffered any stranger to return that had once discovered their towns."

Some persons have supposed that the Batts expedition in 1671 reached the falls of the Kanawha river in Fayette county, West Virginia, and that the abandoned fields were at that place. There is nothing in the Fallows journal to sustain that view, and the outside evidence is all against it. It is not certain, and in fact not probable, that the explorers even reached the present West Virginia line. If they crossed it at all they could have gone but a few miles further which would have placed them in Monroe or Mercer county. The time the explorers were upon the journey toward the west is well known, and it was physically impossible for them to have gone as far as the falls of the Kanawha in the stated time.

Eighty years after the Batts expedition, Christopher Gist found old fields between the mountains and the Ohio which had not yet been totally obliterated by encroaching forests. On March 4, 1752, he found a "great many cleared fields covered with white clover," and elsewhere he spoke of "some meadows" and "an old Indian road." In Tygart's valley, near the western base of the Alleghany mountains, the first settlers in 1753, discovered large tracts over which forests had but lately closed, and smaller areas still in sod; while on Cheat river, forty miles distant, James Parsons in 1769 found trees, apparently a century old, which had taken possession of land that had formerly been cleared, as he judged from the uniform size of the timber, and the fact that trees had grown up through artificial cobblestone floors, perhaps used for drying places for Indian corn, nuts, fruits, and fish.

The land on the Kanawha river, where the Indians made salt and where it is assumed they lived in considerable numbers, subsequently became the property of General Washington. On August 20, 1773, he inserted an advertisement in a Baltimore newspaper offering to lease 20,000 acres to settlers. A hundred years had elapsed since the Indians had abandoned their homes there, and yet large tracts of comparatively open land remained, over which the forests had not yet spread, as may be inferred from General Washington's description. "As these lands," said he, "are among the first which have been surveyed in the part of the country they lie in, it is almost needless to promise that none can exceed them in luxuriance of soil, or convenience of situation, all of them lying on the banks either of the Ohio or Kanawha, and abounding with fine fish and wild fowl of various kinds, as also in most excellent meadows, many of which, by the bountiful hand of nature, are in their present state almost fit for the scythe."

Any openings in the forest in that region were artificial, as the land was naturally covered completely by woods. The meadows of which Washington spoke could have been none other than remnants of extensive cornfields abandoned by the Indians a hundred years before. It is thus seen that clearings made by the Virginia Indians were found in large numbers in all regions that were fairly well explored, but in smaller numbers where explorations were fewer; but no explorer in any extensive region failed to report the openings in the forest, made, or supposed to have been made, by natives for purposes of agriculture.

In that portion of the present State of West Virginia lying east of the mountains clearings were found by the first explorers, and were called old fields. They were in grass, with a few trees here and there on which wild grapes grew in luxuriance. The best known of such places was that in Hardy county, and to this day it retains its name Old Fields. Wild hay was cut on this ground in 1747, as is shown by an entry in the journal kept by George Washington who visited the Old Fields while surveying land for Lord Fairfax. "We camped this night," he says, "in the woods near a wild meadow where was a large stack of hay."

An indirect description of the Hardy county Old Fields is given in a journal kept by Isaac Van Meter during a trip to Ohio in 1801. His home was in Hardy county. He described the Peepee Bottom in Ohio thus: "On our way back to town we passed through the Peepee Bottom on the military side, the longest bottom I have yet seen. Clear prairie is said to contain 900 acres. This bottom has the greatest resemblance to the Old Fields of anything I have yet seen. There are thickets of plum and other shrubs, twined with grapevines, and here and there overtowered by a large elm or cherry tree; and shadowing burr oaks separate open glady spots. Thus the large prairie is surrounded, which is generally dry, and has a very great abundance of strawberries."

There were other old fields on the upper waters of the Potomac, some along the river between Cumberland, Maryland, and Keyser, West Virginia, occupying the rich bottom lands. Other open areas were below Cumberland. One such nearly opposite the mouth of the South Branch was taken possession of by Thomas Cresap whose place is now called Old Town. He was living there in 1747.

The absence of edged tools among the Indians made the clearing of land very slow and laborious. With sticks and stones as their only implements they dug and pulled out by the roots the small bushes. Some which could not be grubbed out were broken off near the ground; but the trees and large saplings could not be handled by the rude tools of the savages, except in a very slow and laborious way. The bark was pounded from the trunks near the ground, and the trees were left to die. They usually lived a year after being girdled, and during the several succeeding years the branches and trunks fell upon the crops beneath. Fire was the Indian's principal agent in clearing land. Trees were burned down and logs were severed by fires kept burning for days at a time to accomplish what an ax or a saw would do in a few hours. The labor was performed by the women. The dead branches that fell as decay progressed were carried to the wigwams for fuel.

Strange as it may appear, Indians who lived in the woods were often hard put to it to secure firewood. We know this from the accounts of travelers who in early times visited Indian towns in the eastern part of Virginia. The woods for long distances around the towns were swept clean of dead saplings and fallen branches which could be broken or carried whole to the wigwams. The savages had no tools with which to cut sound wood, and were forced to depend upon what could be picked up. For that reason, the dead branches which fell from the girdled trees in their cornfields were a welcome addition to their scanty fuel supply. It is not improbable that Indians were occasionally forced to move their villages not only because the soil of their cornfields became exhausted by excessive tillage, but for the reason that the supply of wood for fires was scarce and hard to procure. Early white settlers have been known to move their huts to a more convenient fuel supply, and doubtless the Indians did likewise.

Burnt Woods—During the Indian's occupancy of West Virginia he left his mark in the form of burnt woods. He burned much less than in regions farther west, when large tracts were changed from forest to prairie, but there is no question that he was vigorously applying the torch up to the time he took his departure.

The clearings made by Indians for agricultural purposes, were comparatively large, but they were small in comparison with openings made by fires set accidentally, wantonly, or to the end that more wild game might abound, with improved opportunities for hunting it. Though white men are rated high as destroyers of forests, they are not in the same class with the Indian. He used a little wood, destroyed vastly more to make room for his fields, but his real work of forest destruction was done with fire. He was wasteful and destructive as savages usually are, and the word economy had no place in his vocabulary. When he had abundance, he squandered like a pirate, and when want pinched he stood it like a stoic.

The Indian is by nature an incendiary, and forest burning was his besetting sin. The few trees and poles which he took for use and the thousands destroyed to make his cornfields, were a small drain on the forests in comparison with the millions which his woods fires consumed. It is not known how long he had been burning the valleys and mountains before white men came to Virginia, but the custom was general at the time of the first settlement, and it was, apparently, of long standing and was evidently growing worse. There is reason to believe, though there is no positive evidence of it, that the lesson of destruction was being learned from Western Indians, who, by the agency of fire, were changing forests into treeless plains. If any considerable regions of Eastern Virginia, except swamps too damp to burn, had escaped repeated visitations by fire, the early explorers failed to make note of them. Complete destruction of forests by fire had already occurred over tracts aggregating hundreds of square miles, and undergrowth had been injured or destroyed almost everywhere in the regions early explored. In many localities the mature trees alone remained, and they were frequently so thinned and depleted that the woods resembled parks rather than forests, as is abundantly set forth in contemporaneous writings. Over very large tracts, at the period of discovery, the forests had apparently reached the last stage before their fall. No small wood was coming on to take the place of the old trees, and with the death of the mature timber many regions would have been treeless. Philip Alexander Bruce, in his economic history of Virginia, sums up the evidence contained in the early records by saying: "Freedom from undergrowth was one of the most notable features of the original woods of Virginia."

Conditions do not seem to have been so bad in that part of Virginia west of the mountains as in the eastern section, but that may have been due to the fact that the transmontane region was almost unknown for eighty years after its Indian population had departed. In eighty years burnt woods will recuperate in a damp climate and on rich soil like West Virginia, and when white men entered the country they were not generally impressed with burnt and open tracts as they were further east and further west where the savages were interrupted in the very act of burning.

Doubtless many fires were accidental or resulted from carelessness, but generally the Indians burned the woods to increase food supply, directly or indirectly. So far as they reasoned at all, they doubtless thought the end justified the means. The food supply was directly increased by fires which facilitated hunting operations; indirectly, by opening the way for the growth of grass, nuts, fruits, and berries, thereby causing game to congregate in certain localities. The fruits of many vines and trees were eaten by the Indians. Observation doubtless taught those savages, as it has taught more civilized men, that fruit-bearing trees and plants multiply more rapidly, and yield more abundantly, on the margins of burned tracts than in deep forests. The Indian was cunning enough to put his knowledge to practical account, and sufficiently far-sighted to set fires one year that the burned tracts might yield more sustenance the next year and in future years. The fall of some score millions of feet of prime timber in a forest conflagration meant no loss to the Indian, if briers and grass followed, for they brought together beasts and birds which furnished the Indian with more food than he could have procured in the forests that fell.

More is known of the early condition of the Shenandoah valley, the northern part of which lies in West Virginia, than of the country west of the Alleghanies, because the Virginians came pretty early in contact with that valley and wrote descriptions of it, either from what they saw or from hearsay. No portion of Virginia was more terribly burned than that valley. Its earliest explorer, as far as is definitely known, was Governor Spotswood, in 1716. He wrote no description that has been preserved, the only account of it having been written as a diary by James Fontaine, one of the governor's companions. The diary is more minute in its account of stores of liquors carried and consumed, and the size and number of rattlesnakes seen and destroyed, than in description of the country. Consequently we must depend upon later writers for an account of conditions there when settlements began some years after Governor Spotswood's visit.

The Shenandoah Valley is known to have been a highway for Indian traveling north or south, and camps of natives were in the valley, at certain times at least, until after 1730; but the valley probably had no resident tribes subsequent to the Iroquois conquest about 1672. The worst burning doubtless occurred before that time. A vague account of the region reached John Smith when he was exploring the Rappahannock a hundred years before the first white man is known to have seen the valley. It is worthy of note, and remarkable, that the very earliest reference to the region was misleading in an essential point, for the valley was said to be a place which Indian fires had not yet injured. When John Smith questioned the warrior Amoroleck, whom he captured on the Rappahannock, as to the land beyond the mountains, the Indian's answers showed that he knew of the Blue Ridge, but all he could tell of what lay beyond was that "the woods had not been burnt." If the warrior referred to the lower part of the valley of Virginia, he was mistaken, for the woods had been burnt. An area now occupied in part by three counties, Frederick, Berkeley and Jefferson, was treeless. The burnt lands extended across the present state of Maryland, and into Pennsylvania, and in those states were long called "The Barrens," and occasionally are still so called, on account of the stunted timber which once grew there. The area of the treeless region in the lower Shenandoah valley exceeded 1,000 square miles in one body. This statement depends chiefly upon Samuel Kircheval's "History of the Valley," for its authority though other writers refer to the devastation wrought there. Kircheval could not have had personal knowledge of it, but he might, and very probably did, talk to old men who were eye-witnesses of the conditions he describes. W. H. Foote goes more into details in his sketches of Virginia and says: "A large part of the valley from the headsprings of the Shenandoah to the Potomac or the Maryland line, a distance of about one hundred and fifty miles, embracing ten counties, was covered with prairies abounding in tall grass, and these, with scattered forests, were filled with pea vines. Much of the beautiful timber in the valley has grown since the emigrants chose their habitations."

There is other testimony establishing the fact that what had been open prairie in the Shenandoah valley when white men first saw the region had relapsed into forest less than a century later. There is no reason to suppose that tracts between the Alleghany mountains and the Ohio river did not follow a similar course.

History does not tell of the beginning of forests and forest fires in West Virginia, or anywhere else in America. Indians were doubtless in the country thousands of years ago, and their ancestors hunted the musk ox in the Ohio valley during the ice age.

There is ground for the opinion that the Indian was not always an incendiary. Had he been one, the woods could not have spread so wide and so far. Nothing is more certain than that oft-repeated and long-continued fires will finally destroy a forest and make a prairie or a desert. Had the natives been indulging their habits of firing the woods from time immemorial, they would have kept down the forests, and white men from Europe would have landed upon the shores of a grass continent. That such was not the condition at the time of the discovery is warrant for the belief that the Indians had acquired their incendiary propensities within a comparatively recent period; and at the same time, evidence is apparently conclusive that the fires were gaining the mastery over the woods, and that the primeval forests were disappearing. Nathaniel S. Shaler speaks of the matter thus in "Nature and Man in America:" "If the advent of European folk in the Mississippi valley had been delayed another five centuries the prairie country would doubtless have been made very much more extensive. Thus in western Kentucky a territory of about five thousand square miles in area had recently been brought to a state of open land by the burning of the forests. All around the margin of this area there were only old trees, scarred by successive fires, there being no young of the species to take the place as they fell. It is probable that with another five hundred years of such conditions the prairie region would have extended up to the base of the Alleghanies, and in time all the great Appalachian woods, at least as far as the plain lands were concerned, would probably have vanished in the same process."

The theory that the Indians of the Mississippi valley commenced burning forests when the buffaloes first appeared, finds some support in the records of history and geology. If the theory is correct, the buffalo originated among or beyond the Rocky mountains, and, spreading eastward in search of pasture, reached the forests of the Mississippi valley. That is believed to have occurred in comparatively recent times, perhaps not much more than a thousand years before the discovery of America. Evidence of it is found in the absence of buffalo bones in waste heaps, caves, drift, gravel and bogs of the region until the most recent deposits were made. The moundbuilders pictured almost every animal now found native in the region except the buffalo, and this fact is interpreted to mean that those people were not acquainted with the buffalo. In the fossil deposits about certain saline springs in Kentucky are found the bones of many extinct and still living animals, from the musk ox of the ice age, down to the creatures of the present. They lie in the bogs, layer upon layer, the oldest below, the most recent on top. The bones of the buffalo are found only in the surface layer, showing that this great quadruped came the most recent of all.

It has been supposed that the Indians who built the mounds in the Mississippi valley were agriculturists, and were beginning to rise in the scale of civilization, but with the coming of the buffalo they found it so much easier to live on the flesh of that animal than to cultivate the soil, that they abandoned their fields, turned hunters, and lapsed into savagery. In order to enlarge the grass tracts and afford pasturage for buffaloes they burned the land, killed the timber and the encroachment of prairies upon the forests began at that time.

Certain it is that the buffalo had reached the Atlantic coast at the time of the discovery of America. It is also certain that it was a grass eater and sought open tracts where pastures were good. Buffaloes were much more numerous in Virginia than in Pennsylvania east of the mountains. William Byrd, writing in 1729, said they were seldom found north of the fortieth parallel of latitude. These animals made trails long distances through the wooded regions, connecting one pasture with another. There is no question but that Indians burned the pastures and surrounding woods yearly to improve the range, increase game and make hunting easier. The deer, elk and buffalo were among the finest game animals in Virginia, and quotations from Beverley, Lederer, Fallows, Byrd and others show that these animals congregated in large numbers where grass was found. It was to the Indian's interest to thin and destroy the woods that grass might grow more abundantly, and no one acquainted with his habits has ever charged him with neglecting his interests in this particular.

WEST VIRGINIA INDIANS.

An extended discourse on the traditional Indian occupation of the territory now embraced in West Virginia is foreign to the purpose of this chapter. Such a discussion would be profitless, and it might be carried to great length without exhausting the subject. It may be stated once for all that no man now knows to a certainty what tribe or tribes predominated in this state prior to 1672 when the region ceased to contain a fixed Indian population. The truth probably is that part of several tribes occupied the territory between the Alleghany mountains and the Ohio river, shifting their positions, coming and going, and moving about; but to name a precise date and say what tribes were here then, no man can do it. Within wider limits, however, there is room for speculation as to who they were.

In the Fallows journal of 1671 some of them are called the Salt Indians. Evidently that was not their name, and was used as a descriptive term, based on the fact that they made salt. John Mitchell, who resided in Virginia and wrote about 1760, furnished additional information concerning the Saltmakers who had terrorized the explorers' guides nearly ninety years before. "The Indians they meant," said he, "were the ancient Chawanoes [Shawnees] who lived to the westward and northward of the place where the discoverers were at, and were at that time, 1671, engaged in a hot and bloody war with the Iroquois, in which they were so closely pressed at that time that they were entirely extirpated or incorporated with the Iroquois the year following."

There is other evidence that the Shawnees occupied certain localities in West Virginia at an early time, but it cannot be reasonably asserted that they were the principal people. There were so many Indian tribes in the eastern part of the United States, and since the same name was by no means uniformly applied to the same tribe, a large element of uncertainty is introduced into every attempt to delimit the several tribes and assign them territory. If that could be done for a particular time, it would not hold for another period, because the Indians were constantly shifting positions.

Better success attends efforts to deal with Indians as groups instead of single tribes. A group is made up of several tribes, and might be called a nation if it were compact enough, and firmly established in a particular region. The Iroquois offer the most familiar example of a group composed of several tribes. The Powhatan confederacy in Virginia was another.

The greatest buffalo hunters of all the Indians in America were the Sioux, who occupied seven hundred thousand square miles of territory west of the Mississippi, from the Arkansas river northward. Investigators have been led to believe that the ancestors of these Indians had something to do with prehistoric Virginia. It is not improbable that their buffalo hunting began there, and that they moved west, allured by the greater abundance of those animals, at a period so recent as to form a connecting link between tradition and history. A study of geographic names, of languages and of traditions has apparently indicated that the cradle of the Siouan nation was in the mountains of western Virginia, upon the Monongahela, Kanawha and Great Sandy rivers.

The theory has been advanced, and much evidence in support of it is adduced by James Mooney in his "Siouan Tribes of the East," that when the great western migration of the Sioux occurred, certain remnants remained behind, and moved over the mountains to Piedmont, Virginia. There they were found by explorers a year or two after the founding of Jamestown. They extended from the Potomac at Harper's Ferry southward, near the mountains, to South Carolina. They were warred upon by Powhatan's confederacy on the east, and later by the Iroquois from the north. John Smith fought the Sioux upon the Rappahannock river in 1608. The warrior Amoroleck, who told Captain Smith that the woods behind the Blue Ridge had not been burned, was a Sioux. The Indians whose deserted cornfields Captain Batts found on New river in 1671 were Sioux, and Lederer reported Sioux near the Roanoke river who kept a year's supply of corn in reserve. They were not hunters then as their kindred were later on the western plains, but agriculturists. The belief that the cradle of the Siouan nation was among the mountains of West Virginia is founded partly on the fact that many Siouan names of rivers, mountains, and other natural features were found in that region; and partly on a tradition among the Sioux themselves that their ancestors reached the western plains by descending the Ohio river, or some stream whose description answered to the Ohio.

The suggestion that the Sioux from among the Alleghany mountains reached the western plains by following the migration of buffaloes is not well taken because there is no evidence that the buffalo migrated westward from the mountains, but much evidence to the contrary. A discussion of the Sioux's probable habitat in West Virginia must enter the borderland which lies between authentic history and tradition. The fact has not been established, but it is not improbable. Nevertheless, if the known evidence in the case were deemed sufficiently conclusive to prove that the Sioux once had their homes here, there is nothing to show that they were the tribes driven out between 1656 and 1672, the period usually assigned to the extirpation of the last West Virginia tribes. The migration of the Sioux, if it occurred at all, was probably at an earlier date. It is an historic fact, however, that several tribes of Siouan stock lived in Virginia for sixty years after the Jamestown settlement was founded, and Mooney says: "The great overmastering fact in the history of the Siouan tribes of the east is that of their destruction by the Iroquois."

CONQUEST OF THE WEST VIRGINIA TRIBES.

The country beyond the mountains remained unknown to the colonists on the lowlands of Virginia for a century after settlements had advanced up all the rivers of the east as far as the tides ran. Those broad, deep channels afforded highways for sailing vessels from fifty to one hundred miles from their mouths, and passage up and down was easy by taking advantage of the ebb and flow of the tides; but at the base of the first plateau the navigators encountered rapids, and could sail no farther. The Potomac's rapids were just above Washington, those of the James river were at Richmond. Above those points the movement of the advance of the settlements toward the base of the mountains was slow. While the line of outposts was creeping toward the west, mile by mile, the Indians who lived in the territory between the falls of the rivers and the mountains were meeting their fate. During that period there was generally peace between them and their white neighbors, who were approaching nearer each year; but an irresistible foe was pressing them from another direction. Those Indians who lived between the falls of the rivers and the mountains consisted for the most part of fragments of Siouan tribes, as stated on preceding pages. The enemy which wrought their destruction was the Iroquois, and with the destruction of the tribes between the mountains and the English settlements, occurred also that of the tribes in West Virginia, behind the Blue Ridge, and between the Alleghany mountains and the Ohio river.

The important part which the Iroquois acted in the tragedy which culminated in the extirpation of the inhabitants of fifty thousand square miles in one body—along and on both sides of the mountain ranges from the Potomac river to the borders of South Carolina, demands a brief account of the conquering people. Their center of power was in Western New York. Until about 1716 they were known as the Five Nations, because their confederacy included five tribes, of which the Mohawks were the most important. Soon after the beginning of the eighteenth century the Tuscaroras moved up from North Carolina and joined them, and the confederacy then became the Six Nations, collectively known as Iroquois. The six tribes were the Mohawks, Onondagas, Cayugas, Oneidas, Senecas and Tuscaroras. As far as history affords evidence, that was the most perfect organization of Indian tribes that ever existed in the United States. It was a strong, military government, with a center and branches. Some have seen in it the nucleus or foundation of what promised to develop into a real Indian nation.. Without question, it was a strong organization, and in most things it was ably managed. The directing hand of rare statesmanship was seen in it. It is impossible to say how far it might have gone or what it might have accomplished if it had not met the advancing colonies of white men. In that contact, the Iroquois went down before the superior power of Europeans. As long as the confederacy fought Indians only it was irresistible. The warriors from the north overran the country to the Carolinas on the south, to the center of Ohio, and perhaps farther on the west, and south of the Ohio river in Kentucky; while on the east they carried their victories into Massachusetts.

When, in their early intercourse with the English and Dutch colonies on the Hudson, they procured fire arms, they became stronger than ever. The tribes with which they fought were as yet armed only with bows, arrows and stone hatchets and spears, and they were powerless before their adversaries armed with guns. Some effort was made by the Virginia colonists to put an end to the war which the Iroquois were waging against the tribes in Virginia. Certain neutral zones were laid out, intended to keep the Iroquois north of the Potomac, but the war could not be stopped. The Virginia and Carolina tribes were willing enough to stop, for they fought only on the defensive; but so implacable was the Iroquois' hatred that nothing could induce them to make peace. Their war parties stole through the woods, and traversed forest paths hundreds of miles, fell upon camps and villages by surprise and utterly destroyed them. Early explorers, particularly Lederer and Batts, witnessed this war of extermination waged by the Iroquois. They saw the deserted towns, the abandoned cornfields, the ruined camps of tribes which had perished, or had fled to parts unknown in hope of escaping a fate which was certain if they remained where they were.

The war policy of the Iroquois was like that of the Tartars under Genghis Kahn and Tamerlane. The northern tribes exterminated, destroyed and obliterated everything that fell into their power. Some historians have seen in this policy the weakest point in the statesmanship of the Iroquois. They left solitudes which they were unable to repeople, just as the Mongolian conquerors did who marched westward through Asia, and as was done at a later time in Central Africa by Mohammedan marauders. By pursuing such a course the Iroquois were isolating themselves by creating a waste zone on all sides of them. The appearance of white men on the scene brought their power to a close before the destructive work which they had undertaken was fully executed, and for that reason it cannot be known what the final result would have been had there come no interference.

The Crisis—Having spoken of the tribes which were living west of the Alleghanies, what little is known of them, and having described briefly the enemy that wrought their destruction, it is now in order to give an account of the final crisis. The story must, of necessity, be brief, for of the details, which must have been many, history is silent. The fact that a region of twenty thousand square miles, extending from the mountains to the Ohio river, was laid utterly waste by the northern savages stands out as the one thing known of the closing scenes of that struggle. The Iroquois had been raiding the region for more than ten years, and their last campaign closed in 1672, with the total extirpation of the unfortunate West Virginia tribes.

Doubtless the Iroquois sent their warriors into West Virginia over all the principal trails leading from the north; some probably ascending the Monongahela, others descending the Ohio, while still others moved southward across Maryland and passed the mountains by the four paths described in preceding pages. The most important of these was the Seneca trail, whose very name suggests traditions that it was a highway for those conquering tribes from the north. There is not one word of detail of the last campaign, not one particular. The scenes enacted in the forests and by the rivers of West Virginia in that desperate struggle are lost to history. The Iroquois swept the region and left it a desolation. Nearly a century later their orators appeared in a conference held at Fort Stanwix, now Rome, New York, for the purpose of making a treaty, and declared that "all the world" knew that the land now embraced in West Virginia was theirs because they had conquered it.

How complete the conquest was, and how desolate was the country which they left, is witnessed by the fact that no Indian tribe ever again dared live in it. Seventy years after the conquest John Peter Salley, with a small party of explorers, crossed the entire state without seeing a human being who called the region his home, and nearly ten years later Christopher Gist traveled two hundred miles within its borders and saw no one, though he noted old fields and paths. Indians from Ohio and perhaps from other regions sometimes passed through the region. When Washington was surveying on the Potomac in 1748, he saw a party of thirty savages passing through, and a few years after that time, Ohio Indians repaired to the salt springs on the Kanawha river to make salt. These people were not permanently in the country, and made no attempt to occupy it. With very few exceptions the many Indian graves in West Virginia date earlier than the time of the Iroquois conquest.

When settlers began to cast covetous eyes upon the fertile valleys of West Virginia, they knew they could take the land without dispossessing any one. The Iroquois, by the treaty of Fort Stanwix, had surrendered all claim to it, though some of the Ohio tribes disputed the right of the northern Indians to dispose of the land, and, as will be shown in succeeding chapters, the tribes in Ohio would not submit to the occupation of the region by white men until compelled by force of arms.

FRENCH AND INDIAN WAR

THE FRENCH AND INDIAN WAR.

The rivalry between France and England for possession of the region west of the Alleghany mountains led to the conflict known in history as the French and Indian war. It is so called because the Indians entered into an alliance with the French and fought with them. There were a few exceptions, chiefly in the south, where small parties of Cherokees and other tribes assisted the English, but such help amounted to so little that it may be dismissed with slight mention. The few bands of Cherokees from the region of eastern Tennessee and the western part of North Carolina, appeared once or twice on the eastern frontier of what is now West Virginia, but their efforts were barren of any visible results. On the other hand, thousands of Indians belonging to the region from western New York to the Mississippi river, went on the warpath to help the French.

In a history confined in its scope to a region as small as West Virginia, it should not be expected that a full and minute history of the French and Indian war would appear. A large part of it was remote from any portion of this State, and its activities were of more immediate concern to New York, New England, and Nova Scotia, and nothing more than the briefest mention of events can be given in this chapter.

The Land Contest—The rivalry between England and France in North America was one of the most important that ever occurred where the question was one concerning possession of territory. It was a contest between the two most powerful countries in the world at that time for control of a continent. The English colonies were in possession of the coast from Main to Florida, and were so firmly established between the mountains and the sea that the French saw no prospect of dislodging them and they made no attempt to do so. But behind the mountains, west from the crest of the Alleghanies to the Mississippi valley, and including most of that valley, was a region of vast extent and of unknown but enormous resources. Further north lay Canada, stretching from the Atlantic to the Pacific, and northward to an unknown distance until it was buried in Arctic snows. The western and northern country was a prize worthy of the best efforts of the powerful competitors, and the war was fought for its possession.

That part of West Virginia beyond the summit of the Alleghanies was part of the stake. It was but a small portion in comparison with the whole, but it was one of the best parts. Had this State been all there was to fight for, it is not probable that arms would have been resorted to at that time; but this territory could not be left out of consideration while contending for the rest and it turned out that some of the most important movements in the entire contest occurred in what now is West Virginia.

The French were first in possession of certain points in the disputed territory, but the English based their claim on the discovery and first possession of the coast. They insisted that fact made the whole country theirs as far inland as they might wish to claim it. It was not a question, however, that could be settled by assertion of rights backed up by argument only. It was pretty well understood by both parties to the controversy that sooner or later a settlement of the whole matter would be forced by an appeal to arms. The French were first to prepare for it. Their explorers were almost a century ahead of the English in the west. They penetrated very early, by way of the St. Lawrence river and the Great Lakes, to the Mississippi river. Their explorers in some instances were missionaries, in others they were traders, but in all cases they held in view one common purpose, to possess the country and hold it for France.

The French were very active explorers and traders, and were usually successful in winning the good will of the Indians. They planted settlements and established outposts in places selected with good judgment, and had an eye to the strategic points in the regions which they explored. They knew the value of rivers as highways for travel and commerce, and the use of portages between navigable streams. But there was one defect, one weakness, in the French system of occupation which could not be made good by all their strong points. Their agricultural establishments were small, their farmers few. They did not fix their civilization in the soil as the Anglo-Saxons did. They preferred to trade with Indians for furs, and turn the furs into cash. The English were traders also, but agriculture came first and was made the solid foundation upon which all else was built in America. The French tried to occupy and hold a territory entirely too large for their numbers. Their lines were stretched too far, and when the pressure came, the lines broke. The English along the coast were compact. Their towns were growing, their trade increasing, their ships were well freighted, but back of and beneath it all was the solid ground work of agriculture. Their advanced posts toward the west were not trading stations, but farming settlements. They did not build villages the first thing, as the French did, but they cleared farms, planted corn, and raised cattle, sheep, and hogs. The village was the last thing they thought of, and it came only when a business center was needed for a group of settlements.

During a hundred years the English settlements moved from the coast westward, slowly, steadily, irresistibly. The woods opened and fields appeared, marking the lines and progress of the westward advance. While the English, Scotch, Irish, Welsh, Dutch, and Germans were clearing fields, the French sent La Salle, Marquette, Hennepin, and Balboa to explore. While the Anglo-Saxons were building cabins among the mountain valleys and arriving almost in sight of the western rivers, the French sent Captain Celeron to bury leaden plates, with letters cut on them, along the Ohio, expecting to hold the country that way. The leaden plate was no match for the log cabin and the cornfield in a contest for the possession of the country. The French finally understood this, and they threatened to build forts unless the English movements were stopped at the eastern base of the Alleghany mountains.

The fight by that time was beginning to take form for the possession of Western Virginia, between the mountains and the Ohio. The French threw out a bluff. They threatened to build a fort on the Greenbrier river and another on Holston river in eastern Tennessee. Virginia called the bluff by continuing to push settlements toward the west. Christopher Gist established a colony on the Youghiogheny river, now in western Pennsylvania, but at that time supposed to be Virginia territory; and cabins had made their appearance west of the mountains on the Greenbrier and Tygart's rivers. The French moved soldiers south from Lake Erie and prepared to hold the western valleys by force, if the threat of force proved unavailing. Virginia accepted the challenge, and the appeal to arms was near at hand.

Washington's Mission—It became known in Virginia in 1753 that the French had reached the Alleghany river from Canada and were building forts in that region. That territory was then claimed by Virginia, and Governor Dinwiddie felt it his duty to take steps to protect it against the French. He chose to look upon them as simple trespassers and sent a message to them, asking them to withdraw from that region. The messenger who carried the letter was George Washington, twenty-one years old. Late in the fall of 1753 he set out from Williamsburg, at that time the capital of Virginia, passed across the Shenandoah valley, and through Hampshire county. At the mouth of Wills creek, now Cumberland, Maryland, he left all settlements behind, except one west of the Alleghanies which he reached in a few days. He followed a path through an unbroken wilderness and crossed the mountains, on the summits of which the early snows had already fallen. He was a lone messenger upon a mission of supreme importance. He was sent on ahead of the march of Anglo-Saxon civilization to clear the way for its progress westward. For more than forty years, the apparition of the French power on the western horizon had disturbed Virginia and the other colonies. Governor Spotswood saw the danger before 1716, and sounded the warning that the French were determined to bar the English from the region beyond the mountains. What Spotswood saw dimly had assumed definite form by 1753. The French were actually building forts on the Alleghany river, and rumors of their purpose to build others on the Greenbrier and the Holston were in circulation. It was time for Virginia to look to her frontiers; and as the winter of 1753 was settling its early snows upon the lone and dreary Alleghany mountain summits, the youth of twenty-one was riding westward through that wilderness to serve notice on the French to leave the Ohio valley. The crisis had come. The powers of England and France were about to clash, and a continent was the stake.

When Washington reached Gist's settlement of a dozen families on the Youghiogheny river, near the site of Connellsville, Pennsylvania, he secured the services of that veteran frontiersman as a guide. They pushed on, went by the site of the future city of Pittsburgh, and the observant eye of the youthful Washington noted the strategic importance of the situation. Their horses were left behind, and they ascended the Alleghany river, reached the French post, and Washington delivered the Governor of Virginia's letter to the officer in charge. The notice to quit the country was answered in writing, and with the paper in his pocket Washington and Gist set out upon their return. The weather was intensely cold, and ice was floating in the Alleghany river. Crossing the stream with the greatest difficulty, and in imminent peril of drowning, they pushed on through the snow and ice. Washington fortunately escaped a shot fired at him at close range by an Indian. Gist rushed upon the savage and caught him, and would have immediately killed him, but Washington induced Gist to spare the Indian's life, and he was allowed to make his escape in the forest.

The First Clash—Washington reached Williamsburg in midwinter, and delivered to Governor Dinwiddie the French answer. It was unsatisfactory, and when Washington explained the situation as he had observed it, among other things, that he had counted two hundred canoes drawn upon the bank of the Alleghany river ready for a descent to the Ohio as soon as the ice should go out in the spring, the Governor of Virginia saw that negotiations would amount to nothing, and that quick action in taking possession of strong posts on the Ohio river was necessary, if the French were to be turned back into Canada.

An expedition under Ensign Ward was set in motion toward the Ohio river as soon as possible, with instructions to build a fort at the junction of the Monongahela and Alleghany rivers, where Pittsburgh now stands. A force of soldiers, under Colonel Joshua Fry, was sent on the march to garrison the fort when ready. The builders under Ward went ahead of the soldiers, and when they reached the designated place they began the erection of the fort. Their work was cut short, however, for scarcely had they felled a few trees before an army of one thousand French and Indians, and eighteen cannon, floated down the Alleghany in canoes and boats. The French notified the Virginians to leave in one hour, and there was nothing to do but comply with the demand. The forks of the Ohio thus fell into the possession of the French.

George Washington was second in command of the expedition under Colonel Fry. He soon had the entire responsibility, for the commander was sick and not able to perform the duties of the office. West of the mountains they met scouts from whom they learned of the expulsion of Ward's men from the Monongahela region; but the soldiers who were to have garrisoned the fort, marched on, with the hope that they might arrive in time to dislodge the French before they had fortified the forks of the river. That hope was not to be realized. The enemy was strong in numbers and quick in movement. They did not wait on the site of Pittsburgh to be attacked by the Virginians, but marched east to meet them, and if possible, drive them back. The advance guards came in contact on the Youghiogheny river late in June, and in the first skirmish the French were defeated, and the leader of the party, Jumonville, was killed. That was the first bloodshed in a war which was to involve England and France in a conflict all over the world, wherever their armies and navies met. It is possible, however, to detail in this chapter only the occurrences which were of immediate concern to Western Virginia.

Fort Necessity—When the French took possession of the forks of the Ohio after the retreat of Ensign Ward's party, they commenced the erection of a fortified post which they called Fort Duquesne. Reinforcements arrived from Canada, and a force approximately seven hundred French and Indians was sent east. Meanwhile the brush with Jumonville's party occurred, and the French prepared to fight the Virginian army which had by that time reached the vicinity of the Monongahela river. Washington was in command, owing to the sickness of Colonel Fry who had charge of the expedition. The army contained fewer than four hundred men, largely Virginians, but some were from Pennsylvania and a few from South Carolina. It was already clearly understood that it was not Virginia's or Pennsylvania's quarrel alone but that the contest was between the two nations, England and France. All of the Indians were not on the French side, for a considerable number were with the English army.

When Washington learned through his scouts that the enemy was advancing in strong force from Fort Duquesne, he fell back to a point in Fayette county, Pennsylvania, just north of the Virginia and Pennsylvania line, and about fifty miles west of the site of Cumberland, Maryland. He selected a favorable place for a stand, threw up entrenchments, and called the place Fort Necessity. The enemy soon appeared, in larger numbers and with better arms than the English had. The battle which ensued was severe, and though Washington's troops were in trenches, the advantages were all against them. Heavy rain spoiled much of their powder and rendered some of their guns unserviceable. The trenches were partly filled with water, rendering them nearly untenable. The Indians and French climbed high in the surrounding trees and fired into the fort at an angle which brought the English under point-blank range. Washington kept up the unequal fight until he had lost about one-tenth of his men. He saw the uselessness of sacrificing more lives, and he opened negotiation for surrendering. The French offered liberal terms which were accepted. The soldiers retained their small arms, but not the artillery, and were permitted to march to Virginia. This surrender occurred on July 4, 1754, just twenty-two years before the Declaration of Independence.

The articles of capitulation which Washington signed caused embarrassment afterward. They were written in French, which language Washington did not understand, and one of the clauses referred to the death of Jumonville, and called it "assassination," and it passed that way. The translation made for Washington by his Dutch interpreter did not give the word's correct meaning. The French afterwards took advantage of that misapprehension and claimed that Washington had signed a paper making himself out a murderer.

Startling Proposition by the French—The retreat of Washington's army over the Alleghany mountains left the French in possession of all the country beyond. Their victory seemed to them an important one, and it would have been, if nothing had followed. They miscalculated the effect which the defeat of the few hundred men at Fort Necessity would have on the English, and thought the time was opportune for driving a good bargain. In January, 1755, the English received a startling proposition from the French to the effect that neither should occupy the country between the Alleghany mountains and the Ohio river. That territory now comprises the larger part of western Pennsylvania, and the whole of West Virginia except the eight counties east of the mountains. If the French proposition had been accepted it would have left that region of some forty or fifty thousand square miles, an uninhabited wilderness, separating the French possessions in Ohio and the country beyond, from the English on the Atlantic seaboard.

The design of the French was too easily seen through to deceive anyone. It would have given them all they wanted, and would have confined the English to the country east of the mountains. The English were not deceived, and they replied with a counter-proposition which was equally startling to the French. They proposed that France destroy all its forts in the Ohio valley as far west as the Wabash river; save the forts at Niagara and Crown Point; surrender Nova Scotia; and leave as a neutral strip the region between the bay of Fundy and the St. Lawrence river. France's reply was the dispatch of three thousand soldiers to America, and the English made a similar answer by sending an army under General Braddock.

It is interesting to speculate on what the result would have been if England had accepted France's proposal that the transmontane part of Virginia should be left unoccupied. It is not probable that the combined powers of England and France would have been able to keep settlers out of the region. They would have crossed the mountains at unguarded points, and ten soldiers would have been necessary to hold back one determined settler.

Braddock's Campaign—The march and defeat of General Braddock's army in the summer of 1755 deserve a larger place in the history of West Virginia than can be accorded here. The fate of the region in Virginia between the Alleghany mountains and the Ohio river hung in the balance that year, and for a time it looked as if the country would fall into the hands of France and become a part of Canada or a province like Canada. The English gained some success over the French in the north, but none in the Ohio valley. The defeat of the expedition under Fry and Washington the summer before was but a passing incident compared with the disastrous route of Braddock's army in 1755. It looked for a time as if the French and their Indian allies would not only overrun the western valleys but would overwhelm and destroy the settlements as far east as the Shenandoah valley. After the retreat of the army from Fort Necessity in 1754, the savages poured over the mountains and murdered many defenseless settlers; but in 1755 the whole country along the frontiers from the headwaters of the Tennessee river northward to Pennsylvania received murderous visitations. A volume would be inadequate to recite in detail the horrors that befell the unfortunate people between the Alleghanies and the Blue Ridge. The worst, however, came after Braddock's defeat, and an account of that campaign and defeat should come first in logical order.

Braddock brought an army with him from England, and landed at Alexandria, Virginia, in the spring of 1755. He was joined by troops from different colonies, principally Pennsylvanians and Virginians, and took up the march to the west with a long train of supplies. The general planned an extensive campaign. He said he would be west of the Alleghanies by early summer, would capture Fort Duquesne within three days after coming in sight of it, and would then invade Canada by way of the Alleghany river, and drive the French from their strongest forts in the north. His facility for bragging did not inspire unbounded confidence in his ability to perform. Washington who was one of his aids ventured to suggest how the Indians might best be fought, but his advice was rejected with sarcasm. A few weeks later, however, the dying general admitted that he had been wrong, but it was then too late to profit by Washington's advice.

Braddock sailed from Alexandria up the Potomac to the site of Washington and landed opposite where the White House now stands. The march was immediately commenced and was pushed west through Frederick, Maryland, and to the Potomac at Williamsport. The objective point was Wills Creek, now Cumberland, Maryland, but there being no road up the Potomac, the army crossed that stream and marched nearly due south almost to Winchester where it fell into the highway leading to Wills Creek. This road passed through Hampshire county and crossed the Potomac into Maryland at the mouth of Little Capon river, and followed the Maryland side of the Potomac to Wills Creek.

Vexatious delays made the march slow. It was six weeks behind time at Wills Creek. The distance from that point to Fort Duquesne was one hundred and thirty miles. The whole way led through a wilderness with scarcely a break. There was no road for wheeled vehicles. The Nemacolin path, an Indians' and traders' trail led from Wills 'Creek to the forks of the Ohio, but it was fit only for footmen and packhorses. Braddock set large numbers of his soldiers to work road building. He made a highway for wagons and artillery, but the country was so rough that an average of no more than five miles a day could be finished. The army toiled on. Braddock chafed at the delay but he could not be urged to greater progress by making a temporary road. He insisted that streams and ravines should be bridged and hillsides graded. The idea was firmly fixed in his mind that he was opening a permanent highway between the east and the west for the use of English colonies. He meant it to be a military road for the movement of armies in the years to come. His ideals were high. He was opening the first good wagon road from the Atlantic seaboard into the Mississippi valley. Washington had opened a makeshift of a road part of the way the year before. Although the unfortunate Braddock missed many of his calculations, he builded greater even than he knew when he made that road across the Alleghanies in June, 1755. The star of empire moved west with him as he toiled five miles ahead between the rising and setting of each day's sun. There were to be temporary checks, but the Anglo-Saxon was on the march to the Pacific.

Braddock's march ended suddenly and disastrously on July 9 when within seven miles of Fort Duquesne. The Indians and French set an ambuscade where the town of Braddock is now situated, in the suburbs of Pittsburgh, and attacked so suddenly that the English army was quickly thrown into confusion. It is not believed that the combined French and Indians numbered one-half of Braddock's army. The ambuscade, it is said, was not set in expectation that it would prove more than temporarily successful. All that was hoped was that the English would receive a check. The attack, it is believed, was planned to take place at the river crossing a half mile away, but Braddock was already over when the French arrived, and on the spur of the moment, the ambuscade was set in a ravine which the English army was just entering.

Confusion quickly produced panic. The troops brought from England were soon huddled in helpless fear, firing by volleys into the tree tops, or into the ranks of the Virginia and Pennsylvania troops who were trying to hold the ground. Braddock had placed all his hopes in his regulars. He had declared to Washington that it was impossible that Indians could produce any effect upon them. There is no doubt that the regulars were brave enough, but the suddenness of the attack, its ferocity, and its mystery, utterly bewildered them. They could see no enemy. The deadly rifles of the foe rang in the woods, and men fell fast on all sides, but no foe appeared. To the regulars it seemed like fighting invisible spirits. Some of the survivors afterwards declared they had not seen a single Frenchman or Indian during the entire battle.

The colonial troops, and particularly the Virginians, understood that kind of fighting. They had faced it all their lives. It was precisely the kind of attack against which Braddock had been warned, and he had answered the warning with a sneer and a slur. He saw his mistake when he realized that the battle was lost. Washington had collected the Virginians and had fought until all but thirty of his two hundred and forty men had been killed, and he had succeeded in holding the enemy in the woods until what was left of Braddock's regulars had made their escape from the slaughter pen, had crossed the river, and were in full flight on the back track. Braddock was carried along mortally wounded. He had shown no cowardice or indecision. When the horse he rode was shot, he mounted another and repeated this three times, until he was too severely wounded to fight longer, and then the flying soldiers carried him from the field and across the Monongahela which a few hours earlier that morning he had forded in full expectation that the walls of Fort Duquesne would be in view before sunset.

Washington had two horses shot under him, and four bullets pierced his clothes, but he came off at the head of the thirty Virginians and turned his back upon the field where the battle had been lost. Few of the wounded and none of the dead were brought away. There was no time for it. Flushed with victory the French and Indians swarmed out of the woods which had concealed them, and poured down to the ford in pursuit of the fugitives, until checked by the fire of a few soldiers who had rallied to cover the retreat.

The English left seven hundred and fourteen dead or dying on the battlefield which was one-third of the army. The Indians killed nearly all of the wounded. The bones of the dead lay unburied for three years. The retreating army fled as rapidly as possible in the direction of Fort Cumberland, as Wills Creek was called at that time, its name having recently been changed. Braddock was carried eighty miles before he died. He was buried near Fort Necessity. Colonel Dunbar was on the road with a second army, marching after Braddock. The retreating army met the fresh troops coming up. No rally was attempted, but Dunbar turned about and joined in the retreat. So great was the consternation that stores worth half a million dollars were destroyed to keep them from falling into the hands of the enemy which was not within seventy-five miles. The stores could have been easily hauled back to Fort Cumberland; but so complete and so senseless was the destruction that it became necessary to send to Fort Cumberland and bring up a supply of flour to feed the army while retreating to that place. Colonel Dunbar was then in command. Instead of halting at Fort Cumberland and reorganizing the army, he continued his flight until he reached Philadelphia. When he met the retreating army on the road, if he had, like Sheridan, exclaimed, "turn, boys, we are going back," there is no apparent reason why he might not have captured Fort Duquesne.

Panic on the Frontiers—The consternation which followed when it became known on the frontiers that Braddock's army had retreated and that Dunbar had fled with the troops to Philadelphia, has been many times described in history and story. It was a momentous crisis in the border settlements of Virginia. The frontier stretched from Cumberland, Maryland, to Tennessee. Every settlement and every cabin was in immediate danger. The attacks by Indians had been bold before, but it was apparent to everybody that danger was many fold greater than before the battle. It was believed that the savages would speedily pour over the mountains and fall on exposed settlements, and that belief was soon proved to be well founded.

Washington had halted at Fort Cumberland, and with what soldiers remained, he strengthened the walls and prepared to resist an attack. However, there was no pursuit in force by the enemy, whose army returned after the battle to Fort Duquesne to celebrate the victory. Small parties attacked the settlements and many murders were committed, but no large force invaded the frontiers; and it was with feeling of relief that cold weather came in the fall of 1755 and ended the danger for that time. Indians were poor winter travelers because their clothing was mean and they suffered from cold. Winter was the time when the people on the frontiers felt measurably safe.

Governor Dinwiddie wrote to the Lords of Trade in England recommending as a means of protecting the exposed frontiers that a chain of forts be built along the Alleghany range of mountains from the head of the Potomac to the Holston river. It was believed that with a sufficient number of such forts well garrisoned, the depredations by the enemy would materially decrease. Some time elapsed before arrangements were perfected for building the forts, even after the plan was approved. Washington was placed in charge of measures for defense of the frontiers, and gradually the work went on. The forts were never all built, but several were, and garrisons were placed in them. The correspondence on the subject between Washington and Governor Dinwiddie and others was voluminous and throws much light upon affairs in the troubled region at that time. A perusal of that correspondence at this day will convey the impression that the forts as means of defense fell far short of expectation, and as defensive measures they had little value. The Indians were able to pass between the forts which were necessarily many miles apart, and fall by surprise upon exposed settlements far in the rear of the fortified places.

Expedition to the Ohio—An expedition was planned in Virginia in the winter of 1755, after the defeat of Braddock, for the purpose of striking a blow against Shawnee Indian towns in Ohio. A good deal of mystery has surrounded the affair. It is better understood now than it was a hundred years ago, but still it seems more like a myth or legend than like history. In one particular it is worthy to be remembered, for it was the first English military expedition to the Ohio river south of Pittsburgh.

When Braddock failed, the plan of another invasion of the Indian country was discussed by Governor Dinwiddie and others. The scheme was the Governor's. Andrew Lewis was placed in command of about three hundred and fifty men and was dispatched from Fort Frederick, in Augusta county, to attack villages of the Shawnee Indians supposed to be situated in Ohio, opposite the mouth of the Big Sandy river, which now forms the boundary between West Virginia and Kentucky. The march from Fort Frederick was about two hundred miles, through woods all the way. The start was made February 18, 1756, and the army was in the wilderness about a month, and returned without crossing the Ohio river. Part of the march was through territory now in West Virginia, and it is supposed that Kentucky was touched near the mouth of the Big Sandy river. Tug Fork was named by soldiers on the expedition who cut up buffalo skins there and ate them to save themselves from starving. It is not definitely known why the army turned back without crossing the Ohio. It has been said that a messenger from

Governor Dinwiddie overtook the expedition with orders to return. That is doubtful. The expedition probably turned back because the soldiers were starving. They lost most of their supplies by the overturning of canoes in crossing a river, and were reduced to the necessity of eating their horses. The expedition broke up by desertions before its return, and many of the men perished from cold and hunger. There was a belief prevalent at the time that the expedition had been sent on a fool's errand to attack Indian towns which had no existence. Andrew Lewis, who commanded the expedition, was eighteen years later in command at the battle of Point Pleasant.

The Enemy's Stronghold—The French understood how to use the Indians to the best possible advantage. The savages were kept in close touch with the depots of supplies which were then maintained in Canada and the western valleys. Food was furnished the ever-hungry children of the forest, and blankets and ammunition were supplied with a generosity which won the good will and faithful devotion of the Indians. Their wrongs at the hands of the English were kept ever fresh in their memories, and they were urged to seek revenge for the past and security for the future by breaking up as many settlements as possible. The trading posts established by the French were small and far apart, and they did not excite in the Indian's mind the distrust which was roused by the presence of the English settlements. The French occupied some parts of the region but did not take it all; while the English both occupied and took. The Frenchman's trading post was a fort, a storehouse, and a few huts where Indians were welcome to camp and loaf to their heart's content; but the Englishman's settlement had no place for the Indian and he was made as unwelcome as possible. The result of it all was that the shiftless savages much preferred the French to the English. Some of the far-seeing among the natives, however, would have kept both French and English out of the country if they could, for they recognized both as robbers who were bent on taking the country. One of them stated the matter very plainly to Christopher Gist by asking where the Indians' land lay since the English claimed all on one side of the river and the French all on the other. Another untutored child of the wilderness thought he recognized a similitude in a pair of scissors, and compared the English to one blade, the French to the other, while the Indians were like the cloth that was cut in bits by the contact of the blades.

On the whole, the Indians welcomed rather than resented the presence of the French, and gathered about the forts and depots of supplies, and helping themselves to arms, clothing, and food, they went forth upon the warpath. Fort Duquesne was the central hive from which the savages swarmed to attack the Virginia frontiers. From that stronghold they received their inspiration and their sinews of war. It was clear to thoughtful men in Virginia that little was to be accomplished by fighting the marauders after they had invaded the settlements. Every advantage was on their side. They came in the night, hid by day, and waited for favorable opportunities to attack. They took few chances, for they were able to pick the time and place, and when they had done their bloody work, they could glide back into the forest, and successful pursuit seldom occurred.

Washington was one of those who saw the futility of waiting on the frontiers to be attacked. In season and out of season he urged upon the Virginia government, and upon the English government that no relief was possible until the stronghold at Fort Duquesne was broken up root and branch. He began the agitation immediately after the retreat of Braddock's army. In 1756, and again in 1757, he urged the sending of another expedition over the Alleghany mountains to strike a blow that would end the trouble by driving the French out of the Ohio valley. Expeditions against strongholds further north were urged also, but Virginia's immediate concern was the breaking up of the establishment at the forks of the Ohio.

In 1756 Captain Jeremiah Smith with twenty men met some success in a fight with a much larger party of Indians on Lost river in what is now Hardy county. The enemy was led by a Frenchman who was killed in the encounter, as were five Indians.

A second party of Indians in the region met a reverse a few days later at the hands of Captain Joshua Lewis and a company of eighteen men. Soon afterward, marauding parties of Indians and French committed depredations near the site of Martinsburg, Berkeley county. The success attending the Indians in these affairs was not encouraging, but in almost all other instances where they entered the settlements in large or small numbers, they did great injury. The battle of the Trough near Old Fields, Hardy county, cost the settlers many lives. Captain Mercer fell into an ambuscade on Capon river, Hampshire county, in 1757, and his company was almost annihilated. Many of the French and Indians implicated in that affair were on horseback. They had stolen their mounts from the various settlements. The Indian chief, Killbuck, was very active on the waters of the upper Potomac. For two years he hung about the settlements much of the time, retiring occasionally to Fort Duquesne to procure supplies. He commanded bands of sixty or seventy warriors, and was too strong for the small parties of settlers to pursue with hope of success.

Fort Seybert Massacre—In 1758 Killbuck invaded what is now Pendleton county, coming across the Alleghany mountains over the old Seneca warpath. He first surprised a small fort at Upper Tract, which he burned. Not one of the occupants was left alive to tell the story, and the particular manner of the capture and destruction of the blockhouse was never known, except that the place was left a heap of ashes. A few coins found among the charcoal a century and a quarter later were all that the savages overlooked. They then moved a few miles further to the south fork of the South Branch, now called Moorefield river, where they appeared before Fort Seybert, which occupied a bluff overlooking the valley. The fort was a place of refuge erected by the settlers, who continued to live in that exposed place for two years after prudence should have led them to leave the country. The fort was a log house surrounded by a circular wall of logs planted on end. Even yet the almost obliterated outline of the circular wall can be made out.

The settlers were warned of danger in time to repair to the fort before the Indians appeared. Only one gun was fired in its defense, and that wounded one of the assailants who was crouching behind a rock forty yards away. The place possessed means of defense, and might have held out, but the commandant was seized with fear, and ordered the fort surrendered. Killbuck entered into a parley and promised that the occupants of the fort would be unharmed if they surrendered without further resistance. In spite of protests from some of the inmates, the door was thrown open. One girl concealed herself behind the door, and in the subsequent excitement, slipped into the yard and escaped. The Indians marched the prisoners a few hundred yards up the hill, and under an oak tree which still stands to mark the fatal spot, all were tomahawked but one boy who made a desperate dash for his life and ran a mile before he was overtaken. His expertness as a runner gave him favor in the eyes of the savages, and his life was spared, and he was carried into captivity. Most of the details of the massacre were learned from him when he returned years after. He was James Dyer and his descendants yet live in that country.

At the first alarm, a messenger was dispatched across the Shenandoah mountains for help. The distance to the settlements in the Shenandoah valley, about the site of Harrisburg, was some forty miles. Troops were hurried to the relief of the fort, but arrived too late. The place had been burned, and the trail which was taken by the retreating savages was followed through Greenawalt Gap, thence to the mouth of Seneca creek where Killbuck's band entered the Seneca warpath and crossed the mountains the way they had come. The warrior who was wounded in the attack on the fort was carried seven miles to Greenawalt Gap, where he died. They put the body in a shallow cave, and walled up the entrance with rocks, and a century later parts of his disjointed skeleton filled with fear the mountaineers who were accustomed to peer through the opening in the rude wall. Some part of the wall remains to this day, but all signs of the skeleton have disappeared.

The destruction of the settlements at Upper Tract and at Fort Seybert well nigh completed the breaking up of all signs of civilized man between the Alleghany mountains and the Shenandoah valley. Two forts only held out, except the military posts defended by garrisons, and few settlers remained. Those who had not fled east to places of safety, were killed or carried into captivity. The settlement in the vicinity of Romney, the center of which was Pearsall's Fort, and another some twenty-five miles east, near the forks of Capon river, the center of which was Edward's Fort, still held out.

Places of Refuge—The places of refuge, usually called forts, were often nothing more than log houses with holes cut in the walls through which to fire upon assailants. In time of danger, the people for several miles around hastened to these places of refuge. Usually there was no regular garrison, but the occupants defended themselves the best they could. At times the militia was called into service, and a temporary garrison was placed in the rude forts. Between 1753 and 1760, that is, during the time that the French and Indian war created a constant peril, forts and strong houses were built in all the important settlements in the territory now embraced in West Virginia's eight counties east of the Alleghany mountains. A fairly complete list and brief account of these forts follow. In some instances the exact location of the forts cannot now be determined. In other cases there were more than one fort of a certain name.

Ashby's Fort stood on Petterson's creek, in Mineral county, near the present town of Frankfort. John Ashby, from whom the fort was named, appears to have been living in that vicinity in 1748. The fort was built in 1755 to protect settlers who were on the extreme frontier and exposed to the direct attacks of the first savages who crossed the mountains after Braddock's defeat. Fort Ohio was some ten miles from it on one side, and Fort Cumberland about twenty-five miles on the other, while Pearsall's Fort was thirteen miles east. In the winter of 1755 a garrison of twenty-one men under Captain Charles Lewis was stationed there. In 1756 Indians committed depredations almost under the walls of the fort. An Indian chief whom the English nicknamed "The Crane," because of his unusually long legs, knew Captain Ashby personally, and took it upon himself to kill or capture him. After hanging around the fort several days waiting for an opportunity to accomplish his purpose, he discovered the captain unarmed some distance from the fort, and gave chase. Ashby fled for his life with the Indian in pursuit, but in spite of "The Crane's" reputation for fleetness, he was unable to lessen the distance between himself and the sprinting captain. Finally he gave it up, and in his disgust and disappointment bellowed: "Run, Jack Ashby, run!" Ashby looked back as he replied: "You fool, did you think I had boots on?"

Fort Buttermilk was one of the chain of fortified places built under Washington's supervision to protect the settlers after Braddock's defeat. Captain Thomas Waggoner built it in 1756, and it stood in the South Branch valley, three miles above Moorefield, Hardy county. It was some miles above Fort Pleasant, and it had eighteen men in the disastrous fight, called the battle of the Trough in 1756, and most of them were killed. It was sometimes spoken of as Fort Waggoner, after its builder. A garrison of seventy men was stationed there, under Captain Waggoner, in 1757. The fort seems to have been destroyed or abandoned later in the war.

A small place of refuge which seems never to have had a regular garrison, was located near the forks of Capon river in the present borders of Hampshire county. It was seldom mentioned, and there is reason to believe that it was abandoned about 1757, and that the settlers who built it for their protection moved to a more secure place.

Fort Cox, named as is supposed from Frend Cox, who owned the land where it stood, was built in 1755 at the mouth of Little Capon river. It was a place of considerable importance during the French and Indian war, but was never attacked. It was a depot of supplies for the surrounding region. Twelve years after the close of the war the fort had disappeared.

Fort Edwards, in Hampshire county, stood near the present village of Capon Bridge. It appears to have had a garrison of militia part of the time during the war from 1754 to 1759, and at one time had at least one hundred men within its walls. It was from this fort that Captain Mercer sallied in 1756 to attack a party of French and Indians in the vicinity. He fell into an ambuscade and lost many of his men.

Fort Evans, two miles south of Martinsburg, Berkeley county, was too far east to feel the full weight of Indian hostility, but early in the war it was attacked while few men were in it. The assailants were beaten off, and no other attack was made on the place.

Three miles below Romney, Furman Fort was located on the South Branch. It was built by and named from William Furman, who was afterwards killed by Indians. The fort was never attacked. It was three miles north of Pearsall's Fort.

Early in the war a number of settlers whose farms were in the vicinity of Petersburg, Grant county, built a small place of refuge, called George's Fort. Though it was never attacked, murders were committed almost within rifle shot of it. It is not believed that this fort was occupied later than the year 1757, and there is no account that it was ever garrisoned by soldiers.

Hedges' Fort, a place which seems to have been of minor importance, was situated on Back creek, Berkeley county, on the road which now leads from Martinsburg to Berkeley Springs.

Fort Hopewell was a settlers' place of refuge located on the north fork of the South Branch, about six miles above Petersburg, Grant county. It was there early in the French and Indian war and was attacked, but the date of its building does not appear. The assailants made good their retreat when a relieving force under Captain Waggoner appeared in the vicinity. Hopewell Gap, sometimes called Owers Gap, where the north forks breaks through New Creek mountains, probably perpetuate the name of the fort.

Fort McKenzie, named from Captain Robert McKenzie, was in Hampshire county, and is believed to have been on the South Branch, but its exact site has not been identified.

Fort Maidstone was built near the mouth of Capon river, in the present county of Morgan, in 1755 or 1756. For a short time in 1757 it had a garrison of seventy men under Captain Robert Stewart. There is no account that the Indians and French committed depredations in its vicinity.

Fort Neally, a small place in Berkeley county, stood on Opequon creek. It was one of the few forts captured by assault. In the fall of 1756 the Indians attacked and took it, and murdered most of the inmates, and carried others away.

Fort Ohio, named from the Ohio Company which built it, was originally a frontier storehouse or depot for merchandise on its way to the western Indians. It was built in 1750, and stood near the site of the village of Ridgely, Mineral county, on the Northwestern turnpike. The location of the storehouse at that place has historical importance, not regarding the French and Indian war, but in matters of trade routes across the Alleghany mountains. It has been generally supposed that the Ohio Company transported its Indian merchandise west from Wills Creek, or Cumberland, Maryland, over the old Nemacolin Indian path to the forks of the Ohio. The building of Fort Ohio indicates that the Ohio Company's traders used the route afterwards known as the McCullough's trail as well as the Nemacolin path. Fort Ohio stood on or near the McCullough trail, and at one time it was stocked with sixteen thousand dollars worth of merchandise. The Governor of Virginia in 1754, after Washington's retreat from Fort Necessity, ordered that the

Ohio Company's storehouse be taken possession of and converted into a fort, to be defended with cannon. There is no account that it was ever attacked by the Indians and French.

The fort built near the site of Romney by Job Pearsall has been frequently mentioned in this chapter. The fort was built the first year of the French and Indian war. It was a post of great importance, and part of the time had a regular garrison. Indians committed depredations near it, but never made a direct attack. It was one of a chain of forts only a few miles apart along the South Branch from its mouth upward beyond the present Pendleton county line. Historically, it was the most important of them all.

Fort Pearson or Peterson was near the mouth of Mill creek, Grant county, on the road from Petersburg to Franklin. It was built in the fall of 1756. The place was not often mentioned and it was probably of little importance. It was built by order of a council of war held at Staunton in the summer of 1756. The fort was in Augusta county, two miles south of the Hampshire county line at that time. It appears to have been a link in the chain of forts from the Potomac river to Tennessee, but it is not known that it was ever garrisoned with soldiers. Fort Pleasant stood at Old Fields, Hardy county. Captain Thomas Waggoner built it in 1756 under orders from Washington, and it was a place of considerable strength, consisting of cabins, blockhouses, and palisades. One of the cabins which formed a corner of the fort was reported standing a few years ago. The battle of the Trough was fought in 1756 in sight of this place, and a large part of the garrison, who were lured into the open by the Indians, were killed. The fort was not attacked.

Ruddell's Fort, often written Riddle's, was a small stockade on Lost river, Hardy county, and was built in 1755 or 1756. Information on the subject is not explicit, but the fort was probably named from Stephen Ruddell, who lived in that vicinity. Captain Jeremiah Smith defeated a party of French and Indians in that vicinity in 1756. The

Frenchman in command was killed, and in his pocket was found a commission directing him to attack Fort Frederick, in the Shenandoah valley.

Sellers' Fort, named from Thomas Sellers, on or near whose land it was built in 1756, was situated in Mineral county at the mouth of Patterson creek. It was garrisoned that year by thirty men, and repelled a sudden attack by French and Indians.

Fort Seybert and the fort at Upper Tract, in Pendleton county, have been already described, in the account of their destruction in 1758 by Indians under Killbuck.

Fort Warden, near the present village of Wardensville, Hardy county, was burned by Indians in 1758, but the particulars of the affair are not clear.

Fort Williams stood six miles below Romney on the South Branch. It was not mentioned in connection with any attack by Indians. It was three miles below Furman's Fort.

This list of twenty-three forts, built in West Virginia's eight counties east of the Alleghany mountains during the French and Indian war probably does not include all. Others seem to be referred to in early accounts without naming them. Numerous as they were, they were inadequate to afford security to the settlers near them. One by one the settlements were broken up as the war progressed, until, in the fall of 1758, much of the region had been depopulated. Had the war continued a year or two longer it is not improbable that most of what is now West Virginia territory east of the mountains would have been depopulated. Garrisons might and probably would have continued to hold some of the posts, but the continuance of a farming population would have been impossible. Many of the people had fallen victims to the Indians, but a larger number had returned to the Shenandoah valley or further east. When peace was restored, most of them came back to their abandoned farms to find their buildings burned and nothing but the bare land left of their former improvements.

The Fall of Fort Duquesne—For three years Washington urged upon the Virginia government and upon the British commander-in-chief in America the absolute necessity of destroying the French and Indian power at Fort Duquesne, and in 1758 he was gratified to see a movement set on foot for that purpose. During the three years intervening between 1754 and 1758 the British military forces had not been idle. The war was carried into Canada and the French strongholds in that country were one by one attacked and captured. The French made marvellously effective use of the means at their command. The British over-measured them in resources, but the French fought on the defensive, and contested every step's advance by the British. The French power in America was not wholly broken until Quebec fell into the hands of the British, which occurred after the capture of Fort Duquesne in 1758; but repeated reverses had much weakened them before they were called upon to defend their post at the forks of the Ohio. They did not enter into that campaign with the assurance they had shown during the three preceding years in the Ohio valley. During those three years they had been fighting in offensive warfare along the Virginia and Pennsylvania frontiers; but in 1758 they found themselves fighting upon the defensive, and realized, like Hannibal of old, that "the hope and courage of assailants are always greater than of those who act upon the defensive." The French began to withdraw their war parties from the frontiers in 1758, and prepared to wage a war of life and death near the walls of Fort Duquesne.

General Joseph Forbes was in command of the force that was to march over the Alleghanies to attack the French on the Ohio. He brought across the ocean with him twelve hundred Scotch Highlanders as the nucleus of his army of invasion. Virginia added nineteen hundred militia, and Pennsylvania twenty-five hundred. Four hundred came from other provinces, making a total of six thousand men, nearly three times the force that followed Braddock. The settlers on the long-tormented frontiers watched that army take up its march toward the mountains, over whose summits the Indians had poured for three years, and there was a fervent hope from Pennsylvania to North Carolina that the end of the war was near at hand. It was one of the largest armies which had been set in motion in America up to that time, and it was well equipped with artillery and other supplies. Its progress was followed with keenest interest as it marched through the settlements westward, and in due time Fort Cumberland, now Cumberland, Maryland, was reached. That was the extreme western limit of the frontier, and beyond that lay the same wilderness that had killed Washington's plans in 1754, swallowed up Braddock's dreams of victory in 1755, and it stretched as dark and silent as it did then. One large region in that wilderness was called "The Shades of Death." The anxious people watched General Forbes's six thousand soldiers file past Fort Cumberland, and disappear in the wilderness and among the mountains. Then came the period of waiting for news. The wait was long.

The road which Braddock had opened three years before from Fort Cumberland to the vicinity of Fort Duquesne remained. White men had not since used it, except such of the French as had accompanied bands of marauding Indians in forays against the settlements; but scouts had from time to time reported that the road had become a highway for Indian war parties, and that the grades on the mountains had been tramped hard by the incessant coming and going of moccasined feet. General Forbes decided, against the voices of most of his officers, that he would not go west over the Braddock road. His decision was looked upon as a military mistake, but his decision was the court of last resort, and it was accepted by his army. It turned out that no disastrous consequences resulted from the stubborn Scotch general's determination to cut a new road from Fort Cumberland to the forks of the Ohio; but the margin between success and failure of the expedition was at one time very small, owing to the long time required to open the new road.

In fifty days the army advanced only fifty miles, and the end of the journey was seventy-five or eighty days away, at the rate at which the expedition had moved after leaving Fort Cumberland. General Forbes insisted upon grading all the hills and bridging the ravines and streams. He considered that he was constructing a permanent highway, and he wanted to build it on scientific principles. The fact that the heavy frosts of autumn had already bared the trees on the mountains and had given warning that in a little time the ground would be buried under snow, did not induce the general to increase his speed. He spoke of going into winter quarters and postponing the rest of the march until the following summer. He was sick, and had been ailing nearly all the time during the march. He could not ride on horseback or in the wagons, and it was necessary to carry him on a litter while he inspected the road-building, and kept along with the army's slow march.

Washington acted as second in command, and the transaction of most of the army's business devolved on him. He was a man of remarkable patience, but the slow progress taxed this quality to its limit. Late in the fall information was received that Fort Duquesne was in poor condition and that its garrison was reduced to seven hundred men. It looked like an opportunity to strike, and on November 5 Washington was permitted to take twenty-five hundred men and make a dash for the forks of Ohio. He built eight miles of road in a day, and on November 24 he was near enough Fort Duquesne to hear a heavy explosion at night. The meaning of it was not known at the time, but it was found that the French had blown up their magazine at the fort. They despaired of holding out if they waited for the assault which was sure to be delivered in a few days, and decided to escape while they could. They loaded what their boats would carry, and embarking on the Ohio floated down with the current. They had set the fort on fire and it was soon in ruins. While the embers were yet smouldering, Washington's army came up and took possession. The last boat load of the French was just disappearing round a bend in the river. The fleet was bound for Illinois, where the French still held posts. The Indians who had swarmed in and about the fort saw the handwriting on the wall in time to disperse in the wilderness. Winter was at hand, and they realized that the French would no longer be able to feed and clothe them.

The blow broke the power of the French in the Ohio valley. They held a few posts hundreds of miles further west, but they were too remote to be a menace to the Virginia frontiers. The day of deliverance for the distressed settlements east of the Alleghanies had come. The blow was fatal to the enemies of the settlers. The Indians had lost their leadership and inspiration when the French left them.

A few more blows were delivered against the power of France, and the English became masters of the valleys of the Ohio, the Mississippi, and the whole of Canada as far north and west as they cared to claim it. The continent had been won for the English race. The French began more than half a century before with a scheme to confine the English colonies to the Atlantic coast, while they hoped to hold all west of the Appalachian range of mountains, and all north of the Great Lakes for themselves. Their scheme ended in the loss of every foot of land they had ever held on the North American continent. The war benefitted the English colonies in two ways. It not only opened the west for them, but it taught them to trust one another, and to fight side by side when there was a common interest to serve. From that time the growth of the idea of union among the colonies began, and twenty years later it resulted in the achievement of their independence.

The fate of that part of West Virginia west of the mountains hung in the balance until Fort Duquesne fell. The way was then cleared for colonization which soon followed. Had the territory fallen into the hands of France, the character of the inhabitants would have been different and the whole future history of the region would have been changed. In 1761 the French and Indian war was formally ended by treaty between England and France.

THE PONTIAC WAR.

The Indians refused to abide by the terms of the treaty of peace signed by England and France. The latter country supposed that it was binding its allies, and that the savages would lay down their arms and agree to the peace. The Indians did not at first understand it, and when later they saw what the French meant, they declined to be bound. During the two years from 1761 to 1763 the savages remained comparatively quiet. They knew that the French had left off fighting and that most of the soldiers had quit the country, but they expected the French to come back with new armies and renew the struggle. It at last slowly dawned on the natives that France was gone for good. Then it was that the Indians decided to renew the war on their own account, and the short and ferocious struggle which ensued is known as Pontiac's war, so named from its organizer, who was by birth a Delaware Indian but had been adopted by the Ottawas and ultimately became their chief. He has been considered by some as the ablest Indian on the American continent. Though all do not accord him a place so high, none deny that as an organizer he has had few equals in any race of people.

The war was nearly all outside the borders of West Virginia, and at no time was the existence of the State in jeopardy, and for that reason the events of the war will be here given in brief outline only.

When the English moved west through Canada and the present State of Michigan to take possession of the posts surrendered by the French, the Indians rebelled and refused to recognize the authority of the English or the French either. Pontiac met an English officer on Lake Erie and told him to go back, for the country belonged to the Indians, and the French had no right to cede it or the English to receive it. The English refused to turn back, and from that day Pontiac worked to organize the tribes for war. The profound secrecy of his work was the most amazing part of it. In only one instance did any of his secrets filter through to the ears of the English whom he was about to strike. In that instance an Indian girl betrayed the conspiracy to an English officer in whom she felt an interest, but the betrayal came too late to save more than one of the doomed garrisons.

Pontiac's organization included practically all of the Indians from the Mississippi river to the Alleghany mountains, and from the Tennessee river northward into Canada. His purpose was to massacre all the English in the region, as nearly on the same day as possible. Deception and treachery were to be the means employed. The scheme was executed with diabolical precision.

Fort Sandusky near Lake Erie was surprised and captured May 16, 1763. Nine days later a fort at the mouth of St. Joseph's river was taken, and two days later Fort Miami on the Maumee river fell into the hands of Pontiac. On June 1 Fort Ouatamon in Indiana was surprised and captured, and Machilimackinac, far north in Michigan, was taken by treachery on June 2. Venango in Pennsylvania was destroyed and not one of the garrison escaped to tell the tale. Fort Le Boeuf in the same region shared the fate of Venango on June 18. Four days later Presque Isle, now Erie, Pennsylvania, shared the fate of the rest. Cornstalk, a Shawnee chief from Ohio, penetrated to the settlements on the Greenbrier river, where the tactics which had proved so fatally successful were again tried. The Indians came in the guise of friendship and were entertained and fed by the unsuspecting people until at a given signal, the savages drew their tomahawks and massacred all on whom they could lay their hands. The few that escaped fled across the mountains into Augusta county, and there was not a white person left on the Greenbrier river, or anywhere else west of the mountains in the present territory of West Virginia, except an occasional hunter like the Pringles who at that time were camped in the unbroken wilderness and had cleared no fields to betray their presence.

Three forts held out against the attacks of Pontiac's conspirators, Detroit, Forts Pitt and Ligonier in Pennsylvania. Detroit had warning from an Indian girl, and when the Indians came, expecting to be admitted into the fort without question, they were met with drawn swords. The savages had sawed-off guns under their blankets, but dared not use them when the garrison was found ready. Pontiac besieged Detroit for a year, but failed to starve it out. Fort Ligonier did not fall into the trap, and the Indians besieged that also, but without success. They made a determined effort to take Fort Pitt. They tried treachery, deception, and direct assault. They dug holes in the river bank, and burying themselves out of sight, kept up a fire for weeks. They attempted to set fire to the fort by shooting burning arrows upon the roof. They offered the garrison safe passage across the mountains to the settlements if they would evacuate the fort, but they found negotiations as fruitless as assaults had been.

On the last day of July, 1763, the Indians raised the siege of Fort Pitt and disappeared. It was learned in a short time why they had done so. General Bouquet was marching to the relief of Fort Pitt with five hundred men and a large supply train, and the savages had gone forward to meet him and give battle. As General Bouquet marched west from Fort Cumberland, through Pennsylvania, he found the settlements broken up, the houses burned and the crops unharvested. Desolation was on every side, showing how completely the Indians had carried out, in that region, their purpose to destroy all settlements west of the mountains. When the army reached Fort Ligonier the Indians had abandoned the siege and were gone. Bouquet marched forward to Bushy run, where the savages made a sudden and fierce attack. The battle continued into the second day, and the English found themselves completely surrounded and in danger of annihilation. A stratagem saved the day. The English set troops in ambuscade in an advantageous position, and by feigning retreat, drew the Indians into the trap when they were completely routed, and the way for the westward march was opened. General Bouquet had lost so many of his packhorses that he was compelled to destroy part of his stores for want of means to transport them. After a four days' march the army reached Fort Pitt.

The tide had turned against the savages. They could no longer accomplish anything by treachery and surprises, and in open battle they were unable to stand against the forces which the English were sending against them. General Amherst, the British commander-in-chief in America, gave voice to his rage against the Indians when he declared them "the vilest race of beings that ever infested the earth, and whose riddance from it must be esteemed a meritorious act for the good of mankind." He said they were unfit for allies and unworthy of respect as enemies, and he sent orders to the officers on the frontiers to take no prisoners, but kill all who could be caught. He offered a reward of five hundred dollars to anyone who would kill Pontiac, and caused the offer of the reward to be proclaimed at Detroit.

The end of the war was near. In the spring of 1764 General Bouquet collected an army of two thousand at Pittsburgh and invaded the Indian country in Ohio. The force was more than the savages dared face in fight, and they resorted to negotiations, hoping to persuade the army to turn back. Bouquet received their overtures, but continued to advance upon their towns and settlements. They realized that resistance was useless, and they were obliged to accept the terms which he offered. They made peace, and gave up all the white prisoners held by them. More than two hundred were restored to their people. It is probable that the Indians would not have consented to the peace had they not lost all hope of help from the French. For some time after the war began they believed that the King of France would send soldiers and supplies to assist them. That hope was finally abandoned when De Neyon, a French officer in Illinois, wrote a letter to Pontiac, telling him that peace existed between France and England, and the Indians need expect no help from France. He advised Pontiac to make peace. This letter was received while the siege of Detroit was in progress, and the substance of the communication became known among the tribes and greatly discouraged them. The failure of the three sieges, Fort Pitt, Fort Ligonier, and Detroit, further discouraged the Indians by teaching them that they could not contend against white men in the open, though success might be attained by treachery and ambuscade. Ten years of peace on the Virginia frontiers followed the close of the Pontiac war.

THE DUNMORE WAR

THE DUNMORE WAR.

There was peace on the Virginia frontier from the close of Pontiac's war in 1764 till the Dunmore war in 1774, ten years. During that ten years a wonderful shifting of the frontier had taken place. The line of settlements had moved foward farther in those ten years than in the century that had gone before. The year 1764 found the outposts of the settlements along the eastern base of the Alleghany mountains. Before that time a few adventurers had crossed the barrier and had established camps or built cabins in the wilderness beyond; but such were too few and too widely dispersed to be classed as settlements, and whatever they had been earlier, they had ceased to exist before the peace of 1764 had been declared. The summer of that year found the western part of Virginia uninhabited. In another chapter the history of the pouring of settlers over the mountains prior to 1774 is given. When the spring of 1774 came it found the frontier at the Ohio river instead of at the eastern base of the Alleghanies as ten years before. From their country beyond the Ohio, and southward and northward, the Indians had looked without much concern upon the settlements advancing miles at a bound until they were upon the bank of the Ohio at Wheeling, at the mouth of the Little Kanawha, at many places between, and settlements were creeping down the Kanawha valley from the Greenbrier, but had not yet actually reached the Ohio in that quarter.

Surveyors—The Indians had by treaty relinquished their claims to Western Virginia, between the mountains and the river, and they showed no disposition to interfere with the white people in their occupation of the region; but these people were beginning to show signs that they did not mean to stop at the Ohio, or at least that they did not intend to stop short of Kentucky. The same treaty which transferred West Virginia to the ownership of white people, transferred Kentucky also; but the legality of the transfer was disputed by portions of certain tribes.

Numbers of officers who had fought in the French and Indian war were entitled under Virginia's laws to land west of the Alleghanies. The amount in the aggregate was very large. Surveyors were sent over the mountains in the spring of 1773 and again in 1774 to locate land for the soldiers. The surveyors were not in the employ of the State, but of those who expected to obtain the land. There were certain limits within which the surveys must be made, but those limits were wide and in some parts were vaguely defined. The surveyors were permitted to go pretty much anywhere that good land was to be had, except that they were not supposed to cross the Ohio river. Some did cross it, however, if not to survey land, at least for other purposes. The various parties traveled up and down the Ohio for hundreds of miles.

Surveys were run on both banks of the Kanawha, and above and below, and the bottom land between the Kanawha and the Guyandotte was staked for claims. By the middle of summer, 1774, there was scarcely a good piece of land along the Ohio river, on the eastern and southern side, that had not been staked and plotted for some officer who had seen service in the French and Indian war. There was keen competition to secure the best tracts, but each surveyor scrupulously respected former surveys. If he found himself on located land he immediately withdrew to some other place. Some surveys contained ten or twenty thousand acres, and those of less than several hundred were few. The land parties frequently went in companies of twenty or thirty, and believed themselves strong enough to take care of themselves if the Indians undertook to give trouble. As a general thing, Indians were not often encountered except in the immediate proximity of the Ohio river.

While the surveyors were at work locating lands for soldiers, settlers were entering the country by every path and road. Not only were they building cabins and clearing cornfields in what is now West Virginia, but they were finding their way by hundreds into Kentucky, which was then considered as within the bounds of Augusta county,

Virginia. The land was claimed by Virginia as its territory under the old charter; but the King of England claimed it as his under the terms of the treaty of Fort Stanwix. He claimed that he received it from the Iroquois Indians. There might have been a serious conflict of title, had not the Revolutionary war killed forever the crown's title and confirmed Virginia's. Many of the settlers who built their cabins at that time, finally received title by what was then known as the tomahawk right, which was a sort of homestead.

Indians Suspicious—Such was the state of affairs on the Virginia frontier in the spring of 1774. Some people have claimed that there was no sufficient reason for the Dunmore war, and that it came more by accident than from a deliberate purpose on the part of either side. That view is scarcely justified if the situation on the frontier and the feeling of the Indians at that time are considered. The savages saw the endless tide of immigrants and surveyors moving toward the west, and they had by that time learned that the Anglo-Saxon land hunger was never satisfied. That which he touched lightly to-day he seized with an unbreakable grip to-morrow. Though the surveyors and the settlers had not yet made a serious crossing of the Ohio, which was the boundary line between the Indian lands and the white man's possessions, they were upon that stream and were making it a highway, and it would be but one step more to occupy the north bank. The Indians understood it, and it was that which made them restless in the spring of 1774. Traders returned from beyond the Ohio and reported that the savages were sullen. Word traveled rapidly along the frontiers that the Indians were in an ugly frame of mind. The report lost nothing as it went, and almost before the snows of the winter of 1773-74 were off the ground, the frontiersmen were expecting hostilities. The logic of the men on the border was that what was bound to come, might as well come quickly, and they lost no opportunity to hasten events. A study of the situation along the Ohio river and as far south as the Holston river in

Tennessee at that time must relieve the Indians of a good deal of the blame for the Dunmore war. Both sides drifted into it through each one's suspicions of the other. Acts and reprisals followed in rapid succession until the whole border from Pittsburgh to the Clinch river was in the midst of war.

Murders became frequent along the Ohio in April. A canoe belonging to a trader named Butler was fired into near the mouth of Little Beaver, and two Indians were killed. Traders in the Indian country had been made to feel unwelcome before that time. Threats were many and warnings were sent out. War was being talked of in Williamsburg, the capital of Virginia, as though the formal declaration had already been issued. In crisis like that it often happens that men clothed with a little brief authority, or none at all, precipitate trouble which they are powerless to curb. Such a man was Dr. John Connolly at Pittsburgh at that time. He claimed to represent Lord Dunmore, Governor of Virginia, and in some things he was Dunmore's agent, and may have been in all he did, for the matter is involved in doubt. At any rate on April 21, 1774, at Pittsburgh, Connolly issued a circular to the inhabitants which was virtually, though not formally, a declaration of war against the Indians. It was so understood by the border men.

There chanced to be at Wheeling at that time a number of men waiting for the spring freshet to carry them to Kentucky. Among them was George Rogers Clark, a young man who some years later was the conqueror of Kaskaskia and Vincennes. While the men were waiting at Wheeling, the attitude of the Indians naturally came up for discussion, and most of the men expressed a willingness to turn aside from their Kentucky trip and cross into Ohio and fight the Indians. The leadership of the proposed expedition was offered to Michael Cresap, who, to the surprise of the company, refused it, and argued with the others that there was no just reason for war, and that the peace of the frontier ought to be maintained if possible. On the heels of this came

Connolly's declaration of war from Pittsburgh. Michael Cresap then accepted the leadership, and hostilities were formally inaugurated with wild ceremonies. The same evening two Indians were killed and their scalps were brought into Wheeling. Those who considered the war actually began at Wheeling called it Cresap's war because he was leader of the first outbreak which occurred there. The Indians understood at the time that Cresap was the man who had brought on the first actual fighting, and he was afterwards accused by the Chief Logan with crimes and acts of cruelty which were not his.

That was about the twenty-seventh of April. Three days later five or six Indians, one of them a woman with a young child, were murdered at Yellow Creek, about half way between Wheeling and Pittsburgh. Much has been written of it and several versions have been given of the affair. The facts seem to have been that a party of white men, one of whom was Daniel Greathouse, fired upon the Indians, either without any provocation, or without much, and killed the father, brother, and sister of Logan the chief. Some would date the opening of the war from that occurrence, though only three days had elapsed since Cresap's party had danced round a warpost at Wheeling to celebrate the beginning of the war. It is not necessary to date it from any particular day. The white men took up the gage of war much more eagerly than the Indians who seemed to hang back for some weeks though small parties went at once upon the warpath.

Logan's Revenge—The Indian chief Logan was soon east of the Ohio at the head of a large party and was satisfying his passion for revenge. He did not consider that a state of war existed but looked upon himself as the wronged party and that the affair was personal, as far as he was concerned. He struck for the settlements on tributaries of the Monongahela, and true to the instincts of the wronged savage, he made no distinction between the innocent and the guilty, but killed indiscriminately until he had made good his threat that he would take ten lives for everyone of his relatives killed at Yellow Creek. His bloodiest work was done along Dunkard creek, in Greene county, Pennsylvania, but he turned south into what are now Monongalia and Marion counties, West Virginia. He was still in the field after midsummer when he left at a house near the West Fork of the Monongahela, a letter which a prisoner wrote at his dictation. He still supposed that Captain Cresap was the responsible party for the Yellow Creek murders, and the letter was addressed to him, asking why he committed the deed. Logan stated in the brief note that the Indians had not gone to war, but that he was the only one angry. He made four or five incursions into the settlements, one into southwestern Virginia.

Immediately after the trouble began along the Ohio the settlers in the region from Pittsburgh southward to the Kanawha took hurried measures for their safety. They left their homes by thousands and fled east to places of refuge. It is said that a thousand crossed the Monongahela in one day. There was not a general flight over the Alleghanies, but many went. The people on Cheat river, in the present county of Tucker, built a fort, but though they were nearly as far east as any settlement on the western side of the mountain, they abandoned their fort and fled over the Alleghanies. Westfall's fort was built that year in Tygart's Valley. Most of the settlements, however, held their ground, but forts were provided for times of alarm. As far south as Holston and Clinch rivers, at that time in Virginia, the alarm was great, and it was feared that the Cherokees would take the war path also.

Work of Scouts—As soon as the alarm became general along the frontiers, the militia officers organized a system of scouting. The men who went upon that duty were generally spoken of as spies in the letters and reports of the officers who looked after them. Men were sent into the woods, to be absent often many days. Their duty consisted in watching paths over which Indians attempted to enter the settlements, and upon the discovery of tracks, or if the savages were seen, the alarm was given and the people took extra measures for their safety. Passes through the mountains, or fords where streams were crossed, were points which the scouts watched with the closest scrutiny. A single scout frequently was assigned the duty of guarding several paths or fords, hurrying from one to another in a round of inspection. Many an Indian raid was thwarted by the vigilance of the men who were assigned the dangerous work of outwitting, out-generaling, and out-running the warriors of the wilderness. Sometimes the savages slipped through and fell upon exposed people before warning could be given. The Indians had regular routes of travel, and did not usually wander at random through the woods. A passage from a letter published in Thwaites and Kellogg's Documentary History of the Dunmore War gives an insight into the daily occurrences of that time. The passage is quoted below for that purpose, and not for any particularly important facts it contains: "I have made strict inquiry into the conduct of the spies," writes an officer, "and find it was not their fault, the letting the enemy in undiscovered. The different passes they were ordered to watch lay at such a distance that it took several days before they could go to each. When they came to Sandy river they found the enemy's footing, and immediately ran to the station. But as they were thirty miles off and the enemy had two or three days' start, the damage was done before they got in to give the alarm."

Warning the Surveyors—When it was seen that war with the Indians was inevitable, it became a matter of extreme importance to send warning to the various parties of surveyors in Kentucky and elsewhere in the western country. Otherwise, they would fall victims before they knew of their danger. The Indians had become insolent near the Ohio river, and had announced their purpose of killing every Virginian and whipping every Pennsylvanian found trespassing upon their grounds.

Daniel Boone and Michael Stoner, two experienced woodsmen well acquainted with the western country, were sent to warn the surveyors and advise them to leave the country as speedily as possible. The messengers went as far west as Louisville, Kentucky, and all the surveyors, except one party, made their escape.

Early in summer most of the people had left their farms and were living in forts. There was fear of famine in the regions, for crops could not be cared for, and at the best there was little enough in the country to eat. The officers in charge of the militia were urged to extra effort to afford protection sufficient to allow the men to gather their harvest. Those who could act in concert went in companies to reap wheat and rye, and cultivate corn on which existence during the next winter depended. The Indians learned that by waylaying the paths leading to the fields, or by setting ambuscades near the fields, they could attack the workmen passing to and fro, or while they were at work; and a rather large proportion of the injury of white people that year was done under such circumstances. The situation became unendurable as the season advanced and the demand was general that the war be carried into the Indians' country as the surest means of keeping them out of the settlements east of the Ohio river.

Lord Dunmore was Governor of Virginia at that time. He was the last Royal Governor to hold the office in Virginia. Early in the summer of 1774 he had plans under way for an invasion of Ohio where the hostile tribes lived. He carried on an extensive correspondence with officers in southwestern Virginia, and in the Shenandoah Valley, where he expected to raise the chief part of the army for the campaign in the west. Many obstacles and difficulties were in the way of rapid progress. There was lack of ammunition. The cry for powder was heard from one end of Virginia's frontier to the other. Scouts were sent into the woods to watch Indian paths, and were to be absent many days, and they often had no more than three or four loads of powder each, not enough for a fight of two minutes. Sometimes twenty or thirty men had only a pound or two of powder to be divided among them, and it is sometimes recorded of them that they turned out cheerfully to hunt the savages, though the supply of ammunition was so dangerously low that they dared not waste a single load even to procure food which they always needed.

While Dunmore was communicating with his captains east of the mountains, and was slowly and laboriously organizing the forces, the settlements west of the mountains were overrun with the enemy; and the cry for help was incessant. To meet the emergency as speedily as possible, and at the same time carry on the preparations for the main campaign, Dunmore undertook to send a small, flying column over the Ohio to strike a quick blow against some of the nearest Indiana towns, and then fall back to the eastern side of the river. It was believed that an attack against their own villages would draw the Indians home from their raids in the settlements and give the people a respite from the horrors of savage warfare.

McDonald's Campaign—It was not Dunmore's purpose to send soldiers from east of the mountains to put through the preliminary campaign, but he meant to raise a force on the western rivers for that purpose. Colonel Angus McDonald was given command of the force to be raised. He was a Scotchman, then about forty-seven years of age, and lived at Winchester. He selected his captains, one of whom was Michael Cresap, and Daniel Morgan was another. By the first of July he had raised a force of four hundred men on the Monongahela and Youghiogheny rivers, and was in camp at Wheeling, ready to cross the Ohio and carry the war into the enemy's country.

It was the purpose to strike the first blow at Wapatomica, a group of Shawnee towns on the Muskingum river, Ohio, near the site of the present town of Dresden. These were the nearest of the Shawnee towns and could be reached most quickly. Their inhabitants had feared an attack some weeks earlier and had abandoned the place, but when the attack was delayed they concluded that the reported danger was an exaggeration, and they returned. The tribesmen who made their homes in those villages were very troublesome to the frontiers. They were active in their hostility, and persistent in their attacks.

Colonel McDonald did not encounter an Indian until within six miles of the village, but his advance was evidently well known to the Indians who boldly went out to attack his soldiers. An ambuscade was set near the path, and though the Indians were probably not more than one-tenth of his number, they put up a sharp fight and held their ground about half an hour. They inflicted a loss of two killed and five wounded upon the whites, and lost four of their number killed, and had several wounded. Colonel McDonald left his wounded at that place, with a detachment to care for them, and pushed forward toward the villages. The Indians were unable to make any further effective defense, and their towns fell into the hands of the frontiersmen after some skirmishing at the crossing of the river and a few shots afterward in which one Indian was killed and one taken prisoner. The towns were found abandoned, and five miserable villages were burned. Seventy acres of growing corn surrounded the towns. This was all cut down as a military measure, the purpose being to deprive the savages of that food supply and compel them to hunt and fish for a living which would give them less leisure for raiding the frontiers. Between three hundred and four hundred bushels of old corn were destroyed. The army by that time was short of provisions, and marched across the country to Wheeling, about one hundred miles distant.

It was now early August. Those who had expected the destruction of the Indian towns would afford any relief to the exposed settlements were disappointed. The Indians carried on their raids with more energy than ever. Colonel McDonald's army marched to Brownsville, Pennsylvania, and there awaited the advance of Governor Dunmore's troops from Virginia.

BATTLE OF POINT PLEASANT.

The central point in the Dunmore war of 1774 was the battle fought October 10 at the mouth of the Kanawha river in West Virginia, and known as the battle of Point Pleasant. All movements led up to that, and all results of any importance followed from that event. Two armies were raised. The nucleus of one army, which was led by Governor Dunmore in person, consisted of the four hundred militia under Colonel McDonald on the Monongahela. The Governor marched west in September and collected about eight hundred more, many being from Hampshire county, and with the united forces proceeded toward the Ohio. He spent some time at Pittsburgh which he called Fort Dunmore in honor of himself, having changed its name from Fort Pitt. The forks of the Ohio, and all the region south and west of it were then claimed by Virginia as a part of its territory; but Pennsylvania did not admit the validity of the claim. There were violent disputes on the subject, and Dunmore intended to strengthen and maintain Virginia's hold while on the western campaign. He was playing politics and marching against the Indians at the same time. The common perils of the frontier war had a tendency to overshadow the controversy regarding the boundary dispute, but the dispute could not be wholly put away, and it was constantly coming to the surface.

Governor Dunmore moved his army to Wheeling by two routes. Part marched across the country from the Monongahela and part descended the Ohio from Pittsburgh, and by September 30 the whole force was at Wheeling, ready to invade Ohio at some point which, it would seem, the Governor was slow in deciding upon. It was the announced plan to form a junction with a second army which was then on the march across the Alleghanies and down the Kanawha river to the Ohio. The point of meeting for the two forces was at one time fixed for the mouth of the Kanawha, then the mouth of the Little Kanawha, where Parkersburg now stands; but it was changed to the mouth of the

Hocking river further down the Ohio; and as it finally turned out, the two armies never came together at all. The fighting was done by the southern army, and as far as contributing to the victory was concerned, the force under Dunmore's immediate command could be left out of consideration. Its presence doubtless had much weight in bringing the Indians to terms, after they had lost the battle of Point Pleasant and had retreated to the interior of Ohio. That matter will be further considered in its proper place. The assembling of General Lewis' army and its march westward to the Ohio river will now claim attention.

The Rendezvous—The site of Lewisburg in Greenbrier county was appointed as the place of rendezvous for the army which was to march down the Kanawha river. On July 24, 1774, Governor Dunmore, then at Winchester on his way to Pittsburgh, wrote to General Andrew Lewis, that he had resolved to invade the Indian country beyond the Ohio. It is not probable that the subject was then mentioned between Dunmore and Lewis for the first time, but the plan assumed definite shape from that date. Colonel McDonald's force was then already on the march into Ohio. Governor Dunmore directed General Lewis to raise an army and march either to the mouth of the Kanawha or to Wheeling, as should be determined upon later, but he did not give explicit instructions regarding the number to be placed in the field, or how they should be called together or supplied. The details were left to General Lewis to work out with the help of militia officers in the southwestern part of Virginia. Governor Dunmore saw ahead very clearly in one particular, and one of the sentences in his letter was prophetic. "The Indians," said he, "having spies on the frontiers, may bring all the force of the Shawnees against you in your march to the mouth of the Kanawha." That was precisely what did happen.

General Lewis set about raising the army for the expedition. His brother, Charles Lewis collected several hundred men in Augusta county, and a force came up from what is now eastern Tennessee, but was then a part of Virginia, and in a short time about fourteen hundred men were in the field and on the march in detachments for the place of rendezvous on Greenbrier river.

The army was composed of as fine a body of men as ever assembled in this or any country. They were English, Scotch, Irish, Welsh and German, and many of them were born and had lived all their lives on the frontiers. They had passed through the French and Indian war, many of them as soldiers, and through Pontiac's war, though few of them served in it as soldiers. They knew the dangers and the hardships of frontier life, and their bodies were strong and their spirits courageous. Every man in one of the Augusta county companies stood over six feet tall in his moccasins. They were all expert in the use of the rifle, having handled that weapon all their lives. Most of them had done duty as scouts and spies, and knew how to take care of themselves in the woods, and were at home anywhere, in forest or on the march, in rain or heat, in cold and storm. Every man of them knew what to do when thrown on his own resources, and still had sufficient military training to know the value of acting in concert when occasion required.

They were volunteers. Enforced service was not necessary. They were like Cromwell's soldiers who "put some conscience into the fight." Cowards had been weeded out pretty effectively before the army reached the place of rendezvous on the Greenbrier river; for a few desertions occurred from time to time as the march became harder. In some instances there was cowardice shown while the enlistment was in progress, for it is recorded that occasionally a man who feared that a draft might be resorted to, fled to the woods rather than enter as a volunteer. By that process, the men were sifted, and those who shouldered their rifles and filed to the front could be depended upon to stick through fatigue and in the face of danger.

The collection of supplies for the campaign was attended with much difficulty. The principal articles of food were flour and beef. The cattle were driven, and the flour was carried on pack-horses west of Staunton. The quantity of flour accumulated was one hundred and sixty thousand pounds, or eight hundred barrels. It was gathered from an extensive region, for at that time there were no large stores and mills as at present. Small water mills, scattered here and there, from Staunton to the borders of North Carolina, did the grinding of the wheat, and the contributions of all were hauled by wagons or carried on horses to Staunton and other points. The whole supply could not all be ready at the appointed time; and it turned out that some of the flour was yet in Staunton when the army had reached the Ohio river. The collection of the necessary supply of cattle was less difficult, for the cattle could walk. About three hundred and fifty trailed over the Alleghany mountains, and some two hundred of these reached Point Pleasant, and a small number ultimately accompanied the army into Ohio.

The expedition had eight hundred pack-horses. There being only paths across the Alleghany mountains and westward, it was impossible to use wagons. The load for a horse was about two hundred pounds, or one barrel of flour. The horses were barely sufficient to carry the supply of flour, had there been nothing else, but the flour was only a portion of the stores. There were salt, tools, tents, blankets, and many other things that the army could not go without. The result was, the pack-horses could not carry more than half at a time, and two or more trips were necessary. Loads were carried from Staunton to Warm Springs as one relay; from Warm Springs to Lewisburg, or Camp Union, was another; the next carried the supplies to the mouth of Elk river, the site of Charleston; and from that place to the mouth of the Kanawha much of the stores was transported in canoes by water.

Trouble was experienced in providing kettles for the army. They could not be bought in sufficient quantity in the region, as the country merchants did not keep such a supply on hand. Finally the order went out to "buy, beg, or borrow kittles," for they must be had. The soldiers were made sick if they lived on roast beef without broth. A supply of kettles was procured. The expedition was equipped with about one hundred and thirty ordinary axes, and thirty broad axes. They were hand made, dull, and when delivered to the army, they had no handles. Each company ground its own axes and made handles for them. There was cloth for two hundred and seven tents, and the men made the tents.

Ammunition was very scarce, particularly powder. In fact, powder was the one article always scarce on the frontiers. The supply of that indispensable commodity was pitifully low in the army's magazines. One of the reports states that each soldier was allowed a quarter of a pound, and the inference is that there was little reserve supply. The officers watched over the powder with a vigilance which never relaxed. The butchers were not allowed to shoot beeves, because powder could not be spared for that purpose. The strictest orders were enforced against unnecessarily firing guns. Threats were made that if any company disregarded that regulation, their powder would be taken from them. No matter how wet the weather might be, the rule against the discharge of guns was enforced. Rain was liable to render the flintlock gun temporarily unserviceable, and it was customary to fire the load after a rain, and put in a new charge of powder. Even that precaution had to be dispensed with.

The army was supplied on credit. In the spring of that year Governor Dunmore asked the Virginia Assembly to appropriate money for defending the frontier, but the request was not complied with, and when it became necessary to supply an army about to take the field, there was no fund on which to draw. The Governor acted under an old law which permitted a debt to be incurred for the purpose of repelling invasion. To make the law applicable it was assumed that Virginia was invaded by enemies, and that the military force about to take the field was for defense. It appears that the people generally were willing to sell on credit. Only occasionally did anyone refuse, and when that happened, the person who refused to trust the government was held up to public scorn. "There is two cursed scoundrels," wrote a citizen to Colonel Preston while the army was on the march, "old Pate and his son Jacob, has corn, beef, and old bacon plenty to spare, and will by no means let it go without the ready cash, which I would fondly furnish them; from what I imagine they do all they can to hurt the expedition." Fortunately, there were not many who demanded the ready cash, and the army was not delayed one hour on account of short supplies. There was some delay through the failure of getting supplies up to the front over the long trails.

Early in September the troops began to gather at Camp Union, now Lewisburg, Greenbrier county. The men from Augusta county arrived first and put the camp in order for the forces from Tincastle and Botetourt counties a few days later. Trains of pack-horses filed west across the mountains with flour and camp equipage, and droves of beeves wound their way through the woods, and when they reached the Greenbrier river they were put in pasture to await the next advance.

By some means the Ohio Indians were soon aware that the army was on the march, and they knew the route it would take. Scarcely had the advance guard reached the camp on the Greenbrier before Indian spies were discovered hanging on the outskirts, observing the movements of the troops, and improving any opportunity to pick off stragglers. It became necessary to increase the number of pickets and scouts. The men who herded the cattle were in constant danger of being shot from the surrounding thickets. The Indian spies were on the alert for stray horses, and stole them on different occasions; though sometimes they were so close pressed by pursuers that they were obliged to abandon the horses and take to the woods. As soon as the camp on the Greenbrier was established some of the most skilled woodsmen were sent as spies far down the trail toward the Ohio river to give timely warning if Indians should be advancing in force to attack the camp. Some of these scouts went as far as the mouth of Gauley river, and kept the army informed of what was going on. They encountered no hostile army, but ascertained that Indian scouts, or small companies of marauders, were passing to and fro pretty frequently.

March to Point Pleasant—The officers estimated that the distance from the Greenbrier river to the Ohio, at Point Pleasant, was one hundred and sixty miles. For the most part, the route followed an old Indian trail. It led through the territory of the present counties of Fayette and Nicholas, and reached the Kanawha river near the mouth of Gauley. The plan was to carry the stores on horses to the mouth of Elk, the site of Charleston, and there make canoes in which to transport them to the Ohio. The last part of the army had not arrived on the Greenbrier when the van set out for the Ohio. Colonel Charles Lewis, from whom Lewis county, West Virginia, was named, went first with the Augusta county troops. Colonel William Fleming followed some days later with pack-horses bearing seventy-two thousand pounds of flour, and with tools for making the canoes. Colonel William Christian was left at Camp Union to bring up the rear some days later with four hundred men, and a long train of cattle and pack-horses. When Colonel Christian marched from the Greenbrier, some of the flour and cattle were fifty miles in the rear, and some had not yet left Staunton. It is thus seen that an army of fourteen hundred men and its supplies were strung out fully two hundred miles, all the way from Staunton to the mouth of Elk river. However, the fighting force was massed fairly near the front. Colonel Christian who was the last to leave the Greenbrier was exceedingly anxious to push ahead and overtake the main army before it should cross the Ohio. He was greatly encumbered with stores and gained very slowly on those in front.

At the mouth of Elk river the pack-horses were unloaded and were sent back to the Greenbrier, more than one hundred miles, for the rest of the stores. A hundred chopping axes and more than a score of broad axes were set to work making canoes. Yellow poplars with trunks three feet or more in diameter and forty or fifty feet to the first branch were felled on the bottom land where Charleston has since been built, and in a few days eighteen large canoes were ready for their loads.

Several hundred soldiers had proceeded on foot down the Kanawha valley toward the Ohio, accompanied by just enough pack-horses to carry temporary supplies. Each company was allowed one horse to carry its tents. The country was thoroughly scouted, for danger of an Indian attack increased as the army approached the Ohio. Spies penetrated to the bank of that stream, and for several days some of them lay concealed among the hills within a short distance of Point Pleasant, watching Indians who were hunting buffaloes in the vicinity. Other spies had crossed the Kanawha and were waylaying trails in that quarter. They, too, discovered Indians, who were apparently ignorant of the proximity of the Virginia army.

The van of the invading force moved with constant caution, and whether in camp or on the march, everything was ready for instant battle, should the enemy appear. The canoes kept a parallel course, but behind the army. Two of the canoes upset, and the flour was cast into the water, but the wet bags were recovered. Three or four guns were lost by the upsetting. The precious supply of powder was trusted to the canoes, but a special guard was placed over it, and it went through to its destination without mishap. When the canoes had discharged their cargoes on the bank of the Ohio they returned to the mouth of the Elk for more.

Before the Battle—The army under General Lewis reached Point Pleasant, October 6, and went into camp along the banks of both the Kanawha and the Ohio rivers, and on the point of land where the two streams met. The camp fronted half a mile on the Ohio and a half on the Kanawha. The place was covered with large trees and logs, and much of it was brushy. The men cleared a space in front of the tents, but except that, the camp was buried in the woods. Shelter for the storms was prepared, and the cattle and such of the horses as remained were turned loose to find what they could in the way of provender. The whole army did not arrive at once, but men continued to come up for some days.

General Lewis expected to form a junction there with Governor Dunmore's army that was supposed to be descending the Ohio from Wheeling, and it was thought probable that the northern army would reach Point Pleasant first. When Lewis arrived he found dispatches which had been deposited in a hollow tree by scouts sent down from the upper army. The bearers of the dispatches were Simon Girty and Simon Kenton who subsequently were well known on the frontiers, the first because he became a renegade and joined the Indians, and the latter as one of the defenders of the Kentucky frontiers. When the messengers reached Point Pleasant and found no one, they concealed their dispatches and left a note pegged to a tree telling where to find the papers. They returned to Governor Dunmore who was then at the mouth of the Hocking river. The dispatches informed General Lewis that instead of continuing down the Ohio to the mouth of the Kanawha, Governor Dunmore had changed his plan and was about to march across the country for the Indian towns on the Scioto river. He ordered General Lewis to proceed to that point, and named a certain ridge near the towns for the junction of the two armies. That was the fourth or fifth place selected by Governor Dunmore for the armies to unite.

General Lewis began his preparations for crossing the Ohio. His army was not yet ready for the advance. Four hundred men who were bringing up the rear under Colonel Christian had not arrived, nor were they expected inside of five or six days. Long trains of supplies were likewise on the road and part of them must be waited for, though a portion was too far in the rear to come up in time to be of any service during the outward march. At that time there were two hundred and fifty pack-horse loads of flour still at Staunton, and some at Warm Springs, while others were scattered from the camp on the Greenbrier all the way to the mouth of the Kanawha river. General Lewis did not propose to wait at Point Pleasant for the arrival of all his stores, as that would detain him until the beginning of winter, but he could not advance until Colonel Christian's reinforcements arrived. The army was in good condition. The sick had been left on the Greenbrier, and arrangements were under way for leaving at Point Pleasant such as were not in a condition to march.

At that time the Indian army under the leadership of Cornstalk was marching from the Scioto river to attack the Virginians on the Kanawha. The Indians numbered about eight hundred, according to the judgment of those in the best position to know. Some estimates placed their strength as high as eleven hundred, and some as low as five hundred. About half of the savage army consisted of Shawnees, the remainder of various tribes from Ohio and Michigan—the Ottawas being a Michigan tribe. Their shot pouches were filled with ammunition obtained from traders at Detroit. The charge that the British supplied the ammunition with which the Indians fought the battle of Point Pleasant has been many times heard; but it is not true in the sense usually understood. During the summer the Indians had been carrying their furs to Detroit and buying powder and lead from dealers who probably knew what was to be done with the ammunition. The Indians had a bountiful supply with which to fight the battle. They reached the western bank of the Ohio on the afternoon of October 9, and that night made rafts and crossed over to the Virginia side about six miles above the mouth of the Kanawha. Their movements were so carefully concealed that their presence was unsuspected. They proceeded two or three miles down the bank of the Ohio and went into camp, prepared to attack the army the next morning. A detachment remained on the Ohio, or western bank of the river, and took a position opposite the mouth of the Kanawha to be ready to cut off the retreat of the Virginians should they attempt to escape by crossing the Ohio. Another squad crossed the Ohio below Point Pleasant and posted themselves on the south bank of the Kanawha to cut off retreat in that direction.

It was Cornstalk's plan to surround the Virginians and annihilate their army. It seems that he had no doubt of his ability to do so. Few military men have ever undertaken with an inferior force to surround a superior or even an equal force.

The battle took place on the bank of the Ohio, and it does not appear from the best accounts by those who participated, that the fighting line of the Indians at any time reached the bank of the Kanawha. Therefore, they never succeeded in surrounding the Virginians, though they could have done so by extending their line across the peninsula from one river to the other. At one time the firing line of the Virginians was a mile and a quarter long, reaching from the Ohio river to the hills; but that was after the enemy had retreated a mile or more from their most advanced position. The first part of the engagement, which was the severest fighting, occurred on a front little if any exceeding a quarter of a mile in length.

Though General Lewis had marched and camped in constant expectation of attack for a week past, the enemy came nearly striking him by surprise on the morning of October 10.

Defeat of the Indians—The battle of Point Pleasant has been by many considered the most stubbornly contested fight that ever occurred between white men and Indians. It was by no means the most bloody, but in close-quarter and long-continued fighting it stands without a parallel in border warfare. The captain of the Indians, Cornstalk, expected to win. He knew the number of soldiers opposed to him, and was aware that the odds were against him. He planned a surprise, although he laid his camp liable to discovery, and it was discovered, and his surprise failed. When it is considered how hard put to it the Virginians were to hold their ground in the early hours of the battle, the probable result of a sudden irruption of hundreds of savages into the camp without warning is apparent.

At daybreak on October 10, 1774, two soldiers from the camp at Point Pleasant went about two miles up the Ohio river, on the Virginia side, to hunt. They ran into the Indian camp before they saw it. The savages were eating breakfast. They fired on the hunters as soon as they saw them, and killed one. The other escaped by flight, though pursued some distance. He reached the camp perhaps within fifteen minutes, and gave the alarm. A few minutes later two or three other soldiers, probably scouts or pickets, arrived with the information that the enemy was advancing. The drum beat to arms, and General Lewis ordered two columns of one hundred and fifty men each to march in the direction of the enemy. These two columns were made up of soldiers from every company in the army. Colonel Charles Lewis commanded one, Colonel William Fleming the other. The latter marched near the bank of the Ohio, and Colonel Lewis pursued a parallel course, but some two hundred yards or more inland, near the base of the hills.

Up to that time it was not suspected that an Indian army was at hand, but rather a large raiding party intent on stealing horses and attacking detached parties which might separate themselves from the army. The columns marched through the woods up the Ohio about three-fourths of a mile when the Indians were met advancing. They first fired upon the column of Virginians nearest the hills, but almost immediately delivered a furious attack upon Colonel Fleming's column on the bank of the river. The Virginians quickly broke ranks and took to trees and logs for shelter; but so instant were the Indians to see an advantage that they shot a number of the soldiers before they could cover themselves. Colonel Lewis was exposed for a few moments in an open space of ground, and was picked off and mortally wounded by the Indian sharpshooters who were sheltered behind every log and tree a few rods distant. Colonel Lewis handed his gun to a soldier and walked to the rear. He reached camp, but he died while the battle was still in progress. Captain John Field was ordered to take the wounded officer's place.

Colonel Fleming met a fate nearly similar, and almost at the same instant. Three balls, two of which were supposed to have been fired from one gun, struck him almost at the first fire. The two bullets broke his left arm, and one penetrated his lungs. He walked from the field, and being a surgeon, he dressed his own wounds, with the aid of an attendant, and finally recovered. The Botetourt troops on the bank of the Ohio held their ground in spite of the rushes of the enemy to break the line; but the Augusta men near the base of the hills were less favorably situated as far as natural defenses were concerned, and were forced slowly back from one shelter to another for nearly two hundred yards. There they made a stand and beat off the assaults of the savages who came up with yells and curses. The two lines were often less than twenty steps apart, and individual combats took place hand to hand. The Indians jeered and defied the Virginians, asking them why the fife was no longer whistling, and declaring that they would teach the white men how to shoot.

The heavy firing in front announced to General Lewis at the camp that it was a battle, and not a skirmish with raiders. He sent his captains to the front, one after another, until only one remained in camp, and he was set to work building breast works of logs and brush behind which to make a last stand if driven back. Not one of the captains who led out reinforcements commanded his own men. This caused confusion on the field, for some of the soldiers declined to obey, and waited for commands from their own officers.

When reinforcements arrived at the front, help was first given to the column next to the hills, as that seemed pressed harder than the other; at least it had fallen back while the troops near the river were holding their ground in the face of a murderous fire. The Indians in front of Colonel Field's line, near the hills, were unable to hold their ground when the reinforcements opened on them, and they fell back slowly, from tree to tree, and sheltering themselves behind logs and banks, until they were forced to retreat to the point where the fight commenced an hour before. Here they took a stand in a strong position, and refused to fall back farther. Colonel Field was killed at this place by two Indians concealed among some logs within a few rods of where he stood behind a tree endeavoring to get a shot at another Indian who was talking to him and attracting his attention to give the warriors among the logs a chance to shoot him. The strategem was too successful.

Captain Evan Shelby assumed command of the troops near the river when Colonel Fleming left the field. The two armies were then lined up face to face, extending from the base of the hills across the bottom land to the Ohio river, and for about four hours they fought without either side gaining and holding a rod of ground. Several times the Indians attempted to rush the Virginians and break their line, but they were unable to make any impression although they fought with a courage which won the admiration of those who opposed them and has called forth praise from many military men since. No civilized and trained troops could have done better. The chiefs were constantly running back and forth in the rear of the line exhorting the warriors to "Lie close," "Shoot well," while the voice of Cornstalk was distinctly heard over the entire line, calling to his men, "Be strong," "Be strong." They came up to his expectations in every particular. His only miscalculation was that the Virginians were stronger than he expected to find them. He thought he would be able to force them back, rush their lines, and drive them into the water. His detachments posted on the opposite bank of the Ohio, ready to cut off escape in that direction, watched the fight, and encouraged their kindred on the firing line by repeatedly calling across the river, "Drive the white dogs into the water."

While the battle was hanging in even scale from seven in the morning until after twelve, a hundred axes were sounding in the rear, felling trees to make breastworks across the point from the Kanawha river to the Ohio, behind which the men could retire for a final stand if driven from the field. The constant arrival of the wounded from the front was watched with anxiety, for it was evident that the contest could not be maintained indefinitely at that rate. The felled trees were piled two logs high, and a mass of brush and branches were added, the whole making a breastwork of formidable dimensions. Fortunately, it was not needed as a last resort.

Toward one o'clock the Indian army began to give ground slowly. The line was not broken, but Cornstalk evidently gave up hope of victory at that time and commenced maneuvering to get his wounded off the field in preparation for retreat at nightfall. The warriors fell back from tree to tree, fighting as they went, and not neglecting to curse and defy the Virginians, and challenge them to come on. Something more than a mile in the rear was a dense thicket which had grown on the site of a former Indian town, and Cornstalk had in view that place to make a stand and hold the Virginians in check until he could send his wounded across the river. Some of his dead he buried in shallow graves, some were thrown in the river, and others were scalped to prevent these trophies from falling into the hands of white men. The Virginians closely followed the retiring savages until the thicket was reached on the site of the old town, and there another pitched battle was fought during three hours or more. The battle line was a mile and a quarter long at that place.

The Indians called repeatedly: "Fight on. We have as many men as you have, and will have two thousand to-morrow." That was a bluff. They had their whole available force on the firing line, except a squad of tomahawk men who were in the rear cutting saplings with which to make stretchers for carrying off the wounded. While the fighters were putting on a bold front, the improvised ambulance corps was carrying the badly wounded up the river bottom to the bank of the Ohio where a fleet of seventy rafts was moored in readiness to ferry the army back to the Ohio side.

The retreat of the enemy was hastened an hour or more by a flank movement on the part of the Virginians. A small stream, called Crooked Run, with high banks, flowed southward, between the Indians and the base of the hills. Taking advantage of the concealment which this afforded, a strong flanking party was dispatched along the channel of the creek, and under cover of its banks, to strike Cornstalk's army in the flank and rear. The movement was successfully executed. The Indians found themselves suddenly attacked in the flank and not doubting that it was the reinforcement which they knew Colonel Christian was bringing up, they gave ground and retreated to their rafts about four miles above the battlefield. The Virginians did not know the exact time of the enemy's retreat. The woods were so dense that nothing could be seen beyond a few hundred feet, and when the fire of the Virginians was no longer replied to, reconnoitering parties went forward and the retreat of the Indians was discovered. The sun was then setting, and no attempt at pursuit was made that evening.

It was a victory dearly bought. The Virginians lost forty-six killed and eighty wounded in the battle, and a number afterwards died of their wounds. There is not agreement among different reports concerning the casualities in General Lewis's army. The figures above given are from a letter written from the battlefield six days after the fight. Nor was there agreement concerning the Indian losses. In fact, the exact loss was never ascertained. It is doubtful if the Indians ever knew exactly what number they lost in killed or in wounded. They threw some of their dead into the river, and they scalped others to prevent the white men from doing it; and the soldiers scalped eighteen others. These eighteen had been killed in the early part of the fight while the Indians were trying to rush the camp; and the warriors were soon afterwards forced back so rapidly that they could not remove their dead. The number of saplings cut near the thicket where they held their ground from one to five in the afternoon indicated that they made many stretchers to carry away their wounded.

After the Battle—When General Andrew Lewis discovered that a pitched battle was on, and that victory was by no means certain, he sent messengers upon the trail to meet Colonel Christian who was supposed to be coming down the Kanawha valley, a day's journey in the rear. He had four hundred men, which was a force sufficient to renew the battle in case the Virginians should be worsted in the first encounter. At sunset the messengers met Colonel Christian's troops toiling slowly along the path. They were not expecting to reach Point Pleasant before the afternoon of the following day; but the news that a hard and doubtful battle was in progress brought instant change in the plans, and a night march of six hours brought the reinforcement on the battlefield. The battle was over, but it was not yet known whether the whole Indian force had crossed the Ohio, or whether the battle would be renewed next day.

The camp of the Virginians was in a deplorable condition. The only surgeon in the army, Colonel Fleming, was lying at the point of death, as was supposed, and unable to render any assistance on account of his own wounds. The army had failed to provide for such an emergency, and the wounded were lying about the camp with only such attention as one soldier is able to give another, and the dead were not yet buried. Colonel Christian's account of the scenes and conditions that met his eyes and ears when he arrived at midnight, seven hours after the battle, gives a picture of distress and suffering that appalled the stoutest hearts.

Early on the morning of October 11 strong reconnoitering parties searched the country for the enemy. It was apparent that the retreat was not a feint. Seventy rafts were found where they crossed the river. A search of the battlefield resulted in the collection of twenty-three rifles, twenty-seven tomahawks, eighty blankets, with many shot pouches, powder horns, war clubs, and coats. The spoils were collected at camp, and according to law were sold at auction, and brought nearly five hundred dollars.

Soon after the battle, dispatches arrived from Governor Dunmore repeating the order for General Lewis to march toward the Indian towns on the Scioto river, and there form a junction with the Governor's army. A certain place and a certain day were named for the meeting. It was impossible for General Lewis to obey the order, for he must first take care of his wounded, and secure his stores before he could safely advance into the Indian country. He wrote to Dunmore, informing him of the battle, and promising to march as soon as possible. A temporary fort, hospital, and storehouse were built at the mouth of the Kanawha, and a garrison for defense and nurses for the wounded were left.

Beyond the Ohio—On October 17, General Lewis led his army across the Ohio river and marched toward the Indian towns nearly one hundred miles distant. A mile and a half west of the river they came to the camping place of the Indians on their retreat the night after the battle. A number of articles had been left scattered about the camp when the Indians moved out on the morning of October 11. The Virginians met with no serious opposition on the march. Indians lurking in the woods occasionally fired at long range, but no large parties were encountered.

The defeat of the Indians at Point Pleasant took the fight out of them. They made their way to their towns as expeditiously as possible, impeded as they were with large numbers of wounded. Cornstalk, their head chief, saw the uselessness of resistance. His whole available force was now not more than one-third of that which he must meet, after Lewis and Dunmore had formed a junction, and the Indians were powerless to prevent a junction. Cornstalk called his defeated and discouraged warriors together to decide what they should do. He saw no hope of victory, but he proposed that the warriors kill their own women and children, and then go down to meet the advancing enemy, and fight until the last warrior was dead. The assembled Indians heard in silence. No one had an answer to give. Cornstalk waited for reply, and when none was made, he struck his tomahawk into the tent post, exclaiming that since the warriors would not fight, he would go and make peace.

The day after Governor Dunmore's army reached the proximity of the Indian towns, Cornstalk came to the camp to ask for peace, promising in advance to agree to whatever terms were offered. In Governor Dunmore's report to the Earle of Dartmouth, he said, "The Indians determined to throw themselves upon our mercy; and with the greatest expedition they came in search of the body with which they knew I marched, and found me near their own towns the day after I got there. They presently made known their intentions, and I admitted them immediately to a conference wherein all our differences were settled. The terms of our reconciliation were, briefly, that the Indians should deliver up all prisoners without reserve; that they should restore all horses and other valuable effects which they had carried off; that they should not hunt on our side of the Ohio nor molest any boats passing thereon; that they should promise to agree to such regulations for their trade with our people as should be hereafter dictated by the King's instructions, and that they should deliver into our hands certain hostages, to be kept by us until we were convinced of their sincere intention to adhere to all these articles. The Indians finding, contrary to their expectations, no punishment likely to follow, agreed to everything with the greatest alacrity, and gave the most solemn assurances of their quiet and peaceable deportment for the future; and in return I have given them every promise of protection and good treatment on our side."

Logan's Speech—It was in course of the peace negotiations at Camp Charlotte, where the Indians met Dunmore, that a famous speech was delivered by John Logan, an Iroquois Indian of the Cayuga tribe. He it was whose relatives were murdered at Yellow Creek by Daniel Greathouse's party in April, 1774. Logan went upon the warpath four times during that spring and summer, and killed ten white people for every one of his relatives who had been killed. Considering that he had fully avenged them, he retired to his cabin, and did not take part in the campaign which ended with the battle of Point Pleasant. In the midst of the negotiations between Dunmore and the Indians, the absence of Logan was noticed, and upon inquiry, Dunmore was informed that the Cayuga chief refused to come to camp. Thereupon, Simon Girty, an interpreter, was sent to Logan's cabin to invite him to the council. The chief refused to come and sent by word of mouth a speech to be delivered in his stead. This speech was committed to writing by Colonel John Gibson, and was filed among the papers relating to the treaty. It afterwards fell into the hands of Thomas Jefferson who published it in his notes on Virginia, and a long controversy followed as to its genuineness. Logan was only half Indian. His father was a Frenchman, his mother a Cayuga Indian. Logan spoke English very well. The speech concerning which there has been so much discussion, follows:

"I appeal to any white man to say if he ever entered Logan's cabin hungry and he gave him not meat; if ever he came cold and naked, and he clothed him not. During the course of the last long and bloody war, Logan remained idle in his cabin, an advocate of peace. Such was my love for the whites that my countrymen pointed as they passed, and said, Logan is the friend of white men. I had even thought to have lived with you, but for the injuries of one man, Colonel Cresap, who last spring, in cold blood, and unprovoked, murdered all the relatives of Logan, not even sparing my women and children. There runs not a drop of my blood in the veins of any living creature. This called upon me for revenge. I have sought it. I have killed many. I have fully glutted my revenge. For my country, I rejoice at the beams of peace. But do not harber the thought that mine is the joy of fear. Logan never felt fear. He will not turn on his heel to save his life. Who is there to mourn for Logan? Not one."

Conclusion of Peace—When Governor Dunmore found that the Indians were anxious for peace, and that further fighting would not be necessary, he sent orders to General Lewis whose army was then about twenty miles off, and advancing, to halt and wait the outcome of the negotiations. General Lewis did not obey the orders but marched on. The next day a second order to halt reached him, with information that peace was practically concluded; that the Indians had agreed to all the terms; and that Lewis and his army would be of no assistance, and might hinder. However, Governor Dunmore gave his consent that General Lewis and such of his officers as he chose might repair to Dunmore's camp, but the army must halt.

The camp was then about six miles distant, and General Lewis did not deem it safe for a few officers to proceed that distance alone through the woods, with an Indian army in the neighborhood. Besides, there was no water where the troops then were, and General Lewis gave orders to march on. The guides took the wrong path, and instead of proceeding to Camp Charlotte where Dunmore was, the army marched toward an Indian town, and were within three-fourths of a mile of it before the mistake was discovered. The Indians in the conference with Dunmore at Camp Charlotte became panic stricken. They supposed that General Lewis intended to attack their towns in spite of Governor Dunmore's orders. They broke off negotiations at the camp and fled. Dunmore himself was alarmed, and suspected that Lewis intended to strike the towns in defiance of orders. The Governor, accompanied by a few officers, hastily rode to meet Lewis, and when they met, Dunmore sharply asked what the defiance of orders meant. The matter was satisfactorily explained, the Indians were reassured, and the negotiations proceeded and peace was soon declared.

The return of the troops soon began. General Lewis marched back to Point Pleasant, but not all in one body. The troops broke into small detachments and made their way home by different routes. A garrison was left at Point Pleasant to occupy the fort, and such of the sick and wounded as were unable to proceed to their homes were made comfortable where they were. Some of them remained all winter at Point Pleasant. The various companies and detachments set out for their homes as speedily as they could make arrangements to do so. Most returned by way of Greenbrier river, but some followed different routes, a considerable number crossing the Alleghany mountains into the present county of Pendleton by way of the Seneca Trail, eastward from Tygart's Valley.

THE QUEBEC ACT.

A political movement designed to have far-reaching results was being engineered by the English parliament in 1774 while the Dunmore war was in progress. A bill passed parliament and was known as the Quebec Act, because by its terms it extended the province of Quebec southward to the Ohio river and westward to the Mississippi. West Virginia is concerned in the history of that transaction, for had it succeeded as it was planned, the Ohio river would have become the northwestern limit of the United States, and all beyond that, including the present States of Ohio, Indiana, and Illinois, would have been part of the Dominion of Canada. It was a scheme with a deep and studied purpose back of it. It was a blow aimed by the English government against the English colonies in America. The spirit of independence among them had been growing for fully ten years, and British statesmen foresaw the logical result if the English on the Atlantic seaboard, from New England to Florida, were permitted to push their settlements westward across the Alleghany mountains into the Ohio and Mississippi valleys, and firmly established themselves there. They would become so strong that they would attempt to throw off their allegiance to England and set up an independent nation, reaching from the Atlantic to the Mississippi.

The English government never had encouraged the settlement of the country west of the mountains. Some of the leading statesmen made no secret of their desire to see the Ohio valley, and all beyond it, remain a wilderness, occupied by Indians and wild animals. The only commerce which was desired with that region was traffic in furs, carried on between traders and Indians, as was done up to the time of the Revolutionary war. No such thing as the development of the agricultural resources of the region was wanted. The Alleghany mountains were looked upon as a natural and proper boundary between the English seaboard colonies and the pack-horse country of the west. For several years the English government did all in its power to discourage and hinder any settlement west of the mountains. Finding that the tide was too strong to withstand, partial consent was given—but given grudgingly—that the region between the mountains and the Ohio river might be settled; but no farther. The Quebec Act of 1774 was, therefore, an attempt to forever prevent the settlement of the country beyond the Ohio by the English.

That region belonged to Virginia by charter, but the English government showed no disposition to recognize that colony's charter rights west of the mountains. When it suited the government's purpose to claim it as a part of Virginia's territory—for instance, when the English were combatting the French pretensions to the region—the claim was duly set forth; but when the English government could best subserve its own selfish and short-sighted purposes by denying that Virginia had any rights there, the denial was clear-cut and to the point. In 1774 it suited the government's purpose to ignore Virginia's claim to the region west of the Ohio, and by the Quebec Act the region was cut off and separated from Virginia as completely as it could be done by an act of parliament. About two hundred and forty thousand miles were thus cut from Virginia and given to Canada. That it was not done in fact as well in theory was due to the energetic action of the Virginians themselves, in the Dunmore war and later, in refusing to recognize the validity of the Quebec Act.

The parliamentary act was intended to restore the old French law in the civil courts of Quebec, secure rights to the Catholic inhabitants, and make the boundary of Canada the Ohio and Mississippi rivers. As far as the territory now contained in the States of Ohio, Indiana, Illinois, Michigan, and Wisconsin was to be settled at all, the settlements were to be French, the same as Canada. It was believed that such a condition would make forever impossible any political, social, or business union between the coast and the interior. The two regions would have nothing in common; and in case of trouble between the English colonies and the mother country, which was then actually taking form, the Canadian and the Ohio valley French Catholics would give no assistance to the Protestant colonies; and if trouble should arise between England and her French subjects in Canada, the English on the seaboard would give no help to the Canadians. Thus one-half of America was to be played against the other half; there would be no growth of English settlements westward; and danger of successful resistance to the authority of the British Crown need be no longer feared.

The Quebec Act was not much discussed in America at the time of its passage. In truth, few of the common people knew of it. They were then preparing for the Revolution, expecting to settle once for all the question of England's interference in affairs which should be purely American. When the Revolution ended, and the time came for discussing the boundary between the United States and Canada, the real purpose of the Quebec Act was better understood. England was in no position to insist on the Ohio river as a boundary. The Virginian armies under Lewis and Dunmore, and later under George Rogers Clark, had broken down the parliament-made boundaries, and nobody recognized them, though the British continued for years in an endeavor to hold part of the country south of Lakes Erie and Michigan. Even as late as the war of 1812 some lingering belief remained with certain English statesmen that they would be able to hold some of the region which had been staked off by the Quebec Act of 1774. The last prop to that hope was knocked away when Commodore Perry destroyed the English fleet on Lake Erie.

When Governor Dunmore invaded the country beyond the Ohio river, he builded greater than he knew. He probably thought little about his invasion of the Province of Quebec. He perhaps was scarcely aware that as soon as he set foot on the western bank of the Ohio river he was in Quebec. By leading an army of Virginians into it, he virtually proclaimed that it was still Virginia territory, and that the Quebec Act was nullified. Dunmore was loyal to the home government, and by claiming Virginia's authority still extended beyond the Ohio; he gave the Americans an argument, in later boundary negotiations, which the English could not answer. They were bound by the act of one of their own loyal and credited officials.

Some of the soldiers who served with Dunmore in the campaign which concluded with the treaty at Camp Charlotte, held a meeting on November 5, 1774, at Fort Gower, west of the Ohio river, and near the mouth of the Hocking river. They were on their way home, and for several weeks they had little news from New England and other eastern ports. The Revolution was already gathering head on the Atlantic seaboard, and the Virginian soldiers who had been so long in the western wilderness, were uneasy lest their eastern kinsmen might be uncertain as to where they stood on the questions of the hour. In order to give voice to their sentiments they passed a set of resolutions which they afterwards published. They recited that they were willing and able to bear all hardships of the woods; to get along for weeks without bread or salt, if necessary; to sleep in the open air; to dress in skins if nothing better could be had; to march farther in a day than any other men in the world; to use the rifle with skill and with bravery. They affirmed their zeal in the cause of right, and promised continued allegiance to the King of England, provided he would reign over them as a brave and free people. "But," they continued, "as attachment to the real interests and just rights of America outweigh every other consideration, we resolve that we will exert every power within us for the defense of American liberty, when regularly called forth by the unanimous voice of our countrymen."

The treaty which Dunmore concluded with the Indians at Camp Charlotte was only preliminary. He planned to meet representatives of as many tribes as possible at Pittsburgh the following summer and there discuss various matters concerning the relationship of the two races, and conclude a treaty that should be lasting. Dunmore returned to Williamsburg in December, and wrote an elaborate report of the late campaign and of various other important matters, and forwarded it to the British government. That report let fall no intimation that his tenure of office as Governor of Virginia was not secure, as far as any influence the Virginians might exert was concerned; but he combatted certain adverse criticisms of his administration which came from governmental sources. The chief criticism of his course was that he had encouraged the settlement of the region beyond the Alleghany mountains contrary to the wishes and the policy of the English government. Dunmore entered into a full and fair discussion of the whole question, and showed that he was much better acquainted with the matter than his critics were. He maintained that it was impossible by law or force to prevent the frontier settlements from pushing westward; that the people will move farther into the woods in defiance of laws and proclamations, and that they forever imagine that the land a little farther on is more fertile than that already occupied.

Arguing from that condition, Dunmore maintained that it was better to let the settlers have the vacant land in a lawful way, since they would otherwise take possession of it in an unlawful way. The Dunmore war, he explained, was forced upon Virginia by the Indians themselves who would not keep to their own side of the Ohio river. The Governor believed that the chastisement which the savages had received had impressed them, as they were never before impressed, with the power and resources of white men. For that reason, the Governor hoped that much good would come from the conference with the various western tribes which he had planned for the following summer. Events moved more rapidly than he foresaw. Before the time for the conference arrived, Dunmore had been driven from Virginia by the rising patriots under the leadership of Patrick Henry and the same General Andrew Lewis who served under him in 1774. The treaty with the Indians was held at Pittsburgh, according to arrangement, but Dunmore had no part in it. The result of the treaty will be shown in the chapter on West Virginia's Part in the Revolution in this book.

WEST VIRGINIA
IN THE REVOLUTIONARY WAR

WEST VIRGINIA IN THE REVOLUTIONARY WAR.

In 1775, when troubles began to thicken round Governor Dunmore, of Virginia, and he foresaw his early departure, he took advantage of every opportunity to do injury to the cause of the Virginians with a view to crippling them in the inevitable struggle with the mother country. The Indian affairs on the western border were in an unsettled condition, and Dunmore understood how easy it would be to turn the savages against the frontiers and precipitate a war of such seriousness that the whole forces west of the mountains would be needed to protect exposed settlements from Pittsburgh to Central Kentucky. The governor knew that any diversion in that quarter would weaken Virginia along the seaboard where the contest with the mother country was assuming the form of armed hostility. He, therefore, cast his eyes toward the west to see what trouble he could stir up in that direction.

The first movement was an attempt to turn the Indians against the settlers, and the next was to deprive the settlements of some of their means of defense. During the progress of the Dunmore war he had built two forts and garrisoned them. One was at Pittsburgh, the other at Point Pleasant. Old Fort Pitt had been abandoned several years, and part of the site had been sold in 1772. He took steps to recover ground for the new fort, or have the old repaired, and he called it Fort Dunmore, in honor of himself. Fort Blair was built at Point Pleasant. Dunmore had been criticized by the home government in England for establishing these forts. It was claimed that they were not needed for military purposes, but were meant to assist certain land speculations in the west, in which the governor was financially interested. He defended his course and laid down an elaborate argument to prove that the forts were necessary to impress the Indians with a sense of Virginia's power, and incline them to keep the peace. Fort Fincastle, at Wheeling, named for one of Dunmore's titles, was built in June, 1774, by Major

William Crawford, but a garrison was not maintained there after the close of the Dunmore war.

When Dunmore saw that he would soon find it necessary to depart from Virginia, one of his last acts was to order the abandonment of Forts Dunmore and Blair. The patriots seized the fort at Pittsburgh as soon as it was learned that Dunmore had ordered its evacuation, but there was no force at hand to take Fort Blair into keeping when its garrison left it. The militia in charge held it for some time after the order for its abandonment was issued in June, 1775. The abandonment of that fort was said to have been the last official act of Dunmore as governor of Virginia. The commandant of the fort hoped that some countermanding order would come, but when he gave up hope of such, he evacuated the fort and removed the cattle and other stores over the mountains by way of Big Sandy river. Indians burned the fort soon after.

The Pittsburgh Treaty—Dunmore left an appointment with the Indians in October, 1774, to meet him in Pittsburgh the following summer and conclude a treaty. When business became so pressing that he could not go he delegated his agent at Pittsburgh, Dr. John Connolly, to meet the Indians at the appointed time and place. Connolly immediately busied himself stirring up trouble, and endeavored to array the Indians against the frontiers by enlisting them on the side of the King of England. The Indians were kept posted on events, though they did not very well understand the political issues involved. News of any clash between the Americans and the British troops in Massachusetts or elsewhere quickly reached the western Indians, and excited and confused them. It was a revelation to the natives that white men of English speech did not all stand together. Agents of the English traveled among the Indians and by misrepresentation and otherwise tried to win them to the royalist side. Some of the most active agents of the English in this work were Frenchmen who lived among the tribes or about the frontier posts.

The people west of the mountains took prompt measures to counteract British influence among the savages. Both the English and the Americans have been charged with being first in attempts to stir up the Indians to go on the warpath, and perhaps both sides did it very early in the contest; but it was not the policy of the Americans to do so. Their purpose was to hold the savages neutral, and they carefully impressed that view upon the Indians. It was well understood that if the savages should go upon the warpath the frontiers would lose more than they would gain. No time was lost in getting into communication with the leading chiefs, and explaining the situation to them. In May, 1775, a convention was held at Pittsburgh, attended by leading men from Northwestern Virginia and Western Pennsylvania, and a committee was formed to take necessary measures for the public good. A petition was addressed to the Continental Congress in which the fear was voiced that emissaries of the British were urging the Indians to attack the frontiers.

The Continental Congress received the petition from Pittsburgh and referred it to the delegates from Virginia and Pennsylvania. It was decided that the conference with the Indians at Pittsburgh, which had been appointed by Dunmore for the summer of 1775, should be held, and Virginia named commissioners to take the matter in hand. The congress likewise appointed commissioners. One of those appointed was Benjamin Franklin and another George Washington, but it developed that their other duties would not permit them to attend, and the committee was made up by the appointment of Lewis Morris, James Wilson, Thomas Walker, James Wood, Andrew Lewis, John Walker and Adam Stephen.

James Wood was sent upon a special mission among the Indian tribes of Western Pennsylvania and Ohio to sound their sentiments on peace and to invite them to attend the conference in Pittsburgh. He discovered that the British had been tampering with the savages and were employing French agents to win them over to the side of England in the approaching struggle. Mr. Wood found most of the Indians inclined to peace, but they were perplexed. It had been represented to them that in a contest with England the Americans would ultimately lose. It had been further represented that the Americans were determined to take all of the western land, as they had already taken some of it; but that the English would respect the rights of the Indians. The Virginia commissioner won the day. All he asked of the Indians was that they remain neutral in the approaching war, and this the most of them were anxious to do.

In September large numbers of Ottawas, Wyandots, Shawnees, Mingoes, Delawares and Senecas assembled at Pittsburgh for the proposed treaty. The Ottawas were from the neighborhood of Detroit, and the Senecas were Iroquois from the upper waters of the Alleghany river. They were represented by their chief, Guyashusta, whose influence and authority later proved to be of the greatest value to the Americans. The Shawnees were represented by Cornstalk, who had led them at the battle of Point Pleasant. His influence was also valuable, while he was permitted to live, which, unfortunately, was not long. While the Indians gathered in large numbers at Pittsburgh, the British at Detroit sent a spy in the person of Drouillard, a Frenchman, to watch the proceedings and report what occurred. He did not dare enter the camp at Pittsburgh, but approached within ten miles of the town and remained in concealment, while Indian emissaries came and went between him and the treaty house, and kept him posted concerning all that happened. He lost no time in carrying his news to Detroit.

After a discussion of several days, during which a number of the Indian chiefs made speeches, a treaty was concluded. The Indians agreed to give up all prisoners and property which they had carried from the settlements, and to maintain peace with the frontiers.

So far as West Virginia and Kentucky was concerned the treaty proved of the utmost importance, and only of a little less importance to the rest of the country. Looking back from a distance of nearly 140 years, one is apt to lose sight of what was accomplished by the Pittsburgh treaty of 1775. The revolutionary war was just commencing, and the Indians pledged themselves to neutrality and kept the pledge for two years. That gave the back parts of Virginia, Pennsylvania and Kentucky peace on their borders, and permitted soldiers to cross the mountains and join the patriot armies which were fighting near the seacoast. The first troops that reached Washington's army after he assumed command before Boston were western Virginians. The help which the patriot generals received from the backwoods near the Ohio was of the most substantial kind. That assistance could not have gone to the front had an Indian war been raging on the frontiers.

The two years of peace at that critical time came as a deliverance in another way. It gave the frontiers a chance to establish themselves and prepare for the storm which followed. Had the Indians attacked the border settlements from Pittsburgh to Kentucky at the same time that the British attacked in the east, in all human probability the settlements would have broken up between the Ohio river and the mountains, and in Kentucky. The frontier would have been thrust back where they were twenty years before along the eastern base of the Alleghanies. The two years allowed sufficient time to build forts and prepare for the worst.

Had the frontiers been pushed back, there is no telling what result it might have had on the boundary between Canada and the United States at the close of the revolution. George Rogers Clark would not have led his little army into the Ohio valley and broken up the British authority there. When the time came for the treaty of Paris, which ended the war, the British would have been in possession of all west of the Ohio river, if not all west of the Alleghany mountains, and it is not improbable that they would have been left in possession.

The neutrality of the Senecas on the Alleghany river, stood the Americans, and especially the western settlements, a good turn later. When the British force at Niagara was preparing to march south to attack Pittsburgh the Seneca chief Guyashusta reminded them that his territory, which lay between Niagara and Pittsburgh was neutral, and that if they undertook to march through it he would fight them. The British did not care to stir up an Indian war at that time, and the attack on Pittsburgh was abandoned.

The history of Western Virginia in the revolutionary war is largely a history of hostilities with the Indians upon the frontiers. By the commencement of 1777 it became apparent that the western Indians would not remain much longer at peace. Acts of hostility were becoming frequent on the borders, and the settlers were building forts, and on all sides preparations for war were seen. The British had finally succeeded in winning to their side the wild men of the wilderness.

Connolly's Plot—Dr. John Connolly was an evil genius on the western frontier of Virginia and Pennsylvania in the first year of the revolution. His power for harm was considerable, and that his plans finally failed was due to the vigilance and good luck of the patriots. He was Dunmore's western agent, and he stuck to his chief with a faithfulness worthy of a better cause. Dunmore placed him in power at Pittsburgh and his wide acquaintance with men and conditions on the frontiers made him a hard man to circumvent. He saw as soon as anybody that the colonists would go to war with England, and he was Dunmore's willing and able tool in stirring up trouble with the Indians. He finally failed to start them upon the warpath against the frontiers. Connolly's grip of affairs about Pittsburgh was shaken loose when Dunmore lost his hold of affairs in Virginia. Early in the summer of 1775 Connolly saw that if he struck the Virginia frontiers he would have to do it with force other than Indians.

Dunmore had found it necessary to escape from Virginia on board an English ship, but he was hovering around Chesapeake bay and the mouths of the rivers. Connolly succeeded in escaping from the west and boarding Dunmore's vessel in York river. He there laid before the fugitive governor a plan for breaking up the western settlements of Virginia and so plausible were his arguments that he convinced Dunmore that the plan was practicable. Thereupon Dunmore sent him by sea to General Gage at Boston to submit the plan to headquarters to obtain approval, and to secure the means of putting the scheme through. General Gage approved, and Connolly set out for Canada to begin his destructive work in the neighborhood of Detroit.

The plan contemplated an invasion of western Pennsylvania and Virginia by an army from Canada. The force was to consist of British regulars to be drawn from garrisons in Illinois and Detroit, with Canadians, Indians and such loyalists from Virginia and Pennsylvania as might join. Connolly was to be in command, and was to be supplied with money. Authority was conferred on him to act in any emergency that was likely to arise. He was to have a train of artillery to batter down blockhouses and other fortified places. He intended to march first against Pittsburgh, and when he had taken that place, proceed against Wheeling, which was then the second strongest post on the western frontier, in the Ohio valley. Having taken Pittsburgh and Wheeling, it was not expected that any serious resistance would be encountered west of the mountains, and Connolly believed that a short time would suffice for the subjugation of all the west. He then planned to march his army east to Alexandria, Virginia, where Dunmore was to meet him with a fleet and army.

Connolly set out from Boston for Canada, but American armies were operating about the lakes and he doubted whether he could get through. He, therefore, turned back, and undertook to make his way west through Maryland. He reached Frederick, where he was recognized and placed under arrest. A paper giving the details of the plot was found in his baggage, and his plot was discovered and defeated. He afterwards made his escape and fled from the country.

Indians go on the Warpath—The year 1777 was long remembered on the Virginia frontiers as "the bloody year of the three 7s." At the close of 1775 Governor Hamilton at Detroit wrote to Guy Carleton that he expected to see the Indians upon the frontiers the next summer, but the British were not able to move the savages as rapidly as Hamilton supposed they could, and it was not till 1777 that the western tribes were upon the warpath. Scattering bands of Indians went out months before, and the alarm was general in every exposed settlement from Kentucky to Pittsburgh, and forts and places of shelter were built in many places as a matter of precaution against sudden attack.

Fort Randolph, at Point Pleasant, was built to take the place of Fort Blair, which was abandoned and burned in 1775. As early as May 15, 1776, Captain Matthew Arbuckle, with a company of Virginia troops, left Pittsburgh for Point Pleasant to garrison the fort. There was extended correspondence between officials and men of influence in the east and people of the western country on the subject of equipping forces for the defense of the frontiers.

Fighting in what is now West Virginia occurred in many places during the revolution, but in most instances no British appeared in arms though it was generally understood that the Indians who did the fighting were armed, and in some instances paid, by the British. In a history as condensed as this, it is not practicable to give much more than an outline and a few details of the principal events of the war. It would require a volume for a single county in some instances to present the details of the war. Events in Monongalia, Ohio, Harrison, Randolph or Greenbrier counties would alone fill a book, if written fully as they deserve. All that can be here attempted in one chapter is to single out a few of the leading occurences and omit all that are of comparatively minor importance. The revolutionary war proper in Western Virginia, including only the actual fighting in the state or directly affecting it, extended from September, 1777, to September, 1782, almost exactly five years. There were many important occurrences prior to 1777, and the war with the Indians did not cease with the conclusion of peace in 1783; but the period of five years above named took in most of Western Virginia's share in the revolution within its borders. During the revolution the present territory of West Virginia was three times invaded by forces large enough to be called armies, and narrowly escaped invasion another time. Three of the hostile forces were commanded by white men in British pay, though Indians constituted most of the rank and file. The first invasion was in 1777 when Fort Henry, at Wheeling, was attacked. The second occurred in 1778 when an Indian army marched against Fort Randolph at the mouth of the Kanawha, and continued the invasion as far as the Greenbrier river. The third invasion was planned for July, 1782, against Wheeling, but did not materialize; and the fourth was directed against Wheeling in September, 1782.

In addition to these occurrences there were others in which the destiny of West Virginia was vitally concerned. One was the capture of Kaskaskia, in Illinois, and of Vincennes, Indiana, by a small army, chiefly Western Virginians, under George Rogers Clark. There were numerous raids and pillaging expeditions by the Indians in all parts of the country from Greenbrier river to the Pennsylvania line. These irruptions were not with the fringe of the frontiers alone, but in some cases extended from the Ohio river to the very base of the Alleghany mountains, and on one occasion across the mountains into Pendleton county on the waters of the Potomac. Small raids by the stealthy savages, tried the courage and determination of the settlers more than invasions by armies; for the movements of large bodies could not be long concealed, and the people had time to fight or fly; but the noiseless advance of a few, skulking through the woods, waylaying paths, and falling without warning and without mercy upon the defenseless cabins, struck terror everywhere. No exposed cabin was safe between the mountains and the Ohio, and every rock and tree by the lonely paths were ever-inviting hiding places for assassins. None who have not studied minutely the chronicles of those awful years can form a conception of the desperate situations in which the people were often placed.

The correspondence between the leaders of the people among the western valleys and mountains and the authorities at Richmond give a picture which constantly raises astonishment that people could hold their ground under such circumstances. The petitions to the people in the east to send food, because no crops could be raised; or to send powder, for there was none in the settlements; or to send a bar of lead for bullets; or a piece of steel to mend gun locks; or flints for firing the guns, were numerous and show the straits to which the pioneers were often reduced. Sometimes these appeals were partly granted—they always were if possible—but too often the message came back that it was impossible to do anything. There was nothing to do but fight on, and beat off the savages, or die in the attempt. More than once those appeals for help went across the Alleghanies toward Richmond accompanied with the despairing assertion that unless powder came, or food was found, the settlements must "break." That word meant that all must be given up and the people seek safety in a retreat across the mountains. How nearly that came to pass on more than one occasion is shown in brief sentences in that short and poorly spelled correspondence of which the following are examples among scores of others: "Buckhannon settlement has broke;" "fourteen Tygarts valley familys were on foot yisterday, and others must go;" "not three loads of powder remain."

Appeals that crossed the mountains did not fall on unsympathetic ears. Hampshire county sent its militia two hundred miles to defend the wilderness frontiers along the Ohio; and even Staunton responded in the time of need, though the resources of the valley of Virginia were drained to the limit to fight the British in the east. Militia crossed the Alleghanies to the Greenbrier settlements; went down the Kanawha, penetrated to the mouth of the Little Kanawha; helped the people on Cheat river in Tucker county, where the settlers had only eighteen men; sent soldiers to Tygarts valley, where the hard-pressed settlers were once on the point of giving up the fight. The eastern counties spared militia also for the Wheeling district, and for the Monongahela. The help thus given in the hours of greatest need doubtless saved the day. On more than one occasion the militia that crossed the mountains found it impossible to remain long because of the famine. The settlers were often on the verge of starvation, and there was nothing to divide, even with the defenders who had come to help fight.

It was not the custom among the people on the frontiers to lie still and wait to be attacked. Scouts, who were almost invariably called spies in the early court documents where the records are to be found, were kept in the woods constantly on the lookout for Indians. These men usually remained out ten days at a time, when they were relieved by others. They waylaid the paths by which the savages were accustomed to enter the country, and upon making any suspicious discovery, the settlers within twenty or thirty miles were warned. The very best woodsmen were detailed for that duty, and many a life was saved by their vigilance. The Indians who invariably came from Ohio, had certain routes which they followed. When they were discovered upon a path it was known within a fair degree of certainty what place they intended to strike. It was then the scout's duty to outrun them and spread the alarm. The scouts usually ranged well off toward the Ohio river. They were not always successful. The Indians were quick to learn that the paths were watched, and they deviated from their usual courses, and escaped the watchful eyes of the spies. Sometimes the scouts were waylaid and caught by the very savages they were watching. It would be hard to imagine a life more beset with peril than those of the spies on the frontiers. Some of them never received pay, while many years afterwards some were placed on the pension rolls as revolutionary soldiers.

First Siege of Fort Henry—The larger events in the transmontane revolutionary history of Virginia were opened by the siege of Fort Henry at Wheeling in September, 1777, by an Indian army led by a white man erroneously believed for many years to have been Simon Girty, who was a notorious renegade in the Indian country. It is now known that the leader was not Girty, who at that time was serving in the garrison at Pittsburgh, and who did not desert to the Indians until six months later.

The fort at Pittsburgh was under command of General Hand in the summer of 1777. He was a regular army officer and had been sent west to take charge of military affairs in that district. In August he learned from his spies that the Indians were preparing a formidable attack upon some part of the frontier, and he believed that Wheeling was the objective point. Messengers were sent to warn the settlements near the Ohio from Pittsburgh to Point Pleasant. The fort at Wheeling was an alluring place, in the eyes of the Indians; and in the course of the war they made three attempts to take it. General Hand undertook to discover the line of the enemy's march in time to give specific warning to the place theatened. He sent spies west of the Ohio to watch all the principal parts leading to the river; but in spite of that precaution the Indian army reached the river undiscovered, and appeared before Fort Henry, September 1, as suddenly as if they had risen from the ground. It was afterwards learned that they had made their way to the river in small parties, and by unfrequented routes, and had assembled by prearrangement just below Wheeling on the Ohio side.

Fort Henry had formerly been called Fort Fincastle, from one of Dunmore's titles; but when he became odious because of his activity in combatting the Virginians, they changed the name in honor of Patrick Henry, Governor of the State. Fort Dunmore for a like reason became Fort Pitt again; Dunmore county ceased to exist, as did Fincastle county. The odious ex-Governor was stripped of his namesakes as far as the Virginians could do it. Fort Henry was made a place of considerable strength, but was not calculated for defense against artillery, as the Indians had none. It was made of logs twenty-one feet long, set on end, four feet in the ground, and seventeen above. There were bastions at the four corners, on which the defenders could station themselves to pick off the assailants. It was the purpose to mount small cannon there, but none had been provided. A wooden dummy was set up in a position to make it visible from the outside, and it was hoped that the Indians would be afraid of it. They discovered that it was a sham, and sarcastically challenged the garrison to fire it. The walls of the fort were two high to climb, too strong to break down with any means at the disposal of the Indians, and the plan of defense consisted in preventing the battering in of the gates or setting the fort on fire.

The savages drew near the walls of the fort on the night of August 31, and instead of attacking openly, they set an ambuscade and waited for daybreak. When the people about the fort began to stir, a few of the Indians showed themselves, and pretended to retreat. Captain Mason went in pursuit with fourteen men, and fell into the trap set for him. All of his men were killed but three. The firing called out a rescuing squad from the fort, and Captain Joseph Ogle with twelve men went to the rescue. He fell into the same trap and nine of his men were killed. That left about a dozen men in the stockade to resist the attack of more than three hundred Indians. The fort contained no soldiers, and was defended by men, women, and children of Wheeling and vicinity. In the fighting that followed the women handled rifles the same as the men.

Before the enemy began the assault on the fort, the white man who seemed to be the leader posted himself at the widow of a cabin within hearing distance, and proceded to read a demand for the surrender of the place, and accompanied it with a proclamation which he pretended was signed by Governor Hamilton, of Detroit. The demand for surrender was made in the name of Great Britain, and not the Indians. The King's protection was promised to all who would lay down their arms and submit; and warning was given to all who offered resistance that the savages would attack them, and if they fell into the hands of the Indians their safety could not be guaranteed. Colonel David Shepherd, commandant of the fort, replied that the place would not be surrendered. The white man at the cabin window undertook to show by argument that the fort could not offer successful resistance, but his talk was cut short by a shot fired at him from the fort, and he withdrew.

The assault commenced a few minutes later with a rush against the gate. It withstood the attack. The Indians endeavored to push the posts of the stockade down. In that they failed also. The people in the fort fired at short range with deadly effect. The assailants recoiled; but their courage was not abated. They came up again and again in determined rushes against the gate and the palisades, employing logs and stones as battering rams to break the wall. These attempts met with no better success, and some of the boldest tried to set the fort on fire. Once more they failed. The bullets from the port holes picked off the enemy rapidly and finally drove them away from the walls.

The Indians having spent their rage in fruitless rushes against the logs of the palisades, withdrew to a safer distance, and renewed the attack with less danger to themselves. Their best riflemen ensconced themselves behind shelter, or hid in neighboring cabins, and tried to pick off the defenders by shooting through the port holes. They wasted a large quantity of British lead and powder to no purpose, for they killed no one in the fort. They kept up the fire, with repeated attempts to storm the place, during two days and nights. They amused themselves with burning the cabins and barns of Wheeling, and practically nothing was left. They also drove up the cattle found about the neighboring fields and killed them, and feasted on the spoils. On the third day, when their vigilance was relaxed, fourteen men under Colonel Andrew Swearinger succeeded in landing near the fort, and entered its walls without loss. A second reinforcement arrived soon after in command of Major Samuel McCulloch. His forty men were not so successful in reaching the fort without a fight as Swearinger's had been. The Indians attempted to intercept them, and a sharp encounter occurred, but all reached the fort except the leader. He was cut off, and made his escape by riding his horse down a precipitous bluff two hundred feet high. The Indians saw all hope of success vanish, and they raised the siege and marched off. They had one-tenth of their number killed. They displayed courage of the highest quality in their attacks on the fortified place. Few civilized armies will continue a long and offensive fight which costs them one man in ten.

The Grave Creek Ambuscade—Soon after the Indians departed from Wheeling a disastrous ambush occurred at the Grave Creek Narrows, near the Ohio, a short distance below Wheeling. There seems to be no positive evidence that the Indians concerned in it were part of those who had lately besieged Fort Henry, but such was probably the case. The party must have been large, for they made quick work of Captain William Foreman and twenty-one Hampshire county militia. The remainder of the party was saved from destruction by the alarm of the Indians who mistook the advance of a few men for the van of a large force, and fled. They did not go so precipitately, however, but that they were able to carry off nine guns and twenty blankets belonging to the slain men. Sundry other arms and accoutrements were carried off also, the whole of which was afterwards paid for by the State, amounting to more than five hundred dollars in value.

Assassination of Cornstalk—Though many of the Ohio tribes were openly at war with the Virginians in the summer of 1777, the Shawnees remained at peace. They were probably the most powerful tribe in Ohio. They had formed the strength of the confederacy which had been defeated at Point Pleasant three years before. In the treaty at Camp Charlotte, following the battle, Cornstalk, the Chief of the Shawnees, had pledged that he would keep the peace, and ever since he had tried to do so. His task became extremely difficult as the summer of 1777 advanced and war parties from among the other tribes were constantly going out. The Shawnees were restless, and were restrained only by the influence of Cornstalk. The agents of the British were among them, doing all in their power to turn the Shawnees upon the frontiers. Cornstalk frankly explained to the officers on the frontiers the troubles which the peace party among his tribe was having. Some of the young men had gone on raids in spite of him. Even then he did all he could to repair the damage they did. He conducted to Point Pleasant some of the stolen horses carried off by his people.

Early in the fall Cornstalk came again to Fort Randolph at Point Pleasant, and brought the intelligence that the Shawnees were getting beyond his control, and that some influence which he could not understand was leading them. The influence was undoubtedly British bribes. Red Hawk, another chief of the Shawnees, came with him. Under the circumstances the commandant of Fort Randolph thought it advisable to detain the two chiefs as hostages to secure the good behavior of the Shawnees. The chiefs were not unwilling to be detained, and were well treated during their stay at the fort.

In the fall a number of militiamen arrived at Point Pleasant from the east for the purpose of invading the Indian country. While waiting at the fort, a young Indian, Elinipisco by name, son of Cornstalk, arrived at the fort to learn what had become of his father who had long overstayed his time. Scarcely had the young man reached the cabin where his father was before word was brought that a soldier had been killed by Indians within a mile of the fort. It happened to be one of the militiamen who had lately come. His companions declared their belief that the Indians who killed the soldier had come with Elinipisco, and had concealed themselves in the woods for the purpose of killing a white man. Refusing to listen to reason, they rushed to the cabin where the Indians were, and murdered them on the spot. The victims had warning a few moments before the assassins arrived, and might have saved themselves by flight, but Cornstalk refused to do it, and advised the others to die like men. When the murderers appeared at the door, Cornstalk stood up, and without a word, received the bullet that killed him.

Few lives have been more dearly paid for than the Virginians paid for Cornstalk's. The Shawnees hesitated no longer, but plunged immediately into the war against the frontiers, and few were the Shawnee warriors who did not, during the five succeeding years, consider it his duty to personally avenge the death of his chief by taking ten lives for one, if possible. Four years afterward when Colonel William Crawford fell into the hands of the Indians, he was burned at the stake to avenge the death of Cornstalk, as was expressly declared by some of the Shawnees.

Fort Randolph Attacked—The season was too far advanced when the tribes learned of the death of Cornstalk for offensive movements by large bodies to be carried out before winter. The Indians could not campaign in cold weather because their clothing was insufficient. The frontiers could depend upon peace and security after the first deep snows of the fall until the spring thaws.

In May a force of Shawnees, estimated at two hundred, crossed the Ohio river secretly and approached Fort Randolph in the night. The fort stood on the Point Pleasant battlefield, and the savages came with full recollection of the defeat they had suffered there less than four years before. They repeated almost exactly their tactics of the year before at Fort Henry, but with less success. Early in the morning a few Indians showed themselves in a field near the fort to decoy a party in pursuit; but the trick was suspected, and the plan for an ambuscade came to naught. Finding that the soldiers would not fall into the trap, the savages threw off all disguise, and boldly rose from their concealment, forming an unbroken line from the Kanawha river across the neck of land to the Ohio, cutting off the garrison's retreat by land, should such a step be undertaken. Their purpose had been, as was supposed, to decoy as many of the garrison out as they could, fire on the party, and pursue the fugitives to the fort, and enter at their heels before the gate could be closed. The failure of that plan made an open assault necessary, unless they wished to abandon the purpose of attack.

Several attempts were made to take the fort by storm, but the assaults were weak. The Indians displayed little of the fierce courage they had shown at Fort Henry. Their experience on that occasion had taught them prudence; and, besides, they must have realized from the start that their force was too small to capture the place unless it could be done by treachery or surprise. That turned out to be impossible, and they settled down to a siege, and during one week they closely invested the fort, discharging their guns occasionally in the direction of the stockade. Finally, they packed up their belongings and moved off; but instead of recrossing the Ohio and returning to their own country, they marched up the Kanawha. That meant only one thing—that they intended to attack the Greenbrier settlements, one hundred and sixty miles distant. The region between the Greenbrier country and Point Pleasant had no settlers at that time.

Assault on Donnally's Fort—The commandant at Fort Randolph realized the danger the Greenbrier people were in. If that army of two hundred Indians should fall on them unawares, the settlements would be wiped out. As soon as it became certain that the savages were headed for the Greenbrier, the commandant of the fort called for volunteers who would try to pass the Indians on the way and warn the people. The danger of the undertaking was pointed out, but there were volunteers enough. Two soldiers were chosen for the work. They were dressed and painted like Indians. A sister of Cornstalk, who had remained at the fort since the year before, notwithstanding the murder of her brother and nephew, assisted in painting the scouts and disguising them to make them look as much like Indians as possible.

The scouts traveled day and night, and overtook the Indians on Meadow river, about twenty miles from the Greenbrier settlements. The vacant house of a frontier settler stood at that place. Some of his property remained there, hogs and other things. The Indians were in the act of killing and eating the hogs when the scouts passed them unseen, and a few hours later reached the outlying settlement of the Greenbrier colony. There having been no Indian alarm that spring, the people were in their fields putting in crops. Two forts had been erected for their protection in time of danger. One stood ten miles north of the town of Lewisburg, and was known as Fort Donnally, the other was Fort Savannah on the site of Lewisburg. A few hours after the scouts sounded the alarm, the entire settlement was on the way to the forts. Twenty men with their families assembled at Donnally's before dark, and five times that number were within the walls of Fort Savannah, ten miles distant.

Donnally's Fort was a two-story log house with port holes through which assailants could be fired on from the loft. It has been claimed that the building was enclosed with palisades, but that seems to be doubtful, as the enemy in the attack in 1778 approached the walls of the house, crawled beneath the floor, climbed the corners in an endeavor to reach the roof, and in other ways conducted the assault as though not embarrassed by the presence of palisades.

The Indians, after reaching Meadow river, directed their march toward Donnally's Fort instead of Fort Savannah, because they supposed, and rightly, that the former was weaker. They arrived in the night and lay in wait near the fort till morning. The inmates had prepared for a siege by providing a store of food and water; and strict orders had been given the evening before that the door should not be opened in the morning until an examination had been made to see that the coast was clear. It is strange that in the face of danger which was known to be imminent the occupants of the fort would sleep through the night without posting guards to watch for the enemy. The wonder is that the historian is not called upon to relate how the building was approached in the darkness and set on fire. The Indians lost that opportunity of winning an easy victory; and contented themselves with lying in wait to strike a sudden blow in the morning.

About daylight one of the inmates, contrary to strict orders, went to the yard for kindling wood, and left the door open. One white man and a negro slave were awake in the house, but all others were asleep. The man who stepped into the yard was immediately shot, and the savages rushed for the open door. A blow from the white man's tomahawk killed the first that tried to enter, and the negro discharged a musket loaded with shot, into the faces of the Indians who were pushing toward the door. They were checked, and the door was shut. The savages began to hew it with their tomahawks. Some of them having crawled under the house attempted to raise the puncheons and force an entrance that way; while others climbed the walls.

The first shots waked the men upstairs who fired through the port holes with such deadly effect that seventeen of the assailants were killed so near the walls that their comrades dare not approach to remove them. Those who were climbing the walls mocked the men within whose words could be heard and were repeated: "Aim good," "Shoot 'em sure," "Powder scarce." There was powder enough, however, to dislodge the assailants from their position near the walls and drive them from the vicinity of the fort. They retired to a safer distance and fired at long range for several hours, but without doing any damage. Hundreds of bullets were buried in the logs, but none passed through.

In the afternoon help came from Fort Savannah. As soon as the people who fled for refuge to that place were safely within, they sent out expert woodsmen to get in touch with the enemy. They approached sufficiently near Donnally's Fort to hear the firing, and carried the news to headquarters. Sixty-six men were sent to the relief of the people at Donnally's, and the Indians fled without long sustaining the attack. They left the country without doing further damage. Their campaign as a whole had failed, as they had been able to kill only one person.

The Illinois Campaign—Indiana and Illinois were far removed from what is now the territory of West Virginia, and on the face of it, it might seem that events happening there in 1779 and 1780 would have little connection with West Virginia's history; but such was not the case. It had become apparent by that time that no permanent relief from Indian raids and invasions need be expected as long as the borders fought on the defensive only. War brought no hardships to the Indians, but rather amusement and recreation, if they were permitted to carry it on in their own way. They made a pastime of skulking about the settlements, stealing horses which they were able to sell to the British and to traders, and taking scalps for which the British paid them well. They sometimes met reverses on those raids, but generally not.

An invasion of the Indian country was looked upon as the only means of securing permanent relief. The prompt and satisfactory peace which followed the campaign of 1774 was cited as an example of what a successful invasion of the enemy's country would accomplish. In 1778 Fort McIntosh was built on the north bank of the Ohio below the mouth of Beaver creek, and army headquarters were moved from Pittsburgh to that place in order to be nearer the borders of the Indian country. The same year Fort Laurens was built still nearer the Indian country, on the bank of Tuscarawar creek, and Colonel John Gibson with one hundred and fifty men was stationed there. The building of these forts disconcerted the Indians, and excited their hostility in a special degree. They took measures to harrass the places as much as possible. On March 22, 1779, Captain Byrd, a British officer from Detroit, with a following of eight white men and one hundred and twenty Indians, appeared before Fort Laurens, and besieged it. His force was too weak to assure any measure of success in assault, but he waylaid provision convoys and attacked small parties, and for a month made his presence felt. He retired when he saw no opportunity to do further mischief.

In 1778 a force was raised and placed under command of George

Rogers Clark for an invasion of Illinois. The blow was aimed at British posts in that region whence the Indians received much encouragement in their war against the Virginia settlements. Clark's force was largely made up of West Virginians, from the Monongahela Valley and elsewhere within the present boundaries of the State.' He surprised Kaskaskia in Illinois and Vincennes, Indiana, and captured them. He left Captain Helm in charge of Vincennes.

When Hamilton, Governor of Canada, learned of the success of the Americans, he set out from Detroit, October 8, 1778, with thirty-five British regulars, forty-four irregulars, seventy militia, and sixty Indians to recover the lost ground and restore British influence in that quarter. He increased his force by picking up other Indians on the way, and on December 17 he appeared before Vincennes, and Captain Helm was surrounded and compelled to surrender. Governor Hamilton then dismissed his Indians to their homes, and ordered them to assemble at Vincennes early the following spring to renew the campaign. His designs were ambitious. He expected to drive the Americans out of Illinois, break up and destroy the settlements in Kentucky, repeat the work in Virginia west of the mountains, and capture Wheeling, Fort Randolph, and Pittsburgh. He calculated that he could do more than Connolly had planned.

He calculated without duly considering that George Rogers Clark lay with a small but well-seasoned force a hundred and fifty miles west of him. Winter had come by that time, and Hamilton intended to do nothing till spring, and he expected no movement meanwhile by anyone else; but Clark prepared for immediate action. Marching from Kaskaskia in midwinter he passed undiscovered through the forests and across the prairies of southern Illinois, wading water often waist deep, and before the British at Vincennes suspected the proximity of an enemy, Clark's little army appeared before the place. The British had a force large enough to have fought, even on open ground, with fair prospects of success; but they were deceived concerning the number of the Americans. Clark marched the same companies of troops several times across a rising ground in full view of the fort; and so concealed the movements that he led the British to believe that the force they saw was much larger than it really was.

Demand for the surrender of Vincennes was refused at first by Hamilton, and Clark approached within rifle range, and opened fire. A few minutes sufficed to send up the white flag at the fort, and Hamilton surrendered. The Americans won a victory which, in far-reaching results, has had few equals, if any, in this country. Its full scope was not very clearly understood at the time, and the immediate fruits were looked upon as the chief prize. These consisted of the release of one hundred white prisoners who were found in Vincennes; the capture of military stores worth fifty thousand dollars, and the clearing of the whole country of British from the Mississippi to Detroit. The ardor of the Indians was greatly dampened, and they learned for the first time that the British were not able to protect them. The Americans from that time forward held the country as far west as the Mississippi river.

Governor Hamilton was sent a prisoner to Richmond. He was cordially hated by the Americans by whom he was called "the hair buyer," in allusion to his policy of buying scalps from the Indians. It was claimed that his standing offer of high prices for the scalps of men, women, and children (for he made no distinction) caused many a murder of prisoners taken by Indians. They killed captives for the scalp money. In view of the hatred felt for Hamilton, some relief was felt by those in charge of him when he was delivered safe in Richmond. He remained there a year as a prisoner, and he was the subject of heated correspondence between Thomas Jefferson and British officers who undertook to secure his release on parole. Jefferson contended that Hamilton's conduct had put him outside the pale of civilized war. He was exchanged in 1780, and was again for a time Governor of Canada.

Last Siege of Fort Henry—An expedition was sent against Coshocton, Ohio, in 1781, under General Brodhead, with one hundred and fifty regular soldiers and an equal number of militia. He met with small loss on his part, and inflicted severe damage on the savages.

In the summer of 1782 the Ohio Indians prepared for attacking Wheeling. The town had been rebuilt after it was burned by the savages in 1777. The fort was the same, and the only addition to its strength was the mounting of a small cannon on one of the bastions. A British officer named Caldwell with a few white men appeared in Ohio in July to lead the army of three hundred Indians against Wheeling. Among the white men in this proposed expedition were Simon Girty, the renegade, and his brother George. The expedition was only fairly on foot when a report spread through the Ohio tribes that General Clark with a large army was invading the Indian country and that General Irvine with another army was on his way to Canada. It was a false report, but it broke up the march toward Wheeling. Reinforcements for Canada were asked for, and such Indians as did not feel that their presence at home was absolutely necessary, moved toward Canada to lend their aid. Later the army, or part of it, which had intended to attack Wheeling, crossed the Ohio into Kentucky, and appeared before Bryant's station, August 14, 1782. Caldwell and the two Girtys accompanied that force.

The British did not give up the design of attacking Fort Henry when Caldwell and his three hundred Indians marched off toward Kentucky; but commenced gathering a new force. As a nucleus of an army, Captain Pratt entered Ohio with forty British regulars from Canada. Little trouble was experienced in collecting as many Indians as were needed, and toward the last of August two hundred and eighty-two savages were ready to march with the regulars. On September 11 this force appeared before Fort Henry, and demanded an immediate surrender, which Captain Boggs, the commandant, refused. The experience of the Indians in rushing forts by day taught them prudence, and they remained out of range until after dark.

The delay was of much advantage to the people in the fort. There were less than twenty men within the walls when the enemy appeared, but women and children were numerous. While the foe was waiting for darkness, a boat came down the Ohio under charge of a man named Sullivan. It was loaded with cannon balls for the army operating in Illinois and Indiana, and had a crew of a dozen or more men. Sullivan saw the situation, and succeeded in landing near the fort where he tied the boat, joined the garrison, and assisted in the defense.

The British flag flew over the camp of the enemy and the blowing of the bugle was a constant reminder that a considerable part of the threatening force consisted of white soldiers. Under cover of darkness they made more than twenty attempts to set the stockade on fire. They piled hemp against the wall and applied the blaze; but the hemp was damp, burned slowly, and the savages and their white allies were doomed to witness the repeated failures of their incendiary efforts.

Near the walls of the fort stood Ebenezer Zane's cabin. He considered it near enough to be successfully defended, and he was anxious to hold it, as it was believed that the enemy would burn all the houses in their power as they had done in 1777. Two white men and a negro remained in the cabin with Zane. While the attack was delayed, the discovery was made that keg of powder which was needed in the fort had been left in Zane's cabin. To fetch it while scores of Indians were within shooting distance was extremely perilous, but several volunteers offered themselves for the service. Among them was Elizabeth, daughter of Ebenezer Zane, and upon her insistance, she was sent for the powder. As she ran from the fort across the open space to the cabin, the Indians saw her but refrained from firing, simply exclaiming contemptously, "A squaw." But when she emerged from the cabin door a few minutes later with the powder in a table cloth that had been tied round her waist by her father, the purpose of her mission was suspected and bullets struck all about her as she ran, but she fortunately escaped harm and safely entered the fort.

The firing was very sharp from the fort and the cabin while the Indians were trying to set the place on fire. They were especially galled by the shots from the cabin whose fire raked them in the flank during their assaults on the fort. Late at night they attempted to rid themselves of the cabin by burning it, and an Indian, with glowing brands in his hands, crawled almost to the wall before the negro, who was at that moment on guard, discovered him. The savage had exposed himself to view in the darkness by waving the billets to kindle the embers to a blaze. The moment he exposed himself the negro fired. It was believed that the savage was struck; and at any rate, he dropped his fire brands and hobbled howling away.

A number of Indians took possession of a cabin loft some two hundred yards from the fort, and made night noisy with yelling and dancing. At length the cannon on the bastion was trained on the cabin, and the ball broke a joist, causing the upper floor to fall with all its load of savages, and effectively stopped the revelry in that quarter. The cannon was fired sixteen times during the siege.

The Indians, or more probably their white auxiliaries, conceived the notion of making a cannon of wood. The idea was suggested to them by the capture of the cannon balls in the boat which had stopped there on its way down the Ohio. A hollow maple log was procured, and the balls were found to fit the cavity. With chains procured in a neighboring blacksmith shop the log was securely bound, and the breech was plugged. The improvised weapon was pointed adroitly toward the fort gate, and a live coal was applied to the train of powder set to discharge the piece. The explosion burst the cannon, scattering broken chains and pieces of wood far and near, doing no damage to the fort, but injuring several of the savages who had crowded as near as possible to witness the effect of the shot.

The Indians made several attempts to break the gate open, but failed in all of them. Meantime a relief force had been collecting in the surrounding settlements, and seventy men marched to Fort Henry. The enemy did not stand for a fight in the open, but raised the siege and marched off. A portion of the attacking force appeared before Rice's Fort a few miles distant, defended by a few men. In the attack there they lost four warriors and accomplished nothing. In a few days the last stragglers of the formidable invading force had recrossed the Ohio, and no Indian army ever after that set foot on the soil of West Virginia.

The man who carried the British flag in the attack on Wheeling was shot, and fell with the flag. That was nearly eleven months after the surrender of Cornwallis at Yorktown, and it is claimed that it was the last flag to fly over a British force in fight on American soil during the Revolution. Consequently, it has been claimed that the siege of Fort Henry, in September, 1782, was the last battle in the war of Independence.

The Loyalists—When the Revolutionary War came on, political lines were drawn, and hatred and hostility divided the factions. By no means all of the people were in favor of separation from England, and doubtless many who were apposed to a separation were honest and sincere in their views. The great majority, however, espoused the American cause, and in most parts of the country the tories—the name applied to those who took sides against their country—were in such minority that they were powerless for harm. The greatest strength of the tories was seen in those parts of the country which the British were able to overrun and dominate, particularly parts of New York, New Jersey, and South Carolina. Where it was believed that British protection could be depended upon, large numbers of American citizens declared for England, and some took arms to fight their countrymen who were struggling to gain their independence. It frequently happened that the tories were vindictive, and went out of their way to make trouble for their neighbors who had espoused the patriotic cause. This naturally led to reprisals and retaliations, and finally the animosity between tories and their patriotic countrymen grew intense.

There has been a good deal said by writers of local history in West Virginia, west of the mountains, of tory plots along the Ohio and Monongahela. It was popularly believed that one of the purposes of the Indian and British invasions in 1777 which ended in the siege of Wheeling, was to furnish safe transportation to Western Virginia tories who were anxious to quit the country and go to Canada. No one ever seemed able to name or count any who took advantage of the opportunity to depart. There were rumors of plots in the Monongahela Valley in which tories planned crimes and misdemeanors against the property and lives of their fellow citizens. It was long ago published as history that tories were deported from the country, and that in one instance their leader was drowned—supposedly by design—in Cheat river.

It is not easy, by use of the vague historical and traditional data available, to prove or disprove much that has been asserted. It is probable that the accounts are pretty evenly divided between truth and falsehood. It is evident that in 1775 Dr. John Connolly who was Dunmore's agent, believed that many of the people west of the mountains would come out for the English cause if they dared. In his scheme for invasion from Canada, as narrated in preceding pages, he made provision for those who would be found on his side when his army entered the country. How correct his judgment may have been in that matter is not now known. It is certain, however, from what is well known, that the tories west of the Alleghanies were very far from being in the majority. Most of the men carried arms on the other side, and as it was nearly always free choice with them whether they would go into the army or not, it is reasonable to conclude that they took the field in defense of the cause in which they believed. There were probably fewer tories west of the mountains in Virginia than in any other part of the country, in proportion to the total number of people.

East of the Alleghanies in what is now Hardy, Grant, and Pendleton counties, a tory plot came to a head when it was believed that Cornwallis would subdue Virginia and drive the patriot armies out. The center of the plot was near Petersburg, in Grant county. It is said that a number of the tories implicated in the trouble lived twenty miles above there at Upper Tract, and that some came from Moonfield river, along the base of the Shenandoah mountains. The first intimation of rebellion appeared when they refused to pay their taxes or contribute to Hampshire's quota of men to be raised for the army. Colonel Van Meter with thirty militia was sent from Old Fields to enforce the payment of taxes. Fifty tories armed themselves and assembled at the house of John Brake, a German, and declared that they would resist the demands by force and arms. Colonel Van Meter who knew most of the tories personally marched his men to meet them, but instead of a fight there was a parley. The leader of the militia attempted to convince them by argument that they were in the wrong and must ultimately suffer for it, but they had the best of the argument, as it would seem, for the militia went home and left them in arms and defiant. The fact probably was, Colonel Van Meter saw that he was not strong enough to fight them successfully, and he retired to make better preparation.

They thought themselves victorious and became more insolent and defiant than before. They organized a company, elected John Claypole their captain, and prepared to march off and join Cornwallis as soon as he arrived within reach of them. They seemed to be fairly well posted on the movements of the British army which at that time was threatening lower Virginia. General Daniel Morgan, of the Continental army, happened to be at that time in Frederick county, some sixty miles distant. Learning that the tories had organized a military company he thought it time he took a hand. He collected four hundred militia and did not open parley with the insurgents, but pressed them so closely that Claypole surrendered, and William Baker was shot when he refused to throw down his gun; but he was not killed. After one other had been shot, Brake surrendered, and the tory uprising was at an end. When the tories duly reflected upon what they had done they repented, and in order to make amends, they joined the American army and fought till the end of the war. A cavern is pointed out seven miles from Upper Tract which is still called Tory Cave, because of a tradition that some of the terrified men who escaped General Morgan's militia were hiding in it for some days.

Buying Powder in New Orleans—The scarcity of powder in the western settlements, and for that matter in the whole country, has been spoken of. The friendliness of the Spanish who then held New Orleans, induced the belief that a supply might be obtained in that city, if some way could be devised for bringing it to the colonies. To send it by sea would be to invite almost certain capture by English ships. The only other route was up the Mississippi and the Ohio. John Linn and a number of others were sent in a small boat, with a couple of thousand dollars, to buy powder in New Orleans. They reached that place safely, and the Spanish Governor received them in a friendly manner, but the town was full of British spies who at once surmised that the Americans had come on some secret mission, and they urged the Governor to arrest them. After Governor Galvez had secretly informed the Americans of what he was about to do, and the reason for doing it (to allay the suspicions of the English spies) he had one of the Americans arrested and placed in jail, but left him and the others at liberty, with his consent to buy all the powder they could pay for, provided they kept the transaction secret.

The spies were thrown off their guard, and their vigilance was relaxed. Linn quietly purchased ten thousand pounds of powder for $1,800, had it loaded in a boat, and with his men he pulled off up the Mississippi with it. After several weeks had passed, the Spaniards released the prisoner whom they had held as a blind, and he returned to Virginia by sea. Months passed before any tidings came of the powder boat on the Mississippi. Scouts were sent down the Ohio with instructions to search to the mouth of the river, examining the mouths of all the streams as they passed. In case they could hear nothing of Linn and the powder when they reached the Mississippi they were instructed to go to St. Louis and make inquiries there. An old letter is in existence in which one of the scouts wrote to ask an officer where St. Louis was, and the officer in reply said he had no idea.

Meanwhile, Linn toiled slowly up the Mississippi against the current. Winter had set in by the time he reached a post in Arkansas, and he put in there to wait for spring. He was well treated, and passed several weeks pleasantly, and his men rested in preparation for the long journey ahead of them. They set forward early in the spring and in several weeks reached the mouth of the Ohio, one hundred and fifty miles or more below St. Louis. The Spanish officer in command of the St. Louis Fort had by that time heard of the mysterious boat ascending the Mississippi, and when it turned up the Ohio, he sent Indians across the country to the falls at Louisville to intercept and capture it. The Indians were not fast enough. Before they reached the designated place, Linn's powder boat had passed, and they returned to St. Louis. Linn continued up the Ohio and finally landed the powder at Wheeling, and it was put to good service during the remainder of the war.

SOLDIERS AND SUPPLIES.

It was easier to raise troops for the Revolutionary war than to find their supplies. Factories, as the term is now understood, did not exist in this country then. Small shops and individual workers made nearly all the clothing, shoes, blankets, tents, and a considerable part of the arms. If contractors undertook to furnish supplies, they had to go among the people for them. The weaving and spinning were done by hand; leather was tanned in small yards, and a few hides at a time was generally the capacity. No factory took orders to make army wagons, but the blacksmiths in the villages and at the crossroads made them, and the equipment of a regiment made necessary a call upon all the surrounding country for what was wanted. There was no other way to equip an army and keep it in the field. Braddock lost farm wagons worth $100,000 which the farmers of Pennsylvania had supplied on Benjamin Franklin's promise that he would see that they were paid for. Washington's armies were supplied in the same way—when they were supplied at all. The Congress called on the States for supplies, and the States called on their counties, and the counties had to go to the individuals.

In October, 1780, the Virginia Assembly made a direct call on the counties. The counties in what is now West Virginia supplied clothing, beef, wagons, horses, and drivers. Berkeley's share was seventy-one suits of clothes, each suit to consist of two shirts of linen or cotton, one pair of overalls, two pairs of stockings, one pair of shoes, one hat of wool, fur, or felt, or a leather cap. In addition to that, Berkeley furnished seventy-one cattle each weighing not less than three hundred pounds net; one good wagon, with four horses and harness complete, with a driver whose wages for one month were paid by the county. Other counties furnished supplies in like proportion.

Calls for Troops—Virginia laid levies for troops both for defense on its western frontier and for use of the Continental army. Ten calls were issued during the Revolution, all of which were promptly answered. These were in addition to almost constant calls in the counties for militia to fight Indians who were raiding the settlements, and for scouts and spies to guard the paths by which the savages made their way into the country. The West Virginia counties had a military burden to carry during that time which well nigh reached the limit of endurance. Sometimes it was beyond their power. Greenbrier county fell in arrears $30,000 in State taxes. There was no money with which to pay. The State made arrangements that the sum be worked out in road building, and the Greenbrier people built a highway for their settlement to the Kanawha Valley in lieu of cash taxes.

Virginia's first call for soldiers was in July, 1775, the second in October, 1776, third in October, 1777, fourth in October, 1778, fifth in May, 1779, the sixth was later in the same month, seventh in May, 1780, eighth in October, 1780, ninth in May, 1781, and tenth in May, 1782. It is not possible to determine exactly what was the total number of soldiers raised by the ten calls in the seven years, but it was about thirty-five hundred. It does not necessarily mean that that number of individuals enlisted, for the same men may have joined more than once. Neither is it possible to ascertain where all of these men served. It is known that they fought at Kaskaskia on the bank of the Mississippi river, and at Boston. Some of them were in almost every important battle of the Revolution, and in every campaign against the Indians. A number of West Virginians, though in Colonel Crawford's Pennsylvania regiment, were in the army of Gates at Saratoga, and Gates himself was a West Virginian. Soldiers from the banks of the Monongahela and along the Ohio helped George Rogers Clark win and hold Illinois for the American cause. Captain George Jackson raised a company of one hundred and four soldiers at Buckhannon and marched with them to the west; General Morgan with a much larger number marched from Berkeley county, six hundred miles, to Boston. Wherever fighting and hard campaigning was to be done, the soldiers from the mountains of Western Virginia were on hand to help do it.

Pension Legislation—During thirty-five years after the close of the Revolution, Congress made no provision for paying pensions to the surviving soldiers of that war. In 1818 the first pension law was passed. It was so difficult and so humiliating to comply with its terms that comparatively few availed themselves of its privileges. They must, in the first place, acknowledge themselves paupers, that is, "in need of assistance." They must have served to the end of the war, or at least nine consecutive months at one period. About one hundred ninety-four Western Virginians applied for pensions under that law. They were residents in 1818 of what is now West Virginia, though they may have moved into the State long after the close of the Revolution. About eight thousand Revolutionary applicants for pensions filed their claims in the United States.

Congress became suspicious that many of the applicants were not in need, and in 1820 a law was passed requiring all pension claimants to file schedules of their property, containing their whole estates and incomes. Congress was plainly hostile to Revolutionary pensions, and sought to shorten the rolls by numerous eliminations.

In 1832 the law was amended so that those who had served six months or over might draw pensions proportioned to the length of their services. Under this law four hundred and forty-seven Western Virginians applied. The number of rejections was large. In 1850 there were still living in Western Virginia one hundred and twenty-seven Revolutionary soldiers whose claims for pensions had been rejected. That was sixty-seven years after the war closed, and it is surprising that so many were still living. Most of them must have been very young when the war ended, for the most frequent reason for rejecting their claims to pensions was that they did not serve six months. It was not at all uncommon for boys fifteen years old to serve as soldiers. Some of the other reasons recorded for rejecting claims were the following: "A more perfect narrative of his services needed." "A frontiersman." "Was a wagon master." "Neighborhood service against the Indians." "A frontiersman engaged in garrison duty only." "Service in Indian wars of 1777, 1778, 1779, and 1780." "Collecting beeves for Continental army." "Did not serve six months in his first term and his second requires additional proof."

In 1840 there were two hundred and three Revolutionary pensioners still living in West Virginia.

Fixing the Boundary—As the international boundary between the United States and Canada was finally agreed upon, West Virginia was concerned with it only in common with all the other States; but before the question was settled, and while the negotiations were underway at Paris in 1783, the territory now in West Virginia between the mountains and the Ohio river, was in peril of falling dangerously near undesirable neighbors. For that reason, a brief review of the negotiations which finally fixed the boundary should be of peculiar interest to West Virginia. It is not possible to say with certainty what would have been the historical consequence had the boundary been fixed as some of the parties at the treaty of Paris wanted it; though it is probable that the United States would have grown westward anyhow, peaceably if it could, forcibly if it must, as it did in taking Texas, California, Louisiana, and Oregon. Boundary lines in wrong places are not strong enough to check and defeat the expansion of the growing Anglo-Saxon nation. It never was within the power of any European nation or combination of nations to lay down a line across the fertile plains and navigable rivers of North America, in the path of American growth, and say to the United States, "Hither shalt thou come, and no further." Fortunately for the future peace of the United States, its commissioners at the Paris treaty were men of such foresight, firmness, and diplomatic skill that they did not permit the boundary to be fixed in a place where it would lead to future wars. The way was cleared for westward expansion; and when an English statesman was informed that the Americans would listen to no western line short of the Mississippi river, he exclaimed with prophetic truth, "The Pacific is their goal."

Four nations were concerned in fixing the boundary between the United States and Canada—England, France, Spain, and this country. The principal parties to the treaty were the United States and Great Britain, but France was admitted as an ally of the United States, and Spain insisted on taking an indirect part, because she claimed the territory beyond the Mississippi. It transpired before the close of the negotiations that Spain's ambitions and hopes looked to getting possession of the whole Ohio Valley, nearly if not quite up to the Alleghany mountains. Her schemes to that end were deeply laid, and her claims to the country went back to the discoveries by De Soto. The victories by George Rogers Clark really told more against Spain's pretensions than against England's; because from Spain's point of view, Clark won the country by conquest, and Spain did not dare dispute that conquest gave right. The danger that Spain might get its claim allowed by England lay in the fact that Great Britain would rather see Spain in the Ohio Valley than to have it become a part of the United States. The plot—if it was a plot—was defeated by the firmness of the United States commissioners. They would not listen to it, and they let it be clearly understood that if any such terms were insisted on, there would be no treaty in which the United States was a party. Thereupon, Spain's claim to the Ohio Valley was withdrawn, and England undertook to save the region for herself. First, she insisted that Quebec included all the territory between the Ohio and the Mississippi rivers, and that the Ohio was the line between Virginia and Pennsylvania on the one side and Canada on the other. But that line would leave what is now Kentucky, Tennessee, and the region still south a district still in dispute, and to eliminate it from consideration, it was proposed that a line be drawn from western Georgia to the mouth of the Kanawha river, and the United States be confined east of that line. It may be inferred that Spain was to have the country south of the Ohio and west of that line, and England would be content with what was north of the river. If that arrangement had been carried through, Spain would have come into possession of Kentucky, Tennessee, Alabama, and Mississippi, and Florida; and England would have held Ohio, Indiana, Illinois, Michigan, Wisconsin, and Minnesota. The United States would have been confined to the Atlantic coast, with a little land west of the mountains. What is now West Virginia would have been the extreme western region of the United States. England even claimed part of western Pennsylvania and western New York. One of the French statesmen, who was supposed to be friendly with this country, expressed the opinion that the United States ought to be content with the region drained by rivers flowing to the Atlantic ocean.

Once again the United States commissioners set their seal of absolute disapproval on any such division. England modified the terms to the extent of leaving the Ohio Valley, or part of it, as a neutral region for her Indian allies, who would be under England's protection. These terms were likewise rejected, though it was looked upon more favorably than the proposal to extend the province of Quebec to the Ohio river. It was clearly seen, however, that any arrangement that gave England a protectorate in the Ohio Valley would lead to trouble later, for ultimately England would own it, or it would become necessary to drive her out. Another proposition was brought forward by the English commissioners. They proposed that the loyalists who resided in the United States, or who had been forced to quit the country because of the hostility toward them, be given the Ohio Valley, or a part of it, as a compensation for their loss of property, and as a place of residence. That proposal acted upon the American commissioners like flourishing a red flag in the face of a bull. Benjamin Franklin in particular would hear to nothing of the kind. The Americans hated the tories with an inappeasable hatred. They would rather have wild Indians for neighbors. Franklin declared that, if the tories were to be settled as neighbors over our borders, he would insist on having the border follow the Arctic ocean coast. As to compensating the tories for their loss, he sarcastically suggested that England sell its barren Canadian lands and give them the proceeds, but under no circumstances to settle tories even in Canada.

The United States commissioners at the Paris treaty came forward with two propositions for fixing the boundary, either of which they would accept. One was the forty-fifth parallel of latitude. That corresponded with the present northern boundary of New York and Vermont extended westward across Canada, Michigan, Wisconsin, and Minnesota to the Mississippi river. The United States was to have all south of the line, England all north. The other line proposed was the same as the present boundary, but west of the Lake of the Woods its extension was not definite. The English accepted the second proposition. It has been said that they accepted under a misunderstanding of the country's geography. They thought the Mississippi's source was north of the line, and they expected in the future to claim a right to the navigation of that river, and saw a place for an opening wedge by which they hoped to split away forever the trans-Mississippi country from the United States, and doubtless expected ultimately to come into possession of it southward to Spain's possessions. When it was ascertained that the source of the Mississippi was south of the line, dreams of possession west of the river vanished until years later they came up in another form in the Oregon question.

END OF THE INDIAN WARS.

The Revolutionary war ended in 1783 with the treaty of Paris, and the subsequent trouble with Indians on the Western Virginia frontiers was an independent matter, and can be given only the briefest mention in this chapter.

In July, 1783, Governor De Peyster called the Indians together at Detroit and told them that the war between the English and the Americans was at an end, and he dismissed them from the English service, and advised them to make peace. They obeyed in a sullen manner. In the autumn of 1783 when the order was given for the evacuation of New York by the British, Lord North, acting for an excuse on a petition of the fur-traders of Canada, withheld the order for the evacuation of the posts about the Great Lakes. On August 8 of that year Baron Steuben, who was sent for that purpose by the Americans, demanded of Governor Haldimand, of Canada, that British garrisons be withdrawn from posts northwest of the Ohio. Two years later the British garrisons were yet occupying posts in Ohio and Indiana, and the excuse for so doing was that some of the States, especially Virginia, had not yet opened their courts to British creditors for collection of debts against Americans incurred before the war. Thus the British continued to hold posts clearly within the United States, much to the annoyance of the American people.

The Indians were restless, and the belief was general, and was well founded, that the British were encouraging them to hostility. They became insolent, and invaded the settlements in West Virginia and Kentucky, and in 1790 the United States declared war upon them and took vigorous measures to bring them to terms. General Harmar invaded the country north of the Ohio at the head of a strong force in 1790. He suffered his army to be divided and defeated. The next year General St. Clair led an army into the Indian country, and met with one of the most disastrous defeats in the annals of Indian warfare. General Wayne now took charge of the campaign in the Indian country. When he began to invade the northern part of Ohio, the British about Lake Erie moved south and built a fort on the Maumee river, opposite Perrysville, Ohio. This was in the summer of 1794. The object in building the fort was clearly to encourage the Indians and to insult the Americans. On August 20, 1794, General Wayne found the Indians within two miles of the British fort, prepared for battle. He made an attack on the savages, routed them in a few minutes and drove them. They were crushed and there was no more fight in them for fifteen years.

General Wayne was a Revolutionary soldier, and had little love for the British. The sight of their fort on American soil filled him with impatience to attack it; but he did not wish to do so without a pretext. He hoped to provoke the garrison to attack him, to give him an excuse to destroy the fort. He therefore camped his army after the battle within half a mile of the fort. The commandant sent a message to him saying: "The commandant of the British fort is surprised to see an American army advanced so far into this country," and "why has the army had the assurance to camp under the very mouths of His Majesty's cannon?" General Wayne answered that the battle which had just taken place might well inform the British what the American army was doing in that country, and added: "Had the flying savages taken shelter under the walls of the fort, His Majesty's cannon should not have protected them." Two days later General Wayne destroyed everything to within one hundred yards of the fort, and laid waste the Indian fields of corn, pumpkins and beans for miles around. The country was highly cultivated, there being thousands of acres in corn and vegetables. Finding that his efforts thus far had failed to provoke an attack by the garrison, General Wayne led his soldiers to within pistol shot of the walls, in hope of bringing a shot from his inveterate enemies. But the only reply General Wayne received was a flag of truce with another message, which stated that "the British commandant is much aggrieved at seeing His Majesty's colors insulted." Wayne then burned all the houses and destroyed all the property to the very walls of the fort. This campaign ended the depredation of the Indians in West Virginia.

BRADDOCK'S ROAD AND THE WEST-
WARD MOVEMENT

BRADDOCK'S ROAD AND THE WESTWARD MOVEMENT.

Braddock's road across the mountains from Cumberland, Maryland, to the Monongahela river has been previously considered as a military highway. After its principal use as a war road was ended it had an eventful history as an avenue for trade and travel. Its forerunner, the Nemacolin trail, was marked out as a line over which to carry merchandise some years before its importance for military purposes was seen. The Ohio Company with its storehouse where Cumberland, Maryland, now stands, built a fort also, as was done elsewhere, but only for the purpose of protecting its people from robbers and its property from theft. Trade was the object in view, and the field of trade was the western Indian country, from Lake Erie as far south as its traders cared or dared to go, and there was no limit westward. It was a wilderness except for the wigwams and council houses of the Indians. The wares which that country offered the venturesome merchant were only such as the forest produced. The beaver's lodge, muskrat's den, otter's slide, mink's trail, weasel's skulking place, the bear's feeding ground or hibernating rootpit, and the lick or crossing where the deer fell before the hunter, these were the localities searched for by the wandering merchants with their pack-horses and canoes. The spoil of the redman's chase found its way across the trader's pack-saddles, and, carried in that manner scores or hundreds of miles, it reached the seashores and the overseas. There was profit in it for the Ohio Company, as well as for others, and the establishment grew in wealth and influence. It had frontier camps or houses on the western waters, one at Redstone, on the Monongahela in Pennsylvania, another near Pittsburgh, and others elsewhere. Its traders dared the dangers of the ultra frontiers, and brought rich caravans home.

The Nemacolin trail was marked out to shorten the distance from Cumberland to the Indian country, and it was nothing but a trade route.

The road built on nearly the same location by Braddock in 1755 became a trade route also after it had served its day as a military road. This chapter will treat it as such, and in order to properly understand its importance in the westward movement, it becomes necessary to lengthen the road toward the setting sun, by adding to it a few score miles or a few hundred miles of river. The Braddock road, as a trade highway, properly ended at Brownsville, Pennsylvania, or Redstone as it was then called. The road was never completed to Pittsburgh. It fell seven miles short of that point on July 9, 1755, when the fatal battle occurred, and not another mile was ever added to it. The road which three years and five months later reached Pittsburgh lay further north. It was built by General Forbes and was important for war and trade; but the Braddock road had a separate existence and a history in many ways different. Instead of turning north from the vicinity of Uniontown, Pennsylvania, as the military road had done, the trade route ran on west to Brownsville and ended on the bank of the Monongahela river.

This chapter will trace some of that highway's influences in the years that followed. It is proper, however, to forestall misunderstanding of the matter by stating that as the years went by there were other roads besides Braddock's which were concerned in the movement from the east toward the Upper Ohio river. Braddock's in the early years was the most important of all, and as far as West Virginia's early history is concerned, especially that centered along the Ohio and the Monongahela, it stands out preëminent. Imlay's map published in 1793 showed only two wagon roads crossing the Alleghanies in or near West Virginia's present territory. One crossed into the Greenbrier valley near the present route of the Chesapeake & Ohio railroad, and the other was Braddock's road. Six years later a map in "La Rochefoucauld-Liancourts' Travels" showed only three routes reaching the western country from Alexandria, Virginia, by wagons, and one of these went no farther west than Romney, in Hampshire county. One was

Braddock's road, and the other was a highway from Cumberland to Morgantown, but going no farther.

The Greenbrier road which was on the map of 1793 was not shown on the other of 1799. There may have been, and probably were, some sorts of roads crossing the mountains between Cumberland and Greenbrier in 1799, but they were doubtless too wretched for much commerce to pass over. It is well known that there were wagon roads west of the mountains at that time, but it seems that wagons were able to cross the mountains in very few places.

River Travel—The eagerness with which the pioneers cast aside the slow and laborious means of land travel, and took to the water as soon as they came within reach of it, affords evidence of the badness of land highways and the comparatively good ones by water. Floating down stream was much easier than poling and paddling up, though journeys up stream were many times made long distances. Nature obstructed the white man's progress westward by throwing the unbroken chains of the Alleghany range across his path; but she compensated for it, in a measure, by causing the western rivers to flow the general course the white man wanted to travel. Having toiled over the mountains by Braddock's road, the trader or emigrant might take to the water at Brownsville and float with the current the whole way to Kentucky if he wished to go so far. There was no need to bother about how to get back, for few expected ever to return. They were going there to stay.

The Braddock road, and the roads which paralleled it later, were in existence a long time, and the method of river travel changed much in that time. Traders who went over the Nemacolin trail before the French and Indian war and continued their journeys over the western waters, did not go in the manner of those who came after the Revolution, and down to the war of 1812. The different vessels which carried the settler and the trader came and went with fashion and demand. Each kind met a need, and was usually succeeded by a better.

The Canoe—The simplest vehicle of river travel was the canoe. There were bark canoes used at times on the western waters, but there appears not to have been many. The bark canoe belonged to more northern latitudes and depended for its existence almost entirely upon the paper birch, and this tree is scarce or does not grow at all in the Ohio valley. It is the tree of which bark canoes were made in Canada and New England, and doubtless when Indians and explorers journeyed south into the Ohio valley they frequently carried some of their bark canoes with them. South of the paper birch's range they sometimes made canoes of the bark of slippery elm.

The canoes in the Ohio valley were nearly all made of yellow poplar, a beautiful tree which reaches its best development in West Virginia. Canoes in early times were found along all the rivers, particularly the Kanawha and the Monongahela, and a first class one was good for fifteen or twenty years of service, barring accidents. There was only one accident that was really to be feared, and that was loss by flood. The yellow poplar canoe was hewed from a single trunk, and it was impossible to sink it beyond recovery, for the bouyancy of the wood repeatedly brought it to the surface if forced beneath the water, and so solid was the vessel that it was next to impossible to crush it or stave it in by driving it against rocks. The canoe was an Indian invention, and the name is an Indian word. It was the only vehicle of conveyance given by the native American to the white men, and it was one of the most valuable articles that could have been presented. The Indians hollowed their canoes by the slow and laborious process of fire and rubbing stones before white men gave them edged tools. Canoes made in that way were heavy and clumsy; but when axes and hatchets came into use, the shells were made thinner, and the finished article was light enough to float in shallow water. It then became of the greatest use to travelers who followed the water courses. It was used for war and the chase, which were the principal occupations of the Indians.

The white travelers and traders speedily made the dugout canoe an article of great importance. Some of their long journeys in the Ohio valley would have been difficult if not impossible without it. Where the tedious overland trail ended, the water route began. The trader unloaded his pack-horses on the bank of the Kanawha or the Monongahela after the journey over the mountains; and having packed his wares in the narrow hold of the canoe, the light craft shot away into the stream, and was driven upon its journey four or five miles an hour with easy strokes of the paddle. The pack-horses carried the merchandise scarcely twenty miles from daylight till dark; in the same length of time the canoe covered forty or fifty miles, if the course was down stream, and loads on the West Virginia rivers nearly always went down stream. One good canoe carried as much as ten pack-horse loads, and the bales of merchandise glided over the water without a jar. The pack horses bumped them against trees and rocks, or fell with them in quagmires, or damaged the articles by water in fording deep streams. It was with a feeling of relief that the forest merchant approached the western streams after crossing the mountains, and transferred his wares from the pack-saddles to the canoe.

There were canoes of all sizes, from the smallest for one or two men, to those made for business or war, large enough to carry three or four thousand pounds safely upon long journeys. The canoe in which Washington traveled hundreds of miles upon the western waters in 1770 carried eight persons besides equipments and supplies. It was not unusually large. After General Lewis' army in 1774 had toiled over the mountains with a long pack train, the soldiers halted at the mouth of Elk river where Charleston, West Virginia, now stands, and hewed canoes which carried the army's stores to the Ohio.

The canoe on the waters of the Ohio supplemented the pack-horse on the over-mountain trails. That is, they were, within their respective spheres, the means by which the earliest trade was carried on. It should not be supposed, however, that when the pack-horse went out of business as a carrier, the canoe immediately became an obsolete craft. Other kinds of boats were in use long before the pack-horse quit, and the canoe continued its voyages long after the last over-mountain pack-saddle had been hung on its peg to be taken down no more. The dug-out canoe is not entirely a thing of the past yet in West Virginia, though a person might travel a long time without seeing one. The yellow poplars from which to hew them are scarce along the rivers, and have become so valuable at the sawmills that trunks go there instead of to the canoe-maker. Bridges across nearly every stream have made the use of such canoes of comparatively little necessity now.

The Pirogue—The old books of travel, exploration, war, and trading have frequent mention of the pirogue. That, too, was an Indian word, but its exact meaning was not always kept in view by those who made use of the word. It often meant a canoe, pure and simple, but it was generally something else. Sometimes it was a long, slim boat of planks nailed together. The ends were peaked like the ends of a canoe, both being alike in that respect. The vessels would go with equal ease both ways. The pirogue was sometimes made by sawing a dugout canoe lengthwise, and inserting a wide plank or several short ones nailed across. By this method the capacity of the vessel might be doubled, and at the same time it would ride rougher water without danger of overturning. At times a deck was built over the top to protect the cargo against spray thrown over the gunwales when the water was choppy. Pirogues made by sawing a canoe lengthwise and inserting a plank are mentioned in John Lawson's history of the Carolinas as early as 1714, and one is spoken of which had a capacity of one hundred barrels. Another, fitted with a deck and sail, would have voyaged from the Carolina coast for the Barbadoes Islands, but the custom officers refused to issue clearance papers. It was proved that such vessels were sea worthy, for cargoes were carried by the ocean route in the Atlantic coasting trade, between Carolina and Virginia.

The growth of river commerce in the Upper Ohio valley demanded a vessel larger than the canoe, yet not so large that it could not ascend the currents when business called the trader far up the rivers to the inland settlements. The pirogue answered that purpose well. It was flat-bottomed and floated shallow, and could be navigated in most places where a canoe would go. Though not quite as easily managed as a canoe, and a little more liable to meet misfortune in rapids where submerged stones were to be feared, it carried a larger load, and as a freighter, it was a little superior to the canoe. It was a pirogue which was carrying a cargo of cannon balls from Pittsburgh down the Ohio in 1777 when the Indians captured it and proceeded to fire the balls from a wooden cannon with well-known results.

The pirogue—particularly the kind made by sawing a canoe lengthwise and splicing it—is now obsolete. It is doubtful if a single one exists in the world. Yet, in its day, and that day lasted a century and a half, it was an important adjunct of commerce along the waterways of the eastern part of the United States.

The Keelboat—This vessel was larger than the pirogue, but it was made to go up rivers as well as down, and in that respect resembled the canoe and the pirogue. This was the first vessel in the evolution of river craft in this part of the country that had a white man's name, since canoe and pirogue were of Indian origin. The broad, flat bottom gave this vessel its descriptive name; and it was, besides, designed to steer easily. Its use on rivers often shallow and with rocks to be guarded against all the time, rendered impossible a broad center board extending much below the bottom of the boat. The canoe and the pirogue had none, so even an excuse of a center board in the new craft sufficed to give it a name. It was propelled with poles most of the time, and the boatmen were trained for that particular work. Running boards extended along both sides, and the workmen walked on these, braced their poles against the bottom, and by walking with a steady push from stern to stern, they shoved the boat along. This motion was accompanied by the rhythmic cry, "lift," "set," the whole day or night through. The keelboatmen usually kept near shore to take the benefit of shallower water there than in midstream, particularly if ascending the river. When, in passing round headlands or islands, the water was too deep for the setting poles, the boat was temporarily propelled with oars or paddles.

Keelboats carried from forty to eighty thousand pounds, and of course their operations were confined to streams of considerable size and with channels comparatively free from obstructions. Keelboats were seen on some of the interior rivers of West Virginia up to a few years ago, and possibly a few may still be beating up the currents in localities where railroads are not convenient. After the opening of the nineteenth century keelboats from New Orleans carried coffee and sugar for merchants along the Ohio, Kanawha, and Monongahela rivers. Some classes of merchandise from Philadelphia for towns in West Virginia made the sea voyage to New Orleans and thence up the Mississippi and Ohio to the shadows of the Alleghany mountains within four hundred miles of their starting place. But that phase of the question will be considered more at length in discussing the rivalry between the long water carriage and the short land haul across the mountains.

The Bateau—This boat was somewhat pointed at the ends, and carried a load of about fifteen hundred pounds, but it was a rather clumsy vessel and was not common on the West Virginia rivers. Its sphere of usefulness should be sought in Canada, for it was a French boat.

The Barge—When a barge took a long voyage down stream before the days of steamboats, it was supposed never to return. It was a large, unwieldy vessel, and if the journey was long, the cost of towing back to the starting place was greater than the expense of building a new barge where the finest grades of black walnut and yellow poplar planks could be bought for ten or fifteen dollars a thousand feet, delivered at the boatyard. There was no power by which one of the larger barges could be forced up the rivers of West Virginia, before steam came into use. If the distance was short, horses might wade along near the shore, or walk on the bank, and draw the barge up the river for another load, but there was a limit to this. Sometimes men with poles, using them like keelboatmen, forced barges some distance up stream; but that method was not apt to be tried if the distance was considerable. Besides, if the wind happened to be blowing in the wrong direction, the efforts put forth by the men on board, or horses on the bank, availed little. The barge of early times was only for one trip down stream, and that was the last of it. Except that it served a purpose after it reached its journey's end by being broken up and put to use as material for house-building. Many of the earliest houses in Marietta, Ohio, were built of broken-up barges that had come from Pittsburgh or perhaps from head of navigation on the Monongahela.

The barge was of the utmost importance on the western rivers. Its particular place in the westward movement was to carry families and household goods to new homes. Such commodities included farmstock, horses, cattle, sheep, hogs, and poultry. The emigrants from the east loaded on pack-horses, or in wagons, such of their earthly possessions as could not hoof it over the mountains, but what could walk was obliged to do it. The Braddock road, as well as roads and paths farther north and south, conducted the long caravans across the mountains and delivered them upon the banks of the western rivers at the head of navigation, and there the barge was called upon to do its share in steering the course of empire on its western way. Some built their own boats and barges; some bought them ready made. There were boatyards along the Monongahela from its mouth to the head of navigation. After about 1788 or 1790 it was possible, on an hours' notice, to buy nearly any sort of a boat, from a barge down to a skiff, for the descent of the river. There was much travel earlier than that—almost twenty years earlier—but the business of boat-building was at its height along the Monongahela a little before the opening of the nineteenth century. As early as 1768 at Pittsburgh it is recorded that Iroquois and Shawnee Indians who were visiting the garrison there, cast suspecting eyes on some boats which were building at that time, and were anxious to know if the boats were intended for a down-stream voyage. They need not have asked, for all boats built at Pittsburgh and above there on the water courses, at that day and for thirty-five years afterwards, were expected to take their principal voyages down stream. Not only the river's current, but the current of civilization after it had once crossed the Alleghany mountains, moved down stream.

Some of the barges were large enough to carry dozens of families with such of their household goods as they had been able to carry over the mountains, and also their cattle. Indian sharpshooters hung along the banks of the rivers ready to fire into the boats, and to board them if opportunity offered. Many of the barges and houseboats were of timbers so heavy as to be bullet proof. Some were armed with small cannon ready to shoot away any screens or bullet shields with which the savages might equip their canoes for an assault on the barges.

The houseboat, a common sight in the time of the early river migration westward, was a barge with a roof and partitions. The people lived in one part, the farm animals in another, and the household articles were stowed between.

Sailing Vessels—The river craft listed above floated with the current or were propelled with poles, paddles, or oars, though in some instances sails were tried when conditions were favorable. The abundance of excellent timber west of the Alleghany mountains suggested to boat-makers that ship-building might be made profitable, not only for carrying river trade but for ocean traffic. There were shipyards at Wheeling, West Virginia, Marietta, Ohio, and at Pittsburgh. At the latter place operations began in 1792, and part of the lumber was rafted down from West Virginia. Large quantities of black walnut and yellow poplar were used, both there and lower down the Ohio. The walnut largely took the place of oak, not because oak was scarce or of poor quality, but walnut was considered better. It was nearly as strong, was lighter, and it resisted decay better than oak in the river boats. In course of time the walnut-built vessels of the Upper Ohio won a reputation away from home as well as at home.

In 1792 the vessel "Amity" of one hundred and twenty tons and the "Pittsburgh" of two hundred and fifty tons were completed at the Pittsburgh yard. The small one put to sea in 1793, and sailed for St. Thomas in the West Indies, and the larger one went to Philadelphia. If they were in part constructed of West Virginia timber, as has been claimed, it is probable that their hulls carried the first wood from that region to distant cities and foreign countries. In 1793, the "Nannie" of two hundred tons and the "Louisiana" of three hundred and fifty tons came off the ways at Pittsburgh. The small vessel sailed for France, and the larger carried a load of coal to Philadelphia and sold it for ten dollars a ton. That appears to have been the first coal from the Upper Ohio to reach Philadelphia. The next year a ship of four hundred tons, the "Western Trader," was launched at Pittsburgh. By the year 1800 the ships which were made at the forks of the Ohio were going down the river with cargoes of glass, beef, pork, and with furniture manufactured of walnut, cherry and yellow birch.

In 1805 the schooner "Dorcas and Sally" was built at Wheeling and rigged at Marietta. It was of seventy tons burden. A ship built at Marietta sailed for Italy, and entering a port in that country was detained by the authorities a short time until they could ascertain where the vessel came from. They had never heard of Marietta, but when they satisfied themselves that there was such a place, and that the vessel sailed under regular papers, it was permitted to go. By 1805 many sea-going vessels were yearly dropping down the Ohio, of course, never returning.

The time had arrived when a craft of a different kind was to make its appearance on the Upper Ohio. The first steamboat was built on the Monongahela in 1811.

East and West Trade—Something has been said of the pack-horse trade across the mountains. The business soon passed beyond the pack-horse stage and it then assumed a new aspect. When the Braddock road was built, it was the first wagon highway from the Atlantic seaboard to the Ohio river. It was not many years the only one, but it played an important part in shaping the course of trade and travel between the east and the west. In 1764, at the close of the Pontiac war, the Braddock road was nearly choked in places by sprouts springing up from low stumps left in the ground when the road was built. Danger from Indians had been so great that no one had made use of the road since 1755 when Braddock retreated over it; but soon after 1764 the road was opened to the Monongahela river at Brownsville, Pennsylvania, and travel began. The tide of settlement soon set in toward the west. It did not flow immediately into what is now West Virginia, but it accumulated in Pennsylvania, and when the treaty of Fort Stanwix in 1768 removed obstacles in the way of colonizing the regions between the mountains and the Ohio river, there was little loss of time in opening the wilderness. Wagons carried to the Monongahela articles needed in the western country, but the date of the beginning was not as early as some might be led to suppose. The Braddock road was passable for wagons—or at least had been passed by wagons—thirty-four years before the first recorded load of merchandise reached the Monongahela. In Veach's "Monongahela of Old" it is stated that the first wagonload of merchandise arrived at that river in 1789.

If that last statement is true it may be seriously asked what the Braddock road was hauling, if not merchandise, up to 1789. Doubtless merchandise as the word was used by Veach, was understood to be commodities such as merchants offer for sale. There were stores of rather respectable dimensions in the western country before 1789, and it is difficult to believe that all that went on their shelves was carried from Cumberland, or some other depot east of the mountains, on the backs of pack-horses for full twenty years after settlements began to be numerous in the west. If for any reason, Braddock's road was closed to wagons during part of that time, there remained the Forbes road north of it, the military highway to Pittsburgh from eastern Pennsylvania, and no reason has been given for the non-use of that road for wagoning merchandise to the western country.

The exact date of the first wagonload of store goods is not important. Wagons of household goods, in the long emigrant trains across the Alleghanies, were earlier than 1789. Boats upon the Monongahela and Ohio before that year bore abundant evidence that the wagon roads over the mountains were well patronized by wheeled vehicles, as well as by flocks and herds. It is recorded that from November 13 to December 22, 1785, there passed down the Ohio thirty-nine boats, with an average of ten persons in each. In the last six months of 1787 a count at the mouth of the Muskingum river, on the Ohio side a short distance above Parkersburg, showed that one hundred and forty-six boats passed, with three thousand one hundred and ninety-six passengers, one hundred and sixty-five wagons, one hundred and ninety-one cattle, two hundred and forty-five sheep, and twenty-four hogs. From November, 1787, to November, 1788, there passed down the Ohio nine hundred and sixty-seven boats, eighteen thousand three hundred and seventy people, seven thousand nine hundred and eighty-six horses, two thousand three hundred and seventy-two cows, one thousand one hundred and ten sheep, and six hundred and forty wagons.

This is enough to show the set of the tide. All of these people did not pass west over the Braddock road, but the travel was heavy over that route during those years, as well as after and before.

Commodities—The commodities which made up the trade with the western country after settlements began were quite different from those common there in the days of the Indian occupation. Furs were the principal article then, and had the output of that vast region continued to be furs, little need would there have been for roads wider than trails or for means of transportation better than pack-horses; for no large or heavy bulk would have gone to market. But the Indians and the muskrats, otters, and other wild creatures, passed away, and the new inhabitants found new commodities. A list of ordinary articles in trade at Pittsburgh nearly a century and a quarter ago named flour, whiskey, peach brandy, cider, beer, bar iron, earthenware, cabinet work, boots, hoes, plow irons, mill irons, chains, chairs, biscuit, bread, cheese, bacon, beef, linen, lumber. It is not stated whether these articles were produced west of the mountains, or were carried over from the east. It is apparent that all were not of eastern origin, nor were all products of the western country which was then beginning to turn to manufacturing. The raw materials were so abundant in the west that it was almost impossible not to do something with them. The articles named above were shipped down the river. The first flatboat from Brownsville, Pennsylvania, reached New Orleans in 1782, and there continued to pass down at intervals after that. About the beginning of the nineteenth century some of the boats brought cotton, furs, hemp, lead, and skins up the river.

The merchants in the east looked upon the opening of trade routes over the Alleghany mountains as a sure means of increasing trade. They knew that the Indians in the Ohio valley had bought goods to the extent of their ability to pay; and it was evident that white settlers in the region would be able to buy much more. The obstacle in the way of a large and lucrative business with the over-mountain people was the long, rough road. It was eighty miles from Cumberland to Brownsville, and a hundred years ago Cumberland was a long distance west of the manufacturing centers of this country, and Brownsville was only on the eastern edge of the consuming public which then lived west of the mountains. The eighty miles of steep road which separated Cumberland from Brownsville was only part of the obstacle in the way of profitable trade with the transmontane country. However, except a small quantity of merchandise that came up the Mississippi, the western people looked to the east for what they needed in the way of merchandise. When Daniel Boone was keeping store he bought his goods in Hagerstown, Williamsport, and elsewhere east of Cumberland, and he and his sons transported them across the mountains to the west, making use of waterways and mountain roads. In 1796 the cost of hauling household goods from Alexandria, Virginia, to Morgantown, West Virginia, was about eighty dollars a ton.

Trade and the Flag—The question of trade following the flag was discussed in this country for the first time when population began to grow large west of the Alleghany mountains, and problems came up for solution. At that time it was not so much a prophecy that trade would follow the flag as it was a fear that the flag might not follow trade. Southward and westward were the French and Spanish colonies, on both sides of the Mississippi, and the rivers from all along the west side of the mountains flowed that way. It was a question whether the settlers on the westward slope of the mountains, and all the way across the valleys, would not find it easier to trade down the rivers than over the mountains; and if they once formed a habit of trading in that direction might they not form political alliances in that direction also?

The Revolutionary war had scarcely come to a close before that question became a living one in the east. Business men were afraid of losing the western business, and eastern statesmen foresaw the danger of a new republic west of the mountains whose outlet to the markets of the world would be through the Mississippi river. The mountains stood like a wall between the Atlantic coast and the western valleys, and they threatened to divide the two sections forever. The question was indeed much older than the Revolutionary war. The French saw the mountain range and the western valleys, and they sought political and trade advantages by making the most of the barrier which nature had set between the east and the west. They wanted the western valleys and were willing to let England plant its colonies on the Atlantic seaboard. France did not believe that England would make a serious attempt to cross, but the French and Indian war came on, and England crossed, took the site of Pittsburgh, and drove the French out of America.

England no sooner had possession of the land on both sides of the mountains than she began to scheme against her own colonies, and wished to confine them east of the mountains. It was foreseen that they would grow very powerful if they occupied and developed the western valleys, and might be then tempted to declare their independence. To head such a movement off, England extended the province of Quebec to the Ohio river, intending that the French from Canada and elsewhere should settle west of the mountains, and thus hem the English in their original settlements east of the range. But events again moved faster than the politicians, and the Revolutionary war put the Americans in possession of the western country.

Once more a fear of consequences west of the Alleghanies arose. The Americans had it all, but they were anxious concerning the part of the country west of the mountains. It was well known that the line of least resistance was westward and southward, the way the rivers ran, and there was enough country in that direction to make a republic larger than the thirteen original states. Could the smaller east hold the larger west? There would have been no dividing line between the two sections, except for the unbroken range of mountains; but the mountains were there, and the question of trade and politics could not be settled satisfactorily without making the passage of the mountains easier.

The Braddock road was the first attempt to solve the question. It was the first key inserted to unlock the gates of the mountains. Two wealthy parts of a country cannot be permanently tied together by pack-horse trails. The bond is not strong enough. The endless caravans of men, women, children, wagons, and flocks and herds that streamed across the Alleghanies as soon as the road was opened and made safe, is evidence that it was wanted. But during the first years the travel was nearly all one way, westward. Nothing was coming back. Commerce must flow both ways, or it will finally cease to flow. The eastern business men were willing enough to see tens of thousands of people, with their worldly goods, seeking the western country, but there was a feeling for a good many years that there was too little crossing the mountains in an eastward course.

It is idle to speculate what might have been the effect on the ties between the east and the west, with the Alleghany mountains as the dividing line, had the invention of railroads been postponed a few decades longer. After the Braddock road showed the way, others followed as rapidly as they could be built, but it is questionable whether wagon roads could have much longer held the commerce of the sections together. Railroads saved the day. Washington saw the question in a light as clear as prophecy. He knew that wagon roads would not be sufficient to carry the commerce between the east and the west in a few decades more, and he took up the subjects of canals from the Atlantic seaboard as far into the fastnesses of the Alleghany mountains as they could be constructed and operated, and as far up the slopes on the western side as possible. He hoped to bring the two systems of canals within thirty or forty miles of meeting, with the termini connected by broad and solid highways over which commerce would pass east and west.

One of these canals which Washington planned was to follow the James river and Kanawha river route to the Ohio; another was to ascend the Potomac as high as possible; on the western side corresponding canals were to descend branches of the Monongahela river. Other canals were planned for States north of Virginia. The Potomac canal was actually built as far as Cumberland before railroads made its further building unnecessary. Washington expected it would ascend the North Branch of the Potomac into Grant county, where the Northwestern turnpike crosses that stream. From that point a highway would lead over the mountains to Cheat river, either to Dunkard Bottom, Preston county, or Horseshoe Bend, Tucker county. It was Washington's hope that Cheat river could be made navigable to one or both of the points he had selected for the station at the western foot of the mountains. The James river canal was likewise built far up toward the mountains before the coming of railroads put an end to its extension westward.

Washington's canals would have gone far toward solving the problems they were meant to solve, but in the light of fuller knowledge of the regions through which they would have passed it may be accepted that Washington would have met with graver engineering troubles than he expected. The New river, which he counted on using as part of the James river canal system could not have been made navigable much above its junction with the Gauley, and an over-mountain road more than one hundred miles long would have been needed. The situation was nearly the same in regard to the navigation of Cheat river which stream he hoped to be able to hitch to his Potomac canal system. Cheat river could not have been made navigable above Sandy creek in Preston county, about thirteen miles from its junction with the Monongahela.

GENEALOGICAL AND BIOGRAPHICAL

UPPER MONONGAHELA VALLEY

DAYTON
Judge Alston Gordon Dayton, of Philippi, West Virginia, whose distinguished services as a Member of Congress at the time of the Spanish-American war are still fresh in the memory of his countrymen, is a representative of one of the oldest families of New England, the names of many of its members being inscribed in the annals of the Commonwealth as those of brave soldiers and public-spirited citizens.

Samuel Dayton, founder of the branch of the family represented by Judge Dayton, of Philippi, was one of the first settlers of Setauket, Long Island, New York, the earliest of the name to emigrate to New England having arrived there previous to 1640. The descendants of Samuel Dayton established themselves in Connecticut, and his brother was the progenitor of another branch of the family which included General Elias Dayton of the revolutionary army.

(II) Isaac, son of Samuel Dayton, was of New Haven, and was known as "Honorable." He married, December 29, 1708, Elizabeth, born in 1690, daughter of Michael Tod, of New Haven, born in 1653, son of Christopher Tod, a native of Ireland, among whose descendants of the present day is Governor Tod, of Ohio. To Isaac Dayton and his wife were born twelve children, the daughters being as follows: Rebecca, married Ebenezer Gilbert; Hannah, married Stephen Jacobs; Elizabeth, married Daniel Doolittle; Charity, married Jehiel Tuttle; Sarah, married Benjamin English, who gave his life for his country when New Haven was attacked by the British, July 5, 1779; and Deborah, married Nathan Mansfield. Among the descendants of Mr. and Mrs. Mansfield was Rear-Admiral Hull Foote, U. S. N., whose "Unconditional Surrender" message at Fort Henry was duplicated a few hours later by the message of General Grant at Fort Donelson. Among the descendants of Mr. and Mrs. English was Hon. James E. English, twice governor of Connecticut and in 1875 elected United States senator. Another descendant of Mr. and Mrs. Mansfield was Hon. E. D. Mansfield, of Cincinnati, a noted author, and a son of Jared Mansfield, surveyor-general of the Northwest under President

Jefferson, and long a professor at West Point. Following are the sons of Isaac Dayton and his wife: Giles, served in the revolutionary army, and settled at Blandford, Massachusetts; Jonathan, married Mary Yale, a near relative of the founder of Yale University, and was captain in command of the New Haven troops when the city was attacked by the British; Isaac, served in the revolutionary army, was several months a prisoner of war, and lived at Newport; Israel, married the Widow Clark, and had a son Israel, who was a revolutionary soldier and the ancestor of Hon. H. B. Warner, of Washington, D. C.; and Michael, mentioned below.

(III) Michael, youngest son of Isaac and Elizabeth (Tod) Dayton, was born June 4, 1722, and settled at Watertown, Connecticut. He married, January 29, 1749, Mehitable Doolittle. Children: Charles; David; Miriam; Michael; Justus, mentioned below; Mehitable; Polly; Elizabeth; Isaac; Samuel; Lyman; Abel; and Olive. Like his brothers, Michael Dayton was a soldier in the Continental army, but did not live to witness the triumphant termination of the struggle, dying in the service of his country.

(IV) Justus, son of Michael and Mehitable (Doolittle) Dayton, was born June 30, 1754, and married, June 10, 1777, Hannah Titus. They were the parents of the following children: Spencer; Russell; Rhoda; Jonah; Mehitable; Beulah; Henry, mentioned below; Justus; Chester; Archibald; and Elizabeth. Justus Dayton, the father, served in the revolutionary army as captain in the Twenty-sixth Connecticut Regiment, and in 1777 was one of three hundred volunteers who marched from Connecticut under General Oliver Westcott and took part in the battle of Saratoga, which resulted in the surrender of General Burgoyne with his whole army. Captain Dayton was wounded in this battle, but recovered and died in 1825, at the age of seventy-one. Michael, brother of Captain Justus Dayton, served in the ill-fated expedition against Quebec, but survived for other fields. Jonah Dayton, son of Captain Justus Dayton, was a noted inventor, particularly of musical instruments. At Daytonville, Connecticut (named in his honor), thousands of organs have been built at his factories, and many of the ablest workmen employed in the United States learned their trades under his instruction.

(V) Henry, son of Justus and Hannah (Titus) Dayton, combined the occupations of farming and shoemaking. He married Lavinia Culver.

(VI) Spencer, son of Henry and Lavinia (Culver) Dayton, was born January 22, 1820, in Litchfield county, Connecticut. When about twelve years old he went to live with a relative at whose home he could enjoy better facilities of education. While still young he became an apprentice to the millwright's trade, and succeeded so well that he was able, in a few years, to command the highest wages, $300 a year. While learning his trade he was a constant reader at all leisure hours, and the habits thus formed remained with him through life. Undaunted by obstacles which some would have deemed insuperable, he began the study of law, and in 1846 successfully passed the examination required by the laws of Connecticut. On being admitted to the bar he decided that the South offered a favorable field for practice, and in 1847 set out for Virginia, carrying in his pocket a few hundred dollars, the sum of his savings, and in a valise an extra suit of clothes. At Winchester he was admitted to practice in the courts of Frederick county, but not wishing to settle there he crossed into Greenbrier county, and hearing that the court would soon be in session in Nicholas county, he proceeded thither, and soon after his arrival met for the first time Edwin C. Duncan, judge of the court, with whom he ultimately formed a friendship destined to be lifelong, albeit the first few meetings, though inspiring in each respect for the other, were not calculated to promote strong feelings of mutual attachment. The court of Nicholas county was held at Summersville, and Mr. Dayton's application for a license to practice was granted by Judge Duncan. The next court of the circuit was at Sutton, in Braxton county, and Mr. Dayton applied for a license to practice in that county. The license was ordered, but a few minutes later Judge Duncan recalled the applicant and informed him that the laws of Virginia required one year's residence in the state before the issuance of license to practice law.

Finding that the judge would not admit him to practice, and believing that it was in a measure due to prejudice against him as a Northerner, Mr. Dayton retraced his steps to Summersville. Some of the residents and visitors at Sutton did not conceal their pleasure at what they supposed was the discomfiture of the "young Yankee," but he kept his own counsel and bided his time. At Summersville he procured from the clerk, John Hamilton, a certified copy of the order of Judge Duncan admitting him to practice, and with this document in his pocket he set out for Weston, passed through Clarksburg and Fairmont on foot and crossed into Pennsylvania. There was at that time an understanding (which amounted to a law) between Virginia and Pennsylvania that each would admit to its courts lawyers from the other state. Knowing this, Mr. Dayton proceeded to Somerset county, where Judge Jeremiah S. Black was on the bench, and presented his certificate of admission to practice in Nicholas county, Virginia. Thereupon he was admitted to practice in Pennsylvania. The Pennsylvania license, in its turn, and under the rules of reciprocity, would give him the right to demand license in Virginia and no judge would feel at liberty to refuse the demand. Armed with his Pennsylvania license, Mr. Dayton set out for Virginia. By that time the Randolph court was in session, and Mr. Dayton, on arriving there, presented his papers and asked to be admitted to practice. Judge Duncan examined the papers in evident impatience and ill humor, but seeing that he had been trapped he ordered the clerk to make the entry admitting Mr. Dayton to practice, and then, addressing the members of the bar and the people in the courthouse, he said: "If any of you have dealings with this young Yankee I would advise you to look out for yourselves. He played a genuine Yankee trick on me, and I cannot help myself." Mr. Dayton from that time was known as the "young Yankee that outwitted Judge Duncan."

Not having yet decided where to settle, but being favorably impressed with Clarksburg, Mr. Dayton returned from Beverly to Philippi, and there met John S. Carlile, who then resided in Philippi and who persuaded Mr. Dayton to become his law partner. This arrangement caused Mr. Dayton to make Philippi his permanent home and extended his practice to Randolph, Upshur, Lewis, Taylor, Tucker, Grant and other counties, as well as to the higher courts. His care in the preparation of cases and the information at his disposal soon gave him a high rank among members of the legal profession. On one occasion, in Taylor county, some attorney objected to a paper in the suit, claiming that it was improperly drawn. Judge Samuel Woods (who was not interested in the suit) glanced at the writing and exclaimed: "Why that cannot be so. Spencer Dayton wrote this paper, and in matters and forms of law he is as infallible as the Apostle Paul."

During the agitations which heralded the approach of the civil war and throughout the four years of the conflict, Mr. Dayton was a steadfast champion of the Union cause in Barbour county, hesitating not to uphold that cause at the risk of his life. His acquaintance with the people both of the North and South convinced him that the South must ultimately be crushed beneath the weight of the moral and physical courage, the wealth and the perseverance, of the North. He knew that the North would be slow to begin, but would never turn back nor hesitate when once in the field. Like the large-hearted man he was, he did all in his power to alleviate the hardships of the war for both sides, and when it was ended he was among the first to say: "Let us have peace." During the war he was many times in a position to do acts of kindness to his political enemies, and after the close of the conflict such opportunities were frequent and never did he fail to improve them. More than one man, persecuted because of his actions or opinions, was helped by Mr. Dayton without ever knowing the source from which the help came.

In 1861 he assisted in the Wheeling convention in reorganizing the state of Virginia, which reorganization ultimately led to the formation of West Virginia. In 1869 he was elected to the state senate and took a prominent part in the movement for the reënfranchisement of those who had lost their civil rights in consequence of taking part against the government during the war. The leaders in this movement were called "Let-up Republicans," to distinguish them from the radical and extreme members of the party who considered the movement premature. In the contest upon the question of removing the restrictions then placed upon Southern men, Mr. Dayton was the pivotal member, and his vote and influence turned the scale and led to the repeal of the restriction measures. The Flick amendment was opposed in the legislature alike by the extreme Republicans and the extreme Democrats, and its passage and its good results were due to the moderate members who championed the cause of political toleration.

Mr. Dayton was always an extensive reader, particularly well versed in English literature, and as a recreation acquired a thorough knowledge of French and Greek. He has held the office of prosecuting attorney in more counties, perhaps, than any other man in the State, having been elected to that position in Randolph, Barbour, Pocahontas and Tucker, his election in all these counties taking place on the same day.

Mr. Dayton married, November 12, 1849, Sarah (Bush), born October 3, 1819, daughter of Zadok and Abigail (Dewey) Bush, and widow of Samuel Barrett. Mrs. Bush was a relative of Admiral George Dewey, the hero of Manila Bay. Mr. and Mrs. Dayton were married in Upshur county, West Virginia, and their children were: Eldon Lee, born March 31, 1851; Imogene, December 2, 1853; Ida V., October 19, 1855; and Alston Gordon, mentioned below.

(VII) Alston Gordon Dayton, son of Spencer and Sarah (Bush) (Barrett) Dayton, was born October 18, 1857, in Philippi. He received his preparatory education in the public schools, and subsequently entered the University of West Virginia, graduating in 1878 with the degree of Bachelor of Arts. On October 18 of the same year, his twenty-first birthday, he was licensed to practice law, and entered into partnership with his father. Two years later he was appointed prosecuting attorney of Upshur county, and immediately thereafter received the Republican nomination for that office in his native county. He was defeated by a small majority, but ran ahead of his ticket and in 1884 was again nominated. This time he was elected, being the first Republican to fill the place since the close of the civil war. In 1888 he was a candidate for judge of the circuit court, failing by only two votes of receiving the nomination. Two years later (1890) his name was presented to the Republican convention at Piedmont as a candidate for congress in the Second West Virginia District, which position was then filled by Hon. William L. Wilson, author of the Wilson Tariff Bill. Mr. Wilson was a formidable antagonist and the belief was general that only a man east of the Alleghanies could defeat him. The choice of the convention fell on Hon. George Harmon, a wealthy farmer of Grant county, while Mr. Dayton received a strong support from counties west of the mountains. At the convention held at Elkins in 1894 he was by his party nominated for Congress, and Mr. Wilson, still in congress, was once more in the field, the champion of a party confident of victory. The campaign was fought from start to finish with a bitterness seldom equalled in politics. Mr. Dayton, figuratively speaking, asked no quarter and gave none. He was elected by over 2,000 majority, and, in 1896, 1898, 1900, 1902, and 1904 was reëlected, in all six

consecutive times. However, he served only ten days of his sixth term, resigning in order to accept his present office of United States District Judge for the Northern District of West Virginia.

Mr. Dayton's career in Congress was one of steady increase of influence, his appointment on the naval committee, in the early days of his service as a legislator, bringing him at once into prominence as a working member and later as a leader in the important measures originating in or formulated by that committee. He was a believer in a strong navy, and on every occasion advocated the construction of warships of the most powerful class instead of small vessels which could be built at little expense. We had then three battleships in commission and three in course of construction, and our present navy is due in no small measure to his efforts. The naming of the powerful cruiser, "West Virginia," was, in part at least, a recognition of his services in this direction. The vessel is designed with a displacement of twelve thousand tons and thirty-three thousand horse-power and belongs to the most formidable class of warships in the world. When Mr. Dayton took his stand in favor of battleships as against torpedo-boats and other small craft, there had never been a battleship in action, but at the battle of Santiago, July 3, 1898, the value of that class of vessels was fully demonstrated. Mr. Dayton took a prominent part in the controversy in Congress concerning the construction of dry docks, and was instrumental in the repeal of the ruling which forbade appropriations for dry docks unless a bill had been passed for their establishment. After the reversal of the ruling, dry docks were classed with naval establishments, and the result was that four such docks were provided for at Portsmouth, New Hampshire, Boston, League Island, Pennsylvania, and Algiers, Louisiana.

Mr. Dayton introduced a bill in the House which passed the Senate, providing for the promotion and retirement of Lieutenant R. M. G. Brown, U. S. N., in recognition of his services in saving the ship and the lives of his crew in the great storm at the Samoan Islands. Mr. Dayton was largely instrumental also in securing the appropriation of over $5,000,000 to open the Monongahela river to free navigation and to build locks and dams between Fairmont and Morgantown. He was also prominent in an important feature of the United States Geological Survey, for, while the work of surveying had been in progress over fifteen years, no provision had been made for setting up monuments to permanently mark the limits, so that additional investigation or survey might be taken up anywhere with exact data at hand from which to begin measurements. Mr. Dayton called the attention of Congress to this defect, and provision was made for setting up a stone in every county seat in the United States, on which was to be marked the true north and south line of the place.

Another matter with which Mr. Dayton was conspicuously associated was legislation in Alaska. After the purchase of that territory in 1866, provision was made that the laws of Oregon should be in force in Alaska, and thus the matter stood until 1898, although in many particulars the Oregon laws did not suit the different conditions of the Far North. In 1898 a congressional committee undertook to provide a code of laws for Alaska, and of this committee Dr. Dayton was a member and took an active part in framing this code. The bill containing the code was debated for ten days by the committee of the whole House and was finally passed, in consequence in part at least of Mr. Dayton's championship.

Perhaps the most noted and lasting work accomplished by Mr. Dayton during his congressional career was in connection with the Navy Personnel Bill. The object of this bill was to regulate the line of promotion, to give all an equal chance, to equalize the pay received by navy and army officers, and to change the course of study in the Naval Academy at Annapolis. Graduates of that institution were then arbitrarily divided into two classes, the members of one destined to be engineers and machinists, and those of the others to become officers who might rise to the highest grades. The new law placed all on an equal footing as to promotion. Under the old law it was nearly impossible for an officer to rise above a lieutenant until he was over fifty years old, because promotion was more a matter of age than of service, and the civil war left so many officers that they became lieutenants and seldom rose above that rank. The new law removed this disability, providing avenues for promotion without much increasing the expense of the service. The pay of the officer of the navy was made equal with that of the officer of corresponding rank in the army, and among other important provisions which practically changed the whole service of the navy was one for the enlistment of competent machinists who had never attended the Naval Academy. The unwieldy number of ranks in the navy (about fifty) was largely curtailed. Mr. Dayton was recognized as a leading champion of the bill when it came before the House in 1899. It was of the greatest importance to naval men and they watched its progress with the utmost anxiety. Mr. Dayton made a number of speeches showing that he had thoroughly mastered the subject and had become an authority on naval affairs. The result was the triumphant passage of the bill. The naval officers at Washington gave a banquet to the congressmen whose successful championship had at last brought relief to the navy and had accomplished a work the good results of which will be seen in future years. Rear-Admiral W. T. Sampson, the hero of Santiago, who took a deep interest in the measure, stated publicly that Mr. Dayton's speeches on this bill disclosed the most accurate knowledge of the difficult and obscure details of naval affairs and personnel and the clearest insight into them ever displayed in debate in Congress; and, that this was generally conceded by the naval corps. The full significance of this commendation can be appreciated only by those who know how little the Admiral was given to the bestowal of praise or to the utterance of complimentary remarks.

After the blowing up of the "Maine" in Havana harbor, the first speech in the House of Representatives plainly intimating that Spanish dominion in Cuba must be abolished, was made by Mr. Dayton. His concluding remarks were as follows:

> Two hundred and sixty brave men are dead to-day as a result of the "Maine" tragedy. Over two hundred thousand are dead in Cuba, and two hundred and fifty thousand largely helpless women and children are being held in imprisonment and starved to death there to-day. We do not know as yet that the Spanish authorities blew up the "Maine" and destroyed the lives of our seamen, but we do know that Spanish authority is responsible for this wholesale deadly murder going on within one hundred miles of our shores. With food and raiment in one hand and with its strong power backed by seventy millions of freemen, this administration must intervene, stop this horror, and give Cuba her freedom. This intervention may be done, I hope, peacefully. If so, God be praised! If not, and it can be done only by war, let it come! Humanity, Charity, Mercy, and all the other attributes of God Himself, will be with us, and Cuba will be free.

During his service in congress Mr. Dayton kept up his law practice and engaged extensively in outside business, operating in coal lands and other properties, also holding a directorship in a bank. He belongs to the Independent Order of Odd Fellows and the Knights of Pythias, and is a member of the Presbyterian church. He has always manifested an active interest in education, both in the public schools and the higher institutions of learning. He is a trustee of Davis and Elkins College, at Elkins, where he made the annual address in 1910. He made the annual address to the graduating class of the Fairmont high school in 1912, in the presence of a great audience.

He was married, November 26, 1884, to Columbia, daughter of Arthur Sinsel and Hanna (See) Sinsel, of Grafton, West Virginia; and, they have one son, Arthur Spencer Dayton, who graduated from the State University with the degree of A. B., and afterwards from the Law School of the University, and has been in active practice since in his native county of Barbour, West Virginia.

Mr. Dayton was appointed by President Roosevelt, March 14, 1905, as Judge of the United States District Court for the Northern District of West Virginia, to fill the vacancy caused by the resignation of the late Judge John J. Jackson, who had held the office for more than forty-four years, having been appointed by President Lincoln.

In his seven years service, Judge Dayton has never failed to open each term of his court on the first day fixed for it by law; and, during his service on the bench, the business of the District has increased to more than double, in importance, quantity and variety. In addition to his regular work in his own district, he held the court for a year and a half in the Southern District of West Virginia for Judge Keller, during a prolonged illness of that jurist; and, by designation of the Chief Justice of the Supreme Court of the United States, held four or five terms in aid of the judges in the Pittsburgh (Pennsylvania) District. He has occupied the bench as one of the judges in the Circuit Court of Appeals at Richmond, Virginia, at one of the three terms of that court, each year since his appointment. He has prepared and filed more than one hundred written opinions on diversified and difficult questions arising in the several courts in which he has presided.

In his administration of the United States criminal laws he has been unsparing in his efforts to reach and punish those who are primarily responsible for crime, rather than the "catspaw" for the "man higher up." His public utterances to this effect have given him great strength and support among the people. Judge Dayton is a courageous and upright judge, and in the prime of life has reached eminence on the bench in the short period he has presided. He is thorough in his examinations and exhaustive in treatment of the important questions reaching his court; and, by his industry and faculty for extra work, has kept up with the increasing docket in his large and growing district, to the satisfaction of the litigants and the lawyers who practice in his court. He is affable and approachable either on or off the bench, and most courteous in his treatment of the bar, the officers and others having business in his court.

His large hospitable home in the beautiful little city of Philippi, in Barbour county, is open always to his friends; and is frequently the scene of social functions for the towns people and visiting friends.

Judge Dayton has been in active practice in his native county from the time he graduated from school, representing clients in the many phases of the growth and development of the mountain counties of the northern half of the state, dating from the time the first narrow-gauge branch railroads were built, one from Grafton to Philippi, and one from Clarksburg to Weston; and strongly and naturally sympathized with the native population of these regions, among whom he has always been very popular. In his promotion to wider fields as Member of Congress and Federal Judge, he has shown marked capacity to deal with the larger questions that the marvelous development of these regions are undergoing, developed; but there are no indications that he has forgotten or undervalues his earlier friends and their smaller affairs.

FARNSWORTH
The Farnsworth family here to be considered descends from the English colonial settlers in America.

(I) Thomas Farnsworth was born in Bordentown, New Jersey. He married and had a son named Daniel from whom has descended the West Virginia branch of the family.

(II) Daniel, son of Thomas Farnsworth, was born in April, 1766, died in 1848, aged eighty-two years. He came to what is now Buckhannon, West Virginia, in 1821, and founded the town. He had traded his Staten Island property for fifteen hundred acres of land, including Buckhannon (except eighteen lots that had been sold), and two thousand acres in Pocahontas county, and brought his family with him. The house they built and occupied is still standing—the oldest in Buckhannon. It is still occupied by a descendant. A farm was opened up from out the primeval forests and became a valuable piece of property. Politically Mr. Farnsworth was a Democrat and much interested in all public affairs. He married Rachel Stout, born and reared in New Jersey. They had five sons: 1. James S., died aged eighty-five years; he was a soldier in the war of 1812, and drew a pension until his death; he married Abigail Wilcox, of New Brunswick, New Jersey. 2. Thomas, of whom further. 3. Nathaniel, of whom further. 4. John. 5. Isaac. The father, Daniel Farnsworth, was a farmer and stock raiser and dealer, and his sons all settled in and near Upshur county, Virginia.

(III) Thomas (2), son of Daniel and Rachel (Stout) Farnsworth, was born in 1796 in New Jersey, died about 1870. He was by occupation a farmer. He was a member of the Baptist church, and he voted the Democratic ticket. He married Catherine, daughter of Leonard and Christina (Weatherholt) Simon, a sister of the wife of his brother Nathaniel, Susan P. Simon. Children: Daniel, Clarissa L., Lydia A., Susan P., Caroline E., James R., Thomas Grandison, of whom further; Franklin L., Jane, Lloyd, Joseph R.

(III) Nathaniel, third child of Daniel and Rachel (Stout) Farnsworth, was born in New Jersey, February 22, 1797, died at Buckhannon, West Virginia, in 1868, having removed to Virginia with his parents in 1821. By the death of his father he came into possession of the property, on which Buckhannon is now situated. After the organization of Upshur county in 1852, Buckhannon became the county seat, and many lots were sold by Mr. Farnsworth. He led a very active and useful life. He married Susan P. Simon, born in Upshur county, Virginia, May, 1806, died in 1888, daughter of Leonard and Christina (Weatherholt) Simon. She had been a member of the Methodist Episcopal church for seventy years. Her father was one of the first men to effect settlement on the Buckhannon river, the same being in the eighteenth century. He descended from the early German settlers of Pennsylvania. Children of Nathaniel and Susan P. Farnsworth: 1. Christina, died aged fifteen years. 2. Isaac, died aged seventy years; married Mary Benson. 3. William D., died aged eighty-two years;

married (first) Lucinda Reger, (second) Mary C. Reger (sisters). 4. Thomas Jefferson, of whom further. 5. Leonard S. S., married Catherine Padget. 6. Calvin, died aged seventy years; married a Miss McCreary. 7. Mary, married T. S. Havner. 8. Catherine, married John M. Pinnell. 9. Daniel M., unmarried; was a soldier in the Union army in civil war days. 10. Jackson J., born May 12, 1841, deceased; married Henrietta Wise Fidler. 11. Sallie, married Colonel Edward Frey.

(IV) Hon. Thomas Grandison Farnsworth, son of Thomas and Catherine (Simon) Farnsworth, was born November 9, 1836, in Buckhannon, West Virginia. He obtained his education in private schools, and at the Buckhannon Male and Female Academy. He then took a course in medicine at Jefferson Medical College, Philadelphia, Pennsylvania. He really commenced his career as a contractor at the age of nineteen years and continued this until the civil war came on in 1861. In 1857 he moved to Missouri, returning in 1861, when he engaged in the mercantile business at Buckhannon. The war changed all things in this section of the Union, and young Farnsworth was instrumental in organizing Upshur Militia Company D, One Hundred and Thirty-third Virginia Regiment, and was elected its lieutenant; was also lieutenant of the old Home Guard. Later he raised a company for the United States service, which was sworn into line by Colonel Hughes, of the Third Virginia Regiment. On account of some irregularity the company was disbanded. He then returned to private life and engaged in the practice of medicine, which he continued for several years. He was elected treasurer of Upshur county, and served as a member of the town council of Buckhannon several years. In 1870 he removed to California, but after a short stay returned. He was twice elected a member to the house of delegates—1870-72; was mayor of Buckhannon in 1877-78, 1902-03-05-06-11. In religion he is a Methodist Episcopalian, and a Republican in politics. He was made a Mason in 1862, in Franklin Lodge, No. 7, Free and Accepted Masons, and served as master of this lodge one year.

Mr. Farnsworth married, September 10, 1856, Mary J. M. Marshall, of Bath county, Virginia, daughter of Thomas Marshall, and granddaughter of John Marshall. Children: 1. Ida, born October 26, 1857, in Missouri; married W. N. Poundstone. 2. Charles M., born

July 24, 1862; married Anna A. Shutterly. 3. Rose E., born November 3, 1864; married J. Frank M. Coursey. 4. Gertrude G., born March 28, 1867; married Robert T. Crowley. 5. Mary G., born August 24, 1869; married B. W. Ackles. 6. Hugh B., born April 13, 1874; married Minta Phillips. 7. John W., born September 24, 1876; married Alice Hammer.

(IV) Thomas Jefferson, son of Nathaniel and Susan P. (Simon) Farnsworth, was born on the old home farm, in the house standing as built by the ancestors, May 17, 1829. He was educated in private schools, and remained at home until eighteen years of age, when he served an apprenticeship at the trade of blacksmith; after working at this trade some time in various places, he conducted a shop of his own in Buckhannon for one year. March 8, 1852, he started for California with Dr. William H. Westfall, a cousin, and after reaching the Missouri river a party was made up to cross the plains. Upon reaching Mariposa county, California, September 6, 1852, they at once engaged in mining, and in a few months Mr. Farnsworth had accumulated quite a considerable sum of money. He then rented a shop for a year, after which he bought two shops and continued to work at his trade about seven years, doing a large business and employing many helpers. In 1857 he came home on a visit, because of his engagement to be married, and returned to Buckhannon permanently in 1859, with about thirty thousand dollars, the result of seven years' work. He wisely purchased much property in and about Buckhannon, also stocks of various kinds and extensive droves of horses, cattle and sheep; he engaged in farming and stock raising on a large scale, and is still active in business affairs. After the civil war he became active in politics and held numerous local offices. He was a commissioner by appointment to hold the first election under the new state of West Virginia; was elected the first supervisor of his county, and was the first president of the county board. He was also the first to open a school in the place in which he lived, under the new system. In 1874 he was elected to the house of delegates, and in 1875 was a member of several important committees. In 1876 was reëlected to the office in a county strongly Republican, but at the expiration of his term declined further nomination. In 1879 he was the Democratic nominee for the state senate in the tenth senatorial district. He was elected without opposition and

served in the general assembly of 1880-81. Upon the reorganization of the senate in 1883, he was elected president of that body, serving as such during that year and in 1884. Since that date he has declined to hold political office. In 1877 he was appointed by Governor Matthews as regent for the State University and was successively appointed by Governors Jackson, Wilson and Fleming, serving in all eighteen years. He was made a Master Mason in California, and transferred his membership to Franklin Lodge, No. 7, at Buckhannon, where he served as its master for thirteen years. For several years he has been president of the Buckhannon Bank and still holds that office. His name is inseparably linked with that of Upshur county and its present prosperity.

He married, May 19, 1859, in Upshur county, West Virginia, Mary E. Carper, born May 1, 1833 (see Carper III). Children: 1. Emma, died aged two years. 2. Anna M., married Dr. George B. Edmiston; he died March 28, 1891, leaving two children: Matthew and Georgie Bland. 3. Carrie M., died aged three years. 4. Mary M., married Norval B. McCarty; he died August 23, 1911; they had one child, Mary Elizabeth, born at Buckhannon, West Virginia. 5. Maud Carper, married Benjamin Bassel Jr., who died August 16, 1907. 6. Thomas Benjamin, married Clara Teter.

(The Carper Line).

This family came originally from Germany and settled at Reading, Pennsylvania, in the years just prior to the revolutionary war. Later members of the family found their way to Western Virginia and intermarried with some of the best families of that state, including the Farnsworths.

(I) Paul (Kerber) Carper, a native of Germany, died in Reading, Pennsylvania, in 1777. At the time he was assistant quartermaster and recruiting officer in the colonial warfare. He had a son Abraham, of whom further.

(II) Abraham, son of Paul Carper, was born at Reading, Pennsylvania, 1763, died June 17, 1850. In his early manhood he removed to Moorefield, Virginia, where he was married, and in June, 1800, he moved his family to what was then a wilderness region, and built in a dense forest a rude log habitation, located on a site now the campus of the West Virginia Wesleyan College. This was the first house of any sort ever erected in Buckhannon. By trade this man was a hatter; a man of sterling qualities, honest and intelligent. He was also a most ardent believer in the Christian religion. He was reared in the faith of the Lutheran church and was a recognized leader in his church many years. At the time he came to Buckhannon, Methodist ministers preached at stated intervals, about ten miles distant, near the present Rogers Church, in the house of John Reger, the great-great-grandfather of Dr. R. A. Reger. At first he stoutly antagonized the work of the Methodists, but later he approved of and accepted that faith. He and his good wife identified themselves with the Methodist church and he became a licensed exhorter and a class-leader, continuing more than fifty years. The slaves then in his possession were set free, some of whom, however, preferred to remain with their "Old Master," faithfully serving him to the end of his life.

He married Permelia, daughter of George Harris, of Moorefield, Virginia. Mr. Harris was a wealthy man and on their marriage he gave them the land they settled on, above described as at Buckhannon. They had twelve children: 1. Joseph, born June 21, 1789, died 1867; he moved to Ohio; married Jane Harper and they had two children: Homer M. and Elizabeth A. 2. Abram, born May 2, 1791, died 1880; he moved to Randolph county, Virginia; married Margaret Stewart and they had children: Patsy, Burgess and Nehemiah. 3. George, born August 1, 1793; resided in Upshur county all his life; married Rachel White and they had children: Isaac W., Asa, Daniel J., G. Columbus, Minerva, Sarah, Abram, Permelia and Virginia. 4. Adam, of whom further. 5. Elizabeth, born May 14, 1797, died 1880; married Nathan Davisson and they had eleven children: Melville, Austin, Bergin, Dibby Ann, Olive M., Virginia, Carrie, Harriet, Sarah, Jenette, Martha. 6. Permelia, born February 5, 1799, died 1850; married Elmore Hart and had children: Caroline, Ira and Elizabeth. 7. Sarah, born 1801, died 1886; married William, brother of Nathan Davisson. 8. Jacob, born December 22, 1806, died 1819. 9. David, born December 29, 1808, died September 17, 1897; he being the last to remain at home he came into possession of the old homestead, assuming the care and support of the aged father; on May 21, 1845, he married Sarah Jane, daughter of Colonel Asa

Aquires, of Salt Lick Bridge, Broxton county; children: Abram, Benjamin F., Luther E., Wilbur F. and A. Harris. 10. Bergin, born September 22, 1813, died 1835, unmarried. 11. and 12. Asa and Isaac, died in childhood.

(III) Adam, fourth child of Abraham Carper, was born October 4, 1795, died December 30, 1883. He was a farmer all his life in Lewis county, West Virginia. He married Jemimia, born in Randolph county, Virginia, daughter of William Currence, and granddaughter of William Currence, who was a native of Ireland and an early emigrant to Virginia. He was shot from his horse in Randolph county, by the Indians, in 1770. Adam and Jemimia (Currence) Carper had children: Joseph, William C., Bergin, Emily, Jane, Mary E., married Thomas Jefferson Farnsworth (see Farnsworth IV).

McCARTY

The McCarty family was worthily represented for many years by the late Norval Bushrod McCarty, who was one of the substantial citizens of Clarksburg, public-spirited to the highest degree, ever forward in encouraging enterprises which aided in advancing the interests of his adopted city. To a natural dignity of manner Mr. McCarty added a geniality that won him hosts of friends and made him welcome everywhere. He was hospitable, charitable, generous, with a ready sympathy for those in affliction or need. A keynote to his success in his many undertakings was his executive force and mastery of detail in whatever engaged his attention.

(I) Thomas Grenberry McCarty, father of Norval B. McCarty, was born in Lumberport, Harrison county, West Virginia, and there spent his entire life. He was a farmer of substantial means, and an influence for good in the community. At the age of twenty-two he enlisted in the Union army as a private in Company G, Twelfth Regiment West Virginia Volunteer Infantry, Captain James Moffatt, and was killed at the battle of Winchester, Virginia, June 14, 1862, giving his life in the service of his country, a most noble cause. He married Martha Hildreth, a member of the old Hildreth family who settled in New England in the early colonial period. She died shortly after her husband lost his life. They left one son, Norval Bushrod, of whom further.

(II) Norval Bushrod, son of Thomas Grenberry and Martha (Hildreth) McCarty, was born at Lumberport, Harrison county, West Virginia, June 29, 1859. After the death of his mother he went to live with his Grandfather Hildreth and remained with him until about the age of sixteen, when his grandfather passed away. He was thus early thrown upon his own resources, although he was better equipped than many boys are, having been left a good farm and a substantial capital by his father. He acquired a practical education in the district schools near Lumberport, and pursued advanced studies in the Fairmont Normal School, of which he was an honor student, and in which he later taught one term, and in the University of West Virginia. For a short period of time after completing his education, he taught school near Lumberport, and ever after pointed with pride to the little old schoolhouse where he had to struggle with the unruly boys, some of whom were almost twice his size. During this time he was also conducting his farm, and thus continued until he was about the age of twenty-three. He then removed to Janelew, West Virginia, where he remained about one year. He then engaged in the wholesale lumber business in the lumber sections of West Virginia, making his headquarters during this period of his life at Buckhannon. He remained actively interested in the lumber business for about seventeen years and then sold his principal holdings, although at the time of his death he was an extensive holder of some of the finest timber tracts in the state.

At the age of forty he removed to Clarksburg, West Virginia, and engaged in the real estate business, in which line of work he continued until his decease, which occurred at Atlantic City, New Jersey, after a very short illness, August 23, 1911. He was a man of character and executive ability, and therefore was chosen to serve in positions of trust and responsibility, acting in the capacity of president of the Board of Trade of Clarksburg, and a director of the Empire National Bank of Clarksburg. He was also officially connected with the Chevy Chase Development Company of Washington, D. C. He was a Baptist in religion, and a Republican in politics. This brief resumé of Mr. McCarty's life proved that he was a man of clear mental vision, who strove most earnestly to fulfill every duty and responsibility which devolved upon him.

N. B. McCarty

He married, November 23, 1893, Mary Martha, daughter of ex-Senator Thomas J. Farnsworth, of Buckhannon, West Virginia. One child, Mary Elizabeth, born November, 1902.

GAY-BROWN-STOETZER This family traces its origin in America to Thomas Lamar, who with his brother Peter came to America about 1660. The surname was variously spelled in the early American days, and these founders are called Lamore. They are thought to have come from Wicre, a small village near Lille, Flanders, and were probably Huguenots. The following are Lamar arms: Gules, two lions passant gardant, in pale, or. Crest: A mermaid proper, a mirror in the sinister and a comb in the dexter hand, crined, or. There are several French noble families of similar name. The Lamar family has given to America several distinguished sons, among them being General Maximilian and Colonel William Lamar, of revolutionary fame, and Justice L. Q. C. Lamar.

(I) Thomas Lamore was a planter, and lived in Calvert (now Prince George) county, Maryland. He settled upon fifty acres of land, known as Fishing Place, on the west side of the Patuxent river and the north side of Trent creek. Other adjoining lands were already in his possession; he became owner of extensive property in Maryland and had lands also in England. His will was dated October 4, 1712, and probated May 29, 1714. He married (first), before coming to Maryland, Mary ———, (second) Ann ——— (probably Pottinger). Children: Thomas, probably by first wife, of whom further; John, probably by second wife, died in 1758, married Susan ———.

(II) Thomas (2) Lamar, son of Thomas (1) Lamore, was born probably about 1660 to 1670; his will was dated May 11, 1747, and probated January 31, 1748. At the time of his death he owned about three thousand acres of land, much of which was at Rock Creek, Maryland. According to tradition he married Martha, sister of Rev. John Urquhart, rector in the Episcopal church. Children (order uncertain): Robert, Samuel, Alexander, John, married Rachel ———; James, married Valinda ———; Volenda, of whom further; Mary, married Clementius Davis; Thomas, married Eleanor ———; Elizabeth, born October 26, 1722, married June 18, 1747, Joseph Wilson.

(III) Volenda, daughter of Thomas (2) Lamar, married, about 1747, William Williams; he died in 1788. Children: Amos, Eleanor, a daughter married —— Hardesty; Sarah, of whom further.

(IV) Sarah, daughter of William and Volenda (Lamar) Williams, was born in 1747, died in 1836. She married, November 18, 1765, Lieutenant John Suter (as he was afterward, in the time of the revolution), who was born in 1744, died in 1794. He was appointed by Colonel Zadock McGruder, in 1777, second lieutenant of the Middle Battalion, of Montgomery county, Maryland. Children: William Williams, Volenda, of whom further; John, Mary, Robert, Alexander, Margaret.

(V) Volenda, daughter of John and Sarah (Williams) Suter, was born November 25, 1768, died November 13, 1836. She was married, March 5, 1791, to Alexander Smith, born December 1, 1757, died March 14, 1839. He came from Scotland to Loudoun county, Virginia. Later he settled in Allegany county, Maryland, where he owned and operated a large plantation. Children: George, Margaret, married Matthew Gay; Janet, Delia, Sarah, Isabel, Volenda, Maria, Eleanor.

Matthew Gay was the eldest son of John and Margaret (McCleary) Gay, of county Tyrone, Ireland. He was born 1780, died in 1857. His mother was a sister of Colonel William McCleary, who was born in county Tyrone, Ireland, 1741, died in Morgantown, Virginia, 1821. When Colonel McCleary came to this country is not exactly known, but we find him living in Washington county, Pennsylvania. He was sub-lieutenant of the county, being appointed by the supreme executive council of Philadelphia, December 24, 1781. At the meeting of the same council, October, 1782, William McCleary was returned as one of the justices for Washington county; the council did not accept his appointment as justice because his name was to be returned later as a member of the legislature. At the election in Washington county, December 4, 1782, William McCleary was elected a member of the general assembly, which was the supreme executive council. As late as 1784 we find him serving as sub-lieutenant of Washington county. Soon after this he moved to Morgantown, Virginia, which in 1783 was made the county seat of Monongalia county; he received from the governor a colonel's commission. Here he showed the same spirit of vigilance and bravery that had so distinguished him as a citizen of Pennsylvania.

Colonel McCleary was one of the first attorneys of Monongahela Valley, and held many high positions both of a civil and military character. In 1787 he was admitted to the practice of law in Randolph county. He paid the taxes prescribed by law and was appointed prosecuting attorney.

In 1788 he was recommended to the governor of Virginia for judge of the district court of Monongalia county, and he was also at this time state attorney for Harrison county. In the convention that assembled at Richmond, Virginia, June, 1788, to frame the federal constitution, among the distinguished names in Virginia were Madison, Monroe, Washington, Randolph, Lee and others, and we find Colonel McCleary representing Monongalia county from 1788 to 1790 and again in 1798. During the administration of President Washington he held the office of collector of United States taxes, and continued in that service during the whiskey insurrection and until the repeal of that law.

Colonel McCleary was a prominent figure in the Presbyterian church, and in the records of the old Red Stone Presbytery, October, 1784, we find a record of a number of Bibles being given to him for distribution within the bounds of the Presbytery. In 1792 we find him representing the Presbyterian church at Morgantown as a ruling elder at the meeting of the Red Stone Presbytery.

Colonel McCleary's first wife was Isabella Stocton, of Berkeley county, Virginia, who when a child was captured by the Indians and carried into Canada and sold to a wealthy French family who educated her at a Catholic convent. Later when asked to marry a young Frenchman named Plata she only consented on condition that her real parents gave their consent. The young people made the long journey from Canada to Berkeley county, Virginia, on horseback, but all in vain, so strong were her parents' prejudices against the French that they refused their consent, but one day, while Isabella's father and brothers were away on a fox chase, Isabella and her French lover, Plata, decided to elope, but they were pursued and the young Frenchman was shot. Some years later Isabella met Colonel McCleary, married him, and came to Morgantown to live. After her death, leaving no children, Colonel McCleary sent to Ireland for his young nephew, Matthew

Gay, who came to Morgantown in 1800, studied law with his uncle, and upon his retirement succeeded him in his professional life.

Matthew Gay, in 1814, when the British fleet entered Chesapeake Bay, volunteered in a cavalry company to repel the expected invasion of Virginia. The company made one day's march toward Washington, but their services were not further needed. From 1827 to his death, he was president of the board of trustees of Monongahela Academy. He was a director of the Monongalia Farmers' Company of Virginia, a bank of exchange, discount, and deposit, organized at Morgantown in 1814; in 1840, when it wound up its business, he was appointed an agent to collect and distribute its assets. The next year he was elected president of the Merchants' and Mechanics' Bank of Wheeling, and this position he held until his death.

When on his journey, horseback, in 1807, to Richmond, for examination as to his proficiency, and for obtaining the signatures of three judges to his license to practice law, he stayed over night at the house of Alexander Smith. Here he saw for the first time a young girl, the daughter of his host, named Margaret, whom fifteen years later he married. Children: William M., Alexander Smith, John G., Matthew, Sarah A., all of whom died before 1883; Jane V., married Andrew McDonald; Jennette J., married M. W. Tate; Margaret P., married William Guy Brown; Mary Ellen, married John James Brown.

The Brown family is of Scotch origin. Their first family home was in the neighborhood of Edinburg, Scotland, but many migrated from that place to Ireland and England.

(I) John Brown, the first member of this family about whom we have definite information, was born and educated near Edinburg, Scotland. When he was twenty-one years old he went to England, but not meeting with success, he determined to go to Ireland, whither a branch of his family had gone some years before. Going first to Scotland and marrying, he sailed to Londonderry, and settled near that city. There he managed a large estate, belonging to the father of General Montgomery, who fell at Quebec, and afterward to Lord Beresford. Here he died at an advanced age. He married Ann Morrow. Children: John, James, of whom further; George, Peter, Thomas, Ann.

(II) James, son of John and Ann (Morrow) Brown, while in Ireland, was a sympathizer with the revolting American colonies.

After the revolution, he sought the freedom of Ireland, but becoming discouraged in this project sailed, with his wife's family, from Londonderry in the fall of 1789, and came to Philadelphia, Pennsylvania. The following spring he settled near Kingwood, then in Monongalia county, Virginia; his wife's brothers, Robert and Alexander Hawthorne, came with him, but settled near Morgantown. He married Rachel Hawthorne. Children: John C., died in April, 1852; Robert, of whom further; Joseph; William Guy, born September 25, 1800, married (first), July 3, 1828, Juliet A. R. Byrne, (second), June 5, 1855, Margaret P. Gay; Thomas, born December 25, 1802, died November 13, 1867, married Ellen S. Smith; Jane; Ann M., married Elisha M. Hagans.

(III) Robert, son of James and Rachel (Hawthorne) Brown, married Annie, daughter of John Hawthorne, who was born in Londonderry, Ireland, and came to this country when a young man. Settling in Philadelphia at the breaking out of the revolutionary war, he took the oath of allegiance and enlisted in Thomas Proctor's artillery regiment of Pennsylvania. This regiment was formed primarily for the defense of Philadelphia, but as early as April, 1777, it became a part of the regular army, distinguishing itself at Bound Brook, Brandywine, Germantown, Monmouth and many other places. John Hawthorne, about 1790, married Mary Calvery, to whom was born one child Annie. Mary (Calvery) Hawthorne died in 1793. The children of Robert and Annie (Hawthorne) Brown were: Rebecca, married Rev. John A. Regar; Eliza, married Rev. James Dolliver; John James, of whom further. At the close of the war John Hawthorne became captain in the trading ship commerce and was drowned during a storm, July 4, 1796, the little daughter Annie being left an orphan. Her uncle, Alexander Hawthorne, came from Kingwood, Virginia, to Philadelphia and brought her back to Virginia on horseback.

(IV) John James, son of Robert and Annie (Hawthorne) Brown, was born at Kingwood, November 19, 1825, died August 11, 1905. In early boyhood he was sent to Monongalia Academy, during the administration of Rev. Thomas Martin, a learned English and classical scholar, who had been educated at the college of Belfast, Ireland. He afterward entered the junior class of Washington College, Washington, Pennsylvania, from which institution he graduated in 1845.

Then he was deputy clerk of the circuit and county courts of Preston county, and at the same time studied law under his uncle, Hon. William Guy Brown, of Kingwood. In November, 1848, he was licensed, and in the following April he began practice with his uncle, their partnership continuing until 1861. The firm Brown & Brown was engaged in nearly all the greater and most important and difficult cases in that part of the state. Both were recognized as able attorneys, accurate and safe counsellors, and eloquent, ready and most forceful orators. At the bar he was well beloved by his associates. He was ever courteous, patient and considerate of the rights and feelings of others, and never permitted the zeal and the acrimony of the trial court, too often engendering ill will and sharp and caustic criticism, to obscure his judgment. He was ever charitable to the short-comings of others, and by his refinement, purity of life and sweet disposition endeared himself to all who came within the sphere of his influence. He was scrupulously honest in all his affairs, and a man to be fully trusted.

In the days preceding and opening the civil war, the stress was especially felt in the border states, which also were the scenes of many armed conflicts in the course of the struggle. The western part of Virginia had its peculiar difficulties, which form an interesting chapter in American history. Mr. Brown was an intense and steadfast Union man, and had a prominent place in the exciting events of the day. By speeches and other means he earnestly opposed the attempt at secession and the adoption of the ordinance. The Union men of Preston county sent him as a delegate to the convention at Wheeling, which formed the "Restored Government of Virginia." He was also chosen to represent his county in the constitutional convention which met at Wheeling a few months later, and which framed the first constitution of the new state. At the first general election in West Virginia, he was elected to represent in the state senate the district composed of Preston, Monongalia and Taylor counties. To this office he was reëlected. He served with credit as a member of the important committees on finance and the judiciary.

He inherited the warm heart and ardent nature of the Irish, tempered with the hard and practical common sense of his Scotch ancestry. To the former he doubtless owed much of that almost matchless gift of oratory that charmed and delighted his hearers. His charming style of expression and nobility of thought may be seen in the following extract from his speech delivered at Morgantown on the Fourth of July, 1876, when a great multitude gathered to hear him speak:

> Who will say, standing this day beneath his country's flag and witnessing the universal joy of a free and happy people, that the wars, the tears and the blood of a century have been a costly sacrifice? Who will say that if it has taken a hundred years to give practical interpretation to the great charter of American freedom and to present every citizen in this year of jubilee before high heaven, redeemed, disenthralled and regenerated by the spirit of universal liberty, that the cry will not ere long be heard from the tops of the mountains:
> "Watchman, what of the night?" And in ten thousand answering voices echoing around a ransomed world the welcome response will be: "The morning cometh to usher in the meridian splendor of the Sun of Righteousness to whom not only all the honors of all the centennial years of earth and time, but the excellent glory of the eternal ages belong."

In presenting a flag in 1861, made by the ladies of Preston county, he gave expression to the following eloquent and patriotic sentiments:

> Your mothers and wives and sisters have handed to me "the glorious ensign of our republic," with "not a stripe erased or polluted, and not a single star obscured"—wrought by their own patriotic hands—and desire me to present it in their name, to you, my fellow countrymen of Preston county, and to say to you, "it is our country's flag—the emblem of our national Union." I can find no more suitable response to the patriotic Union-loving ladies than by giving utterance to the beautiful sentiment of the patriotic poet of our country:
>
> > A union of lakes and a union of lands,
> > A union of States none can sever;
> > A union of hearts and a union of hands,
> > And the flag of our Union forever.
>
> It is not the flag of Virginia, nor of Pennsylvania, nor of Massachusetts, nor of South Carolina. It is the flag of our country—the flag of our Union; and there are clustering around it ten thousand hallowed associations and memories. It is the flag to which the gallant Lawrence turned his eyes in death and exclaimed, "Don't give up the ship." It is the flag that Perry grasped from the prow of his sinking vessel, and through the deadly broadsides of the enemy bore aloft to victory. It is the flag our gallant countrymen unfurled in triumph over the palaces of the Montezumas.
> Go, my countrymen, baptize it in the morning sunbeams, and give it to the breeze; and if the time shall ever come (which God forbid) when it must be bathed in blood, these mothers and wives and sisters and daughters,

whose gift it is, bid me say to you, their fathers and husbands and brothers and sons, "Go to the tented field, stand by this flag, fight for your country under your country's banner, and die in its defense, if death shall come, like the gallant Jasper, enshrouded in its folds."

Mr. Brown served in the old One Hundred and Forty-eighth Regiment of the Virginia militia, and was not promoted from the ranks until in 1858, at the reorganization of the Virginia militia, he was commissioned major, and served as such until his removal to Morgantown, in 1864. He was there director and afterward president of the Merchants' National Bank of West Virginia. For more than half a century he was a consistent member of the Methodist Episcopal church and his records of the official board, of which he was secretary for the greater part of that time, are still preserved and are models of neatness, accuracy and beautiful penmanship. He was a devout Christian and exemplified in his life the teachings of the Divine Master.

He was initiated a Mason in Preston Lodge, No. 14, in 1858, and when he removed to Morgantown became a member of Morgantown Union Lodge, No. 4, June 24, 1867, and was elected secretary in 1869, and served until his death continuously, a period of thirty-four years. He was as regular in his attendance on his lodge as upon the stated services of his church, so long as health permitted. For many years he was secretary and kept with pride and care the minutes of the lodge proceedings which were always on time for inspection. In wise counsel, in brotherly intercourse and in all that makes the good Mason he was without spot or blemish. He recognized that Masonry is not a religion, but that it is a system of ethics consistent with all true religions. He acknowledged its only religious test is a devout belief in the existence of the one true and living God. He believed in its teachings of brotherly love, relief and truth of its motto of "Faith, Hope and Charity," and practiced them in his daily work, conduct and conversation. Mr. Brown was a man of liberal education, a wonderfully accurate and retentive memory, stored with the facts of history, the choicest literature and the most beautiful imagery. His was a noble and cultured soul, a loving spirit and an attractive personality which charmed alike young and old, and his lovely character and gracious conduct were a daily benediction.

He married (second), September 30, 1868, Mary Ellen, daughter of Matthew and Margaret (Smith) Gay. Children of John James and Mary Ellen (Gay) Brown: Margaret Annie, married Rev. Herman G. Stoetzer, see forward; Alexandria Gay, died February 23, 1899; John Matthew Guy, prominent real estate dealer and business man of Morgantown, married Mary, daughter of Worthington H. and Virginia Bannister, children: Mary Virginia and John Guy.

(I) Martin Stoetzer, father of Rev. Herman G. Stoetzer, came from Germany in 1871, and settled in Wheeling, West Virginia. He married, in Germany, Louise Koenig. Among their children was Herman G.

(II) Rev. Herman G. Stoetzer, son of Martin and Louise (Koenig) Stoetzer, was born in Germany. At the age of eight he came with his father and sister to America. He attended the public schools, the Business College at Wheeling, West Virginia, the Normal School at Fairmont, and in 1889 graduated from the University of West Virginia. During his course at the University he took prizes in oratory and debate, and was one of the founders of "The Athenæum." For one year he taught at the University; in 1892 he received the degree of A. M. from Princeton University. The next year he graduated from the Princeton Theological Seminary, and he then took one year's graduate work in Princeton University and the Theological Seminary. The degree of Doctor of Divinity was conferred upon him in 1911. He is a Presbyterian minister. His first charge was the Dickinson Presbyterian Church, near Carlisle, Pennsylvania, where he remained for six years. From 1900 to the present time he has been pastor of the First Presbyterian Church at Fairmont, West Virginia. He was elected commissioner to the general assembly of the Presbyterian church in the years 1899, 1904, and 1910. He was moderator of the Synod of West Virginia in 1910. He was president of the Alumni Association of the University of West Virginia, 1910, and is a member of the Phi Beta Kappa Society.

He married, March 21, 1894, Margaret, daughter of John James and Mary Ellen (Gay) Brown. Mrs. Stoetzer attended the public schools at Morgantown, West Virginia, and is a graduate, in the class of 1888, of the seminary at Washington, Pennsylvania, also a student of Wilson College, Chambersburg, Pennsylvania. She has had an excellent musical education. Child, John James Brown, born February 5, 1895; he graduated from the Fairmont high school, 1912.

JOLLIFFE

The Jolliffe family has a lineage as old and honorable as any in the Valley of the Monongahela. It is able to trace its ancestry with an unusual degree of certitude to men who did noteworthy public service in England as far back as the early part of the sixteenth century. In all works of family history the name seems to have originally been spelled Jolli or Jolly, meaning in the old Norman French, gay, gallant, handsome. Burke's "Landed Gentry of Great Britain" says: "The family of Jolliffe (originally Jolli) is of considerable antiquity in the counties of Stafford and Worcester, and the pedigree in the possession of the senior members comprises intermarriages with many eminent and noble houses. One branch, established in the north, enjoyed, it appears from authentic records, power and affluence even before the institution of hereditary honors." Another account says, "Descended from an ancient and honorable family which dates its origin from the incursion of the Norman Conquerors, and collaterally allied to some of the chief nobles of the kingdom." During the troublous times of Charles the First and the revolution under Cromwell they were staunch royalists, and adherents of the Established Church, one of them attending Charles to the place of execution. For their loyalty and religious convictions, they were made to suffer by being deprived of their rank, position and estates. At the Restoration their property was restored to them, and they were reinstated in royal favor. They furnished from their number magistrates and sheriffs of the counties of Stafford and Worcester during the reigns of Charles the Second and later kings. They have been aldermen and lord mayors of the city of London, members of Parliament, and governors of provinces. Many of them were men of note as authors, physicians, soldiers, and above all as philanthropists. One of the grammar schools established here and there throughout England by private means was that founded at Stratford-on-Avon by a Thomas Jollyffe, a native of the town, who had gone up to London and become lord mayor. It bore on its rolls the name of William Shakespeare, who but for the good fortune and generosity of his townsmen might have died mute and inglorious. The arms borne by the English family are: "Argent on a pile azure, three Dexter Gauntlets of the Field. The crest, a cubit arm erect vested and cuffed, the sleeve charged with a pile argent, the hand grasping a sword ppd." The motto, *"Tant que je puis."*

The old records have a notice in 1680 at St. Michael's, Barbadoes, of a Thomas Jolley who owned two hundred acres of land, three hired servants, ten bought servants, and seventy negroes. It is probable this was Thomas Jolley, of Cofton Hall, who was a known adherent of Charles the First, probably after his execution was compelled to leave home with his son John, following Prince Rupert to the West Indies. After the accession of Charles the Second he was reinstated in his estates, and in the office which his father had held before him of high sheriff of Stafford county.

(I) John Jolliffe, the American heir of Thomas Jolliffe, of Cofton Hall, and Margaret Skinner, his wife, was born in England about the year 1642, and came to this country when very young, soon after the execution of Charles I. He settled on the western branch of the Elizabeth river, Norfolk county, Virginia, and on January 22, 1662, bought of John Lawrence one hundred acres of land. Other lands were soon acquired by purchase and grants under the law that gave fifty acres apiece for those servants brought over at a master's expense. He built one of the first gristmills ever erected in Virginia, having first received a permit from His Majesty's Council. About the year 1662 he married Mary, only daughter and heiress of Peter Rigglesworth, of Norfolk county, Virginia. They had four sons and three daughters: Joseph, John, Thomas, Peter, Sarah, Elizabeth, Mary. John Jolliffe seems to have been a man of education notwithstanding the vicissitudes of his youth, and possessed of some wealth when he came to the colony to which he added so largely that he was able to provide handsomely for all of his children. At his death he was about seventy-six years old. He seems to have always resided in Virginia, on the Elizabeth river, in Norfolk county.

(II) Joseph, son of John and Mary (Rigglesworth) Jolliffe, was born at his father's house on the Elizabeth river, Norfolk county, Virginia, about the year 1663. He was well educated and there is reason to believe was a lawyer, or held some position about the county clerk's office. He married (first) Ruth —————— and left a son William, born about 1695, and other children of whom there is no record. He married (second) Elizabeth ——————, about the year 1732. In 1737 Joseph

Jolliffe sold the old home place left to him by his father in accordance with the law of primogeniture. It is not known when Joseph Jolliffe went from here. There are serious gaps in the court records of the Virginia colony during this period due to the vicissitudes attendant upon the change of the capitol to Richmond, and to the losses from invasion and threatened invasions in the revolutionary and civil wars.

(III) William, son of Joseph and Ruth Jolliffe, was born at his father's plantation on the western branch of the Elizabeth river, Norfolk county, Virginia, about the year 1695. He was carefully educated and named to the profession of law. His father had been executor for many large estates and seems to have had much to do with courts, and it is probable that he saw to it that at least one of his sons should be trained to the profession. William Jolliffe was one of those who in the great movements toward a wider settlement of the country inaugurated by Governor Spottswood in 1710, left their homes and sought their fortunes in the new regions then opened up. He settled first in Orange county, and upon the formation of a court was among the first to take the oath as attorney. Records show that shortly after this date he was possessed of five hundred acres of land near Winchester. When he was twenty-five years of age he married Phoeby ———, by whom he had sons, William, James, John Edmund, and perhaps daughters.

(IV) James, son of William and Phoeby Jolliffe, was born about 1720. He came with his father and his brothers, William and Edmund, to the Valley of Virginia about 1743. It is probable that his father's home was on the five hundred acre tract of land north of the present town of Winchester, and adjoining the land of Alexander Ross. He joined the Society of Friends at an early age, but was disowned, March 26, 1759, probably for marrying outside of the society. He married, in 1759, Hannah Springer, granddaughter of Dennis Springer, who had a grant of lands from Lord Fairfax. Shortly after their marriage they moved from Winchester to Uniontown, Pennsylvania, where he remained up to the time of his death in 1771. They had six children: William, of whom further; Ann, born August 15, 1762; Drew, September 2, 1764; Elizabeth, June 16, 1766; John, July 6, 1768; Margaret, October 23, 1770. James Jolliffe was a man of high character and deep religious feeling. Though he did not have the large possessions of others of the family, he left behind the memory and the abiding influence of a good man. His descendants are very numerous, having settled in West Virginia and Pennsylvania; from there some moved to Ohio and then west.

(V) William (2), son of James and Hannah (Springer) Jolliffe, was born near Uniontown, Pennsylvania, May 30, 1761, the eldest of the six children of his parents. Soon after his first marriage he removed to Monongalia county, West Virginia, then a county of the old state, and took up his residence in that wild and beautiful region at the mouth of Paw Paw creek on the banks of the Monongahela river, and there his first wife, Catherine, died in 1804. He was a man of strong convictions and deeply patriotic feelings, and when the war of 1812 broke out, as a result of the tyrannical aggressions of Great Britain, he threw himself with ardor into the conflict. From the wounds he received in this service he suffered to the end of his days, being accorded a pension in recognition of its cause. He was interred in the burying ground, which according to the old custom formed part of the "Willey Farm," near Rivesville, in what is now Marion county, West Virginia. He married (first), August 1, 1779, Catherine, sister of Joseph Collins. After her death in 1804 he married (second) Charity Prickett, with whom he lived until his death, May 1, 1827. William and Catherine (Collins) Jolliffe had twelve children: James, born July 17, 1780; William, July 25, 1781; John, July 20, 1783; Thomas, November 15, 1785; Hannah, July 5, 1787; Aaron, September 15, 1789; Amos, of whom further; Levi, September 2, 1793; Elizabeth, May 20, 1796; Joseph, May 20, 1798; Job, June 15, 1800; Nathan, May 3, 1802.

(VI) Amos, son of William (2) and Catherine (Collins) Jolliffe, was born July 6, 1791, in Monongalia county, where he resided during his lifetime, about three miles from Morgantown. He followed the occupation of farming, and served the county as deputy sheriff for twenty years. His political opinions were Republican, a belief in which he carefully brought up his sons. He died February 8, 1859, and was buried in the Morgan graveyard. He married ——— Miller, who died seven years after him, in 1866. To them were born twelve children: Eliza, born October 6, 1817; Rebecca, October 10, 1820; Catherine, December 20, 1822; Sarah A., September 13, 1824; Dorcas, December 20, 1825; Oliver Perry, of whom further; Matilda O., September 12, 1832; John N., August 20, 1834; Sisson H., February 7, 1836; William T., May 22, 1840; James S., December 12, 1842.

(VII) Captain Oliver Perry Jolliffe, son of Amos and ——— (Miller) Jolliffe, was born December 20, 1827, on his father's farm near Morgantown, in what is now Clinton district, Monongalia county, West Virginia. He was one of those boys whose intellectual ambitions develop at an early age. Making the best use of all the advantages afforded by the public schools in the vicinity, he secured what was an excellent education at that day and entered the profession of teaching. This he followed for ten years, when upon the breaking out of the civil war, he considered that the call to arms took precedence of private duties and interests.

Entering the Union army he served until the close of the war, participating in some of the fiercest contests of the time. He enlisted August 16, 1862, in Company C, Fourteenth West Virginia Volunteer Infantry, at Clinton Furnace, in Clinton district, and was honorably discharged June 27, 1865, at Cumberland, Maryland. Though he enlisted as a private, he was elected captain upon the organization of the company, receiving his commission from Governor F. H. Pierpont, serving with that rank until he was mustered out. He held an enviable record, taking a brave part in sixteen regular engagements and numerous skirmishes. A remarkable good fortune attended him throughout the whole time; he never received a wound and never was absent from duty. His company was assigned to the Fifth Brigade, First Division, Eighth Army Corps. The regiment fought at Greenland Gap, in General MacDowell's expedition in December, 1863; in General Crook's expedition; at Cloyd Mountain, Virginia, May 9, 1864; New River Bridge; Lexington, Virginia, June 11, 1864; Lynchburg, June 17 and 18, 1864; Carter's Farm, July 20, 1864; Winchester, July 24, 1864; Martinsburg, West Virginia, July 25, 1864; Halltown, West Virginia, August 24 and 26, 1864; Berryville, Virginia, September 3, 1864; Winchester, Virginia, September 19, 1864; Fisher's Hill, Virginia, September 22, 1864; and Cedar Creek, Virginia, October 19, 1864. He witnessed Sheridan's memorable ride and took part in the fighting that followed.

After the surrender at Appomattox he returned home and purchased a farm of two hundred acres on Independence Road, a short distance out of Morgantown. Here he has since resided, engaged in agricultural pursuits and identifying himself with various charitable and religious movements, and all affairs that concern the welfare of the community. Politically it is hardly necessary to say of a valiant old Union veteran, he is a Republican. He has filled the position of county commissioner of schools, and has been poor director for ten years. In religious beliefs he is a member of the Methodist Protestant church. He is an active and generous supporter of all the good works, superintending and partially paying for the construction of a church near his house in 1877. He is a member of Hoffman Post, No. 62, Grand Army of the Republic, at Morgantown, of which he is past commander.

Captain Jolliffe married, March 26, 1856, Sarah A., daughter of Leonard Selby, of Clinton district, Monongalia county. Eight children were born to this marriage: 1. Ethelbert Oliphant, in the employ of the Standard Oil Company, in Mannington, West Virginia; married Ida B. Fast. 2. Charles E., of whom further. 3. Jennie, married Frank R. Sapp, in the employ of the Baltimore & Ohio railroad at Fairmont. 4. Thayer M., a farmer of Clinton district; married Emma McBee. 5. William S., teller of the Exchange Bank of Mannington. 6. George C., a carpenter, residing in Mannington. 7. Joseph A. 8. Frank C.

(VIII) Charles E., son of Captain Oliver Perry and Sarah A. (Selby) Jolliffe, was born in Monongalia county, West Virginia, 1859. He was educated in the public schools of the neighborhood, and after leaving school taught until 1883. He then decided to enter business and was for three years engaged in mercantile interests. From 1886 to 1888 he served as deputy clerk of the circuit court of Monongalia county. His faithfulness and ability won recognition in financial quarters, and in 1888 he was elected teller of the Bank of Monongahela Valley, Morgantown, and served in that capacity until 1892, in which year he was elected cashier of the Exchange Bank of Mannington, the position he now holds.

OSBORN

The Osborn family, which is a very ancient one, of the Presbyterian faith, may well feel proud of the record which they have achieved, both in the public annals of their country and in their private lives. One of the present representatives, who has ably added to the prestige of the family name, is William Bland Osborn, of Clarksburg, West Virginia. The family lived for many years in Fayette county, Pennsylvania.

(I) Joseph Osborn was a well-known resident of Fayette county, Pennsylvania, and was born in that section of the Keystone State.

(II) Rev. Andrew Gillespie Osborn, son of Joseph Osborn, was born in Fayette county, Pennsylvania, where his death also occurred. He was educated for the ministry and labored successfully in the interests of the Presbyterian church throughout his life. He had a number of children: Alexander H.; Joseph Freeman (see forward); Dr. William F.; Sarah Ann; Linn; Louisa; Cambell; Margaret Jane; Dr. Wilkins; Matthias; Beason; Mary Virginia. Of these, six served bravely in the cause of the Union during the civil war, while their father served as chaplain during the same struggle.

(III) Joseph Freeman, son of Rev. Andrew Gillespie Osborn, was born in Fayette county, Pennsylvania, May 28, 1829, and died at Clarksburg, West Virginia, August 18, 1885. The greater part of his life was spent in Harrison county, West Virginia, where he was engaged in the foundry and machine business, and was engaged in this business at the time of his death. He was a member of the Presbyterian church, and gave his political support to the Republican party. Mr. Osborn married Anna Frum, born in Monongalia county, September 6, 1834, now living in Clarksburg, West Virginia. Of their children, two died before attaining maturity, and the others are: Alexander C., engaged in the machinery business in Clarksburg; William Bland (see forward); Mrs. John Moroso, of New York City; Mrs. Harry P. Chambers, of Washington, Pennsylvania; Mrs. Georgia O. Johnson, of Mobile, Alabama; Mrs. Dr. Henry Coggeshall, of New York City; Richard L.; Dr. Robert Linn, of Clarksburg, West Virginia.

(IV) William Bland, son of Joseph Freeman and Anna (Frum) Osborn, was born in Weston, Lewis county, West Virginia, June 11, 1859. His preparatory education was acquired in the public schools of Clarksburg, to which city his parents had removed in 1863. Mr. Osborn has devoted his business energies in a large measure to financial matters, in which he is regarded as an authority. He is a stockholder in the Erie City Iron Works of Erie, Pennsylvania, the Empire National Bank and the Union National Bank of Clarksburg, and is owner of the W. B. Osborn Machinery Company, of Clarksburg. As an owner of a large amount of real estate in and about Clarksburg, he has been an important factor in developing these interests for the city, and his private residence, No. 309 Clark street, is one of the finest in the city. He has been staunch in his adherence to the principles of the Republican party, has served efficiently as recorder of his city, and is now (1912) a member of the board of school commissioners. His religious affiliation is with the Presbyterian church.

Mr. Osborn married, in 1886, Mollie P., born in Grafton, Taylor county, West Virginia, in 1860, daughter of W. H. and Mary Ellen (Smith) Freeman. Mr. Freeman, who died in 1903, was at the time of his death the cashier of the West Virginia Bank of Clarksburg, and his wife, who was born in Taylor county, is living at the age of seventy-seven years. Mr. and Mrs. Osborn have had children: William Freeman, a machinery salesman in New York; George Morris, a student in the engineering department of the West Virginia State University; Mary Virginia, a graduate of Clarksburg high school, living at home; Anna, died September 6, 1905; Frances Amy and Alexander Bland, attending school; Katherine Linn.

O'BRIEN Ireland has furnished this country with many illustrious families, including the one now under consideration—the O'Briens. They easily trace their lineage back twenty-five generations to that famous O'Brien family of Ireland, noted in history, and connected with the Emmets of whom Robert Emmet was the most eminent. In this country by intermarriage, they connect with the family of General Washington.

(I) Bryan O'Brien was born in Ireland, early in the eighteenth century, in county Clare, being a descendant from the O'Briens of Inchiquin in direct line. He married Mary O'Brien, a daughter of Torlough O'Brien, a descendant in a direct line from Murrough O'Brien, Earl of Thomond and Baron of Inchiquin, and they had two sons, including Daniel.

(II) Daniel, son of Bryan and Mary O'Brien, was born in the year 1764, in county Clare, Ireland, died in 1844, in Beverly, then Virginia, buried at a point near Volga, Barbour county, then Virginia. He emigrated to America in the year 1796, resided in Baltimore eight years as a merchant, traveled to Tygart's Valley, in Randolph county, by the way of the Seneca Trail, in the year 1804, and resided in Beverly, where he engaged in the mercantile business. February 16, 1815, he married Hannah, daughter of John Norris, of Lewis county, then Virginia, a descendant of the Norris and Jones families of Farquier county, Virginia. She was born in Virginia, and was a second cousin of General George Washington, connected through the Ball family. She died in Upshur county, West Virginia, in 1880. Among the children of Daniel and Hannah (Norris) O'Brien was a son, Emmet Jones, of whom forward.

(III) General Emmet Jones O'Brien, son of Daniel and Hannah (Norris) O'Brien, was born in Beverly, Randolph county, now West Virginia, died near Weston, West Virginia, in 1887. He was a stonecutter and mason by occupation. With his brother Daniel he constructed the abutments of the bridge now standing across the Tygart's Valley river at Philippi, West Virginia, about 1858, and also the abutments to the bridge across the Buckhannon river, near its mouth, in Barbour county, West Virginia. He was a member of the first constitutional convention of West Virginia from Barbour county, and state senator during 1867-68 from the sixth district. He was commissioned brigadier-general of militia by Governor Wise, of Virginia. He was a Methodist Episcopalian in religion, and a Democrat in politics. He married Martha Ann, daughter of Jonathan Hall, of Big Skin Creek, Lewis county, Virginia, and a descendant of the Reger and Hall families of Upshur county. Her mother's maiden name was Elizabeth Reger, daughter of Abram Reger Sr., who was one of eleven children of Jacob Reger, who settled on the Buckhannon river, near Burnersville, now Volga, about 1776. Joseph Hall, the immigrant, father of Jonathan Hall, settled at an early day on Pecks Run, Upshur county, and married Ann Strange, whose first husband was named Martin, her maiden name being Ann Hitt. She was a French Huguenot, originally from Virginia. The families of Hitt, Martin, Strange and Hall produced many noted Methodist preachers; also prudent business men are found among the descendants all over the central and western country. The Halls are of English-French, and the Regers of German descent. Both families came across the mountains and settled on the waters of the Buck-

hannon river, on the waters of Big Run and Pecks Run, now in Barbour and Upshur counties, in the latter part of the seventeenth century. They both remain prominent families. Emmet Jones and Martha Ann (Hall) O'Brien had four children: 1. Lieutenant Alonzo Lee, was of the United States cavalry, now deceased. 2. Captain Daniel U., was an officer in the war with Spain in 1898-99; is now a prominent farmer and grazier of Glenville, West Virginia. 3. Mary Lillian, born in 1865; married Hon. William M. Arnold, stock dealer, of Roane county, West Virginia; she is deceased. 4. William Smithe, of whom forward.

(IV) William Smithe, son of General Emmet Jones and Martha Ann (Hall) O'Brien, was born in Barbour county, West Virginia, January 8, 1862. When quite young his parents moved from Barbour county to Weston, Lewis county, West Virginia, where he matured into manhood. His early life was spent on his father's farm, in brickyards and in the public schools nearby his home. Early in the eighties he commenced teaching school in Lewis county, continuing for about ten years. While engaged in teaching, he commenced the study of law, securing his law books and gaining his instructions from the late Hon. John Brannon, of Weston, then one of the most able and distinguished lawyers and jurists of the state. He graduated in the law department of the West Virginia University in 1891, having the degree of Bachelor of Laws conferred upon him. He located at Buckhannon, West Virginia, for the practice of his profession in 1892, and has continued to the present time (1912). In 1903 he formed a law partnership with Hon. William D. Talbot, under the firm name of Talbot & O'Brien. The firm was doing a large business when it was dissolved February 21, 1907, by the death of the senior member, who died in Charleston, West Virginia, while serving as state senator from the thirteenth senatorial district of West Virginia. Since then Mr. O'Brien has been without a partner in his law business. He is identified with the industrial interests of his home city, and has been director in the People's Bank of West Virginia at Buckhannon, being one of the founders of that institution. At this time (1912) he is a candidate for district judge of the twelfth judicial circuit. Politically he votes with the Democratic party, and in religion is of the Methodist Episcopal faith. He is a Mason—a member of Franklin Lodge, No. 7; Upshur Chapter, No. 34; St. John's Commandery, No. 8; Knights of Pythias, Columbia Lodge, No. 54.

He married, October 14, 1896, Emma White, born near Camden, Lewis county, West Virginia, January 31, 1864, eldest daughter of Alexander Perry and Mary Catharine (Fetty) White. Mr. White is a prominent farmer and grazier of Lewis county; is of Scotch-Irish descent, and is of the White family of Maryland and the East Pan Handle of West Virginia. Mr. White's mother's name was Jackson, an aunt of the famous civil war commander, "Stonewall" Jackson. Mr. and Mrs. White's children were: Rebecca, deceased; Emma, wife of William S. O'Brien; Georgia, wife of A. A. Rohrbough, of Camden, West Virginia; Delphia, wife of W. S. Gibson, of Canton, Ohio; Dr. Cummings Edward White, of Buckhannon, West Virginia; Alice, deceased; Pitt Fetty, of Bellingham, Washington; Henry Middleton, of Bellingham, Washington; Evelyn, deceased. The children of Mr. and Mrs. O'Brien are: Perry Emmet, born August 2, 1898; Daniel Pitt, born August 31, 1900; Mary Martha, born November 30, 1902; and William Talbot, born August 29, 1904.

INDEX

ADDENDA AND ERRATA

The following addenda and errata were received after the narrative matter had gone through the press:

Farnsworth, page 373; wherever name Simon appears in this sketch, it should be Simons.

Jarvis, page 929; for Davidson, read Davisson.

Koblegard, page 800, 16th line; date of marriage should be August 9, 1897; birth of Jacob, October 21, 1898.

Loving, page 784, par. 3; for James Frances, read James Francis.

Rainey, page 698; William W. Rainey died July 3, 1912, at the home of Charles W. Brandon, in Philippi.

Randall, page 1224, 33d line; name Lloyd J. should read "Lloyd I."; 34th line, date of birth of Carrie L. should read March 20, 1872; 35th line, name Rosa Bell should read Rosalee Bell, born April 19, 1880; 36th line, birth of Luther H. should be March 30, 1882.

Riedy, page 1182, 12th line; instead of coal mining, read iron ore mining; 13th line, instead of coal mine, read iron ore mine. Owen G. Riedy is a member of the German Reformed church, and votes the Democratic ticket. His children are: Cora Alice, born in Heidelberg township, Lehigh county, Pennsylvania, October 24, 1869; Annie Messura, born in Heidelberg township, December 18, 1871; James Abraham, born in White Hall township, November 16, 1872; Maggie Louisa, born in White Hall township, August 5, 1880. Maiden name of mother of these children was Leanna Lobach. 34th line; name of company should be Consolidation Coal Company, instead of Consolidated Coal & Coke Company. Names of children of Dr. Riedy, all born in Monongah, West Virginia: James Noble, born December 20, 1906; Owen Lobach, August 15, 1907; Eugenia Traverse, April 5, 1911.

Van Voorhis, page 949; in last paragraph, name Daniel Davidson is correct; this is a masculine name, but in this case was given to a female.

Williams, page 858, 17th line; Mark Williams, born October 22, 1798, died March 25, 1847; Jane Tate, born August 15, 1803, died December 10, 1856. Date of death of William J. Williams should read November 21, 1901; birth date of Elizabeth J. Riley should be January 25, 1825, and date of death should be November 12, 1895, instead of November, 1896; 32d line, name Jahn should be Jehu; page 860, 11th line, date of marriage should be October 22; 11th, 12th and 15th lines, name should be Conaway, instead of Conway; 11th line, date of birth of Ollie Edna Conaway was June 10, 1869; 14th line, date of death March 17, 1910, aged seventy-six years; 18th line, date of birth of Glenn Foster, June 2, 1892, and of Alice Merle, January 27, 1897, in the third year in high school.

INDEX

*Against a name refers to note in Addenda and Errata.

Abbaticchio, A., 1026
  Raymond J., 1026
Alexander, 853, 976
  George, 853
  George, 976
  George M., 854
  John, 853
  John, 976
Alfred, Charles J., 1382
  Perry G., 1382
Allen, 465, 634, 817, 1055
  Barnes, 1055
  David, 467

David, Dea., 467
  Ezra, 467
  James, 465
  James F., 1057
  John B., 468
  John J., 818
  John, Rev., 465
  Joseph, 466
  Joseph, 817
  Joseph M., 818
  Joshua, 634
  Judson W., 468
  Nehemiah, 467

Osburn, 634
  Silas B., 634
  Stephen, 1056
Allender, 597
  George, 597
  George M., 597
  John, 597
Amos, 544
  Clay D., 546
  George, 545
  George E., 545
  George M., 546
  Henry Sr., 544

Stephen H., 545
Anderson, 592
  Benjamin F., 592
  George W., 593
  Robert R., 592
Anthony, 1141
  Conrad, 1141
  John D., 1142
  John F., 1142
Armstrong, 864
  Alexander H., 864
  John, 864
  Roscoe G., 864
  Marshall C., 864
Arnett, 520, 569, 747, 1187
  Andrew, 1187
  Amos S., Rev., 1189
  Curtis T., 748
  Eleazer, 1189
  James, 569
  James, 1187, 1188
  John, 520
  John, 1188
  John B., 1190
  Jonathan T., 520
  Lonna D., 1189
  Luther C., 570
  Solomon, 747
  Thomas, 1187
  Thomas, 1189
  Thomas C., 747
  Thomas W., 521
  Ulysses N., 520
  William C., 1188
  William E., 569
  William M., 569
Arnold, George J., 1331
  Jackson, 1332
Ashcraft, 1031
  Amos, 1031
  Ephraim, 1031
  John, 1031
  Marshall E., 1031
Atchison, Herbert W., 805
  Singleman, 805
Avis, Braxton D., 668
  Braxton D., Dr., 669
  John, 668
Bailey, 644, 675
  Benjamin F., 676
  James H. Jr., 756
  John, 675
  Robert, 644
  Silas P., 675
  William H., 644
Baker, 1083
  Andrew C., 1084
  George, 1083
  George C., 1085

John N., 1084
  Peter, 1083
Barncord, John, 612
  Norman R., 613
  Oliver P., 612
Barnes, 1106
  Abraham, 1106
  James W., 1106
  Peter T., 1106
  William, 1106
Barrickman, 1324
  Henry, 1324
  Nimrod, 1325
  Van A., 1325
Bartlett, 866
  Jedediah W., 866
  Josiah, 866
  Meigs J., 866
Batten, 1000
  Henry C., 1001
  Richard, 1000
  Thomas, 1000
Beaty, 524
  Alexander, 524
  Carlton, 527
  Harry B., 526
  James C., 524
  James F., 526
  Lawrence, 527
  Margaret A., 526
  Newton S., 525
Bender, 1306
Bennett, 1335
  Jonathan M., 1336
  Joseph, 1335
  Louis, 1340
  William, 1336
  William G., 1337
Bentley, 586
  John, 586
  Joseph, 586
  Samuel R., 587
Bevington, Lorenzo D., 1218
  Lorenzo K., 1219
Bice, 1117
  Harrison W., 1117
  Henry A., 1117
  John F., 1117
Black, 508, 573
  Belinda, 574
  James M., 573
  William, 573
  William S., 508
  William T., 574
  William W., 508
Blackshere, 504
  Ebenezer, 504
  Elias, 504
  John, 505

Zana V., 505
Bland, 835
  Edward S., 835
  Frank G., 836
  Newton B., 1358
  Robert L., 1358
  Thomas, 835
Bond, 979
  Booth, 979
  Brumfield, 979
  Xenia E., Dr., 979
Boso, Frederick M., 771
Bowcock, 1142
  John J., 1143
  J. McCue, 1144
  John O., 1143
Bowman, 555
  Frank L., 555
  James, 555
  John, 555
  Josiah A., 555
Boydston, 1078
  Eugenis, 1078
  Frank, 1079
  Walter J., 1079
Boyers, 447
  Cyrus F., 448
  Jacob, 447
  Lee B., 451
  Leonard, 447
  Morgan L., 447
  William F., 450
Brand, 549, 556, 730
  Clyde, 730
  Edmond W., 549
  Franklin M., 556
  Hosea M., 556
  James, 549
  James, 556
  James C., 557
  James E., 730
  John, 549
  John, 556
  John J., 730
  William H., 550
Brandon, 695
  Charles W., 696
  Eugene, 696
  William, 695
Britton, 1194
  Asbury S., 1196
  Horatio, 1195
  Luther S., 1196
  Wilson, 1194
Brock, 1039
  Fletcher, 1039
  Luther S., 1040
  William, 1039
Brown, 384, 626

Charles M., 629
James, 384
Jefferson S., 630
John, 384
John B., 628
John J., 385
Robert, 385
Robert M., 627
Thomas, 626-7
Thomas F., 628
William, 626
Brownfield, 463
Archie F., 465
James, 463
James H., Dr., 464
John, Judge, 463
John M., 465
Thomas, 463
Buchanan, 974
Aaron M., Rev., 975
James, 974
John, 974
Joseph K., 975
Buchanan, A. M., Rev., 975
Bumgardner, David, 757
James A., 757
Burdett, 676
Abraham W., 680
Frederick, 677-8
Frederick J., 680
James W., 678
Burnside, 1220
John, 1220
John S., 1220
Robert, 1220
William C., 1220
Burton, 1230
Joseph, 1230
Perry D., 1230
William, 1230.
Butcher, 1121
Bernard L., 1125
Eli, 1123
Eli B., 1124
Samuel, 1121-22
Callahan, 905
Isaac, 905
James M., 905
Martin I., 905
Campbell, James, 1301
Carder, John W., 599
Carpenter, John W., 760
Carper, 377
Abraham, 377
Adam, 379
Paul, 377
Carr, 518
Hugh H., 518
Hugh H., Dr., 519

Larned P., 519
Lloyd L., Dr., 519
Richard, 518
Carter, 709, 824
David, 824
David J., 824
Jackson V. B., 710
Robert, 710
Robert, 824
Robert M., 824
Thomas, 824
William, 709
William H., 710
Casey, Martin R., 942
Thomas, 942
Casselberry, 772
John, 772
Melville L., 772
William, 772
Church, 719
Clyde P., 720
George, 719
Henry, 719
William, 719
Clark, 500, 756
Harry B., 502
Hezekiah, 756
Jason, 757
John A., 500
John A. Jr., 502
Joseph, 756
Kenna, 502
Clayton, 1367
Elisha, 1368
John W., 1368
Thomas M., 1368
Ulysses A., 1369
Clifford, 661
James, 661
John H., 662
Philip, 661
Coffman, 590, 768
Abraham, 768
David, 768
George W., 590
Henry, 591
Ira W., 590
James M., 768
John G., 591
Luther H., 591
Samuel, 768
Truman J., 590
Cole, 671, 1277
Amasa, 1278
Benjamin F., 1278
Henson, 1278
John, 671
Will H., 672
William L. 671

Conaway, 733, 946
Alfred, 733
Andrew, 946
Benjamin F., 733
John, 946
Joshua B., 947
Thomas, 946
Walter B., 947
Conley, 456
Joseph, 456
Joseph X., 456
Rollo J., 457
Conrad, 778
George, 778
James F., 778
John H., 779
Joseph, 778
Cordray, 1019
Isaac, 1019
Thomas, 1019
William E., 1019
Corley, 781
James M., 782
Minoah, 781
William, 781
Costello, 1381
Daniel P., 1381
John, 1381
Cox, 550, 1226
Abraham, 550
Abraham, 1227
Boaz B., 1227
Frank, Judge, 551
Henry L., 551
James A., 1228
Moses, 550
Crile, 1033
Christian, 1033
Conrad, 1033
Daniel, 1033
Lafayette C., 1034
Cunningham, 758
Alexander M. T., 758
John, 758
Cure, Mortimer D., 782
Currey, 1120
Clarence, 1121
Fenton L., 1120
James, 1120
Danser, George S., 1030
William C., 1030
Davidson, 1167
Henry A., 1168
Jeremiah, 1167
Jeremiah 1168
Davis, 631, 685, 723, 761, 810,
825, 862, 1047
Caleb, 724
Caleb, 1047

Claude M., 688
Cornelius C., 827
Dorsey B., 688
Earl W., 810
Edgar S., 810
Edward, Dr., 868
Francis M., 687
Granville H., 685
Hannibal H., 685
Herman B., 862
Jacob, 762
James, 631
James B., Rev., 684
James H., 868
James N., 632
Jesse, 810
John, 724
John, 825
John, 1047
John J., 725
John J., 1048
John, Rev., 631
John W., 725
Lodawick H., 862
Marion H., 819
M. Wardner, 762
Resin, 687
Rezin, 868
Samuel B., 686, 687
Samuel D., 762
Warren M., 826
William, 825
William, 862
William B., 819
William F., 862
William M., 825, 826
Dayton, 363
  Alston G., 368
  Henry, 364
  Isaac, 363
  Justus, 364
  Michael, 364
  Samuel, 363
  Spencer, 365
Dean, Elisha, 1352
  Isabelle F., 1353
  Samuel, 1351
  Samuel A., 1352
DeBolt, George W., 488
  John H., 488
DeForest, 1271
  Abraham, 1273
  Isaac, 1272, 1273
  Isaac, 1274
  Jean, 1271
  Jesse, 1271
  Johannes, 1273
  Theodore R., 1274
  William C., 1274

Demain, 622
  Edward, 622
  Francis, 623
  Frank A., 623
  Robert, 622
  Robert H., 624
  Robert L., 622
Dent, 1309
  John, 1309
  Marmaduke, 1310
  Thomas, 1309
  William M., 1311
Despard, 748
  Burton, 749
  Burton M., 749
  Richard 748
Devison, John, 1225
  John W., 1225
Dille, 1313
  Clarence B., 1315
  Ezra, 1313
  John A., 1313
  Oliver H., 1314
  Thomas R., 1315
Doheny, John, 845
  William T., 845
Dorsey, George W., 873
Douthat, 625
  David G., 625
  Robert W., 625
Douthitt, 1148
  Carl C., 1149
  Thomas J., 1149
  William, 1148
Downs, 968
  Ashbel F., 969
  David, 968
  Harry R., 971
  Jeremiah, 968
  Jonathan, 968
Dudley, 534
  Albert L. B., 538
  Asa, 537
  Benjamin F., 538
  Enoch, 537
  Fleming, 537
  Guilford, 534
  Samuel, 535
  Sarah A., 537
  William, 534
  William, 535
Duff, 713
  Alexander, 713
  John, 713
  William, 713
Duncan, 689
  Edwin S., 689
  George L., 689
  James, 689

James J., 689
Dunnington, Noah, 787
  William L., 788
Durbin, 1006
  Charles R., 1008
  Francis M., 1006
  William, 1006
Durrett, 490
  B. B., 490
  James J., Dr., 491
  John H., 491
Dye, George W., 860
  James F., 861
  Walter, 860
Eddy, 1159
  Andrew L., 1160
  Goian, 1159
  Henry D., 1160
  Joshua, 1160
Edmondson, 636
  Richard C., 636
  Richard H., Dr., 637
  Samuel, 636
Elder, George W., 589
  John A., Dr., 589
Elliott, 1035
  Abraham, 1035
  A. Judson, 1037
  John, 1035
  Lucy A., 1038
  William, 1036
Ernst, Charles M., 682
  Marcus J., 682
Evans, 484, 1316
  Charles W., 485
  Hugh, 484
  Isaac, 484
  John, Col., 1316
  Samuel, 484
Faris, 1186
  George T., 1186
  Humphrey, 1186
  James, 1186
  Samuel S., 1186
*Farnsworth, 373
  Daniel, 373
  Nathaniel, 374
  Thomas, 373, 374
  Thomas G., 375
  Thomas J., 376
Ferguson, George A., 1239
  Oliver, 1239
Ferry, James W., 776
Fife, 1082
  Cyrus K., 1082
  Kinsey R., 1082
  Samuel, 1082
Findley, 1144, 1360
  Adam F., 1360

Ai J., 1361
Jackson, 1144
John, 1143
William, 1145
William, 1360
Finly, 867
  George, 867
  George C., 867
  John A., 867
Finnell, Charles W., 558, 559
  Harry W., 560
Fisher, 521, 651, 907
  Dorothy F., 524
  Frank C., 524
  Fred G., 524
  Fred G., 907
  Jacob, 522
  John, Capt., 521
  Lillian, 907
  Parks, 651
  Robert E., 524
  Robert W., 652
  Willard N., 524
  William, 651
  William H., 524
Fisk, 1302
  Charles B., 1304
  John, Dr., 1303
  Simon, 1302
Fitch, 871
  Arthur, 871
  Dorsey P., 871
  Enoch P., 871
Flanagan, James H., Rev., 681
  Patrick, 681
Fleming, 401
  Alfred, 411
  Allison, 414
  Arch, 423
  Archibald, 411
  Aretas B., Gov., 401
  Benjamin, 412
  Benjamin A., 417
  Benamin D., 416
  Benjamin F., 412
  Benoni, 410
  Boaz, 410
  Brooks, 406
  Donald H., Dr., 424
  Franklin J., 413
  Harrison, 415
  James R., 415
  John, 406
  John A., 420
  John C., 418
  John S., 411
  John W., 423
  Joseph M., 416
  Joseph P., 425
  Matthew, 411
  Nathan, 410
  Oliver J., 420
  Rufus E., 426
  Solomon S., 413
  Thomas, 410
  Thomas, 411
  Thomas W., 421
  Thurston W., 419
  William, 409
  William, 410
  William H., 419
  William M., 424
Fletcher, 981
  Alexander J., 981
  Charles, 981
Ford, 882, 1091
  Eugenius, Rev., 1071
  Gene W., 1072
  George, 882
  Henry, 1071
  Lanty, 882
  Skelton, 1071
  William, 882
Francis, Michael J., 1259
  Thomas, 1258
Francois, Claude, 1199
  Jerome M., 1200
Furbee, 1241
  Benjamin, 1241
  Bowers, 1241
  Caleb, 1241
  George, 1242
  Howard R., 1245
  James, 1242
  James H., 1242
  James S., 1243
Gandy, 1087
  Amos, 1087
  Edward, 1087
  John P., 1088
  Otho P., 1087
Garlow, 1275
  Aaron J., 1276
  Andrew, 1275
  Christopher, 1275
  John, 1275
Garrett, 1108
  Hugh, 1108
  James M., 1109
  John, 1108
  Robert A., 1110
Gaskin, Andrew J., 1115
  Willie, 1116
Gaston, 869
  George, 870
  William, 869
  William, Dr., 870
Glancy, Michael, 823
  Patrick, 823
  Patrick J., 823
Glasscock, 1044
  Charles, 1045
  Daniel, 1045
  Hezekiah, 1045
  John, 1045
  Samuel F., 1046
Goff, 961
  Job, 962
  Nathan, 962
  Nathan, 963
  Waldo P., 962
  Waldo P., M. D., 966
Goodwin, 983, 1267
  Charles A., 984
  Elmer F., 1268
  Eppa D., 1267
  John, 983
  John, 1267
  Joseph, 983
  Samuel, 984
Gordon, 712, 891
  Frank, 891
  George H., 712
  John, 711
  John, 891
  Robert T., 891
  Samuel W., 711
Gore, 1269
  Claude W., 1270
  Solomon D., 1269
  Truman, 1269
  Truman E., 1270
Grant, 634, 1137
  Chapman, 1138
  Dale, 636
  Edward M., 635
  Joseph, 796
  William, 634
  William L., 1139
Greene, 1322
  William, 1322
  William H., 1323
  William H., Dr., 1323
Gregg, 554, 787
  John, 554
  John M., 554
  Thomas, 787
  Thomas M., 554
  W. R., 787
Griffin, 936
  James A., 937
  James S., 937
  Samuel, 936
  Sheridan R., 938
Green, 616
  Ethiel S., 617
  Henry S., 617

Jared, 616
Seymour B., 616
Hale, 855
　Abraham, 855
　Curtis P., 857
　Presley M., 855
　Roy R., 857
　Thomas, 855
Hall, 457, 1098, 1334, 1365
　Allen, 1098
　Asa, 458, 1098
　David, 457
　Edward T. W., 1334
　Hal, 1098
　James M., 1365
　Jesse, 457
　Jesse C., 1098
　John, 458
　Moses, 457
　Richard, 1365
　Samuel G., 1366
　Sylvanus W., 459
　Thomas, 457
　Thomas, 1098
　Thompson, 1334
　Warfield, 1307
　W. Dexter, 1334
　Willey H., 460
　William, 1308
　William H., 1308
Halterman, Charles W., 770
　William, 769
Hanes, 1152
　Abram, 1152
　Alva M., 1153
　David, 1152
　David O., 1154
Hardesty, 1237
　Guy A., 1238
　James, 1237
　James H., 1237
　Joseph M., 1238
　Robert R., 1238
Hardy, 1050
　Irvin, 1051
　Isaac, 1050
　James M., 1050
　William, 1050
Harmer, 698
　Benjamin T., 699
　Harvey W., 699
　Jacob, 698
　Jacob, 699
Harr, Merrick R., 473
　Rufus E., 473
Harrison, 1116
　Samuel R., 1024
　Charles R., 1116
　Thomas W., 1024

William R., 1116.
Hart, 1059
　Charles M., 1063
　Daniel, 1061
　Edward, 1059
　Elmore, 1061
　Ira, 1062
　John, 1059
　John B., 1064
Hartley, 736, 1154
　Edward, 736
　Edwin, 1155
　Guy B., 737
　Joseph, 1154
　Joseph M., 1155
　Peter M., 736
　Peter M., 1155
　Samuel W., 737
Hatfield, 652
　Abraham, 653
　David, 653
　George W., 653
　Hiram, 654
　John L., 654
　Matthias, 652
　William, 652
Haught, 1114
　Evan, 1114
　Francisco T., 1114
　Wilson, 1114
Hawkins, Abraham, 581
　Lawrence E., 581
Hayden, 531
　Benjamin, 533
　Jacob S., 533
　John, 531
　John, 532
　Nehemiah, 532
　Samuel, 532
　William, 531
　William, 532
Hayes, 901
　Albert E., 902
　Alexander, 901
　Henry S., 902
　Manliff, 901
Haymond, 527, 803, 1093, 1118, 1254
　Alpheus F., 529
　Daniel F., 804
　Daniel S., 1118
　Hall H., 804
　Henry, 1257
　John, 527
　John, 1118
　John, 1254
　Lee, 1094
　Luther, 1093
　Luther, 1257

Luther Dr., 1094
Maria F., 531
Odbert J., 1118
Thomas, 1118
Thomas, 1257
Thomas S., 528
Thomas S., 531
William, 528
William, 1118
William, 1254
William, Maj., 528
William S., 531
Haynes, 828
　Isaac, 828
　James M., 829
　James, Rev., 830
　Robert A., 830
　William, 828
Heavener, 908
　Clark W., 910
　Elias, 909
　Jacob, 908
　Jacob W., 909
　Nicholas, 908, 909
Hefner, Henry S., 792
Heinze, George P., 669
　Henry, 669
　Henry A., 670
Hennen, 495, 719, 1212
　Earl M., 496
　Enoch, 495
　Enoch, 496
　Enoch, 1213
　Frederick A., 719
　Matthew, 495
　Matthew, 719
　Matthew, 1212
　Ray V., 1213
　Robert P., 719
　William, 495
　William, 496
　William, 1213
　William H., 495
　William H., 496
　William H., 1213
Henry, Charles O., Dr., 56.
　Lawrence, 564
Hess, 1089
　Abraham, 1090
　Abraham T., 1091
　Balsar, 1090
　W. Melvin, 1091
Higginbotham, 773
　Coleman C., 775
　John, 773
　John, 774
　John C., 775
　William T., 774
Higinbotham, Charles H., 5

Highland, Jacob, 618
  John E., 618
  Virgil L., 618
Hiner, 1013
  Charles E., 1014
  Joseph, 1013
  Samuel, 1013
Hite, George W., 733
  Ralph M., 733
  Thomas R., 733
Hodges, 435
  Charles E., 437
  John H., 436
  John R., 435
  Thomas E., 436
Hoffman, John, 702
  Robert J., 702
  Stingley F., 702
Hogg, Charles E., 931
  Peter, 931
Holden, Minter J., 808
  Wilson B., 808
Holland, Capell, 643
  James W., 644
  Rezin, 643
Holt, 923
  Alfred T., 924
  James W., 923
  James W., 924
  John H., 925
  John W., 923
Hood, 1104
  Charles P., 1105
  John, 1104
  William, 1104
Hornor, 1264
  Charles S., 1265
  Ferdinand Y., 1265
  James Y., 1264
  Paul S., 1265
Hough, 657
  James A., 658
  Joseph, 658
  Mary J., 659
  Thomas, 657
Howard, 471, 502
  Alfred C., Dr., 506
  Charles H., 502
  Edward W., Dr., 502
  George L., 502
  John, 471, 472
  John C., 507
  J. M., 502
  Leroy D., Dr., 507
  Lindsay G., 507
  Orville M., 506
  Paul, 502
  Thomas L., 502
  William G., 502

Huey, 940
  George W., 940
  Jacob B., 940
  John O., 940
Hughes, 784
  Allin C., 785
  Houston J., 784
  Stephen J., 784
Hursey, 792
  John A., 792
  Lloyd R., 792
  Walter S., 792
Huston, 1200
  Chambers, 1201
  Charles R., 1201
  Peter, 1200
  Samuel P., 1201
Hutton, Jonathan, 1127
  Moses, 1127
Ice, 1020
  Adam, 1021
  C. Herschel, 1023
  Fredericke, 1020
  Henry W., 1022
  Rawley, 1022
Irvin, John H., 484
  John W., 483
Jackson, 753
  Edward, 753
  James W., 754
  John G., 754
  Stephen, 753
  Stephen G., 755
  Stephen P., 753
Jacobs, 683
  Daniel B., 683
  Daniel W., 683
  John, 683
  William, 683
Jarrett, 1009
  Absalom M., 1010
  John, 1010
  William N., 1010
Jarvis, 928, 1158
  Cecil C., 930
  Granville E., 1158
  *Hugh, 929
  John, 928
  Joseph, 928
  Josiah W. P., 1158
  *Lemuel D., 929
  Solomon, 928
  Solomon, 1158
Jenkins, 739
  David, 739
  Ezekiel C., 739
  Frederick L., 739
  John C., 739
Jolliffe, 390

Amos, 393
  Charles E., 395
  James, 392
  John, 391
  Joseph, 391
  Oliver P., 394
  William, 392, 393
Johnson, Henry R., Dr., 538
  J. H., 538
Johnston, Job W., 572
  John, 572
Jones, 560, 874, 904
  Clement R., 880
  Daniel J., 904
  Harry H., 879
  Jacob, 874, 875
  James C., 560
  James R., 560
  John P., 904
  Samuel, 878
  Thomas A., 560
  Uriah, 879
  William, 878
Kellar, James C., 649
  James U., 649
  John, 649
Kelley, Aaron, 893
  Franklin P., 894
  Pierce, 894
Keener, 1191
  George, 1191
  George I., 1191
  Joseph L., 1191
Kessler, Calvin M., 585
  Peter, 584
Kincaid, John C., 791
  John W., 790
  Joseph, 790
King, 796, 1253
  Charles, 1253
  John H., 796
  Mount Joy, 1253
  Ossie D., 1253
  Wessie P., 796
*Köblegard, Bert A., 799
  Jacob, 799
Krebs, 989
  John, 990
  Louis T., Col., 991
  Simon, 989, 990
Lane, John, 751, 752
  Peter, 752
Langfit, Frank V., 809
  Valentine, 808
  William, 808
Latham, George R., 704
  John, 703
  Robert, 703
Law, 1032

Francis E., 1032
John, 1033
Thomas, 1032
Layton, Abraham, 1100
  Albert, 1101
  Peter A., 1100
Lazear, John W., 728
  Joseph, 728
  Joseph S., 728
Lazier, 619
  Albert E., 619
  Elza C., 619
  Henry, 619
  John, 619
Lazzelle, 1079
  Isaac G., 1080
  James, 1080
  Thomas, 1079
  Thomas, 1080
Leahy, William J., 977
Lee, 919
Leonard, William, 763
  William E., 763
Leps, Clay W., 507
  George E., 507
Lewis, 437, 1015, 1178
  Arthur E., 1015
  Arthur P., 1015
  Burton, 1015
  David, 437
  Elmore D., 438
  Ernest D., 438
  Evan, 1178
  James S., 1179
  Jonathan, 438
  Jonathan, 1178-79
  Mordecai, 1178
  Mordecai, 1179
  William, H., 1015
  William H., 1179
Lightburn, Harry W., 795
  J. A. J., Gen., 794
Lilley, George M., 539
Lockwood, Ephraim, 607
  George E., 608
  Lyman G., 607
Lodge, 1229
  Aaron, 1229
  Aaron J., 1229
  Robert, 1229
Long, 1053
  Jacob Z., 1054
  Martin, 1053
  William M., 1054
Lorentz, 973
  Adams W., 973
  Jacob, 973
  John, 973
Lough, 632

Isaac N., 632
Matthew W., 632
Robert, 632
Roy A., 633
Loving, 783
  James F., 784
  Richard S., 783
  Richard S., 784
  William, 783
Lowe, John, 588
  John, 1384
  John B., 1383
  Orville L., 588
Loyd, 1180
  George, 1180
  William C., 1181
  William F., 1180
Lucas, 580, 1266
  Basil H., 1266
  Charles F., 580
  George R., 580
  James E., 580
  R. G., 1266
Lyon, Ellis, 833
  James M., 832
  William E., 832
McCarty, Mary M., 381
  Norval B., 380
  Thomas G., 379
McCleary, William, Col., 382
McClelland, 714
  Elizabeth E., 717
  Henry T., 715, 716
  James H., 715
  Mary B., 716
  William, 716
McCray, 1164
  Andrew, 1165
  Francis M., 1165
  John, 1165
McDaniel, 492
  Aaron, 492
  A. J., 492
  Charles A., 492
  Elmer E., 492
  Francis, 492
  Henry C., 492
  Presley, 492
  W. A., 492
McDonald, J. W., M. D., 517
  William, 517
McGraw, John T., 1350
  Thomas, 1350
McGregor, James C., 802
  John, 802
  William, 802
McGrew, 717
  James, 717
  James C., 717
  James H., 718

Patrick, 717
William C., 718
McGuire, John, 694
  John P., Dr., 695
McIntire, 846, 1217
  Charles, 1217-18
  Enoch, 846
  Enoch, 1217
  Isaac, 846, 847
  James, 1217
  Lewis H., 846
McKinley, 1211
  Alexander S., 1211
  George C., 1212
  Thomas, 1211
McKone, John J., 1333
  John J. Jr., 1333
McLane, 1172
  Charles, 1172
  Charles H., 1173
  Joseph A., 1172
McNeely, Dr. Jacob O., 503
  John, 503
  Robert, 503
McNeill, 1101
  Chauncey S., 1104
  Ed W., 1102
  Daniel, 1102
  Daniel R., 1102
  Karl, 1104
  Llewellyn B., 1103
McReynolds, John D., 980
  Richard P., 980
McVicker, 620
  Duncan, 620
  George W., 621
  James, 620
  James M., 620
  John C., 621
Madeira, 645
  Bernard H., 648
  Christopher, 646
  Christian, 647
  Ester, 646
  Francis, 647
  George, 646
  George, 649
  Jacob M., 646
  John D., 645
  John W., 647
  Sebastian, 646
  Walter, 647
Maloy, Jesse S., 577
  Patrick, 577
Malloy, 1359
  James M., 1360
  Patrick, 1359
  Richard V., 1359
Manown, James, 726

James H., 727
Martin, 884, 1041, 1263
  Arthur G., 1177
  Benjamin F., 885
  Charles, 1174
  Elias, 1092
  Frederick T., 1177
  Harry D., 1264
  Henry, 1092
  Isaac, 1263
  James, 885
  Jesse B., 1176
  Jesse S., 886
  John, 1041
  John V., 1176
  Joseph, 1041
  Joseph A., 1041
  Philip, 1041
  Presley N., 1263
  Robert L., 1093
  Samuel, 884
  Spencer, 1175
  Spencer, 1263
  William, 884
Mason, 1295
  George, 1295-96
  George, Col., 1295
  James M., 1296
  Selma M., 1297
Mathers, 604
  Eugene L., 604
  Joseph R., 604
  Max, 604, 605
Maxwell, 844, 943, 985
  Abner, 944
  Cyrus H., 987
  Edwin, 844
  Franklin, 944
  Haymond, 844
  Lee, 946
  Levi, 986
  Porter, 945
  Rufus, 986
  Thomas, 944
  Thomas, 986
  William B., 945
Meredith, 451, 461
  Absalom P., 461
  Aubrey W., 456
  Davis, 461
  Francis M., 453
  James A., 462
  Thomas, 451
  William, 452, 453
  Winfield S., 454
Miller, 886, 1279
  Abner, 1279
  Charles E., 1280
  Ebenezer, 887

Edmond T., 1280
James, 887
Noah, 887
Thomas C., 889
William, 886
William E., 888
Mills, 1001
  David, 1001
  Joseph H., 1002
  Robert, 1001
Mitchell, John S., 789
Moreland, 812
  Alexander, 812
  John, 814
  Joseph, 815
  William, 813
Morfit, 1297
  Charles C., 1300
  Charles M., 1299
  Henry M., 1298
  Henry P., 1297
Moore, 621, 663
  Alexander C., 663
  Andrew, 1193
  George H., 664
  Michael, 659
  Noah A., 661
  Perry W., 660
  Richard W., 663
  Robert, 621
  Samuel, 621
  Samuel P., 663
  Solomon, 659
  William H., 622
Morgan, 513, 596, 949, 1008, 1069
  Aaron, 956
  Achilles, 956
  Albert M., 958
  Charles S., 958
  C. Ray, 596
  David, 514
  David, 950
  David, 1069
  David C., 952
  David, Capt., 951
  David L., 1008
  David P., 1070
  David, Rev., 1008
  Ephraim F., 956
  Francis, 514
  Francis A., 596
  George P., 959
  Haze, 953
  Henry B., 958
  Henry S., 957
  Jacob, 1069
  Jacob B., 1008
  James, 951
  James E., 955

John, 954
John O., 515
John P., 514
Marcus, 955
Morgan, Capt., 951
Morgan, Col., 513, 605
Morgan, Rev., 950
Nimrod, 1009
Oliver P., 954
Stephen, 956
William A., 1009
William S., 958
Zacquil, 606
Zackwell, 514
Zackwell G., 515
Morris, 1192
  Andrew J., 1192
  Ezekiel, 1192
  Oliver E., 1192
Morrison, 700, 1169
  Andrew J., 700
  Arphad P., 701
  David, 1169
  Edward, 1169
  Isham A., 1169
  James, 700
  Otto L., 700
  Wilbur C., 1169
Mount, 839
  Benjamin, 840
  Ezekiel, 839
  George, 839
  John H., 839
  Margaret J., 840
  Matthias, 839
Mumford, 847
  Charles E., 848
  Esau M., 848
  Thomas, 848
Musgrave, 546
  Arthur W., 547
  Clarence L., 547
  Eli, 547
  Elijah, 546
  Job, 546
  Zebulon, 546
Neely, 1073
  Guinn, 1074
  John, 1073
  Matthew, 1074
  Rufus, 1074
  William R., 1074
Neptune, 1029
Newcomb, 895
  Andrew, 896
  Ethan, 897
  Joseph, 897
  Joseph, Capt., 897
Newlon, 608

Charles W., 610
Creed O., 611
James, 609
John S., 608
Nathaniel, 608
William, 609
Nichols, 475
　Francis E., 477
　Henry, 475
　James W., 476
　Thomas, 475
Nutter, Matthew, 806
　Matthew H., 806
　Thomas L., 807
O'Brien, 397
　Bryan, 397
　Daniel, 397
　Emmet J., 398
　William S., 399
Offner, Isaac H., 481
　John E., 482
　Reuben, 481
Ogden, 600, 614, 672, 1249
　Chester R., 673
　Daniel M., 601
　Howard N., 1252
　Jonathan, 1249
　Marshall W., 1251
　Nathan, 600
　Nathan, 1250
　Presley B., 614
　Robert S., 673
　Thomas, 1249
　Van B., 1250
　William, 1251
　William R., 673
Orr, 516, 993
　Charles, 517
　George, 998
　Hiram, 997
　James, 998
　John, 993
　John, 996
　John, 515
　John D., 993
　Lawrence H., 517
　Morgan D., 516
　U. N., 997
　Uriah N., 999
Osborn, 395
　Andrew G., 396
　Joseph, 396
　Joseph F., 396
　William B., 396
Parkes, James J., 570, 571
　Thomas J., 570
Parrish, 1016
　Roy E., 1019
　Richard, 1016

Silas N., 1016
Thomas J., 1016
Parsons, Marshall J., 1321
　Jonathan, 1321
　William L., 1322
Patterson, Robert, 1206
　Robert H., 1206
　Robert W., 1206
Paul, John E., 472
　Nicholas, 472
Payne, 720
　Genius, 721
　Thomas, 720
　Thomas T., 721
　Turner, 720
Peck, Chesley R., 842
　Josiah, 842
Pepper, 982
　Earl, 983
　Johnson, 982
　Samuel D., 982
　William, 982
Perine, Doctor L., 811
　Isaac, 811
　Richard, 811
Phillips, 497, 910
　Burton, 915
　Charles, 497
　Charles R., 498
　David, 914
　Ernest, 916
　Horace A., 915
　James, 497
　James I., 499
　John, Capt., 912
　Nicholas, 912
　Philip, 913
　Richard, 915
　Sylvester B., 916
　Thomas, 913
Pierpont, 919
Pickenpaugh, 603
　James C., 604
　Nicholas, 603
　Thorton, 603
Pigott, 1119
　Elam F., 1119
　Ernest L., 1120
　Jesse, 1119
Post, George, 766
　Howard, B. F., 766
　Jacob, 766
Potter, 561, 892
　Clyte, 892
　David, 893
　Eric, 561
　Henry, 561
　John, 893
　John L., 561

Luvenia M., 893
Powell, 656
　Frank M., 657
　Joseph, 656
　Samuel R., 656
Pratt, Samuel A., 1203
　William S., 1202
Price, 583, 642, 1096, 1276
　George R. C., 1276
　John E., 642
　John E., Dr., 584
　Michael, 642
　Owen, 1096
　Richard C., 1276
　Sanderson, 584
　Thomas G., 1097
　William, 642
Proudfit, 1194
　George, 1150
　Hezekiah, 1150
　Montgomery B., 1150
Purinton, 1052
　Daniel B., 1052
　David, Rev., 1052
　Jesse M., Rev., 1052
　John A., 1053
　Thomas, Rev., 1052
Race, 615
　Agnes K., 616
　James L., 615
　James S., 616
　Joseph N., 616
　Less G., 615
Rainey, William R., 697
　*William W., 698
Randall, 1223
　*George F., 1224
　Martin M., 1224
　Norman M., 1223
Randolph, 926
　Charles A. F., 927
　Fenton F., 926
　Jonathan F., 926
　Peter F., 926
Reay, 1170
　David C., 1171
　George M., 1171
　John O., 1170
　Thomas P., 1171
Reed, 493, 667, 1173
　Benjamin F., 493
　Charles E., 493
　David, 667
　David K., 667
　Frederick R., 1173
　James M., 1231
　John R., 493
　Robert, 493
　Roy F., 1174

Thomas A., 667
Thomas F., 493
William T., 493
Reeder, Emory E. E., 1205
  Jacob, 1204
Rice, 1151
  Abram, 1151
  Curtis R., 1151
  Jacob, 1151
Riedy, 1182
  Abraham, 1182
  *James A., Dr., 1182
  *Owen G., 1182
Rightmire, 959
  Adolphus, 959
  Alpheus, 959
  Byron W., 960
  James, 959
Roane, 1347
  James, 1347
  John C., 1349
  Timothy F., 1347
Robinson, 575, 967
  Christopher, 575
  James W., 967
  John, 575
  John C., 576
  John T., 576
  Joseph B., 967
  Joseph H., 967
  Joseph L., 576
  Paul M., 576
  William, 967
Rodeheaver, 1196
  John, 1197
  John, Col., 1197
  John F., 1198
Rogers, 541, 638, 1042
  George, 640
  George E., 1043
  Harold F., 542
  John, 541
  Thomas, 638, 639
  Thomas, 1042
  Timothy R., 541
  William, 639
  William, 1042
Rohrbough, 745
  Commodore P., 746
  Jacob, 746
  Orr L., 746
Rosier, John W., 568
  Joseph, 568
Ross, 972, 1065
  Edward, 972
  Francis, 1065
  George H., 972
  James P., 1067
  John, 1066

  John F., 1067
Ruhl, 690
  Henry, 692
  Johannes, 691
  John, 692
  John L., 693
Rumbaugh, John, 585
  Roy D., 586
  Simeon, 585
Satterfield, 917
  Eli, 917
  George M., 917
  Lee N., 918
Schwaner, Ernst, 508
Schwenck, 737
  Lawrence S., 738
Scott, 1112, 1355
  Amos C., 1112
  Archibald, 1355
  Buckner F., 1357
  John A., 1356
  Stanhope M., 1356
  William N., 1356
  William W., 1112
  Winfield S., 1112
Shaver, 1222
  James O., 1223
  William, 1222
  Winfield S., 1222
Shaw, 741
  Alexander, 742
  Benjamin, 741
  Leroy, 742
  Samuel, 741
Shields, 1145
  Andrew J., 1146
  James, 1145
  Patrick H., 1146
Shinn, 602, 1207
  Abel W., 602
  Absalom, 1208
  Clement, 1207-08
  Fred L., 602
  George H., 1208
  James, 1207
  James E., 1208
  John, 1207
  Joseph M., 602
  Moses, 1208
Short, 582
  Charles A., 582
  John, 582
  Samuel, 582
Short, 582
  Charles A., 582
  John, 582
  Samuel, 582
Showalter, Ulysses W., 1068
  William U., 1068

Shriver, Cannon, 1240
  John, 1240
Shuman, 960
  Albert, 961
  John, 960
  John, 960
  Jonathan, 960
  Philip, 961
Simmons, 1328
  Alexander C., 1328
  David, 1328
  Israel, 1328
Simpson, 1095
  David B., 1095
  Julius C., 1095
  Waitman T., 1095
Sivey, 837
  Milton A., 837
  William, 837
  William M., 838
Skidmore, 779
  Andrew, 780
  James, 780
  Joseph, 780
Slater, 1330
  Charles N., 1330
  Samuel, 1329
  Samuel N., 1330
Sloan, Elias, 1183
  Herbert E., 1183
Smalley, 1184
  James D., 1184
  Jonas, 1184
  Samson W., 1185
Smith, 542, 594, 624, 640, 1128
  Alfred, 624
  Alfred K., 624
  Carl H., 641
  Charles, 1136
  Charles L., 499
  Edward G., 1140
  Harvey F., 1128
  Henry, 640
  Henry F., 499
  Henry N., 640
  Hugh F., 543
  John H., 624
  John L. R., 594
  John S., Capt., 542
  Joseph, 1233
  Thomas, 1132
  Thomas M., 1137
  Timothy S., 542
  Timothy S., 542
  Walters, 1134
  William, 594
  William R., 595
Smoot, 469
  Charles H., 470

James R., 470
John, 469
Joshua, 469
Snider, 511, 1262
  David N., 511
  David R., 511
  Edwin, 1263
  James F., 1262
  Stephen, 1262
Snyder, 777, 1099, 1379
  Ashville S., 1380
  Elias T., 1099
  Enoch E., 1099
  George, 777
  George S., 777
  Harry E., 1099
  Robert S., 777
  Samuel B., 1380
  Samuel J., 1380
Sommers, 1363
  Camden, 1363
  Jacob, 1363
  Samuel M., 1363
Southern, George C., 579
  John, 578
  John C., 579
  Samuel, 578
Sperry, Clarence B., 1377
  Ezra C., 1377
Spindler, Andrew, 1225
  Charles, 1225
Steel, 821, 822
  James, 821
  Lloyd, 822
  Samuel R., 821
Steele, 722
  Louis H., 722
  Wesley L., 723
  William H., 723
Stewart, 552, 1233, 1345
  David B., 1235
  Edgar B., 553
  Ezrael, 1346
  Francis R., 1346
  James, 1345
  John, 1234
  John S., 552
  John T., 553
  Terence D., 1236
  William, 1234
Stockert, 705
  Gustavus F., 706
  Julius F., 705
Stockton, 731
  Claude E., 731
  Fred E., 731
Stoetzer, 389
  Herman G., 389
  Martin, 389

Stout, 1245
  Benjamin, 1245
  Lemuel E., 1246
  W. Frank, 1246
Strosnider, 836
  Homer, 837
  Jackson, 836
  Rezin, 836
Strother, 1354
  John B., 1355
  John J., 1354
  Samuel E., 1354
  William, 1354
Stuart, 883
  Franklin C., 883
  John W., 883
  William, 883
Sturgiss, 1283
  Alfred G., 1283
  George C., 1283
Supler, 831
  James B., 831
  John, 831
  William, 831
Sutherland, 991
  Alexander, 992
  Charles F., 992
  William, 991
Sutton, 1161, 1375
  David, 1162
  Eugene K., 1163
  Felix, 1375
  Felix O., 1376
  Isaac, 1162
  James E., 1163
  John, 1162
  John D., 1376
  Reuben, 1162
  Richard R., 1163
  William, 1161
Swager, 939
  George, 939
  James T., 939
Swartz, 988
  Jacob G., 988
  Jacob M., 988
  Samuel, 988
Swiger, 509, 562
  Charles O., 510
  Christopher, 562
  Edmond, 509
  Henry, 562
  Jacob, 563
  John, 509
  John, 509
  John, 562
  John B., 562
  Muta U., 563
  Thomas L., 563

Swisher, 706
  David W., 707
  Howard L., 708
  John, 707
Tate, 740
  Oscar H., 740
  Thompson, 740
  William E., 741
Taylor, 1116, 1210
  Benjamin, 1166
  Charles P., 1210
  David, 1166
  Jasper, 1166
  John E., 1166
  Joseph K., 1330
  William, 1210
  William H., 1331
Tetrick, 1214
  Henry, 1214, 1215
  Joseph, 1215
  Lucius E., 1216
  Ozias, 1216
  Willis G., 1216
Thomas, Clarence S., 495
  George C., 495
Thorn, 834
  Arthur K., 834
  John, 834
  John U., 834
Trach, 1110
  Elias S., 1111
  Jacob, 1110
  John M., 1111
Turney, 548
  Daniel, 548
  Jacob, 548
  Peter, Chief Justice, 548
Vance, 731, 1281
  Addison S., 1282
  Fred W., 732
  John E., 731
  Robert A., 1282
Vandervort, 734
  Emery M., 735
  Jacob S., 735
  James G., 734
  Nicholas, 734
  Paul, 734
Van Voorhis, 948
  Daniel, 948
  Elgy, 948
  *H. Morris, 949
  Jerome F., 948
Wade, 1075
  Alexander L., 1076
  George, 1075
  Spencer S., 1078
Walker, 749
  Donald, 749

Kephart D., 750
John P., 750
Peter, 749
Ward, Duncan, 786
  Rush J., 786
Warder, 1232, 1378
  Abraham S., Dr., 1378
  Abraham S., Dr., 1379
  Francis S., 1232
  Henry, 1232
  Hugh, 1233
  James, 1232
  Noah, 1378
Wardwell, 1038
Warman, 650
  Altha, 650
  Thomas, 650
Washington, 898
  Edward, 900
  Edward, 901
  George W., 901
  John, 898
  John, Col., 900
  Lawrence, 899
  Lawrence, 900
  Robert, 898
  Robert, 899
Watkins, 840
  James, 841
  Lettie A., 842
  Stephen, 841
  Thomas, 841
  William H. H., 841
Watson, 439
  Albert T., 446
  Clarence W., Hon., 444
  George T., 446
  James, 439
  James E., 443
  James G., 439
  James O., 440
  James O., 445
  Sylvanus L., 442
  Thomas, 439
  William H., 442
Weaver, 1260
  Frank P., 1262
  George, 1260
  James, 1260
  John, 1261
  Joseph, 1261
  Joseph F., 1261
Wendel, 729
  Conrad F., 729

Jacob, 729
Whetsell, 1342
  George, 1343
  Horatio S., 1343
White, 426, 797, 902, 1002, 1343, 1371
  Alexander, 1344
  Alexander H., 1003
  Alexander P., 1344
  Charles, 435
  Grafton, 432
  Hiram, 1374
  Isaac, 798
  Israel C., 432
  John, 430
  John, 798
  John, 1344
  John, 1371-72
  John, 1373
  Joseph, 1373
  Joshua, 430
  Malissa C., 798
  Michael, 432
  Prescott C., 1375
  Robert C., 1374
  Samuel L., 1003
  Stephen, 426
  Stephen, 429
  Stephen, 431
  Thomas, 1002
  Thomas C., 798
  Thornton, 903
  William, 432
  William, 902
  William T., 903
Whitehill, 478
  Alexander R., Dr., 479
  James, 478
  Stephen, 479
Whiteman, Everal J., 598
Whitescarver, 665
  Frederick, 665
  Frederick W., 665
  George M., 666
  Henrietta A., 667
  John S., 665
Wiedebusch, 486, 1001
  A. L., 486
  Adolph L., 1011
  Edward C., 1012
  Henry, 486
  Henry, 486
  Henry, 1011

Lewis, 1011
William A., 487
Williams, 655, 827, 858
  Homer W., 827
  Jeremiah, 655
  Jesse F., 655
  John W., 655
  Mark, 858
  Perry C., 859
  Samuel, 827
  Thomas, 827
  *Thompson H., 859
  William, 655
  William J., 858
Willis, 941
  D. M., Hon., 941
Wilson, 1209
  James E., 1209
  James W., 1209
  Levin, 1209
  Levin J., 1209
Wilt, 1004
  David S., 1004
  Jacob, 1004
  Michael, 1004
  Oscar C., 1005
Withers, 920
  Alexander S., 921
  Enoch, 920
  Henry H., 921
  John, 920
  John S., 921
  Thomas, 920
Wood, 764, 1058
  Edward J., 1058
  James A., 1058
  John, 1058
  John S., 764
  Joseph M., 764
Woodley, Oscar I., 1228
Worley, William G., 1207
Yeager, George, 489
  George G., 490
  Samuel S., Capt., 489
Young, 800
  John T., 800
  John W., 800
  Ralph W., 801
Yost, 1026
  Aaron, 1027
  Henry S., Dr., 1028
  John, 1026
  John, 1027
  Jorier, Dr., 1028

www.ingramcontent.com/pod-product-compliance
Lightning Source LLC
Chambersburg PA
CBHW020634300426
44112CB00007B/112